Learn Design Patterns with Game Programming

Philippe-Henri Gosselin

Contents

Design Patterns are powerful tools for the creation of robust and scalable software. Presented one by one, patterns are easy to understand, even for a beginner. However, using and combining them in a complex application is much more difficult.

In this book, we focus on the creation of video games: a complete example game and our own game. During the presentation of these developments, we see concepts from the most simple to the most complex. We start with the basics of data representation and elements of graphic user interfaces. In this scope, we make use of popular patterns. Then, we see more advanced patterns for the design of the video game engine. At this step, we create combinations of existing patterns and techniques to solve all problems. To succeed, the software architect has to develop skills in design that lead to new patterns dedicated to its current project. This work continues with even more advanced cases with the implementation of artificial intelligence and network gaming.

Only basic knowledge of object programming is required to start reading this book. A complete game example, divided into many sub-steps, is provided with this book. Beginners can use parts of the game example to create their game, and more experimented programmers can work from scratch.

Who this book is for

This book is for beginners and experienced programmers who wish to improve their skills in software design. The main approach of this book is practical: the reader quickly tries what he reads, and theory comes when it has to.

Students are the first targeted readers: they are generally not yet aware of the main issues in software design. Their usual first approach is to open their favorite IDE and start typing the code, and then face unsolvable problems when the project becomes too large. It is not easy to convince most students that software design is not tedious and is very exciting once you know it. Thanks to the practical approach of this book, and the creation of their own video game, students take this training with ease and pleasure.

Experienced programmers find very interesting content, also because of the practical approach, different from most books on the same topic. This approach differs from a long list of uncorrelated patterns and techniques, usually illustrated by small independent examples. Abstract presentation and small examples are relevant - we propose many of them in this book. However, they do not illustrate the main motivation behind advanced software design techniques: handle large projects and complex combinations of features. Experienced programmers are pleased to rediscover patterns and learn new ways to use and combine them. Note that these points also hold for beginners who can learn more techniques during a second reading of the book.

This book also targets game programmers: even if software design is the first topic, this is a game programming book as well. A lot of common problems in game programming are considered, with offered solutions based on design patterns. The book also proposes an overall approach that allows the designing of robust, stable, easy to maintain games. Most books and tutorials on the Internet focuses on graphics and user interaction, and usually ignore all design aspects. In the best case, the Game Loop pattern is used, but only using this one, we are far, so far from truly robust solutions! Simple presentations are relevant to introduce concepts (as it is done in this book). However, they are not enough to feel the true problems and the motivation of solutions based on software design. In this book, advanced solutions are proposed and offer many design ideas to game programmers. Finally, this book also considers advanced features in games, like artificial intelligence and networking, with robust and scalable solutions.

About the author

Philippe-Henri Gosselin, Ph. D., is a Software Architect and a Data Scientist at Interdigital. Before this position, he was a full professor at ENSEA, an engineering school on informatics and electronics. He was the head of the last-year "Informatics and Systems" specialty and designed all the courses and related content for the learning of advanced software engineering. These courses include more than 100 hours of lectures and supervised practical work, and served as a basis for this book.

CHAPTER **1**

Design a large application

1.1 Objectives

The main aim of this book is to acquire skills to design a large software application. The approach taken to achieve this goal is to make a video game using software design. Each stage of this realization is punctuated by the presentation of these tools and some exercises to better understand them. The Pacman game developed throughout the book serves as an example for each introduced concept. The Pacman game is a well-known simple game: it illustrates concepts without losing the reader in issues specific to a particular video game. Note that pedagogical and fun reasons motivate the choice of making a video game instead of a more traditional application. For instance, it is possible to use notions introduced in this book to make a merchandise inventory management software. However, this kind of realization is less likely to motivate the acquisition of skills!

The most generic tools presented in this book are *Design Patterns*, applied in all stages of development. These patterns are proven recipes that solve many computer design problems without having to reinvent the wheel. Once gained, they save valuable time in design and implementation. They also solve complex problems that, without this approach, are very difficult or impossible to model, even for the greatest coders. More specific tools are also presented according to the needs of the game, such as data structures, algorithmic, display, networks... As presented in this book, design patterns improve these tools.

The method followed in this book also makes it possible to design large applications. Past a certain size or a certain level of complexity, it becomes very difficult to create an application that combines performance and scalability - while ensuring the achievement of requested features. If the problem of computer design has to be summarized to a single question, it would be this one: how to implement functionalities whose complexity exceeds human understanding? This problem has, until proven otherwise, only one solution: the division of complex problems into simple sub-problems. The presentation of this problem is the main subject of this chapter, which we motivate, present, and finally put into practice in the following sections.

The acquisition of all these tools requires some energy. The first tools are the simplest, and their presentation is very detailed to be accessible to beginners. Then, as time goes by, we see more and more complex tools. Readers with more experience will judge the first chapters too simple and find more relevant content in the following chapters. If ever a chapter seems too difficult, we recommend reading the previous chapters again and do all the exercises. All presentations and exercises have a specific pedagogical function, which the reader will only realize once he has improved its skills. Finally, if a feeling of repetition sets in, do not worry! It can happen if the new concepts presented do not seem so new, as if we constantly repeat the same pattern. Such a feeling means that you acquired the design skills and that this book achieved its main aim!

1.2   Software design: a considerable time savings

1.2.1   A simple example

Implementing a large application requires a lot of work time dedicated to software design. When you start in software development, the energy claimed for this stage is not natural. It is a normal feeling: why waste so much time when it is - a priori - much more effective to dive right into the code? People who have tried this naïve approach will testify that it is not the right one - except perhaps for very simple problems. However, it is difficult to convince oneself without having experienced this.

To reproduce the experience of implementation without conception, we consider a simple example: the checkers game. This game has eight black and eight white pieces placed on a checkerboard of eight by eight squares. Only black squares can accommodate pieces.

The initial state is as follows:

There are two types of movement: moving to an adjacent free square and capturing a piece of the other color. We do not consider the creation of king pieces in this example.

Implementing this without design, we produce the following code:

```java
import java.awt.BorderLayout;
import java.awt.Color;
import java.awt.Dimension;
import java.awt.Graphics;
import java.awt.event.MouseEvent;
```

```java
import java.awt.event.MouseListener;
import javax.swing.JComponent;
import javax.swing.JFrame;
import javax.swing.Jlabel;

class BoardComponent extends JComponent {
    public BoardComponent() {
        setPreferredSize(new Dimension(80 * 8, 80 * 8));
    }
    @Override
    public void paint(Graphics g) {
        for (int j=0;j<8;j++) {
            for (int i=0;i<8;i++) {
                if (((i+j)%2) == 1)
                    g.setColor(Color.WHITE);
                else
                    g.setColor(Color.BLACK);
                g.fillRect(i*80, j*80, 80, 80);
                int p = board[i][j];
                if (p >= 0) {
                    if ((p%2) == 0)
                        g.setColor(Color.BLACK);
                    else
                        g.setColor(Color.WHITE);
                    g.fillOval(i*80+5, j*80+5, 70, 70);
                    g.setColor(Color.WHITE);
                    g.drawOval(i*80+5, j*80+5, 70, 70);
                }
            }
        }
    }
}

public class Checkers extends JFrame implements MouseListener {
    private int board[][];
    private int currentPlayer;
    private int selectedPiece[];
    private JLabel statusBar;

    public Checkers() {
        currentPlayer = 0;
        board = new int[8][8];
        for (int j=0;j<8;j++) {
            for (int i=0;i<8;i++) {
                board[i][j] = -1;
```

```java
        }
    }
    board[0][0] = board[2][0] = 0;
    board[4][0] = board[6][0] = 0;
    board[1][1] = board[3][1] = 0;
    board[5][1] = board[7][1] = 0;
    board[0][6] = board[2][6] = 1;
    board[4][6] = board[6][6] = 1;
    board[1][7] = board[3][7] = 1;
    board[5][7] = board[7][7] = 1;

    setDefaultCloseOperation(JFrame.EXIT_ON_CLOSE);
    setResizable(false);
    setTitle("Checkers");
    setLayout(new BorderLayout());
    getContentPane().add(new BoardComponent(),
        BorderLayout.CENTER);
    statusBar = new JLabel("Current player");
    getContentPane().add(statusBar,BorderLayout.SOUTH);
    pack();
    redraw();
    addMouseListener(this);
}
public void redraw() {
    String msg = (currentPlayer==0)?"Black":"White";
    statusBar.setText("Current player: "+msg);
    repaint();
}
@Override
public void mouseClicked(MouseEvent e) { }
@Override
public void mousePressed(MouseEvent e) {
    int i = e.getX() / 80;
    int j = e.getY() / 80;
    if (board[i][j] == currentPlayer) {
        selectedPiece = new int[2];
        selectedPiece[0] = i;
        selectedPiece[1] = j;
    }
    else {
        selectedPiece = null;
    }
}
@Override
public void mouseReleased(MouseEvent e) {
```

```java
        if (selectedPiece == null)
            return;
        int i = e.getX() / 80;
        int j = e.getY() / 80;
        if (board[i][j] < 0 && ((i+j)%2) == 0) {
            boolean doMove = false;
            int i0 = selectedPiece[0];
            int j0 = selectedPiece[1];
            if ( (i==i0+1 && j==j0+1) || (i==i0+1 && j==j0-1)
               || (i==i0-1 && j==j0+1) || (i==i0-1 && j==j0-1)) {
                doMove = true;
            }
            else if (i==i0+2 && j==j0+2 && board[i0+1][j0+1]
                    == 1-board[i0][j0]) {
                board[i0+1][j0+1] = -1;
                doMove = true;
            }
            else if (i==i0-2 && j==j0+2 && board[i0-1][j0+1]
                    == 1-board[i0][j0]) {
                board[i0-1][j0+1] = -1;
                doMove = true;
            }
            else if (i==i0+2 && j==j0-2 && board[i0+1][j0-1]
                    == 1-board[i0][j0]) {
                board[i0+1][j0-1] = -1;
                doMove = true;
            }
            else if (i==i0-2 && j==j0-2 && board[i0-1][j0-1]
                    == 1-board[i0][j0]) {
                board[i0-1][j0-1] = -1;
                doMove = true;
            }
            if (doMove) {
                board[i][j] = board[i0][j0];
                board[i0][j0] = -1;
                currentPlayer = 1-currentPlayer;
                redraw();
            }
        }
        selectedPiece = null;
    }
    @Override
    public void mouseEntered(MouseEvent e) { }
    @Override
    public void mouseExited(MouseEvent e) { }
```

```java
public static void main(String[] args) {
    Checkers checkers = new Checkers();
    checkers.setLocationRelativeTo(null);
    checkers.setVisible(true);
    }
}
```

The code above is complete and can be compiled and run with no other dependency than the standard Java library. The corresponding Java file is available in the Java Project provided with this book (see Section 1.3.3), in the folder examples.checkers.

→ To run it, open the Java project with Netbeans, locate the Java file "examples/checkers/Checkers.java" in the source packages. Right-click on this file and select **Run File** from the context menu.

→ To play, drag a piece of the current player.

1.2.2 Divide and conquer

This first roll is functional and allows us to play the game in its simplest version. Is the design necessary?
One could claim that it is not the case because the complexity of the problem is so low that we don't need any design. However, if we want to enrich the solution with new features, serious problems will arise.

Graphic library

The first solution uses the display features present in the standard Java library. It is relevant for office software and simple cases like the checkers game. To propose a more pleasant display, one should get closer to the graphics card of the machine. Lower level libraries like LWJGL (*Lightweight Java Game Library*) can provide such a display. To use one of these libraries, you must change the initial code in several places. More precisely, it is necessary to start with a first step of identifying the zones interacting with the graphic elements of the standard library. With no structure to find them quickly, this poor design forces the developer to review all the code. This example code is only about 150 lines, and the identification will be fast. In real cases, you have to go through thousands, tens, hundreds of thousands of lines of code. Once this identification is established, almost all identified sections will have to be rewritten completely.

This issue of graphic library change is not the most important. Indeed, it can be very interesting to be able to deploy the game on different platforms (pc, mac, console, mobile, ...), each needing a specific graphic library. An approach without design is to produce a code specific to each platform. It involves changes for each of these versions, resulting in a loss of time and a significant risk of errors.

Design patterns and software engineering can easily solve these problems. They make it possible to isolate the problems of display of the rest of the logic of the game. The result is a solution that can easily switch from one graphics library to another.

To conclude: it is relevant to isolate display features from the rest of the game.

Controls: User Interface, Artificial Intelligence and Networking

In the initial example, the mouse controls the pieces. It may be interesting also to propose other controls like gamepads on consoles, whose logic is very different from that of the mouse. To do this, you must identify corresponding code areas and modify them accordingly. For example, you will have to produce a method equivalent to `mouseReleased()`, surely something like `gamepadBoutonPressed()`. Furthermore, the analysis of the mouse handling method shows that two features are mixed: the management of the mouse and the rules of the game. Actually, it is at this level that movement rules and piece capture are implemented. To get a similar result with a gamepad, you need to reproduce these rules in the gamepad handling method. In the case of the checkers game, this is quite simple, but for many other games, the rules are much more complex. It results in a significant risk of errors: some actions may be possible using one device but not in the others.

In a game, it is often interesting to propose artificial intelligence (AI) to play as a human player. In this case, AI replaces the mouse or the gamepad and controls the game with a mechanics of an even more different nature. As we will see in the corresponding chapter, AI can control the game at a lower level, without going through button press mechanics or other. Adding an AI in our simple implementation of checkers is like creating an additional method, which will also need to apply the rules of the game. It increases the risk of errors again.

One last way to control a game is by networking. In this case, it is generally more interesting to only transmit on the network the commands of each player than the entire data of the game. In doing so, network packets control remote players, as if their devices were directly attached to the local machine. With a naive approach, this new control is used via new methods to implement, with the same risks that come with it.

To conclude: it is relevant to isolate the controls from the rest of the game.

Game data

Working with a single class to produce a large software solution is quickly unmanageable. It is quite natural to distribute the implementation in different classes. Finding the optimal distribution is less obvious. To do this, we must use indicators. The first ones are those found during the steps taken in the paragraphs above: if we introduce a new feature, what problems or risk of error will it cause? According to the previous analysis, it is relevant to isolate the controls and the display from the rest of the game. With similar reasoning, we can conclude that it is interesting to isolate all the data. Thus, whoever needs to read or modify the data can do it very easily, without being lost in the middle of the display, controls, network, etc. For the checkers game, the checkerboard and the current player form this data. Warning: other attributes, such as the selected piece, are not part of the game data.

To conclude: it is also necessary to isolate the game data from the other elements such as the display, the controls, the AI, the network, etc.

Scaling and teamwork

Another way to find a good distribution of functionalities is the consideration of teamwork. To better work together, it is best to limit as much as possible the dependencies between the skills of each person. For example, if a member of the team has a good background to use a specific graphics library, it may be interesting to isolate everything that concerns this graphic library. This library can be "hidden" behind a software interface, as presented and detailed in subsequent sections and chapters. For other developers, who only see the software interface, the library does not exist. The constraints can also be geographical: it is always easier to interact with people physically close to you. Depending on the case, it is relevant to guide the distribution of tasks according to the specificities of team members.

For simple cases, isolating the functionality can be summed up as creating a new class. For more complex cases, it is more interesting to create packages that contain all classes of a feature. When the level of complexity is really important, a hierarchy of packages may be needed.

1.2.3 An example of improvement

This section offers an improved version of the checkers game, with the same intending to convince the mind of the relevance of software design before implementation. The approach followed in this section is not the right one: it would have been better to start by designing this improvement, and then to implement it. Once again, the goal here is to motivate the need to design before coding.

The proposed enhancement is to isolate the data and rules of the game in a separate
Board class:

```java
public class Board {
    private int board[][];
    private int currentPlayer;
    public Board() {
        currentPlayer = 0;
        board = new int[8][8];
        for (int j = 0; j < 8; j++) {
            for (int i = 0; i < 8; i++) {
                board[i][j] = -1;
            }
        }
        board[0][0] = board[2][0] = 0;
        board[4][0] = board[6][0] = 0;
        board[1][1] = board[3][1] = 0;
        board[5][1] = board[7][1] = 0;
        board[0][6] = board[2][6] = 1;
        board[4][6] = board[6][6] = 1;
        board[1][7] = board[3][7] = 1;
        board[5][7] = board[7][7] = 1;
    }
    public int getCurrentPlayer() {
        return currentPlayer;
    }
    public int getPiece(int i, int j) {
        return board[i][j];
    }
    public boolean movePiece(int i0, int j0,int i, int j) {
        if (board[i][j] < 0 && ((i + j) % 2) == 0) {
            boolean doMove = false;
            if ((i == i0 + 1 && j == j0 + 1)
              || (i == i0 + 1 && j == j0 - 1)
              || (i == i0 - 1 && j == j0 + 1)
              || (i == i0 - 1 && j == j0 - 1)) {
                doMove = true;
            } else if (i == i0 + 2 && j == j0 + 2
              && board[i0 + 1][j0 + 1] == 1 - board[i0][j0]) {
                board[i0 + 1][j0 + 1] = -1;
                doMove = true;
            } else if (i == i0 - 2 && j == j0 + 2
              && board[i0 - 1][j0 + 1] == 1 - board[i0][j0]) {
                board[i0 - 1][j0 + 1] = -1;
                doMove = true;
```

```java
        } else if (i == i0 + 2 && j == j0 - 2
          && board[i0 + 1][j0 - 1] == 1 - board[i0][j0]) {
            board[i0 + 1][j0 - 1] = -1;
            doMove = true;
        } else if (i == i0 - 2 && j == j0 - 2
          && board[i0 - 1][j0 - 1] == 1 - board[i0][j0]) {
            board[i0 - 1][j0 - 1] = -1;
            doMove = true;
        }
        if (doMove) {
            board[i][j] = board[i0][j0];
            board[i0][j0] = -1;
            currentPlayer = 1 - currentPlayer;
            return true;
        }
    }
    return false;
    }
}
```

This class contains the `board` and the `currentPlayer`. There are two ways to get this information: `getCurrentPlayer()` and `getPiece()`. They allow, for example, to get the necessary elements for the display. The `movePiece()` method contains all the logic of the game: it allows to move a piece according to the rules of the game. If the move is valid, the method executes it, and returns `true`. Otherwise, it returns `false`.

The `Board` class has no dependencies: there is no import. This property is very interesting because any external element can not influence the implementation of this class. The class interface, namely the name and the arguments of its public methods, defines its use. Indeed, people who use it expect to find specific methods with specific behavior. It is the designer that is responsible for defining the names and arguments of the methods (a.k.a. the API). It plays a very important role because any change will have implications in the code of any user of that class. On the other hand, the implementation of these methods can be modified freely, as long as they respond to the expected behavior.

Using the `Board` class, it is possible to make a `Checkers2` class that handles the display and control aspects without having to worry about the data and rules of the game:

```java
import java.awt.BorderLayout;
import java.awt.Color;
import java.awt.Dimension;
import java.awt.Graphics;
import java.awt.event.MouseEvent;
import java.awt.event.MouseListener;
```

```java
import javax.swing.JComponent;
import javax.swing.JFrame;
import.javax.swing.JLabel;

class BoardComponent extends JComponent {
    public BoardComponent() {
        setMinimumSize(new Dimension(80*8,80*8));
        setPreferredSize(new Dimension(80*8,80*8));
        setMaximumSize(new Dimension(80*8,80*8));
    }
    @Override
    public void paint(Graphics g) {
        for (int j=0;j<8;j++) {
            for (int i=0;i<8;i++) {
                if (((i+j)%2) == 1)
                    g.setColor(Color.WHITE);
                else
                    g.setColor(Color.BLACK);
                g.fillRect(i*80, j*80, 80, 80);
                int p = board.getPiece(i,j);
                if (p >= 0) {
                    if ((p%2) == 0)
                        g.setColor(Color.BLACK);
                    else
                        g.setColor(Color.WHITE);
                    g.fillOval(i*80+5, j*80+5, 70, 70);
                    g.setColor(Color.WHITE);
                    g.drawOval(i*80+5, j*80+5, 70, 70);
                }
            }
        }
    }
}

public class Checkers2 extends JFrame implements MouseListener {
    private Board board = new Board();
    private int selectedPiece[];
    private JLabel statusBar;

    public Checkers2() {
        setDefaultCloseOperation(JFrame.EXIT_ON_CLOSE);
        setResizable(false);
        setTitle("Checkers");
        setLayout(new BorderLayout());
        getContentPane().add(new BoardComponent(),
```

```java
                BorderLayout.CENTER);
        statusBar = new JLabel("Current player");
        getContentPane().add(statusBar,BorderLayout.SOUTH);
        pack();
        redraw();
        addMouseListener(this);
    }
    public void redraw() {
        String msg = (board.getCurrentPlayer()==0)
            ?"Black":"White";
        statusBar.setText("Current player: "+msg);
        repaint();
    }
    @Override
    public void mouseClicked(MouseEvent e) { }
    @Override
    public void mousePressed(MouseEvent e) {
        int i = e.getX() / 80;
        int j = e.getY() / 80;
        if (board.getPiece(i,j) == board.getCurrentPlayer()) {
            selectedPiece = new int[2];
            selectedPiece[0] = i;
            selectedPiece[1] = j;
        }
        else {
            selectedPiece = null;
        }
    }
    @Override
    public void mouseReleased(MouseEvent e) {
        if (selectedPiece == null) {
            return;
        }
        int i = e.getX() / 80;
        int j = e.getY() / 80;
        if (board.movePiece(selectedPiece[0],
            selectedPiece[1], i, j)) {
            redraw();
        }
        selectedPiece = null;
    }
    @Override
    public void mouseEntered(MouseEvent e) { }
    @Override
    public void mouseExited(MouseEvent e) { }
```

```java
public static void main(String[] args) {
    Checkers2 checkers = new Checkers2();
    checkers.setLocationRelativeTo(null);
    checkers.setVisible(true);
}
}
```

The code above is complete and can be compiled and run with no other dependency than the standard Java library. The corresponding java file is available in the "examples/checkers2" folder of the Java example project.

The implementation of the `Checkers2` class is very close to that of `Checkers`:

- The data attributes (`board, currentPlayer`) have been replaced by a reference to an instance of the `Board` class
- Data initialization has been removed from the constructor
- The display is based on the methods of the `Board` class
- The management of piece displacements in the `mouseReleased()` method has been replaced by a call to the `movePiece()` method of the `Board` class

These changes make it easy to add new controls safely. For example, to handle a gamepad, one only has to implement the corresponding methods and then call the `movePiece()` method of the `Board` class. In doing so, there is no risk of introducing differences in the implementation of the rules of the game.

1.2.4 Model-View-Controller Approach (MVC)

The design initiated in the example above is a primary version of the Model-View-Controller (MVC) approach. This approach, proposed in the 1970s, is very common for designing software that interacts with a user.

According to this approach, the software is divided into three main parts:

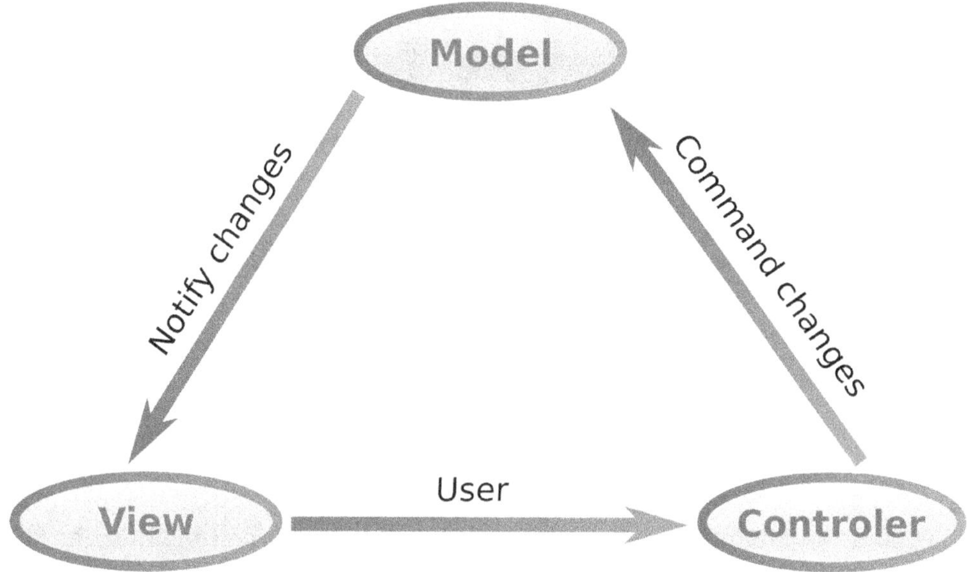

- The model: it contains the data and the logic that accompanies them. In the case of the checkers game, it is contained in the `Board` class. For most games, the model is the set of information about the world in which players play. Added to this is the set of "valid" modifications of the model. For example, you can only ask the model to move a piece if it follows the rules of the game. For office applications, a database like SQL is usually part of the model. So-called "business objects" often represent these databases. All possible changes to this database and their implementation are also part of the model: it is often called "business logic".
- View: It contains the elements to present the data to a user. The most classic case is a visual presentation on a screen. In the case of the checkers game, calls to the graphic elements of the standard Java library form this part. For most games, the view is a visual and sound representation of all or part of the world in which the player moves. For office applications, it is the part of the graphical interface that presents the data, such as a table, a page of a text, and so on.
- The controller: it is at the origin of the changes of the model. In the checkers game, mouse handling forms this part. In video games, devices such as the mouse or the gamepad control the player's data. The controller typically

receives signals from the view, such as mouse movements or when the user presses a button. Then, it transforms these received signals into high-level commands that modify the model data.

These three parts interact together:

- The model indicates the view that is modified. As a result, the view displays the model data in their new state.
- The view allows the user to browse the model data, and to choose the changes he or she deems necessary. The user expresses these changes through the GUI controls.
- The controller receives signals from devices and graphical controls and forms the commands that will produce model changes. Then, it submits these commands to the model.

There are also modified or improved versions, such as the Model-View-Presenter approach. For the video game design presented in this book, we use a modified version of the Model-View-Controller approach. We present this approach in the next chapters.

The first step of this presentation begins in Chapter 2, with the game state as the model, but only for the data representation part. Then, in chapter 3, the problems of display and controls of the game are presented and correspond to the view part. Finally, in Chapter 4, the game changes according to its rules are presented, as well as all aspects of interaction and synchronization between the different parts. Unlike the Model-View-Controller approach, we move the "business logic" part from the model part to the controller part. The implementation of artificial intelligence and network gaming, presented in Chapters 5 and 6, motivates this difference.

1.3   Preparation

This section presents the necessary elements to start the design and the realization of the video game.

1.3.1   Choice of the game

The choice of the developed video game will have a significant impact on the acquisition of skills presented in this book. It may be relevant to follow the book while developing a first simple game, then do a second reading for a more ambitious game. The following elements will help the reader to anticipate possible difficulties.

Graphics

When we think about video games, the first thing that comes to mind is graphics. The simplest and fastest choice is to do everything for a text display, but the result is very limited. Then, the choice of 2D graphics according to a regular grid, like the Pacman game presented as an example, is not much more difficult than with text graphics. Besides, it is easy to find 2D sprites on the Internet, so you do not have to produce the textures yourself. In the case of 3D graphics, things are more complicated. Without an advanced graphics engine, it is necessary to go through low-level libraries, such as OpenGL or DirectX. This approach requires a high level of skills, which risks to lost the untrained reader in this area. With an advanced graphics engine, design choices will likely be imposed. This situation does not allow to make its own experiences in design, the main objective of this book being to be able to design complex solutions. In other words, one of the book's goals is to be able to create an advanced graphics engine, not just to be able to use one. In conclusion, make a 3D game by following this book is only interesting when you already have a good level in game development. It is also more interesting without an advanced graphics engine, working directly with OpenGL or DirectX.

Audio

The audio aspects are not essential to design and make a small video game. The simplest way is to ignore this aspect. In the opposite case, it is very easy to produce sounds, and there are many free sound files.

State machines and real time

A common design approach in video games is to consider the program as a state machine. It means that the game is always in a very specific state, and next to any event, the game will go from this state to another state. This approach facilitates the creation of artificial intelligence since one can represent and traverse a set of states of the game. It also allows great robustness when synchronizing network games.

This approach is also very common in network databases. A database at a time t forms a specific state. A set of queries, called a transaction, is used to change the database, and therefore to move from the state before the transaction to the one after the transaction. No other queries are possible during the transaction, and if a query for the transaction fails, the database engine cancels the previous queries and rolls back to the initial state. A very interesting consequence is that the database is always valid - if all transactions meet the specifications, the database can not be in an invalid state.

This state machine property has mostly consequences for real-time games. For turn-based games, this is not a problem, as the game is by nature a state machine. For real-time games, the state constantly changes, usually 60 times per second, the refresh time of screens. It involves a work of synchronization between the display and the evolution of the game. It is not a difficult exercise but still requires a certain amount of extra energy. It is therefore advisable to avoid real-time games at first, especially those with a very high frequency of change of state, such as fighting games.

Game world

The elements of a video game usually evolve in a world. The most classic case is a two-dimensional world according to a regular grid, like Mario and Zelda games. We should note that we consider the nature of the world and not its visual representation. For example, in the Mario game, we see the world from the side, while we see it from above for Zelda. There are also cases where the visual representation uses 3D meshes, while the world is based on a regular grid. The display often gives the illusion of a continuous world, whereas it is cubic and regular. The characters who evolve in this world do not have to align themselves with the axes of the grid of the world. They are free, and this freedom reinforces the illusion of a continuous world.

The more regular the game world, the easier it will be to manipulate it. It is therefore strongly advised to start with a game with this kind of world. If not, you have to deal with complex problems, such as collisions between objects and sets. An external library can ease it. However, as with graphics, design choices will certainly already be made and limit the acquisition of skills.

Artificial intelligence

Most games require artificial intelligence. It starts with the non-player characters with basic behavior, like the monsters in Mario. One can also find a little less basic cases, like the ghosts in Pacman who can flee or hunt Pacman. For all these cases, there is no particular difficulty. Things are more complex when it comes to playing in the place of a human being.

For games with pieces or cards, such as checkers or chess, current algorithms can offer very good AIs if the space of possibilities is not too large. For some games, like the game of Go, the space of possibilities is so great that it requires very advanced AI techniques, mentioned but not detailed in this book.

For platform games, like Pacman or Mario, the difficulty depends on the character's degrees of freedom. For Pacman, the choices are simple: turn or not at the next intersection. For Mario, the choices are more numerous, given that Mario can go wherever he wants. For descendants of platform games, like FPS or open-world RPGs, the difficulty will depend on the complexity of the game. With a simple FPS like Quake, simple heuristics can be very effective. In the case of open-world games, like Skyrim, there are no proven algorithms to play in the place of a human. However, replacing the main player character is not necessarily interesting, and heuristics may be sufficient for non-player characters.

For strategy and management games, implementing an AI is often required to play against the computer. The difficulty in these cases depends on the complexity of game rules and how much planning is required. For small games where you only have to move a few units or build a few buildings, an AI is not very difficult to implement. For more complex games, where you have to anticipate in the very long term, things can be much more complicated. It can become even more complex if you have to deal with real-time issues, and therefore make a lot of decisions.

Examples of games

It may be appropriate to take inspiration from a known game and create a personalized version. The following list shows various games with their properties:

Game	World	Graphics/ Real-time	AI	Diff.
Checkers	Cubic	2D/No	Simple	Low
Chess	Cubic	2D/No	Simple	Low
Belote	Cubic	2D/No	Simple	Low
Go	Cubic	2D/No	Extreme	High
Pacman	Cubic	2D/Yes	Simple	Low
Mario	Cubic	2D/Yes	Average	Low
Quake	Cubic	3D/Yes	Simple	Ave.
Skyrim	Free	3D/Yes	Average	High
Advance Wars	Cubic	2D/No	Simple	Low
Battle for Wesnoth	Hexa	2D/No	Average	Ave.
Starcraft II	Cubic	3D/Yes	Extreme	High
Heroes of M&M	Cubic	2D/No	Average	Ave.
Civilization 5	Hexa	3D/No	High	High
Transport Tycoon	Cubic	2D/Yes	Average	High
Street Fighter 2	Free	2D/Yes	Average	High

1.3.2   Development environment

To illustrate the notions seen in the various chapters, we choose the Java language and Netbeans code editor with the EasyUML plugin. There are several ways to install it: we show these procedures below. You can choose other environments, such as the ones we present at the end of this section.

1.3.2.1   Netbeans with EasyUML

Java Development Kit (Java SE)

The standard Java SDK is available on the Oracle site. We used version 8 of Java during the writing of this book. The more advanced versions of the kit can also be used, such as Java EE.

Netbeans 8.2 with EasyUML: Quick Installation

Installers of Netbeans 8.2 with EasyUML are available here:

`https://github.com/philippehenri-gosselin/easyuml/releases`

To install the software, you must download and run the installer corresponding to the operating system of your machine (Windows, macOS or Linux). For instance, `nbuml-windows.exe` is the installer for Windows.

The EasyUML plugin contained in these installers is an improved version of the official plugin. It contains enhancements, including a more UML compliant display and better code generation. Source code is available here:

`https://github.com/philippehenri-gosselin/easyuml`

Warning: This all-in-one version does not contain all the features of Netbeans, such as profiling or versioning.

Netbeans 11.2 with EasyUML: Two-Step Installation

Netbeans in a basic format, without plugins, can be downloaded at the following address:

https://netbeans.apache.org/download/index.html

The installation of the standard EasyUML plugin, not improved for the book, is possible from the **Tools - Plugins** menu. Then, on the **Available Plugins** tab of the dialog, select EasyUml, and click the **Install** button. Warning: the standard plugin does not contain all the features of the improved plugin. It will still be possible to display the diagrams provided with this book, but code generation will not always work properly.

To install the improved EasyUML plugin:

→ Download and extract the file in "nbmuml.zip" here:

`https://github.com/philippehenri-gosselin/easyuml/releases`

→ Open the dialog from the **Tools - Plugins** menu and select the **Downloaded** tab:

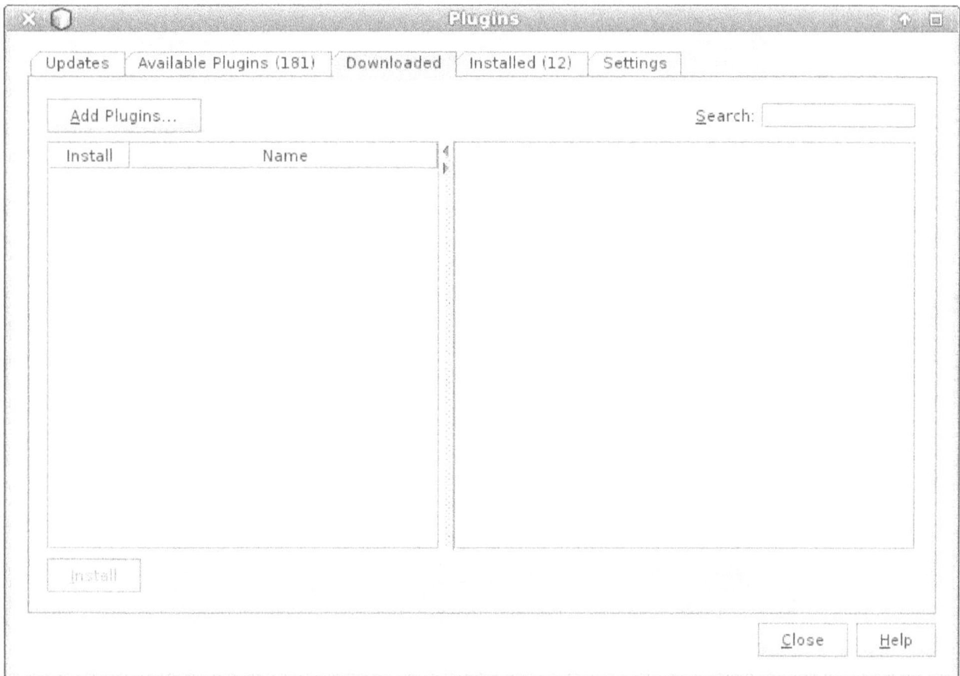

→ Click the **Add Plugins ...** button, and select all .nbm files:

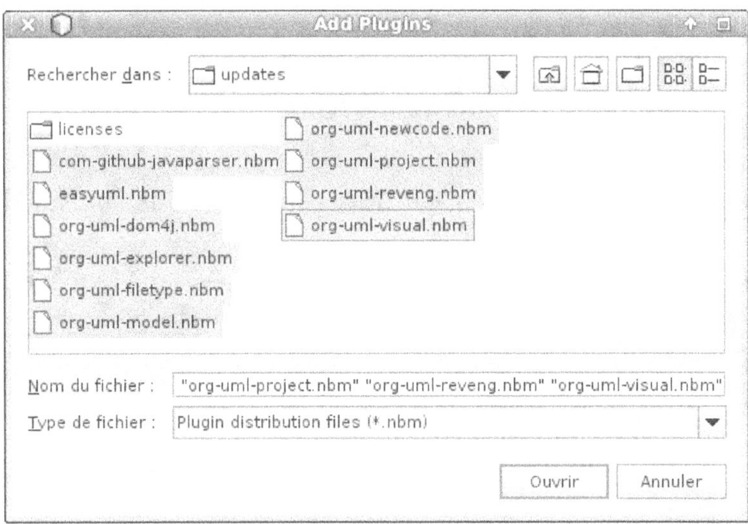

→ Click **Open**.

→ Then click on the **Install** button:

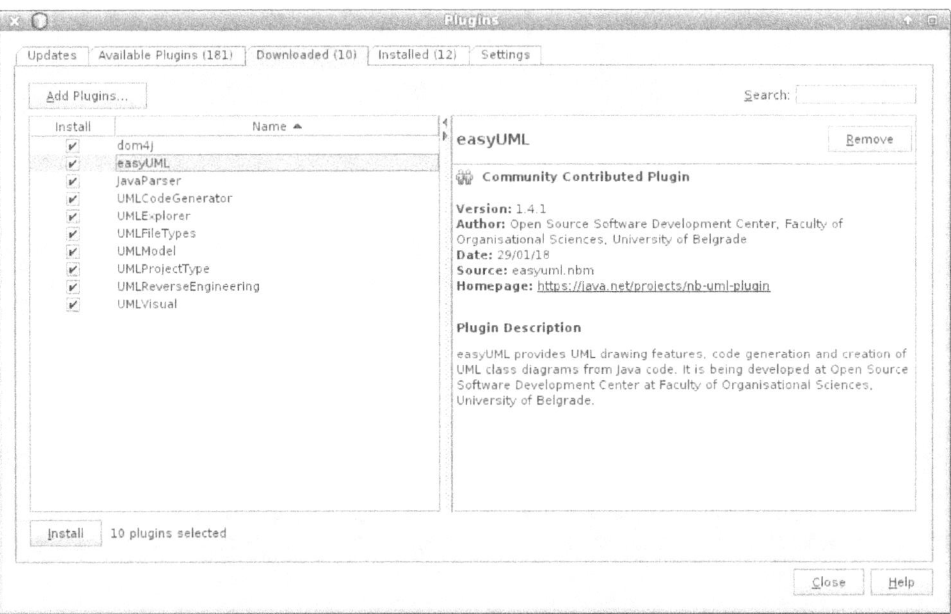

→ Click **Next**:

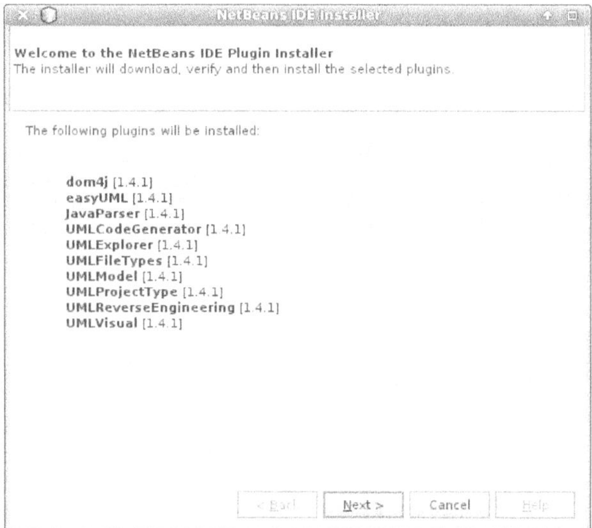

→ Check the **I accept the terms of the license agreements** box and click the
Install button:

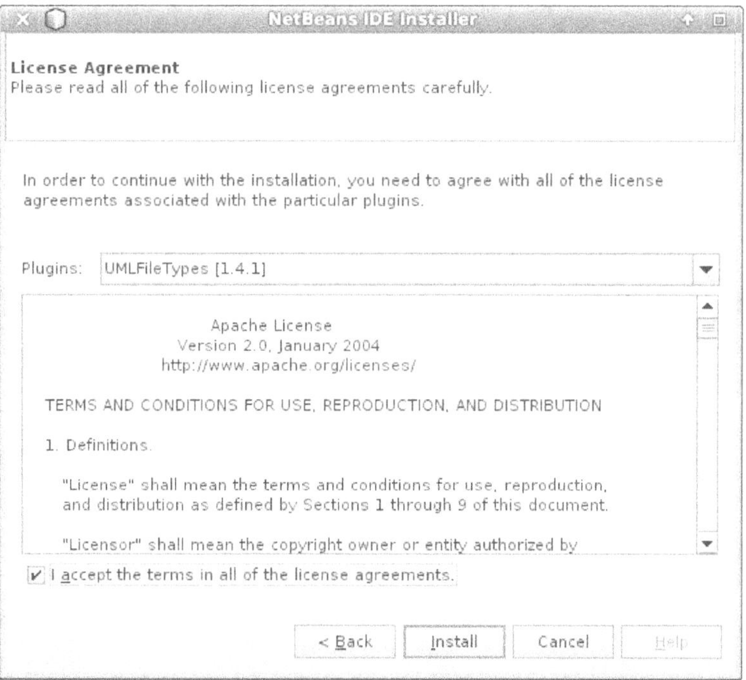

→ Click **Continue**:

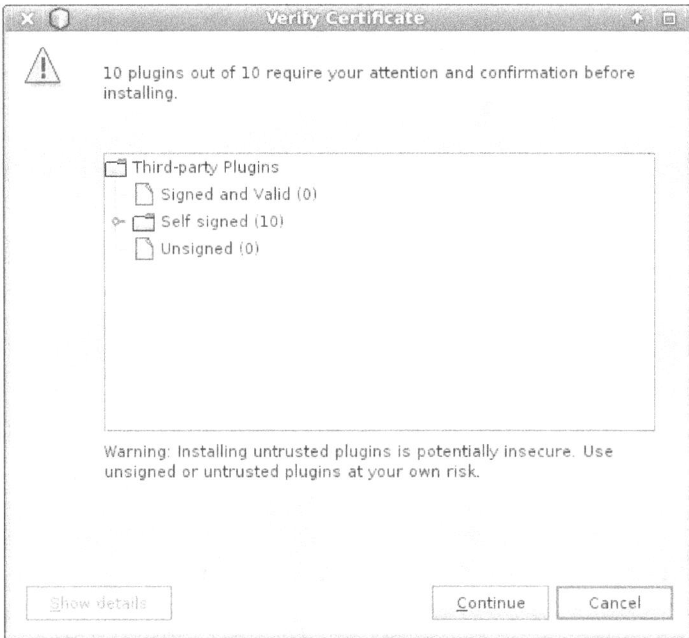

→ Finally, click **Finish**:

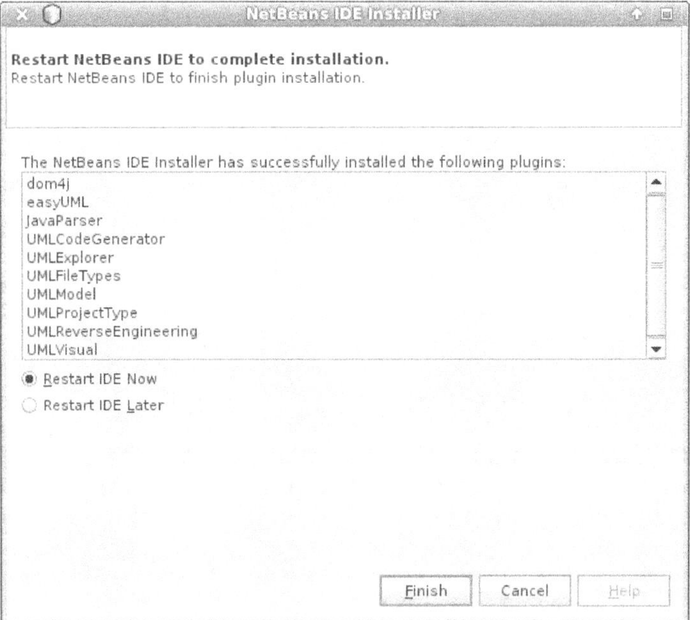

1.3.2.2 Other environments

The Eclipse editor is also a free and open-source solution for editing Java programs. Besides, there are many programs for editing class diagrams and generating Java code. For editing, the Papyrus plugin is one of the best. For code generation, UML2 Extender SDK is a good choice. Warning: Eclipse and its plugins are much more powerful, and therefore much more complex to use. When starting, it's best to use solutions like Netbeans / EasyUML.

Another popular Java editor is IntelliJ IDEA. It is richer than Netbeans and relatively easy to handle. However, only the "Ultimate" version supports UML features.

There are other Java editors, but unfortunately, none contain well-implemented UML features. We highly recommend these features for designing software solutions easily and quickly.

1.3.3 Example projects

We provide two sample projects with this book: a Java Project and a UML Project, available here:

`https://github.com/philippehenri-gosselin/patternsgameprog`

Click the green button "Clone or download" and then click "Download ZIP".

Both projects can be directly opened with Netbeans 8.2 or higher. By default, the LWJGL library for Windows is selected in the Java project. For another operating system, you must remove all associated .jar from the Libraries folder of the Netbeans project and add the ones from the target operating system. The different versions of LWJGL are available in the "lib" folder of the "Java Project" folder.

⇒ Note: When opening the sample Java project for the first time, Netbeans compiles all classes. There are thousands of classes, and it can be very long!

It is possible to open the Java project in another environment, knowing that:

- The src and extern files contain the main Java sources

- The test folder contains Java sources for unit tests

- The res folder contains the resources (images)

- The lib folder contains different versions of LWJGL depending on the operating system:

    - The lib/lwjgl-windows folder contains the library for Windows
    - The lib/lwjgl-linux folder contains the library for Linux
    - The lib/lwjgl-mac folder contains the library for Mac

CHAPTER 2

Represent the state of the game

2.1 Data representation

2.1.1 Initial design

The goal at this stage of the project is to find the best way to represent all the useful information for the game. Although it may seem easy, this step is essential and has consequences on the whole project, until the last stages. Therefore, it is important to devote considerable energy to it - while keeping in mind that it is never possible to plan everything.

Before starting computer concepts, it is strongly recommended to prepare this work on paper, by listing useful information for the game. It begins with the summary description of these, and then, while the list becomes large, it is relevant to start to make groupings.

This work can be done on a paper sheet if you are one or two, or on a whiteboard, if you are three to five. Beyond that, you will need more advanced project management techniques (not described in this book).

2.1.2   Types of information

The types of information required to represent the data are very numerous. Among these, it is often necessary to choose a way to represent the position of an element in the world. In the case of the Pacman game, it boils down to 2D coordinates (x, y). A concept of the relative position may also be needed, as in the Pacman game, where a moving character can be between two boxes. For games whose world is in 3D, a third coordinate is required, for example (x, y, z). To this can be added notions of places, such as level and/or floor in a building. It is also necessary to ask the question of the superposition of the elements. In some cases, elements can have similar coordinates, but in a certain order. For example, in strategy games, units can stack on the same cell, like in Civilization. In these cases, we need a position attribute in the stack.

There are then a large number of properties that can qualify an element or a group of elements. For example, in role-playing games, there are notions of life or mana. These attributes often have minimum and maximum values, which this stage of design must define. It is also necessary to specify if it is possible to have duplicates of properties and/or elements: this will have an important impact on the computer design that follows. There can also be notions of the lifetime of elements: these are most often represented by a time counter, like the "super" mode time for Pacman.

2.1.3   Example with the game Pacman

This section provides an example of a description of the elements of the Pacman game, in a simplified version.

A set of static elements (the world) and a set of moving elements (Pacman and ghosts) forms the game state. All elements have the following properties:

- Type of element
- Coordinates (x, y) in the grid

2.1.3.1   Static elements

A grid of elements called "boxes" or "cells" shapes the world. The size of this grid is set at the start of the level. The types of cells are:

Wall cells. They are impassable elements for moving elements. The possible textures are:

- Upper left corner, upper right corner, lower left corner, lower right corner
- Horizontal, vertical

The choice of the texture is purely aesthetic and does not influence the evolution of the game.

Space cells. The moving elements can cross space cells. The space types are:

- The empty spaces
- The gum spaces
- The super gum spaces
- The cemetery spaces, which serve to define the places where ghosts appear at the beginning of the game, but also places where those devoured by Pacman can resume a normal form.
- The start spaces, which define a possible initial position for Pacman.

2.1.3.2 Mobile elements

Moving elements have a direction (none, left, right, up or down), a speed, and a position. A position at zero means that the element is exactly on the cell. For the other values, it means that it is between two cells (the current one and the one defined by the direction of the element). When the position is equal to the speed, then the element moves to the next cell. Thus, the greater the numerical value of speed, the more the character will have a slow movement. Thanks to these mechanics, character movements are always synchronized with a global clock.

Pacman moving element. The player controls this element, thanks to the direction property. Pacman also has a "super counter", which is used to determine the remaining time before returning to a normal state. Finally, we use a property that we will name "status", which can take the following values:

- "Normal" status: the most common case where Pacman can move around the maze, and avoid ghosts
- "Super" status: Pacman can eat ghosts
- "Dead" status: A ghost caught Pacman

Ghost moving elements. The direction property also controls these elements, whether it comes from a human or an AI. These elements have two particular properties. The first one is "color", which is purely aesthetic. The only rule regarding this color is that it is unique for each ghost. The second particular property is the "status", which can take the following values:

- "Normal" status: the most common case where the ghost can kill Pacman.
- "Flee" status: where the ghost can be killed by "super" Pacman.
- "Eyes" status: where the ghost has been devoured by "super" Pacman.

⇒ Note: This example is intentionally incomplete: it is rare to imagine every possible case from conception. These definitions must be enhanced during the project.

2.1.4 Video Game Development: Specifications

It is now time to start the design of the game you have chosen:

→ Put on the paper the list of items you will need to represent a state of your game. Note that it is not necessary to define the rules of the game for the moment - even if you can start to think about it!

2.2 Basic information

Once the information is on the paper, one can begin to think about how to represent it from a computer point of view. At this stage, there is no programming yet, only design work on the structure of the representation.

2.2.1 Classes

Each application has a specific data structure, and it is not possible to offer a single recipe for all cases. However, we can highlight several common tools. The first of these tools is the representation of basic information, such as the users of a system or the different types of characters in a game. In this scope, the naive approach proposes to make representations independent of each other. With this approach, classes can represent one or more types of data.

⇒ Note: There are several ways to design these classes. The first and most natural is to draw them on a paper sheet. This old support may seem outdated when discovering software design; it is not the case! It remains infinitely faster to scribble a few classes and their relationships on paper, rather than consider alternatives. Do not hesitate to use it, and even more when working in a group. Once your essay begins to converge, it becomes interesting to use UML software. These allow you to represent your classes in a very clean way, but also to generate some of the corresponding source code.

2.2.1.1   Create a new class diagram with Netbeans / EasyUML

→ Click on the menu **File - New project . . .**, then choose the category **UML** and the type of project **UML Diagrams Project**:

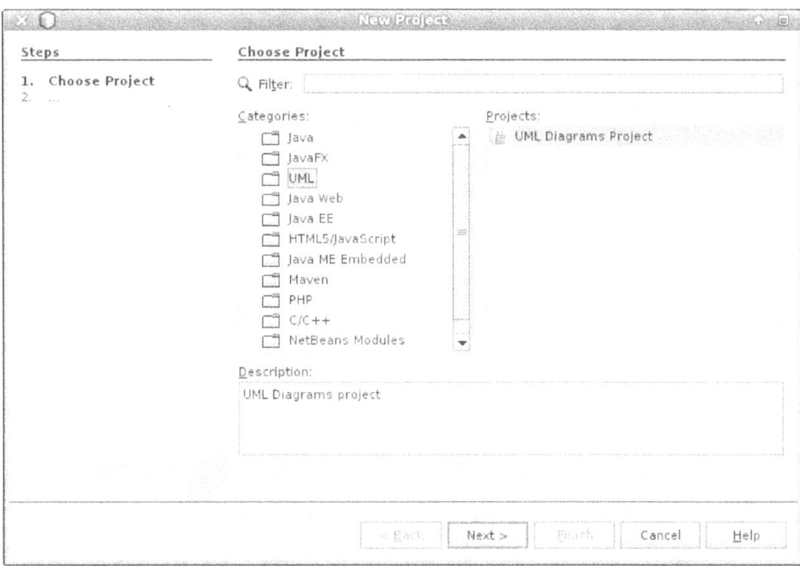

→ Click the **Next** button, and then enter the project name in the **Project Name** box and its folder in the **Project Location** box:

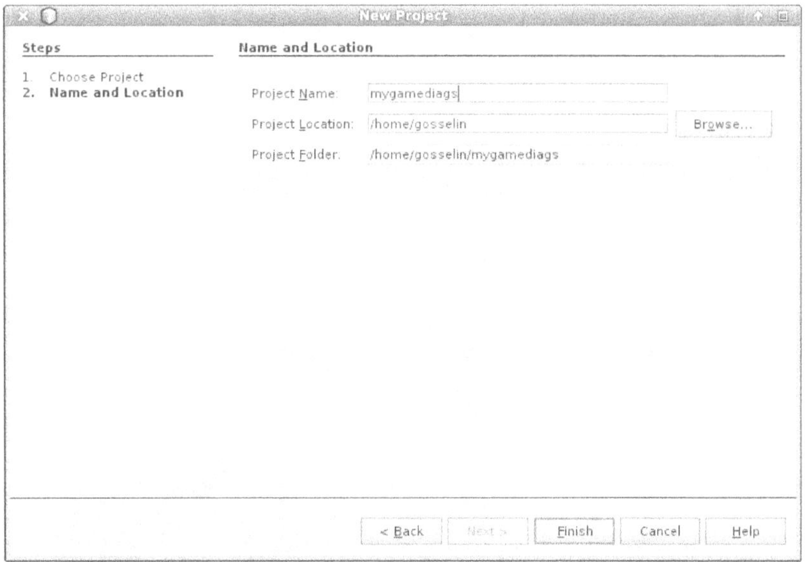

→ Click the **Finish** button.

After the UML project creation, it is possible to add class diagrams.

→ Right-click the **Class Diagrams** folder in the UML project. → This brings up the context menu: choose **New - Other ...**:

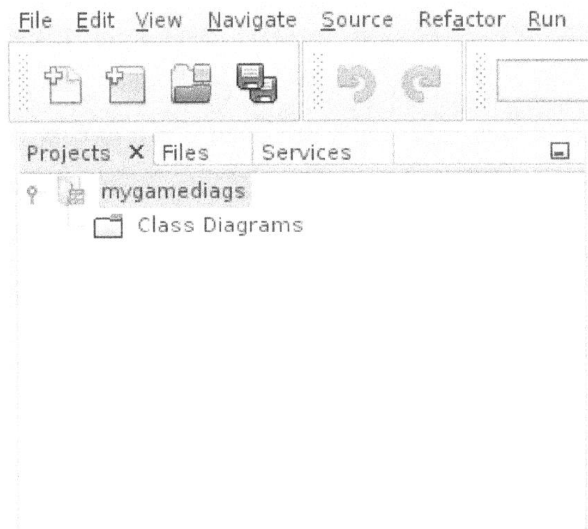

→ Choose the **UML** category and the **Class Diagram** file type:

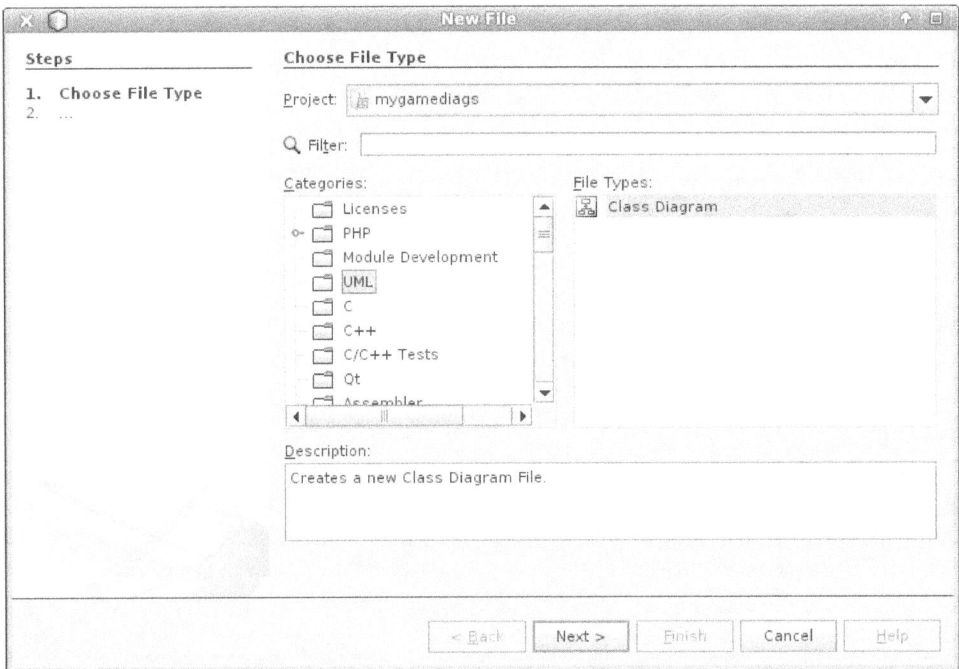

→ Click the **Next** button

→ Define the diagram name in the **Name** box:

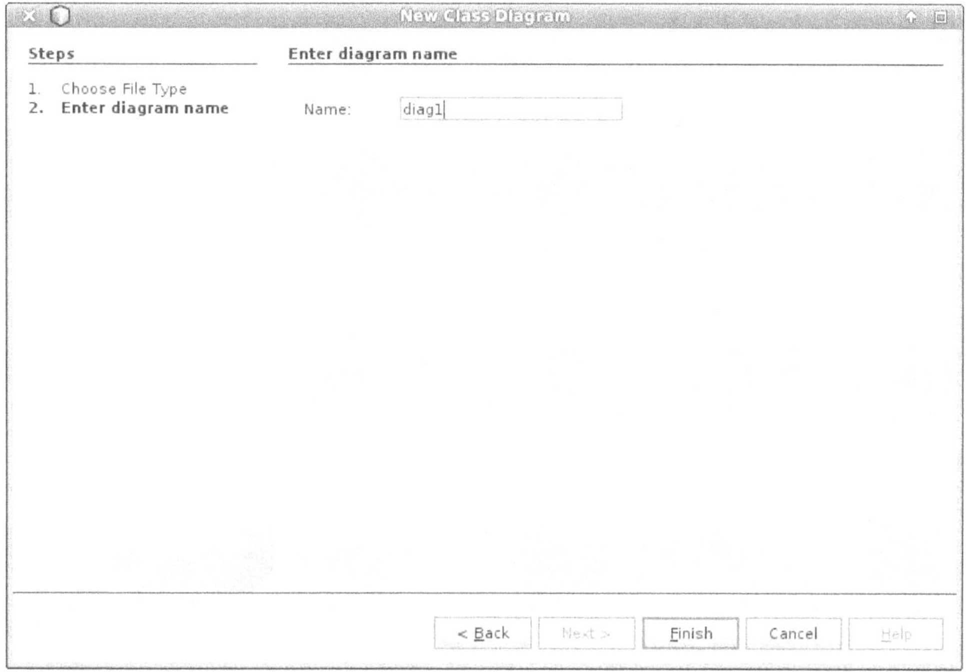

→ Click **Finish**

→ Open the class diagram by double-clicking on its file in the **Project** window.

It brings up several windows:

- The central window is the diagram window (empty in this example).

- The window at the top right is the tools palette to form the diagram.

- The window at the bottom right contains the properties of the currently selected element (if any, none in this example).

- The window at the bottom left provides an overview of the diagram.

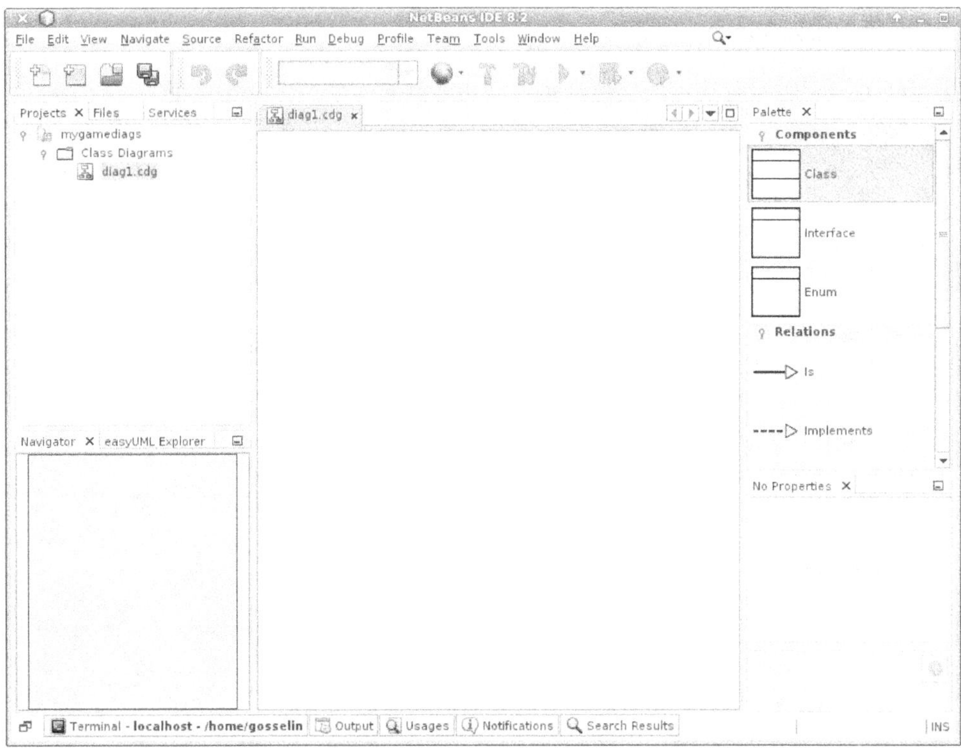

2.2.1.2   Adding a class

Creating classes with EasyUML is very simple, for example, to create a `Pacman` class with two integer attributes x and y:

→ Click the **Class** tool from the palette to the diagram;

→ Double-click on the title of the new class, then enter "Pacman";

→ Double-click in the box under the class title (you should see **double-click to add field**), then enter "int x";

→ Double-click in the box under the x attribute, and enter "int y".

The following result is expected:

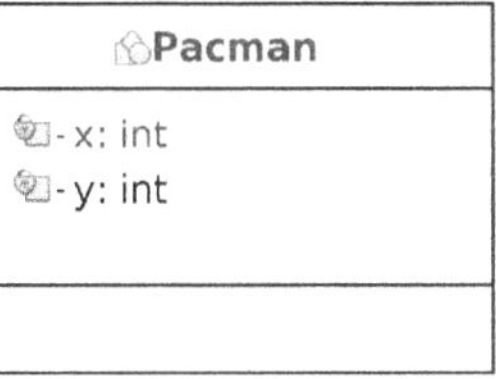

2.2.1.3 Adding an enumeration

Among the properties of Pacman listed in the previous section, there is the direction. Since there is only a fixed number of directions (North, South, East, West), it is useful to use an enumeration of these directions rather than using integer values. This approach reduces the risk of error since it is no longer necessary to memorize the numerical values corresponding to each direction.

Enumeration creation is very similar to classes:

→ Create an enumeration by dragging the **Enum** tool in the palette to the diagram.

→ Double-click the title of the new enumeration, and type "Direction";

→ Add the four directions "NORTH", "SOUTH", "EAST" and "WEST" as well as the value "NONE" to represent the absence of direction;

→ To do this, double-click in the box under the title, and enter the values.

It should give you the following result:

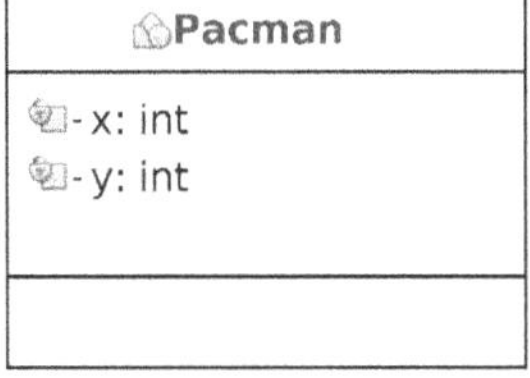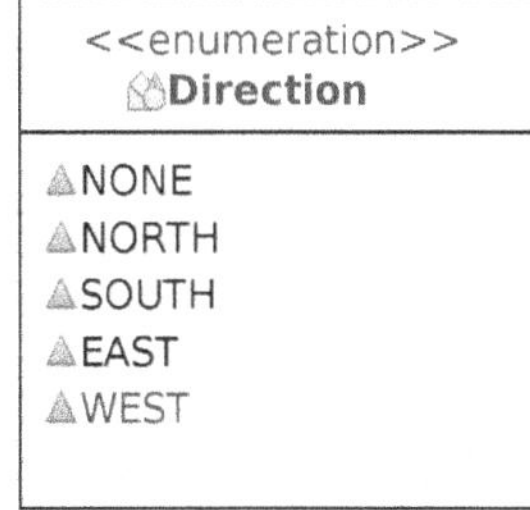

→ Now add a Direction attribute of type `Direction` in the `Pacman` class.

→ Click-drag the icon **Has** with an arrow in the palette to the right to the Pacman class.

→ Reproduce the values in the above dialog: fields **Field name** with the value "direction" and **Target** with the enumeration Direction.

→ Validate to obtain the following diagram:

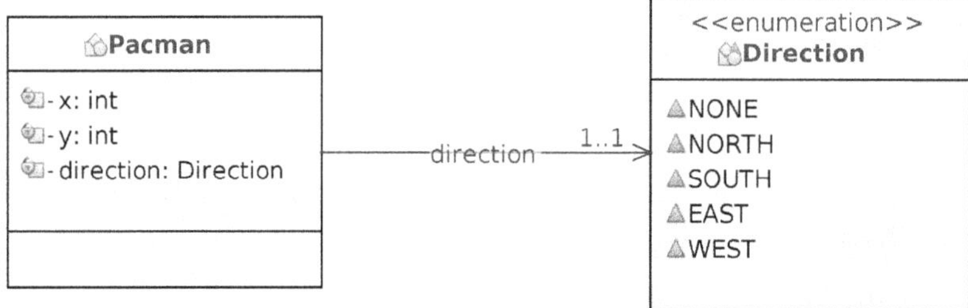

The arrow from the Pacman class to the Direction enumeration is an association. The object pointed to by the arrow indicates that the Pacman class has a Direction attribute, whose name is "direction". The expression "1..1" indicates that the class has 1 and only 1 reference to an instance of this enumeration.

2.2.2 Hierarchy of classes (Polymorphism)

A naïve approach to element representation is to create an independent class for each element. It does not follow one of the major rules of software design: the pooling of solutions. Indeed, several classes can need the same information. It is advisable to identify the information common to the different elements and to use a hierarchy of classes to gather them in parent classes.

2.2.2.1 Parent/Super class

For example, in the Pacman game, the coordinates (x, y) are information common to all the elements. Therefore, we can create an `Element` parent/super class that contains them:

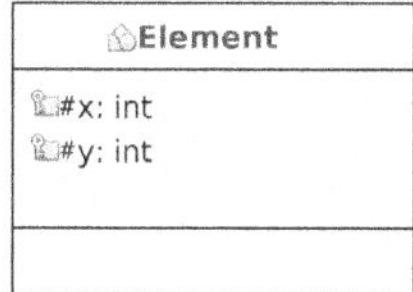

→ Add the `Element` class to your diagram, with the two attributes x and y.

In the figure above, an icon with a key precedes the attributes, as well as the symbol "#". It means that these attributes are protected: only the `Element` class and its child classes can access them. To achieve this result with EasyUML:

→ Click on the attribute we want to modify: the **Properties** window on the bottom right shows its properties:

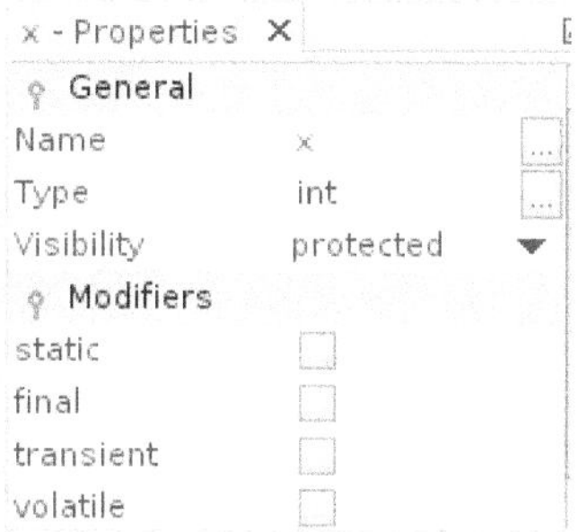

→ Reproduce the above properties by changing the value of **Visibility** to "protected".

The diagram is now modified to trace the attributes and indicate that `Pacman` is a child class of `Element`:

→ Delete the x and y attributes of the `Pacman` class by right-clicking on it and then by clicking **Delete Field** in the context menu.

→ Drag the icon **Is** with an arrow in the palette to the right to the `Pacman` class.

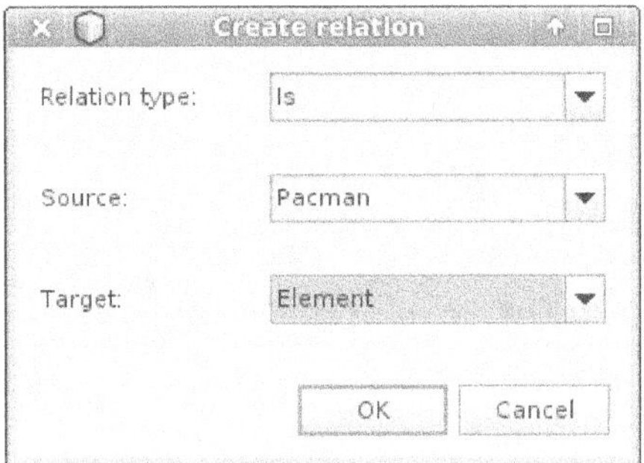

→ Reproduce the values in the dialog above, then validate to obtain the following diagram:

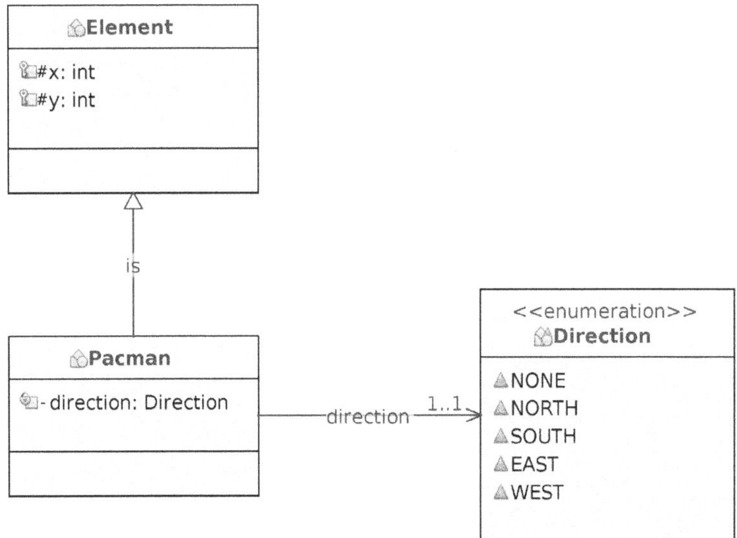

This work can be generalized with the addition of the `Ghost` class: it also contains information shared with all moving elements. As a result, we expand the hierarchy with a `MobileElement` class. By adding all the properties defined in the specifications, and using the principles presented so far, we obtain the following result:

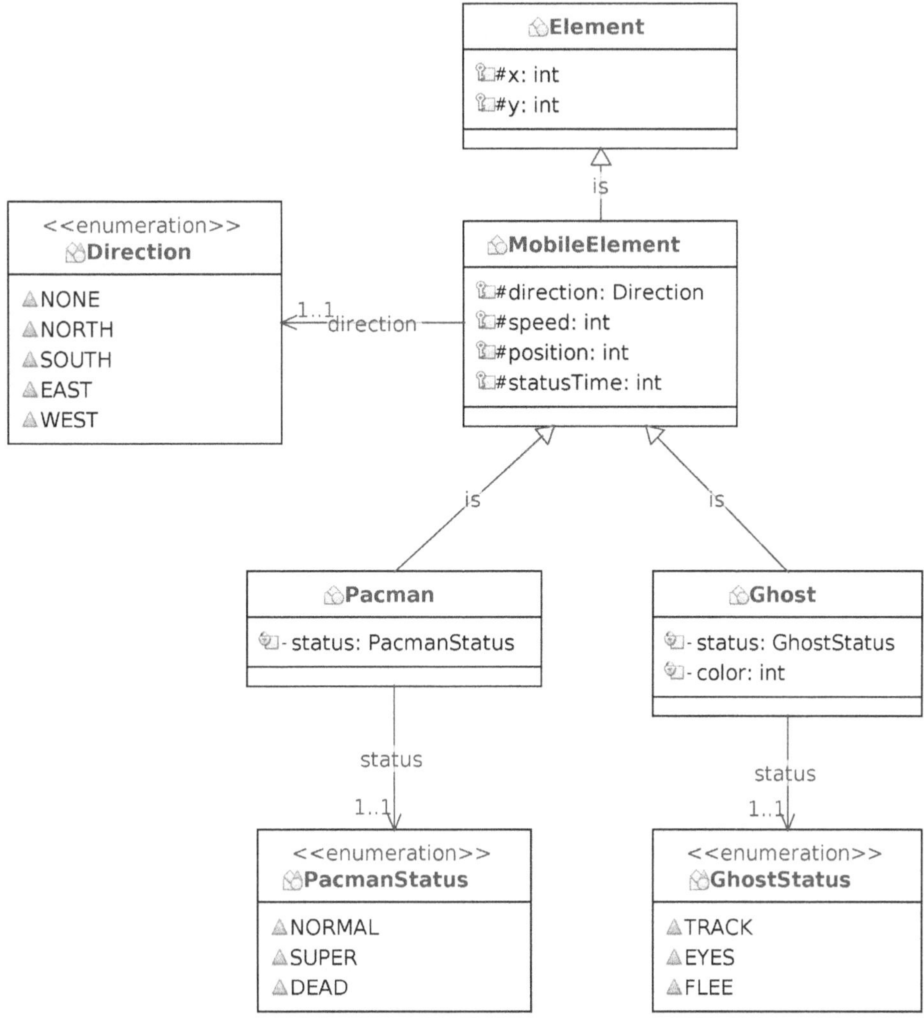

2.2.2.2 Static elements

The case of walls (impassable elements) and spaces (places where characters can move) is discussed in this section. Following the class hierarchy principle, you can start by creating a `StaticElement` class for all classes of fixed elements, a `Wall` class for walls, and a `Space` class for spaces:

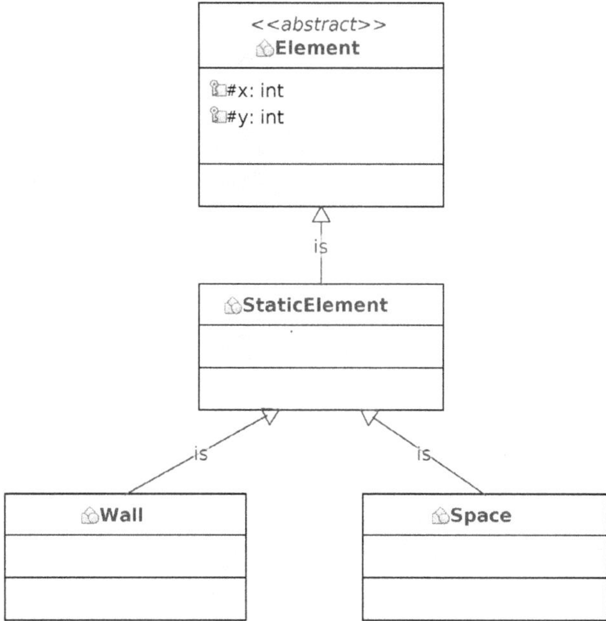

Then, a first approach can be to propose a class for each type of wall and space, all wall types inheriting a `Wall` class, and similarly for spaces. This army of classes for each subtype is debatable since no attribute or method is introduced in these new classes. A similar but much simpler result can be obtained by using the `Wall` and `Space` classes with an attribute that defines the specific nature of the element.

Enumerations are used to define the different types of walls and spaces. These allow to name the different possibilities, instead of numbers or symbols, and thus make the code much more readable:

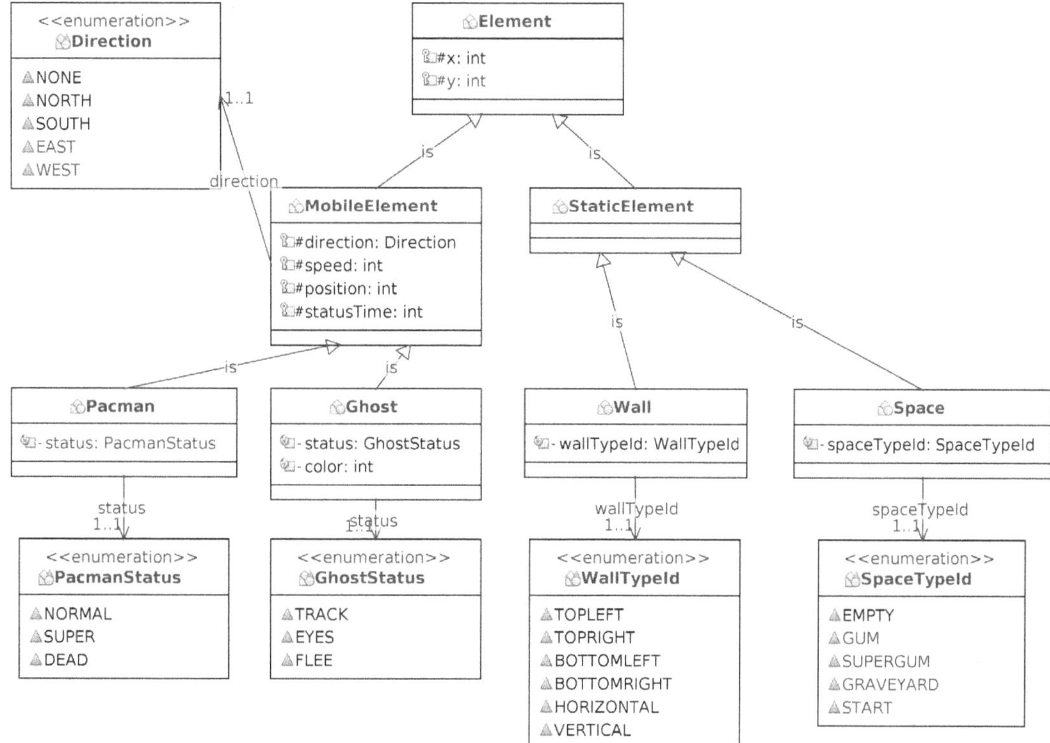

⇒ Note: In this example, we are facing a usual problem in class hierarchy design: when do we need to create child classes? To help answer this question, one should start by asking if the child class requires a new attribute or method. If the answer is positive, then it is likely that its creation is relevant. If not, you may introduce unnecessary complexity - using enumerations can be an interesting alternative.

2.2.2.3 Accessors and mutators (*getters and setters*)

The classes defined above do not have public attributes: without methods, it is not possible to modify them. To do this, accessors (*getters*) are added to allow access to the value of an attribute. By convention, the name of an assessor method is `getAttributeName()`. For example, for the x attribute, the assessor is `getX()`, for `status`: `getStatus()`, and for `spaceTypeId`: `getSpaceTypeId()`. The purpose of an assessor is, in most cases, simply to return the value of the attribute, for instance:

```java
public int getX() {
    return x ;
}
```

The mutators (*setters*) allow modifying the value of an attribute. By convention, their name is setAttributeName(). For example, for status: setStatus(). Their implementation is in most cases a simple update of the attribute, for example:

```java
public void setX(int x) {
    this.x = x;
}
```

Modern development environments, such as Netbeans, are capable of automatically generating these methods. In general, it is not necessary to overload the class diagram with their definition. There are, however, cases where their presence makes sense, like the one of the next section.

The real usefulness of accessors and mutators is a legitimate question when you start in software design. Indeed, it seems simpler to use public attributes and to work without this unnecessary complexity. There are many reasons to motivate these methods, and the first of these is the need to separate the interface from the implementation. The interface, in this case, is the set of accessor and mutator methods. The implementation is the name and types of the attributes. As long as the interface remains unchanged, the implementation developer can freely modify the internal components: for example, modify the type of an attribute. If an attribute is public, all the code outside the class that uses this attribute must also be changed. It can be complex internally, and even more if you have people outside the local development team. In the case of using getters/setters, modify their implementation so that the new type of attribute is supported. This kind of change is common in the design of an application, so it is always safer to use these methods. Furthermore, modern tools can generate them very easily, so there is no reason not using them! In terms of computational cost, the current compilers are so efficient that the call to these methods has no overhead.

Another case that motivates the creation of getters/setters is the one presented in the next section.

2.2.3 Combination of properties (Composition)

This section introduces advanced notions, and can be ignored at first reading.

2.2.3.1 Interfaces

The hierarchical model works as long as the elements have exclusive properties. This model is not relevant if there are common properties in various places in the hierarchy, without the possibility to find a common superclass.

Imagine the following case: we have three types of vehicles:

- Tanks that can move on land thanks to their wheels.
- Boats that can move on water thanks to their propellers.
- Submersibles that can move on land and water thanks to their wheels and their propellers, which they use according to the situation.

A design attempt using a hierarchy could be:

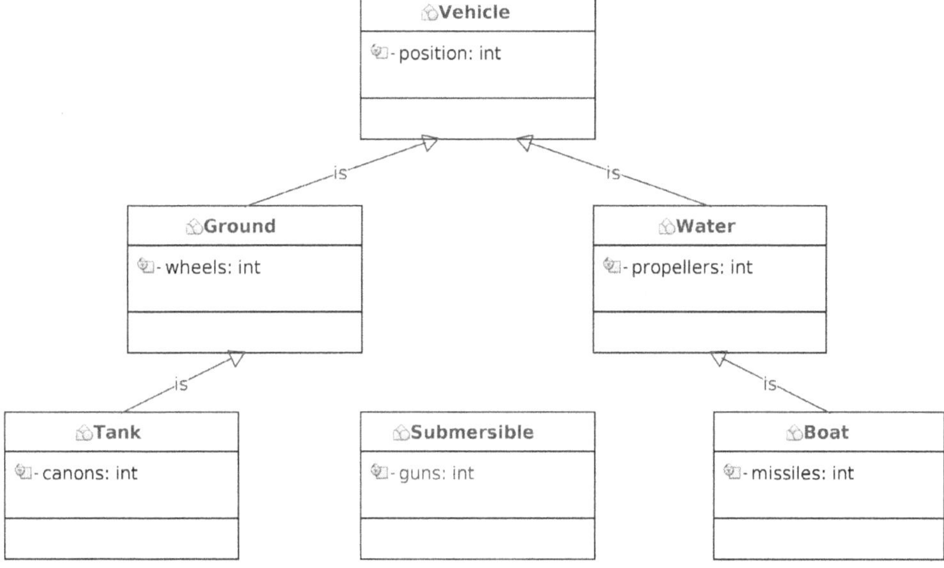

However, there is one major problem: Is the submersible a land vehicle or a water vehicle? The answer is simple: it is both, but we can not inherit two classes at a time.

The first solution is to use interfaces for common properties. In our example, this relates to the terrestrial (`Ground`) and marine (`Water`) properties. Then, the classes concerned by these properties implement the interfaces. For our example, this can give the following result:

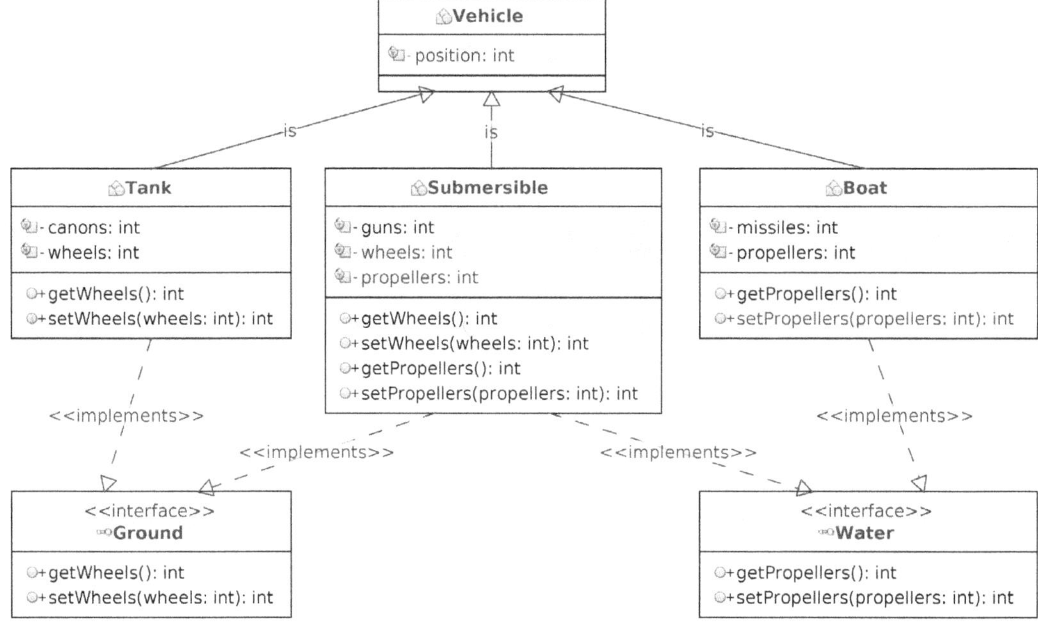

The `Tank` class implements the `Ground` interface: it responds to its properties, namely to own wheels.

The `Boat` class implements the `Water` interface: it has propellers.

Finally, the class `Submersible` has wheels and propellers, and it implements both interfaces.

This approach does not prohibit the hierarchy when it is justified. In this example, we keep the parent class `Vehicle`, there is no reason to modify it.

⇒ Note: If you want to reproduce the diagram above with Netbeans / EasyUML, the principle is the same as with the classes: drag "Interface" from the palette. Similarly, for the relationship "Implements", proceed as for the relation "Is".

This type of design offers advantages; for example, it is easy to identify and process all elements that have a particular property. For example, if all marine vehicles must be processed:

```java
List<Vehicle> list = new ArrayList();
for (Vehicle vehicle : list) {
    if (vehicle instanceof Water) {
        Water water = (Water)vehicle;
        System.out.println(water.getPropellers());
    }
}
```

2.2.3.2 Composition

In the previous approach, we repeated attributes in each class. For example, the `wheels` attribute is in the `Tank` and `Submersible` classes. It is not a problem in this example because there is only one attribute. In other more complex cases, the same interface may contain dozens of attributes, which can quickly become time-consuming to reproduce. A second approach avoids this repetition, this time using the composition:

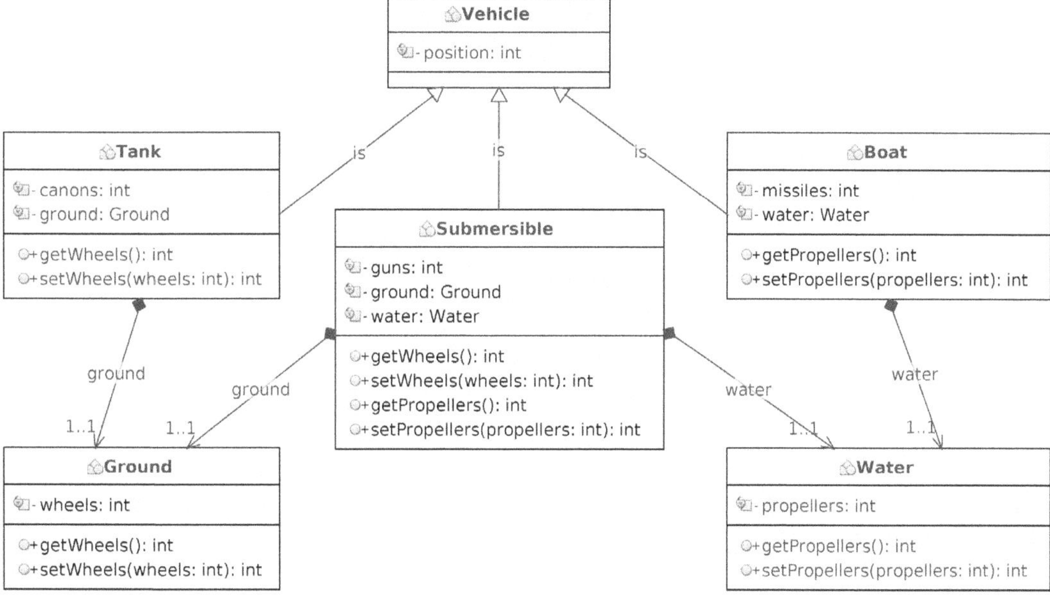

In this case, there is a `Ground` class and a `Water` class and no interfaces. Compositions (solid arrows with a diamond) replace implementations (dashed arrows). The solid arrows also point a class attribute. For example, in the `Tank` class, there is a `ground` attribute of type `Ground` . The expression "1..1" on the dialing arrow indicates that there is only one and only one `Ground` attribute. The composition also indicates that the item designated by the arrow is part of the container: destroy the container also destroys the contents. For example, if you destroy a tank, you also destroy its wheels. From a conceptual point of view, you can not have wheels without a vehicle that can contain them, like a tank.

The implementation of methods of classes with ground properties (like `Tank` or `Submersible`) is very simple since it is enough to repeat the call to the same methods of the property class (like `Ground`). For example, in the `Tank` class:

```java
public int getWheels() {
    return ground.getWheels();
}
```

2.2.3.3 Interfaces and Composition

The second approach loses the ability to easily identify elements that have particular properties, as in the code example above, where water vehicles are processed. The solution is to combine the two approaches, mixing interfaces and composition:

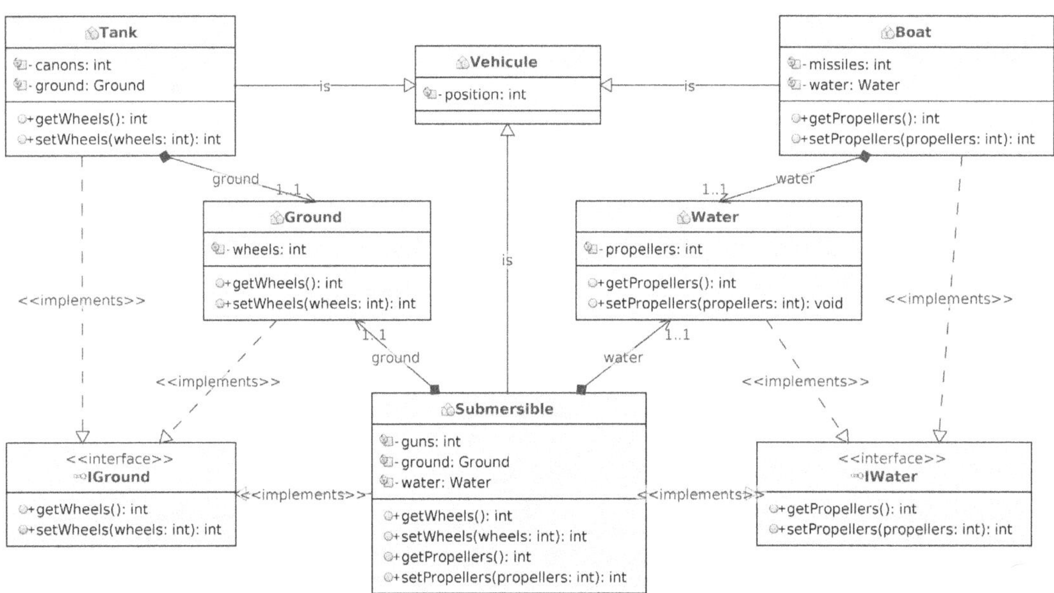

This solution combines all the advantages: the properties are defined once and only once (in a class like `Ground`), and it is possible to consider any vehicle at the desired angle (via an interface like `IGround`). The main disadvantage of this approach is its complexity: it is, therefore, important to judge the need for the features provided. In practice, the first approach is enough to answer most of the problems.

These approaches can seem very tedious. Keep in mind that the energy spent on design is time saved in the long run. For example, when implementing the logic of the game, the ability to identify and manipulate instances according to their properties is a considerable time saver. Otherwise, each class must be treated independently and duplicate the code for each case with similar properties. The risk of erroneous code duplication is usually high enough to justify the energy spent on these interfaces and/or composition approaches.

2.2.4 Exercices

2.2.4.1 Exercise: Role-playing game

We propose here to find a representation for the characters of a role-playing game. We have the following information:

- All characters have a name and a level.
- There are two main categories of characters: mages and bruisers.
- Mages need a resource called "mana" to cast their spells. It has a certain amount at any time and maximum capacity.
- Magicians are either priests or sorcerers.
- The bruisers are either warriors or rangers. Warriors must accumulate rage to use their abilities. Rangers are always accompanied by a pet, who owns his name and his level. The pet and the ranger are related to life to death: if one disappears, the other too.

→ Propose a class diagram that addresses these constraints. Note that there are no expected methods, only classes, their attributes, and relationships between them.

2.2.4.2 Exercise: Roleplay game with multi-classing

This advanced exercise requires having read and understood the section on combinations of properties.

We propose here to find a representation for the characters of a role-playing game. We have the following information:

- All characters have a name and a level.
- There are two great character abilities: magic and strength. Magic requires mana, and strength requires rage.
- There are three types of characters: mages, warriors, and paladins.
- Mages can only do magic with their mana
- Warriors can only use strength through their rage
- Paladins can do magic with mana as well as use strength with their rage

→ Propose a class diagram that addresses these constraints. The only expected methods are accessors and mutators (*setters/getters*).

2.2.5   Video Game Development: Element classes

The goal here is to find classes to represent the elements that were defined in the paper in the previous step.

→ Determine whether a class hierarchy is sufficient to meet the constraints. For beginners, it is strongly advised to follow a hierarchy and to return to the paper definition of the game if this one is too complex for a hierarchy. In other cases, opt for the model with a combination of properties.

→ Make a class diagram. The simplest is to scribble a sketch on paper. Once this first test is successful, it must be reproduced with UML software, like Netbeans / EasyUML.

At this stage of the design, it is not yet a question of game rules, but only of the state, e.g., the data necessary to represent any element of the game. In general, we don't need to define methods at this step.

2.3   Containers

2.3.1   Lists and associative arrays

Once the basic information is defined, it is necessary to store them in containers (or *collections*). For cases where we only expect a small number of elements, attributes in a class is a good choice. In other cases, we require a data structure. There are many possibilities, each with its advantages and disadvantages.

2.3.1.1   Lists

Lists allow storing a variable number of elements according to an index between 0 and the number of elements minus 1. These indices are obligatorily continuous: if you want to ignore one of the locations of a list, it is necessary to place a null reference there. The two main operations of the lists are the addition (*add*) and the access (*get*), both present in the interface `java.util.List`.

There are two main types of lists: arrays (`java.util.ArrayList`) and linked lists (`java.util.LinkedList`). Both types can perform the same operations but differ in their speed of execution. Accessing an element of an array is very fast and does not depend on its size. However, adding or removing an element depends on the size of the array: adding a new element to an array can take a very long time to complete. Conversely, linked lists can be modified very quickly. However, access to the elements depends on the size of the linked list: when it is very large, the accesses are very expensive in computations.

`java.util.List` variables can either refer to a table or a list:

```java
List<String> list = new ArrayList();
```

or :

```java
List<String> list = new LinkedList();
```

In both cases, the access methods are the same. For example, the `add()` method adds an element:

```java
list.add("cherry");
list.add("banana");
```

It is possible to modify an existing element with the method `set()`. For example, to change the element at index 1:

```java
list.set(1,"apple");
```

The index must exist: otherwise, an exception is thrown.

The `get()` method retrieves an element from its index:

```java
String cherry = list.get(0);
String apple = list.get(1);
```

The `indexOf()` method retrieves an element from its value:

```java
int zero = list.indexOf("cherry");
int one = list.indexOf("apple");
```

It is possible to browse a list with the *for each* syntax:

```java
for (String element : list) {
    System.out.println(element);
}
```

The choice between arrays and linked lists is very important: in case of error, a slowdown can be observed, only for reasons of bad design. You should wonder if you spend more time accessing the elements of the container or adding/removing these elements. In the case where there is no real preference, there are data structures such as the chained array. Unfortunately, the standard Java library does not contain chained arrays. You can use associative arrays instead (presented later in this chapter).

The arrays have an *O(1)* access complexity, and an element addition/deletion complexity is *O(n)*. Conversely, linked lists have an access complexity *O(n)* and an element addition/deletion complexity *O(1)*.

⇒ Note: We use the mathematical notation *O([function])* to represent the complexity of an operation. For example, if the container has *n* element, a complexity noted *O(n)* is linear: doubling the size of the container doubles the complexity or processing time. A complexity noted $O(n^2)$ is quadratic: increasing the size of the container makes the processing time unmanageable. A complexity denoted *O(1)* is the smallest possible: it does not depend on the size of the container. Ideally, a design exploits only operations with a complexity *O(1)*. Finally, there are many algorithms with a complexity noted *O(log n)*. Although larger than *O(1)*, it offers a very interesting speed of execution, and is much lower than *O(n)*, even when n is very large.

As part of the design of the state of the video game, the lists allow storing most elements that do not have a particular position in the space. For example, all the objects a character carries or the composition of an army.

2.3.1.2 Stacks and Queues

Stacks and queues are particular cases of lists, where only two operations are involved: add (*push / add / offer*) and remove (*pop / remove / poll*) an element. These operations are present in the `java.util.Queue` interface. Double ended queue (*deque*) structures are capable of efficiently performing both types of operations. Based on this restriction, implementations provide a very fast processing time: *O(1)*. Each type of stack/queue removes the elements according to their own rules. For example, the default stack always removes the last added item. The regular queue always removes the first element added. The priority queue removes the element that minimizes a freely defined criterion.

Depending on the nature of the chosen stack/queue, you can reference a stack or queue with the `java.util.Queue` interface. The behavior is different, but the calls always the same. To create a queue:

```java
Queue<String> queue = new ArrayDeque();
```

To create a stack:

```java
Queue<String> stack = Collections.asLifoQueue(new ArrayDeque());
```

An instance of `java.util.ArrayDeque` is also created: it can produce a queue and stack behavior with the same efficiency. The default behavior is the queue, to get the one of a stack, the `Collections.asLifoQueue()` static method allows you to switch from one to the other.

To create a priority queue:

```java
Queue<String> queue = new PriorityQueue();
```

Now, the same methods can be used to modify these containers. The `add()` method is used to add an element:

```
stack.add("cherry");
```

The `poll()` method is used to remove an element:

```
String cherry = stack.poll();
```

The element removed depends on the choice of the container. For the following code:

```
Queue<String> stack = // Choose one queue type
stack.add("cherry");
stack.add("apple");
stack.add("banana");
while(!stack.isEmpty()) {
    System.out.println(stack.poll());
}
```

If the container is a queue, the display order is that of adding:

```
cherry
apple
banana
```

If the container is a stack, the display order is reversed:

```
banana
apple
cherry
```

If the container is a priority queue, the display order is the lexical order:

```
banana
cherry
apple
```

⇒ Note: Just like lists, it is possible to browse the elements of a queue/stack with the *for each* syntax. The traversal order with this method does not depend on the type of the queue/stack. It is necessary to use the `poll()` method to obtain a behavior according to the nature of the container.

For video games, a stack can be interesting to represent an accumulation of properties on a cell of the world or for a character. A queue can be interesting to memorize all the units that a building must produce. Priority queues are often used for the resolution of advanced algorithms, such as those used for the creation of artificial intelligence.

2.3.1.3 Associative arrays

Associative arrays allow containing elements referenced by any type of index (or almost), called keys. The two main operations are the addition of a pair (key, value) (*put*) and the access function using a key (*get*). These operations are present in the interface `java.util.Map`.

There are two main types of associative arrays: red-black trees (`java.util.TreeMap`) and hash tables (`java.util.HashMap`). Ordered keys are mandatory for trees. To ensure this, one can use classes for keys that implement the `java.util.Comparable` interface. The red-black trees rely on this property to build a fast index. In addition, it allows browsing the elements of the tree in the order defined by the ordering.

Hash tables do not require ordered keys, but do not offer the ability to browse items in a well-defined order. Hash tables require a hash function, implemented in the `hashCode()` method of the key class. Defining this function is usually quite simple since it is often the combination of hash functions on standard classes, whose hash function is already defined. There is also a `java.util.LinkedHashMap` class with the properties of the hash tables and the preserving of the insertion order.

To create a red-black tree, here with `String` keys and `Integer` values:

```java
Map<String,Integer> map = new TreeMap();
```

For hash tables:

```java
Map<String,Integer> map = new HashMap();
```

And finally hash tables with linked lists:

```java
Map<String,Integer> map = new LinkedHashMap();
```

Adding values is done with the `put()` method, which requires a key and the corresponding value:

```java
map.put("cherry",2);
```

The `get()` method allows to find the value corresponding to a key:

```java
int two = map.get("cherry");
```

It is possible to browse all the pairs (key, value) with the syntax *for each* and the method `entrySet()`:

```java
Map<String,Integer> map = // choose a type of
                          // associative array
map.put("cherry",2);
map.put("apple",4);
map.put("banana",7);
for(Map.Entry<String,Integer> pair:map.entrySet()){
    System.out.println(pair.getValue()+" "+pair.getKey()+"(s)");
}
```

Depending on the type of table chosen, one obtains a different ordering. For example, with red-black trees, the ordering is the lexical order of the keys:

```
7 banana(s)
2 cherry(s)
4 apple(s)
```

With hash tables, the order is unpredictable, and can change after each element insertion or deletion:

```
4 apple(s)
7 banana(s)
2 cherry(s)
```

Finally, with hash tables with linked list, the insertion order is preserved:

```
2 cherry(s)
4 apple(s)
7 banana(s)
```

In terms of computational complexity, trees are a little slower than hash tables - assuming that the hash function is well chosen. On the other hand, hash tables have an important memory overhead, which can be problematic for very large volumes of data. The case of linked list hash tables has an even greater memory cost. In all cases, accessing and modifying an associative array has a better execution time than the worst case of an array or linked list. It makes it a good compromise when you need both access and quick changes.

We can also note the associative sets, which contain only keys and no values. They allow noting the presence of elements easily. One find `java.util.TreeSet<K>`, an equivalent of `java.util.TreeMap<K, Boolean>` and `java.util.HashSet<K>`, an equivalent of `java.util.HashMap <K, Boolean>`.

For the creation of a game, an associative array is interesting to draw up a list of properties, like all the buildings built in a city. In this example, keys can be the building names. For the value, if the buildings have no properties, we use associative sets. Otherwise, if a class represents the buildings, we use associative arrays.

Here is a synthesis of the properties of the different conventional containers:

Type	Java class	Order	Access	Add/ Remove	Memory Overhead
Array	ArrayList	No	O(1)	O(n)	very low
Linked List	LinkedList	No	O(n)	O(1)	low
Stack	ArrayDeque	No	O(1)	O(1)	very low
Queue	ArrayDeque	No	O(1)	O(1)	very low
Priority Queue	PriorityQueue	Yes	O(1)	O(1)	low
RB Trees	TreeMap	Yes	O(logn)	O(logn)	low
Hash Tables	HashMap	No	O(1)	O(1)	high
Hash + Linked	LinkedHashMap	No	O(1)	O(1)	high

2.3.2   Store sparse elements (Decorator Pattern)

The first kind of distribution of elements is the sparse case, where the elements are not arranged regularly. For the Pacman game, the characters (Pacman and the 4 ghosts) correspond to this type of distribution. It is also the case for most platform games (Mario, Sonic, ...), first player shooters, role-playing games, for units in strategy games, etc.

The usual solution is to use lists (`java.util.List`), and in particular arrays (`java.util.ArrayList`). Indeed, the number of these elements is generally stable. Stable means changes at most one time per second, which is already a very long time for games where we display 60 frames per second. Furthermore, many random accesses are required. The simplest solution is, therefore, to create an array of elements. For example, for the Pacman game, we can create an array of type `ArrayList<Element>`.

Even if `java.util.ArrayList` already has a lot of nice features, it misses functionalities dedicated to the game we are creating. For example, in the case where the elements have coordinates (x, y), it may be interesting to have a method that returns all the elements to given coordinates. To do this, you can use the *Decorator Pattern*, which extends the functionality of an existing class.

In this pattern, we assume that we have an interface that defines a certain number of functionalities, as well as existing implementations:

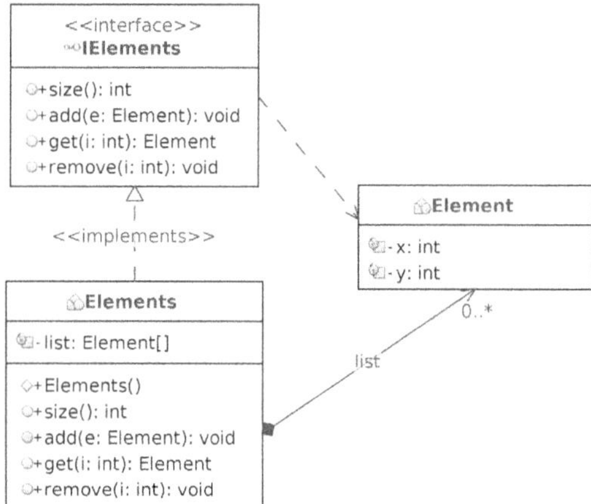

In the above example, it is the `IElements` interface that defines the features: it allows you to manipulate a list of `Element`. Then, we assume that there are direct implementations of this interface. In the example above, the `Elements` class plays this role. It relies on a native array with the `list` attribute.

Implementing the Decorator pattern amounts to creating a new class that enriches the functionality of an existing layout. For example, adding a `Characters` class:

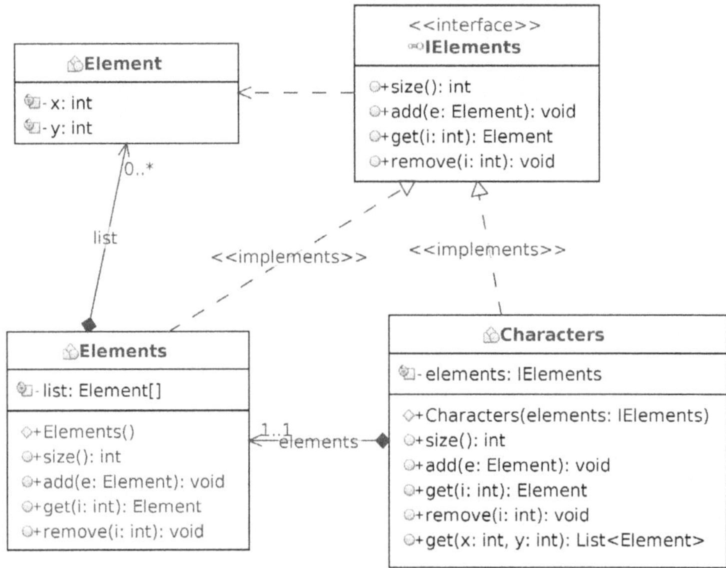

The `Characters` class is the class that decorates any `IElement` implementation. It replicates all existing features and adds a new feature with the `List<Element>` `get (int x, int y)` method. This returns the list of elements to the coordinates (x, y).

The `Characters` constructor initializes the `elements`. This list is the one decorated by the `Characters` class:

```
public Characters(IElements elements) {
    this.elements = elements;
}
```

The implementation of the `Characters` methods that inherit `IElements` is very simple, just invoke the `elements` methods, for example:

```
public Element get(int i) {
    return elements.get(i);
}
```

For the case of the new methods, we are free to add any new functionality, for example:

```java
public List<Element> get(int x, int y) {
    List<Element> list = new ArrayList<Element>();
    for (int i=0;i<elements.size();i++) {
        Element element = elements.get(i);
        if (element.getX() == x && element.getY() == y) {
            list.add(element);
        }
    }
    return list;
}
```

The above example uses a native array to ease the presentation of the Decorator pattern. In practice, it is better to use the lists of the standard library: no need to reinvent the wheel. For example, we can decorate an implementation of `java.util.List<Element>`:

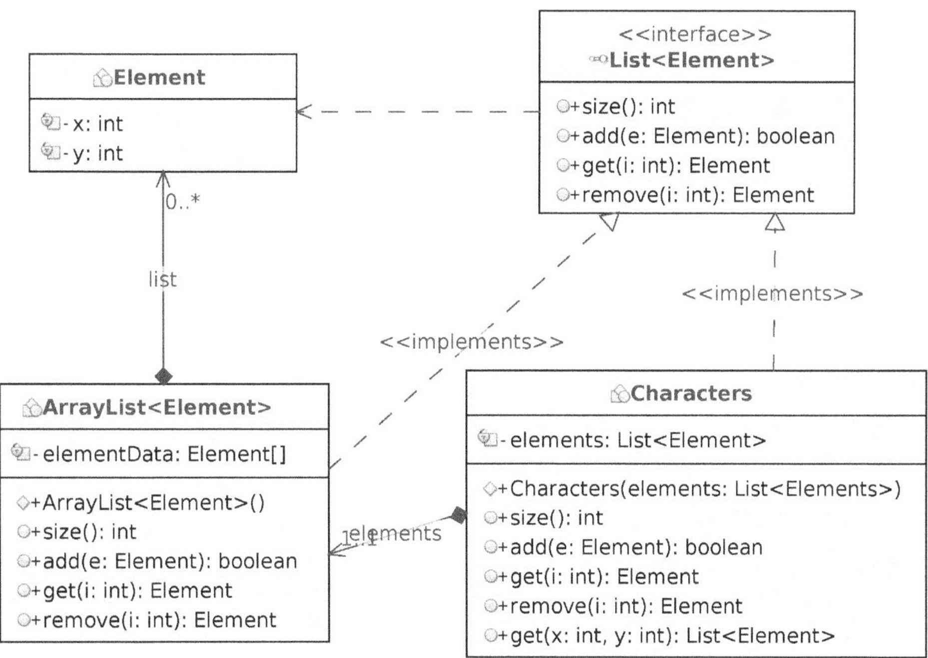

In the diagram above, all methods of the `java.util.List<Element>` interface are not represented for readability.

In many cases in this book, the class and interface methods of the standard library will not always be presented in the diagram. It allows lightening the diagram without risk: the classes of the standard library are well known. The light version of the example above gives:

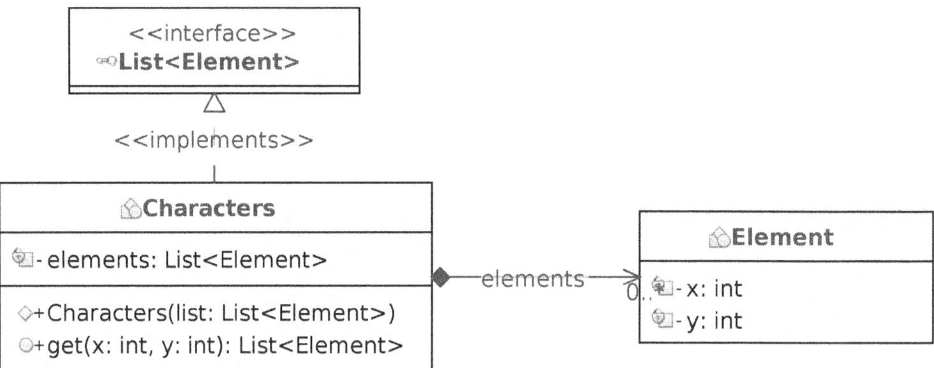

In the `Characters` class, the methods of the `java.util.List` interface are not presented: only the new methods are shown. The result still follows the decorator pattern, even if it is less visually striking.

2.3.3   Graphs of elements

Some element representations require the ability to memorize relationships between elements. It is the case for games with a world map, such as Risk: each country has particular properties and a specific number of neighbors. For space management games, like Stellaris, the world is composed of solar systems, and each is connected to several neighbors. Graphs are also interesting for representing a network of connections even in a regular world, such as railway stations and rails in a transport game like Transport Tycoon.

There are very good free libraries to work with graphs. It is better to choose a library that focuses primarily on algorithmic aspects, such as JGraphT. You don't need a library dedicated to game creation. Often, the fact that the world is a graph is not always visually obvious.

It is also possible to develop graphs by yourself. It can be for reasons of intellectual curiosity, to treat cases that are not offered by libraries, or for reasons of performance: the libraries are generic, and are not necessarily optimized for the very particular case of your game.

The usual approach to represent a graph separates the values from the graph itself. For example, you need a class for elements and a class for vertices that reference elements. Similarly, for neighbors, you need a class for data between elements/vertices, and a class for relations, which reference the data class between elements/vertices.

Then, there are several ways to combine this information. The most common and most compatible format with existing algorithms is a list of element vertices and a list of edges or arcs between vertices. For example, here the `Vertex` class represents a vertex with an `Element`, the `Edge` class represents an edge/arc with data of a `Relation` (here with a notion of distance), and finally, the `Graph` class contains both lists:

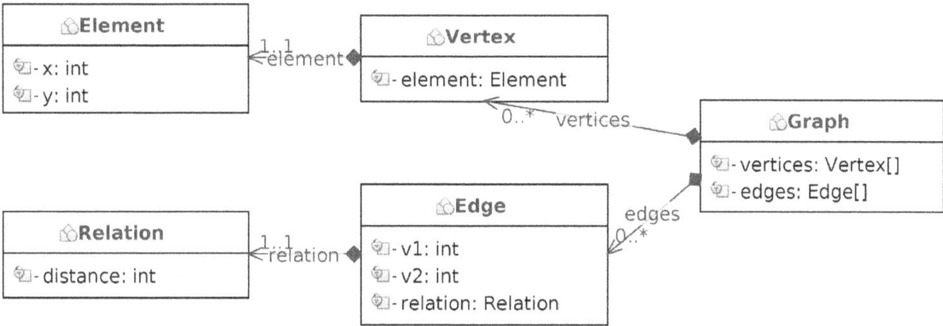

Then, there are still choices to make. For example, we can either place two references to vertices or two indices in the list of vertices to encode the vertices in an edge/arc. In the example above, we select the second choice for performance reasons.

At this stage of the design, only these classes are necessary (manual or in an external library), the functionalities can be added during the project.

2.3.4 Multidimensional arrays

Many games have a world that follows a regular grid: it is interesting to exploit it in the representation. It allows a more compact representation, but also easily solve problems like looking for adjacent elements. In this scope, multidimensional arrays are often a very good choice. The simplest case is a two-dimensional world, like the Pacman game. It can also be interesting to have multiple layers in a two-dimensional world. The addition of a third dimension can represent these layers. An additional dimension can also be added for full three-dimensional games, such as the Minecraft game. Finally, for "sparse" three-dimensional games, where three-dimensional meshes represent the world, vertexes and edges are generally represented by matrices, which are two-dimensional arrays.

⇒ Note: We consider the game world in this chapter, not its visual representation. The display and shape of the world can be different. For example, in Wolfenstein, the world is in 2D, but the display in 3D. In Starcraft II, the world is in 2D with layers, but the display in three-dimensional meshes.

For many cases, a multidimensional array of elements allows these representations. For example, if we want to create for the Pacman game an array of 20 x 10 elements filled with empty spaces:

```
int n = 20, m = 10;
Element[][] array = new Element[n][m];
for (int j=0;j<m;j++) {
    for (int i=0;i<n;i++) {
        array[i][j] = new Space(SpaceTypeId.EMPTY);
    }
}
```

The use of native tables of Java is quite limited: apart from access to the elements, there are no features. An elegant solution to this problem is to use the composition again. We define a class that contains the native array, as well as a series of methods to handle it:

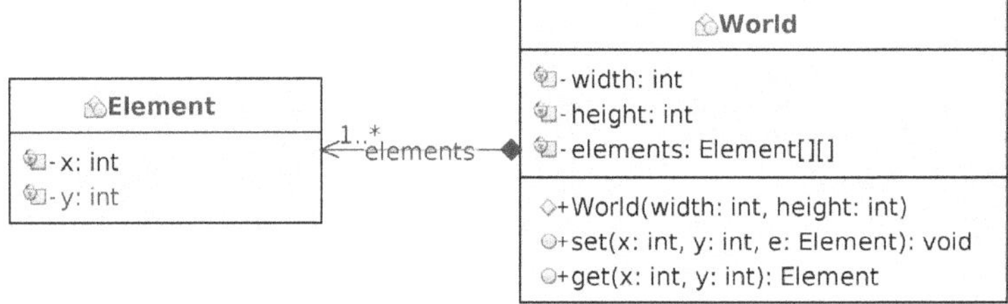

In this example, the presence of the x and y attributes of the Element class is questionable: we can deduce the position of the elements from their position in the multidimensional array. Besides, for the Pacman game, only static elements are stored in this class: it is possible to make an array of StaticElement directly. On this basis, it is possible to present a classic feature that allows easy browsing of adjacent boxes:

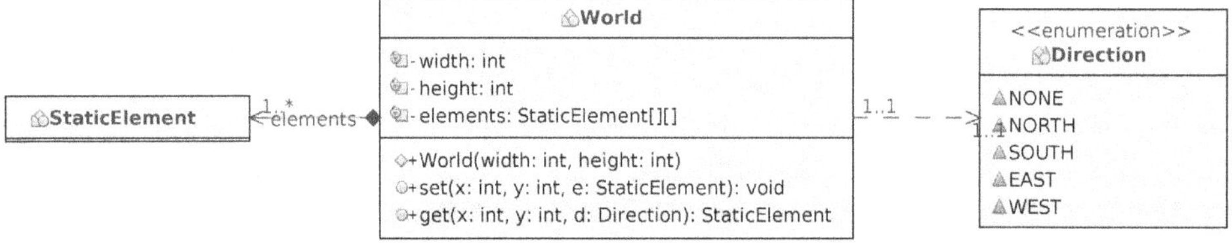

⇒ Note: The Direction enumeration is pointed by a dotted arrow: it is a simple dependency. Unlike the solid line arrow (association), there is no attribute involved. This arrow indicates that the World class uses the enumeration but does not contain it. This principle would be the same if Direction were a class.

Notice, in particular, the get() method, which allows accessing a cell of the array with the coordinates x,y in a direction d. This method is very useful when you have to go through the adjacent boxes, without having to discuss according to the different cases. The example below finds a space in all possible directions around the cell at coordinates (5,6):

```
World world = new World(20,10);
for (Direction d : Direction.values()) {
    if(world.get(5,6,d) instanceof Space) {
        System.out.println("There is a space to the "+d);
    }
}
```

The implementation of this get() method is very simple:

```
public StaticElement get(int x,int y,Direction d) {
    switch(d) {
      case NONE :
        if (x < 0 || x >= width || y < 0 || y >= height)
            throw new IllegalArgumentException(
            "Coordinates "+x+","+y+" are invalid");
          return elements[x][y];
      case NORTH: return get(x,y-1,Direction.NONE);
      case SOUTH: return get(x,y+1,Direction.NONE);
      case EAST: return get(x+1,y,Direction.NONE);
      case WEST: return get(x-1,y,Direction.NONE);
    }
    throw new RuntimeException("Invalid Direction");
}
```

For the NONE direction, a test has been added to test the validity of the (x, y) coordinates. It throws an exception with a clear message, which makes it easier to correct errors.

2.3.5   Iterating containers (Iterator Pattern)

It is often necessary to browse all the contents of a container. For example, to apply similar processing to each item, search for certain items, count/sum information, and so on. Rather than having to write specific code for each type of container, it is possible to use the Iterator Pattern, which formalizes this procedure. Thanks to this pattern, we can traverse any container meeting this criterion.

The Java language offers a native interface for this pattern, here with an implementation for `java.util.ArrayList`:

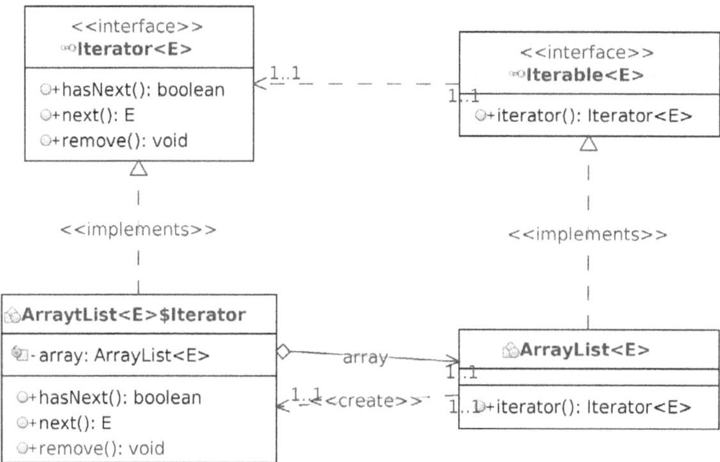

⇒ Note: For the dependency relationship between `ArrayList<E>` and `ArrayList<E>$Iterator` (dotted arrow), the expression `<<create>>` has been added. It allows us to specify the nature of this dependency: here, `ArrayList<E>` create `ArrayList<E>$Iterator`. It does not change the generated code but helps to understand the nature of the relationship better.

⇒ Note: The arrow between `ArrayList<E>$Iterator` and `ArrayList<E>` with a clear diamond is an aggregation. It is the same principle as the composition (with a black diamond), except that the two elements are not related in their life cycle. If we destroy one, the other does not have to be destroyed. In this case, a list iterator is not a part of a list. This information is also purely semantic and makes it easy to understand the nature of the association between the two classes.

The interface `Iterator<E>` has two main methods: `hasNext()` which allows knowing if there are still elements to iterate, and `next()` which returns the next element. All containers of the standard Java library follow this pattern. As a result, whatever the container is, it is possible to browse it in the same way:

```
Collection<Integer> collection ;
collection = new <any standard container>();
collection.add(3);
```

```
collection.add(12);
collection.add(9);
Iterator<Integer> iterator = collection.iterator();
while(iterator.hasNext()) {
    int value = iterator.next();
    System.out.println(value);
}
```

It is also possible to use the *for each* syntax, which works with all classes that implement `Iterable`:

```
for (Integer value : collection) {
    System.out.println(value);
}
```

The above code works with `ArrayList`, `LinkedList`, `TreeSet`, `ArrayDeque`, ... The only difference is the ordering, for example, for all list-based containers, the display is :

```
3
12
9
```

For `TreeSet`, we get the numerical order:

```
3
9
12
```

For associative arrays, which are not `java.util.Collection`, there are several solutions. The first is to browse only keys or values, via `keySet()` and `values()` methods. In each case, a collection is returned, and use the `iterator()` method as in the previous case. For example, to iterate on the keys:

```
AbstractMap<String,Integer> map = new TreeMap();
map.put("apple",3);
map.put("banana",12);
map.put("cherry",9);
Iterator<String> iterator = map.keySet().iterator();
while (iterator.hasNext()) {
    System.out.println(iterator.next());
}
```

It is also possible to browse the (key, value) pairs with the `entrySet()` method. The principle remains the same, if not the fact that we go through pairs instead of simple values:

```
AbstractMap<String,Integer> map = new TreeMap();
map.put("apple",3);
map.put("banana",12);
```

```java
map.put("cherry",9);
Iterator<Entry<String,Integer>> iterator =
    map.entrySet().iterator();
while (iterator.hasNext()) {
    Entry<String, Integer> entry = iterator.next();
    System.out.println(entry.getKey()+":"+entry.getValue());
}
```

For the Pacman game, we add this feature so that we can browse all cells in a level. To do this, simply implement the methods of `Iterable<StaticElement>` interface:

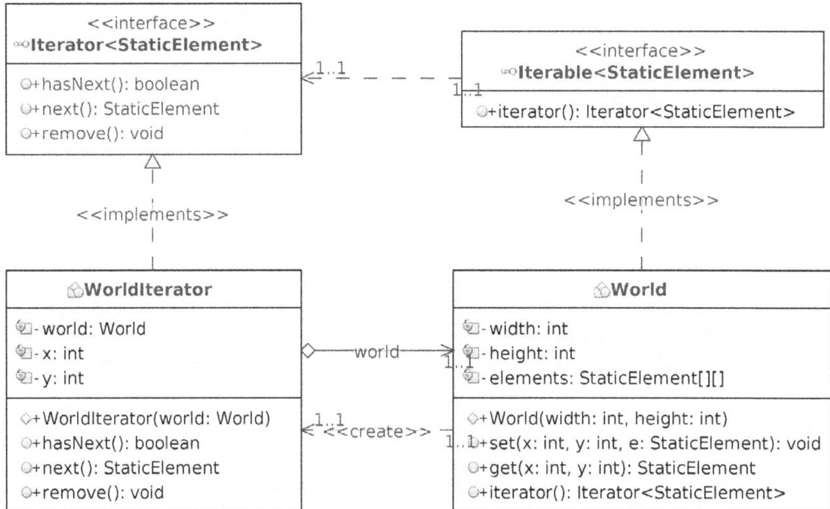

For the `World` class, the implementation of the `iterator()` method is very simple, and returns an iterator on itself:

```java
public Iterator<StaticElement> iterator() {
    return new WorldIterator(this);
}
```

For the `WorldIterator` class, there are three attributes: the world to iterate, and the current (x, y) coordinates. For the construction of the iterator, we consider coordinates (-1,0), just before the first cell, since the `next()` method goes to the next cell:

```java
public WorldIterator(World world) {
    this.world = world;
    this.x = -1;
    this.y = 0;
}
```

For the `hasNext()` method, we ensure that we can go to the next cell, either in x or in y:

```java
public boolean hasNext() {
    if (x+1 < world.getWidth())
        return true;
    if (y+1 < world.getHeight())
        return true;
    return false;
}
```

Finally, for the `next()` method, we go to the next cell, either in x or in y, if possible:

```java
public StaticElement next() {
    if (x+1 < world.getWidth()) {
        x++;
    }
    else if (y+1 < world.getHeight()) {
        x = 0;
        y ++;
    }
    else {
        throw new NoSuchElementException();
    }
    return world.get(x, y);
}
```

In this book, the methods of the well-known interfaces of the standard library are not repeated in the diagram. By adding the static element classes of the Pacman game, we obtain the following result:

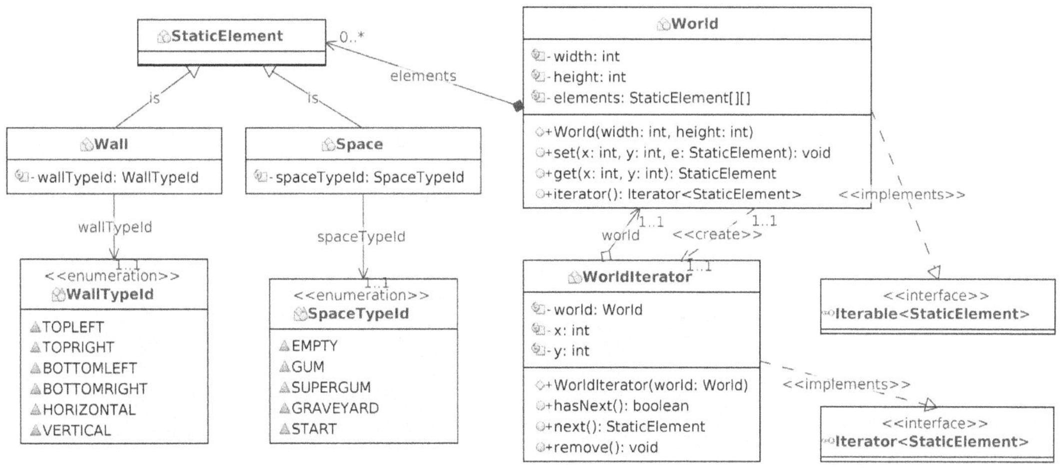

2.3.6 Main container

If we want to allow access to the game data, it is advisable to use a class that provides access to all items. For the Pacman example game, a `State` class is defined to access the world and characters, and therefore to all elements:

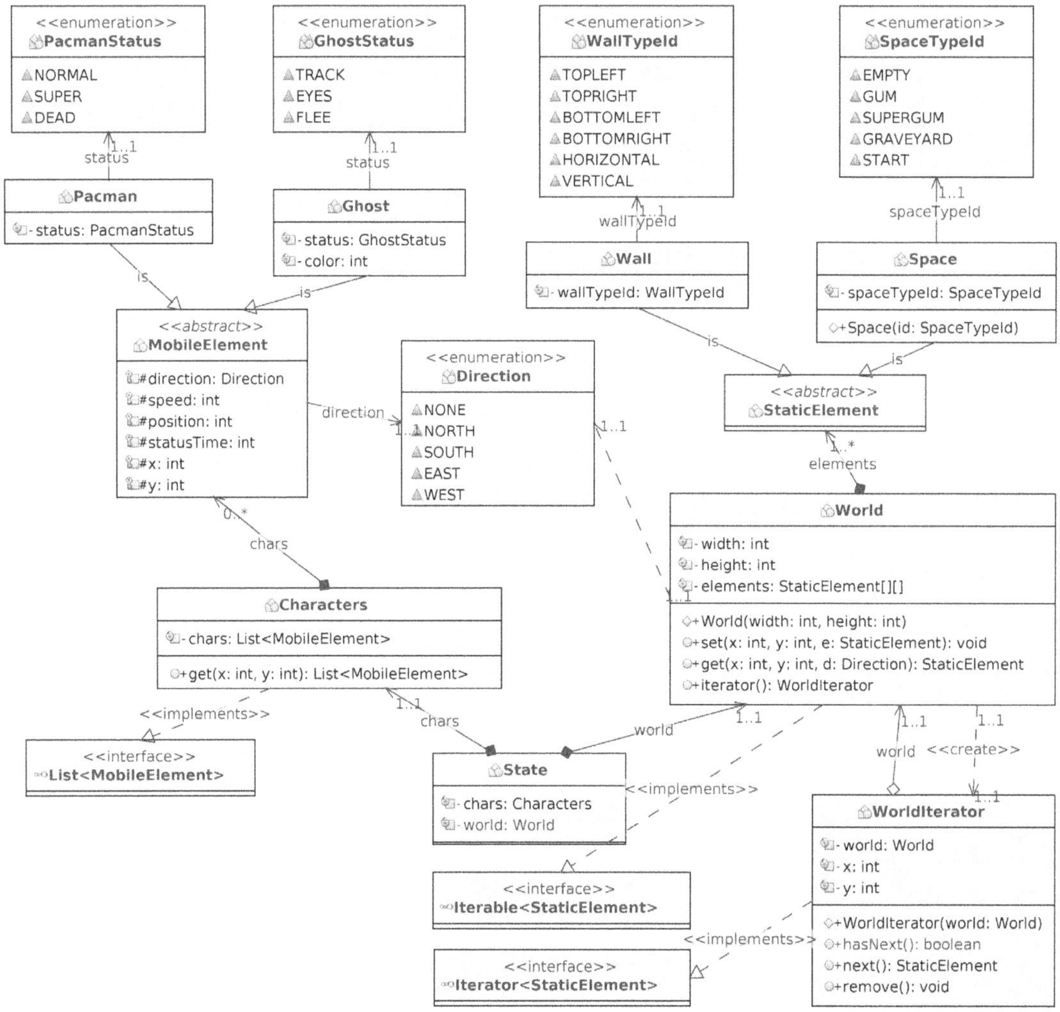

Within the `State` class, we find the two main containers: `Characters` for the characters, and `World` for the world/level. This diagram is available in the EasyUML sample project with the file "Class Diagrams/chap02/pacman_state.cdg".

To separate these state aspects of the game from the rest of the program, we put all the elements of this diagram in the package named `state`. We change the class packages as follows with EasyUML:

→ For each element of the diagram, click on it to display its properties at the bottom right of Netbeans. For example, for the `World` class:

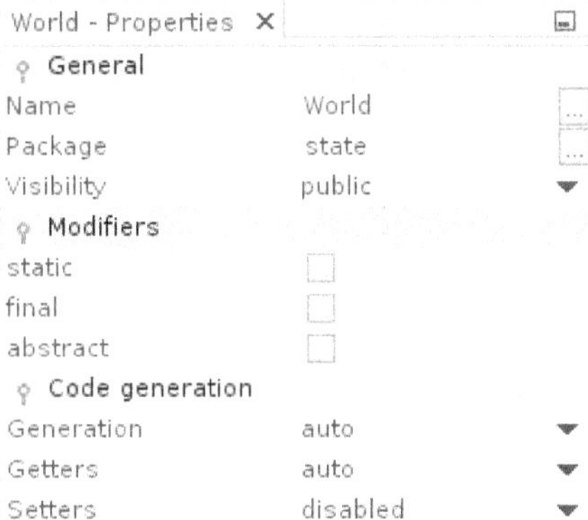

→ In the **Package** field, enter "state". Repeat for all elements of the diagram.

→ It is advised to make the `MobileElement` and `StaticElement` classes abstract. Thus, it is not possible to make instances. To do this, click on a class to display its properties, then check the "abstract" box.

2.3.7   Exercices

2.3.7.1   Exercise: Civilization

We want to represent cities in a game similar to Civilization. We are only interested in cities, and we ignore other aspects such as territories and armies.

Each city has the following information:

- A name
- A number between 1 and 50 that represents its population
- (x,y) coordinates
- Buildings that have the following properties:
    - A type name (library, barracks, ...).
    - The type name is unique, there can not be two libraries for example
- A list of buildings to build

We want to have, via methods, the following functionalities:

- We can add a city to all cities
- You can quickly and easily find a city according to its coordinates (x, y)
- We want to be able to iterate on all cities; the iteration order must be the one of insertion
- For a city, you want to be able to browse all the buildings in alphabetical order

→ Propose a class diagram that represents a set of cities with all their properties. There is no need to put the setters and getters.

2.3.7.2   Exercise: Stellaris

The objective is to represent the planets of the systems of a galaxy, in the manner of the game Stellaris:

Each Planet has the following properties:

- A name
- A type of planet: Habitable or Gaseous
- Habitable planets can have buildings
- A planet can have several buildings of the same type

The buildings have the following properties:

- A type of building: either a factory or a power plant
- A building level, from 1 to 10

Each Planetary System has the following properties:

- Coordinates (x, y) in the galaxy
- A list of planets, in a very specific order

Finally, a galaxy includes a set of planetary systems. Each system is connected to its neighbors by connections. These connections have a certain distance, measured in parsecs. Propose a class diagram to represent these elements. No method is expected.

2.3.8   Video Game Development: Containers

→ Select the most relevant containers for your game:

- For sparse data, such as characters, units, or buildings: a list of items with their coordinates is usually appropriate.
- For sparse data with relationships between them, such as cities in a country or systems in a galaxy: graphs are the best solution.
- For regular data, such as cells in a 2D world: multidimensional arrays are usually the right solution.
- It should also be kept in mind that there are often containers in the containers, and they may own other containers. The exercises illustrate these cases.

→ Once your containers are chosen, draw the class diagram to represent all possible states of the game. For now, few features are required (except the setters/getters), and therefore few methods are present in the diagram at this stage of the design.

2.4   Unit tests

2.4.1   Implement unit tests

2.4.1.1   Generate accessors / mutators (getters / setters)

To generate the getters/setters, two solutions:

→ If you have the improved version of EasyUML: bring up the easyUML diagram explorer at the bottom left of Netbeans. To do so, click on the **easyUML explorer** tab:

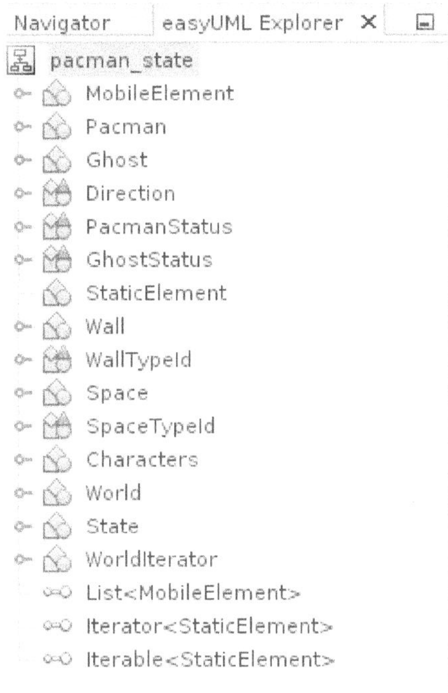

→ Select the root of the displayed tree: in the example above, it is named "pacman_state". This brings up the properties of the diagram:

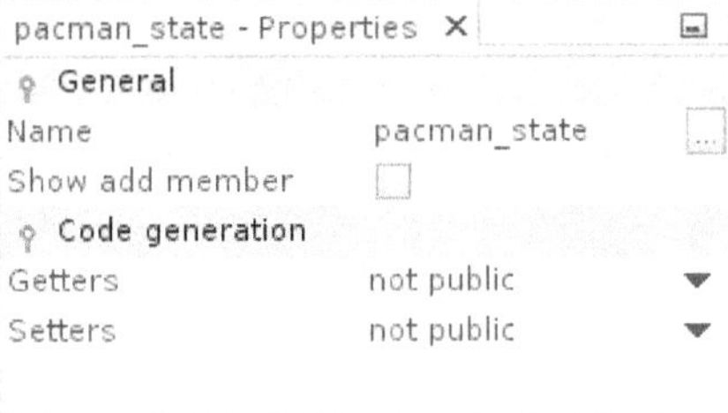

→ For "getters" and "setters" properties, choose "not public". It generates accessors/mutators for all non-public attributes.

→ For the `World` and `WorldIterator` classes, it is better not to have a setter: the user of these classes does not have to modify their attributes. To disable their generation, click on a class to bring up their properties, then select "disabled" for the **Setters** property. For example, for the `World` class:

→ If you do not have the enhanced version of EasyUML, generate the Java files (see below), then for each class, right-click on the class name. It brings up a context menu: click on **Insert code...** A second pop-up menu appears: click **Getters and Setters...** A dialog appears: check all the getters and/or setters you want to generate.

2.4.1.2   Generate Java source code

To generate the Java source code:

→ First you need a Java project (in addition to the UML project). To do so, click on the **File - New project...** menu. In the first part of the project creation wizard, select the **Java** category and then the **Java Application** project type.

→ Click the **Next** button.

→ On the second page of the wizard, enter a name for your project in the **Project Name** field.

→ Select a folder in the **Project Location** field.

→ Click on the **Finish** button.

→ In the Project Explorer or the Files Explorer (at the top left of Netbeans), right-click on the UML diagram file and select **easyUML generate code**.

→ A dialog appears: select your Java project from the drop-down list.

→ Click on the **Generate Code** button

→ If you generate the code for the "pacman_state.cdg" diagram, the code appears in the "Source Packages" folder of the Java project in the "state" package. Several errors appear. Some may be due to input errors in the diagram, for which the diagram needs to be corrected. Other errors are expected, for example some methods use elements of the standard library, such as the `Characters` class that uses `java.util.List`. For these cases, we need to add the corresponding imports. The easiest way to get them with Netbeans is to click on the light with a red circle in front of the line of code. Then, select the relevant option, for example **Add import for java.util.List**.

Once the code we generated is error-free, it becomes possible to implement the different methods. An example of implementation of the class diagram above is available in the example Java project, in the folder "Source Packages/examples/chap02/pacman".

2.4.1.3 Writing unit tests

Any implementation requires a minimum of tests to ensure its proper operation. When you start, you usually choose to write pieces of code on the fly, run them, modify them slightly to do other tests, and then forget them. This approach is questionable since the energy spent to test the code is not profitable over time. In addition, if any changes are made, it is necessary to test the code again.

A very common approach in the computer world is to gather these tests following a predefined framework. For this book, we use the very popular *JUnit* framework. Netbeans integrates it by default, as well as in most Java development environments. To create tests for a class in Netbeans, follow these steps:

→ Right-click on the class to test;

→ The pop-up menu appears, select **Tools**;

→ A popup submenu appears, select **Create / Update Tests**, the following dialog appears:

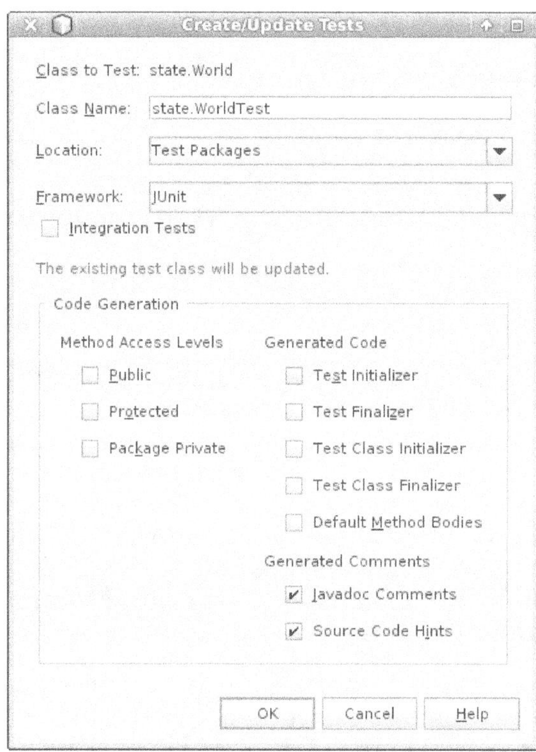

By default, Netbeans proposes to create a class that bears the name of the tested class, extended with "Test". For example, for the `World` class, the test class is `WorldTest`. The new class is created in the same package, here `state`. This class appears by default in the "Test Packages" folder of the Java project, which makes it possible to separate the test codes from the code of the application.

→ Uncheck all boxes in the **Code Generation** box. In this example, we only want to create some specific tests;

→ Click **Ok**;

→ The new class appears in the "Test Package/state" folder, for example for the `WorldTest` class:

```java
package state;
import org.junit.Test;
import static org.junit.Assert.*;
public class WorldTest {

    public WorldTest() {
```

```
    }
    @Test
    public void testSomeMethod() {
    }


}
```

The `testSomeMethod()` method preceded by the `@Test` annotation is a test. We will rename it `testAccess()` to test access methods of the `World` class. For example :

```java
package state;
import java.util.Random;
import org.junit.Test;
import static org.junit.Assert.*;
public class WorldTest {
    Random rand = new Random();

    public WorldTest() {
    }
    @Test
    public void testAccess() {
        int width = 3+rand.nextInt(10);
        int height = 3+rand.nextInt(10);
        World world = new World(width,height);
        assertEquals(width, world.getWidth());
        assertEquals(height, world.getHeight());
        for (int repeat=0;repeat<10;repeat++) {
            int x = rand.nextInt(width);
            int y = rand.nextInt(height);
            world.set(x,y,new Space(SpaceTypeId.GUM));
            StaticElement se = world.get(x, y, Direction.NONE);
            assertTrue(se instanceof Space);
            Space space = (Space)se;
            assertEquals(SpaceTypeId.GUM,space.getSpaceTypeId()
            );
        }
    }
}
```

The `rand` attribute has been added to allow the generation of random numbers. It is often better to put some randomness in the tests, to increase their number.

The first three lines instantiate a `World` with a random size:

```java
int width = 3+rand.nextInt(10);
int height = 3+rand.nextInt(10);
World world = new World(width,height);
```

Then, we do two checks right after. These ensure that the width and height of the world are indeed the expected ones:

```
assertEquals(width, world.getWidth());
assertEquals(height, world.getHeight());
```

The checks are done by the `assertEquals()` method of the package `org.junit.Assert`. It compares two values, and if they are not equal, it reports the problem in a visual interface presented later.

These two checks may seem so obvious that they seem useless! They are, however, a typical case of verification that must be performed, and it is not uncommon for such simple cases to be erroneous. For example, they can fail if you forget to implement the `World` constructor. The other function is to ensure that some properties are valid for the next checks. Here we have the assurance that the `width` and `height` attributes are correct so that we can focus on other potential problems. The next block repeats the same checks ten times, but randomly modifies the parameters:

```java
for (int repeat=0;repeat<10;repeat++) {
    int x = rand.nextInt(width);
    int y = rand.nextInt(height);
    world.set(x,y,new Space(SpaceTypeId.GUM));
    StaticElement se = world.get(x, y, Direction.NONE);
    assertTrue(se instanceof Space);
    Space space = (Space)se;
    assertEquals(SpaceTypeId.GUM,space.getSpaceTypeId());
}
```

Repeating the same checks with random settings is highly recommended, and does not cost much in development time. Another verification method, `assertTrue()`, is used here: it is one of the many methods offered in the package `org.junit.Assert`.

Once the test is written, just right click on the Java file (either in an explorer or in the code itself), and select **Test File**. The tests are then run, and a results window appears. If this is not the case, a bubble on the bottom right proposes to display it, or you can go through the **Window - IDE Tools - Test Results** menu. If everything went well, we get the following display:

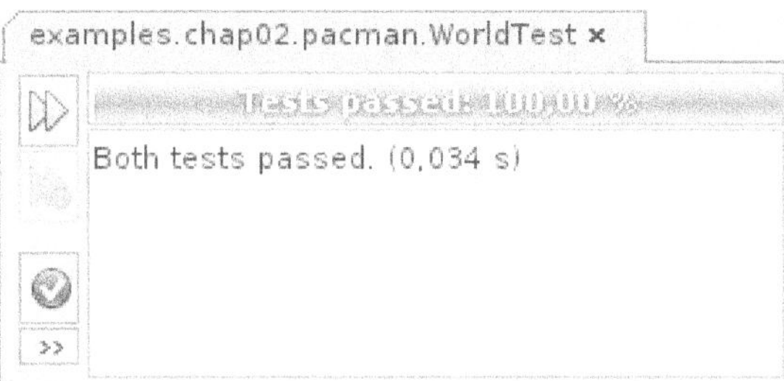

In the opposite case, we obtain a display of the type:

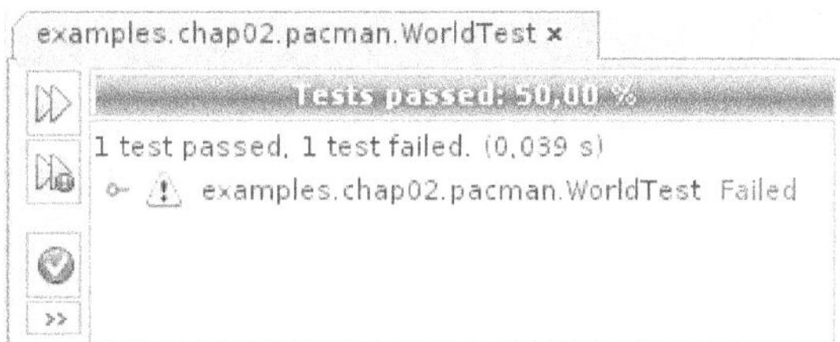

By developing the line with the exclamation mark in a red circle, the reason for the failure appears. By double-clicking on this new line, we are transported to the line where the verification failed. We can then correct the problem, then by right-clicking on this line in the results window, a contextual menu appears. By clicking **Run again**, the test is restarted.

It is possible to add other tests to the `WallTest` class by adding other methods preceded by the `@Test` annotation. For example, if you want to add a test for the iterator, just add a method like this:

```java
@Test
public void testIterator() {
    ...
}
```

We can then run the two tests as before, by selecting **Test File** in the context menu of the java file. You can also run a specific test by right-clicking the test method (its title or content) and selecting **Run Focused Test Method** from the context menu.

Other classes can be tested by following the same procedure. You can then run all tests of all classes via the **Run - Test Project** menu.

An example of test classes is proposed in the example Java project in the "examples/chap02/pacman" folder of the test packages. These test the code in the "examples/chap02/pacman" folder of the source packages.

2.4.2 Exercices

2.4.2.1 Exercise: Civilization Test

We want to implement a test with the following checks for the `Cities` class from the civilization exercise solution:

- Build an instance of `Cities` named `cities`
- Add two cities (instances of `City`):
    - The city "Paris" with coordinates (1,2)
    - The city "New York" with coordinates (5,3)
- Check that the number of cities in `cities` is 2
- Retrieve the city at coordinates (1,2), and check that its name is "Paris"
- Retrieve the city at the coordinates (5,3), and verify that its name is "New York"
- Iterate on all cities of cities:
    - Check that the first is called "Paris"
    - Check that the second name is "New York"
- Add to the city "Paris" the following buildings: "Library", "Barracks" and "Cathedral"
- Iterate on all the buildings of the city "Paris":
    - Check that the first is "Barracks"
    - Check that the second one is "Cathedral"
    - Check that the last one is "Library"

2.4.2.2 Exercise: Stellaris Test

We start from the "Stellaris" exercise solution, to which we must add the following methods:

`Planet` class:

- Constructor function of name

Class `Habitable`:

- Constructor function of name

Class `Gaseous`:

- Constructor function of name

`Building` class:

- Constructor function of type and level

`Connection` class:

- Constructor function of parsecs and coordinates

`System` class:

- Constructor function of name and coordinates
- `Int getPlanetCount()` method that returns the number of planets in the system
- `Planet getPlanet(int index)` method that returns the planet at the index `index`
- `Int findPlanet(String name)` method which returns the planet of name `name`, or -1 if it does not exist
- The `planet addPlanet(String name)` method that builds and adds a planet to the system. There can not be two planets with the same name.

`Galaxy` class:

- Constructor
- Method `Int getSystemCount()` that returns the number of systems in the galaxy
- Method `System getSystem(int index)` that returns the system at the index `index`
- Method `Connection getConnection(int index)` that returns the connection to index `index`
- Method `int findSystem(String name)` that returns the system with the name `name`, or -1 if it does not exist
- Method `int findConnection(int index1, int index2)` that returns the connection between index systems `index1` and `index2`, or -1 if it does not exist. Warning: this must work in both directions, if there is a connection between `index1` and `index2`, it is also true for `index2` and `index1`.
- Method `System createSystem(String name, int x, int y)` that builds and adds a new system to the galaxy. Warning: there can not be two systems with the same name.
- Method `Connection connectSystems (String name1, String name2, int parsecs)` that builds and adds a connection between two systems. Warning: there can not be the same connection twice, in one direction or the other.

Many methods are likely to fail: for example, for creating a planet that already exists in the system. For these cases, throw an `IllegalArgumentException` specifying the nature of the problem, for example: "The system" + name + "already exists".

For accessors (getters), all attributes must be accessible except containers in `System` and `Galaxy`. In doing so, it is ensured that the user of these classes can not manipulate these containers: this guarantees the unique property of the planet and system names.

For mutators (setters), only those of the `Building` class are allowed. For others, all properties should not be editable outside the class.

Once the diagram is updated, generate the code and then implement all the methods. Then, the following checks are expected:

- Create a galaxy
- Add to the galaxy an "Alpha" system with coordinates (10,20)
- Add to the galaxy a "Beta" system with coordinates (12,4)
- Add to the galaxy a "Gamma" system with coordinates (23,17)
- Retrieve from its name the index of the system "Alpha" (method `findSystem()`), then:
    - Check that the returned index is correct
    - Request the system for this index (`getSystem()` method)
    - Check the name and coordinates
- Repeat the checks below for other systems
- Connect the "Alpha" and "Beta" systems with 1 parsecs
- Connect the "Alpha" and "Gamma" systems with 2 parsecs
- Connect "Beta" and "Gamma" systems with 3 parsecs
- Check that the `findConnection()` method finds these three connections in both directions (2x3 = 6 checks in total)
- Check that creating a connection between two systems throws an exception
- Check that creating an existing connection throws an exception

2.4.3   Video game development: state test

→ Resume your class diagram with game elements and containers:

- Move all classes, interfaces, and enumerations in a single package, for example, "state".
- Add any methods that allow you to edit the content. There is no need at this stage of development to bring classes in line with the rules of the game. We only wish to be able to represent and modify any valid state of the game.
- If you are using the enhanced version of EasyUML: When relevant, enable the generation of accessors (getters) and mutators (setters) for the entire diagram. For special cases, set this activation parameter for classes and/or attributes that require it.

→ Once these tasks are done, you should have a diagram similar to that of the Pacman example "Class Diagrams/chap02/pacman07.cdg" present in the sample UML project.

→ Create a Java project, and start generating the code for this diagram.

→ Correct the input errors in the diagram, and regenerate the code.

→ Also add the missing imports.

→ Repeat these steps until you obtain source code without errors.

→ Implement all methods.

→ Create a test file for each class that requires it (usually container classes).

→ Implement and validate all your tests.

2.5   Exercises solutions

2.5.1   Exercise 2.4.1: Role-playing game

The following diagram responds to the constraints:

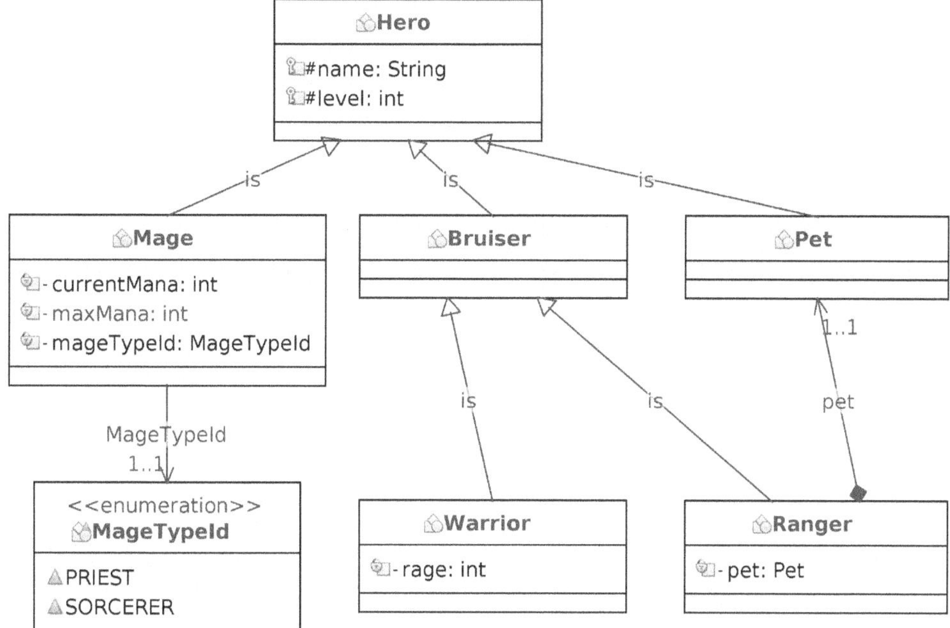

A hierarchy makes it possible to represent everything without conflict or duplicate.

Hero class: parent class of all others, it contains the common properties (name and level).

Mage class: represents the two types of mages: priests and sorcerers. It is not necessary to create a class for each type of magician, an enumeration suffices.

Bruiser class: allows identifying the bruisers, who have no mana.

Warrior class: represents a warrior with his rage.

Ranger class: represents the ranger, accompanied by his pet. The pet attribute is a composition "1..1" to the Pet class, since according to the definition of the game, they are bind to life to death. In the opposite case, if the pet and the ranger could separate, an aggregation (white diamond rather than black) would have been relevant.

Pet class: since it has the same properties as any character, it can be inherited from Hero. Another solution would have been to inherit the Bruiser class, or evenWarrior, if its mechanics are similar. There is not enough information in the description of the game to know it, and it may be interesting to rework this.

2.5.2   Exercise 2.4.2: Roleplay with multiple classes

The following diagram responds to the constraints:

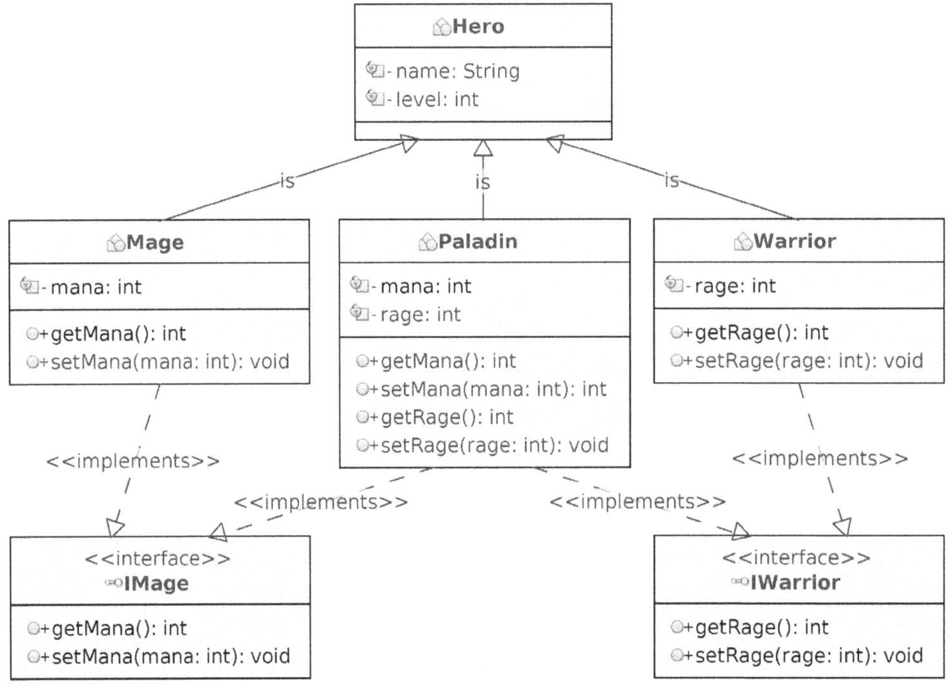

To meet multiple criteria, we followed the first approach presented, which uses only interfaces. It is also possible to follow one of the other two approaches with the composition.

Hero class: main superclass, contains the common properties.

IMage interface: handles the mana property.

IWarrior interface: handles the rage property.

Mage class: implements the IMage interface and contains a mana attribute to handle it.

Warrior class: implements the IWarrior interface and contains a raga attribute to handle it.

Paladin class: implements both interfaces and contains an attribute for each case.

2.5.3   Exercise 3.6.1: Civilization

Here is a possible solution:

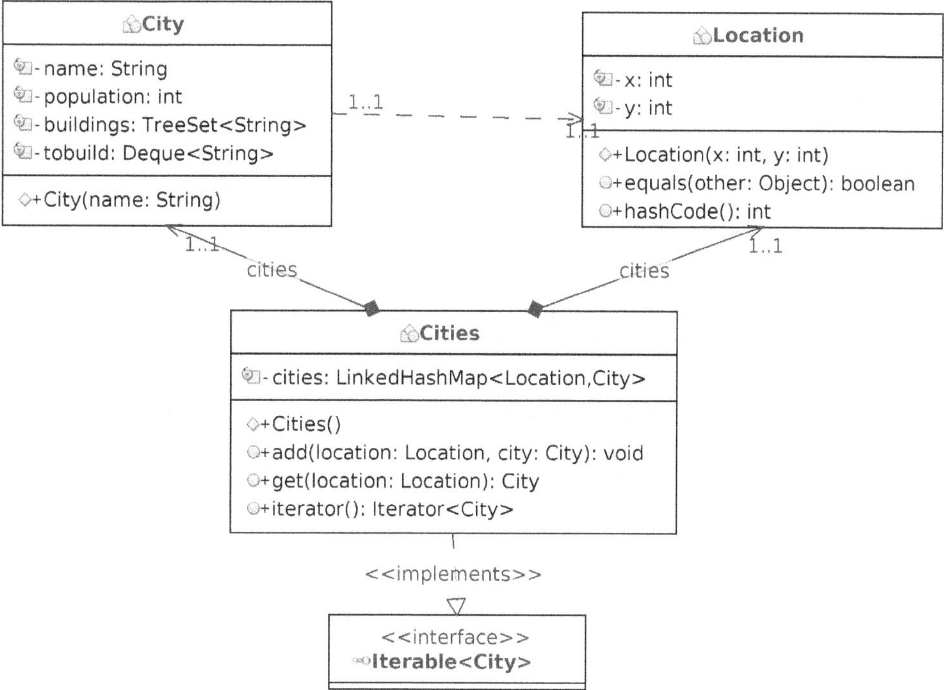

'City' class:

- Represents a city with its name (name) and population (population)

- The list of buildings is held by the buildings attribute. It's a java.util.TreeSet, whose iterator always goes through the elements in lexical order. So, if we do:

```java
City city = new City("Paris");
city.getBuildings().add("Library");
city.getBuildings().add("Barracks");
city.getBuildings().add("Cathedral");
```

```
for(String building : city.getBuildings()) {
    System.out.println(building);
}
```

We see the list of buildings in lexical order:

```
Barracks
Cathedral
Library
```

- The queue of buildings to be built is held by the `tobuild` attribute. We instantiate a `java.util.ArrayDeque` to get the queue behavior: first added, first built.

`Location` class:

- Used to represent a position (x, y) on the map.
- The `equals()` and `hashCode()` methods of the `Object` class are overridden: they allow you to use this class in a hash table (`java.util.HashMap` or `java.util.LinkedHashMap`).

`Cities` class:

- The `cities` attribute contains all cities according to their `Location`. This makes it easy and quick to find a city based on its position: the complexity of this operation with `java.util.LinkedHashMap` is *O(1)*.
- The `add()` and `get()` methods meet the specification. If the other methods of the `java.util.AbstractMap` interface were also implemented, we would be facing a Decorator pattern. In this case, it is a kind of simplified version but still follows the principle.
- The `iterator()` method allows iterating on all cities. It returns the iterator of `java.util.LinkedHashMap`, which iterates in the adding order.

2.5.4   Exercise 3.6.2: Stellaris

Here is a possible solution:

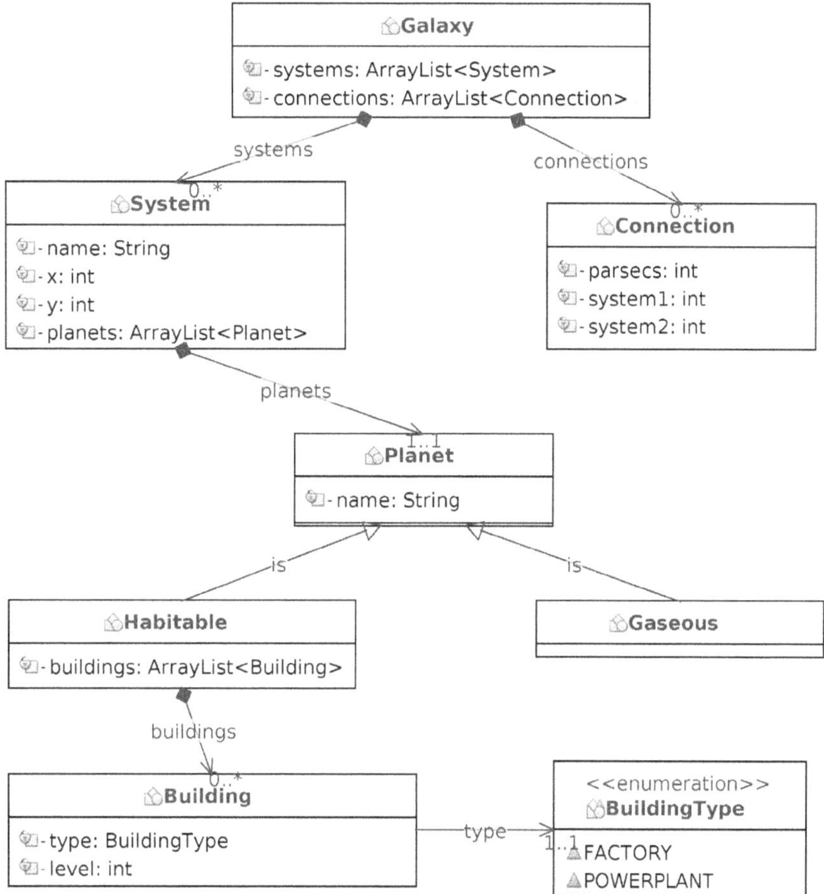

Hierarchy `Planet`, `Habitable` and `Gaseous`: represents both types of planets.

The `Habitable` class contains a list of `Building`. These have a type defined by the `BuildingType` enumeration, as well as a `level`.

The `System` class represents a planetary system, with its coordinates (x, y) and its planet list.

The galaxy is represented as a graph, with its vertices (`systems`) and its edges (`connections`). Each vertex contains a system, and each edge contains a `Connection`, which itself defines the `parsecs` distance between two systems.

2.5.5　Exercise 4.2.1: Civilization Test

A solution is proposed in the "examples/chap02/ civilization" folder of the source packages of the Java example project. A class diagram is available in the file "Class Diagrams/chap02/civilization.cdg". The unit tests are located in the CitiesTest.java class in the "examples/chap02/ civilization" folder of the test packages.

A new test is made with a method whose implementation is:

```java
Cities cities = new Cities();
cities.add(new Location(1, 2),new City("Paris"));
cities.add(new Location(5, 3),new City("New York"));
assertEquals(2,cities.getCities().size());
City paris = cities.get(new Location(1, 2));
assertEquals("Paris",paris.getName());
City newyork = cities.get(new Location(5, 3));
assertEquals("New York",newyork.getName());
int i = 0;
for (City city : cities) {
    if (i == 0) {
        assertEquals("Paris",city.getName());
    }
    else if (i == 1) {
        assertEquals("New York",city.getName());
    }
    i ++;
}
paris.getBuildings().add("Library");
paris.getBuildings().add("Barracks");
paris.getBuildings().add("Cathedral");
i = 0;
for(String building : paris.getBuildings()) {
    if (i == 0)
        assertEquals("Barracks",building);
    else if (i == 1)
        assertEquals("Cathedral",building);
    else if (i == 2)
        assertEquals("Library",building);
    i++;
}
```

2.5.6   Exercise 4.2.2: Stellaris Test

A solution is proposed in the "examples/chap02/stellaris" folder of the source packages of the Java sample project. A class diagram is available in the "Class Diagrams/chap02/stellaris.cdg" file. Unit tests are implemented in the GalaxyTest.java class in the "examples/chap02/stellaris" folder of the test packages.

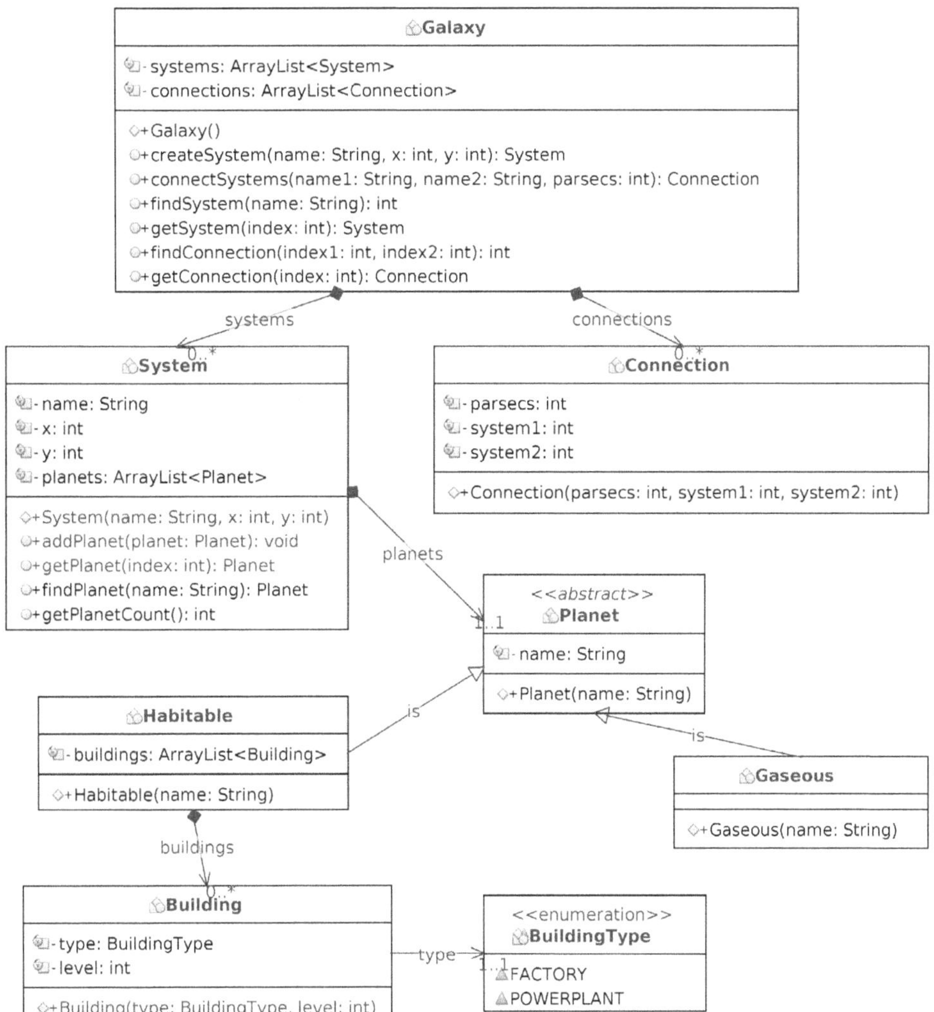

The tests can be implemented as follows:

```
Galaxy galaxy = new Galaxy();
galaxy.createSystem("Alpha", 10, 20);
galaxy.createSystem("Beta", 12, 4);
galaxy.createSystem("Gamma", 23, 17);
```

```java
int alphai = galaxy.findSystem("Alpha");
assertTrue(alphai >= 0);
System alpha = galaxy.getSystem(alphai);
assertEquals("Alpha",alpha.getName());
assertEquals(10,alpha.getX());
assertEquals(20,alpha.getY());
int betai = galaxy.findSystem("Beta");
assertTrue(betai >= 0);
System beta = galaxy.getSystem(betai);
assertEquals("Beta",beta.getName());
assertEquals(12,beta.getX());
assertEquals(4,beta.getY());
int gammai = galaxy.findSystem("Gamma");
assertTrue(gammai >= 0);
System gamma = galaxy.getSystem(gammai);
assertEquals("Gamma",gamma.getName());
assertEquals(23,gamma.getX());
assertEquals(17,gamma.getY());
galaxy.connectSystems("Alpha", "Beta", 1);
galaxy.connectSystems("Alpha", "Gamma", 2);
galaxy.connectSystems("Beta", "Gamma", 3);
assertTrue(galaxy.findConnection(alphai, betai) >= 0);
assertTrue(galaxy.findConnection(alphai, gammai) >= 0);
assertTrue(galaxy.findConnection(betai, gammai) >= 0);
assertTrue(galaxy.findConnection(betai, alphai) >= 0);
assertTrue(galaxy.findConnection(gammai, alphai) >= 0);
assertTrue(galaxy.findConnection(gammai, betai) >= 0);
try {
    galaxy.connectSystems("False", "Gamma", 45);
    fail("An exception should have been thrown");
}
catch(IllegalArgumentException ex) {
}
try {
    galaxy.connectSystems("Alpha", "Beta", 45);
    fail("An exception should have been thrown");
}
catch(IllegalArgumentException ex) {
}
```

CHAPTER 3

User interface

3.1   2D User interface with AWT

This section introduces the elements necessary to create a two-dimensional game with the standard AWT library. This library is included by default in all editions of Java, which allows porting to all platforms. It is also very easy to use, which is particularly interesting when you start.

This section also introduces several common concepts in the design of a video game - so it is relevant to browse it, even if you already know AWT. In this section, we implement graphics components with a naïve approach. In the last part of this chapter, they are formalized to produce an advanced design, capable of managing larger projects.

The source code for the various examples in this section is available in the sample Java project, in the "examples/chap03/awt" folder of the source packages.

3.1.1   Synchronous display with double buffering

3.1.1.1   Display a window

Showing a window in AWT is very simple (file "E01Window.java"):

```java
public class E01Window extends Frame {

    public void init() {
        setTitle("Display and controls with AWT");
        setSize(200,200);
        setResizable(false);
        addWindowListener(new WindowAdapter() {
          public void windowClosing(WindowEvent e){
            dispose();
          }
        });
    }

    public static void main(String args[]) {
        E01Window window = new E01Window();
        window.init();
        window.setLocationRelativeTo(null);
        window.setVisible(true);
    }
}
```

The result is a basic window:

The `init()` method prepares the window. We first defines the title with the
`setTitle()` method:

```java
setTitle("Display and controls with AWT");
```

We define a size with the `setSize()` method:

```java
setSize(200,200);
```

We indicate that the window can not be resized with the `setResizable()` method:

```java
setResizable(false);
```

Finally, we manage the closing of the window with a window listener which destroys the window with the `dispose()` method when we ask it to be closed (button in the interface or key as Alt + F4):

```
addWindowListener(new WindowAdapter() {
    public void windowClosing(WindowEvent we) {
        dispose();
    }
});
```

The `main()` function instantiates and displays the window. We instantiate the window:

```
E01Window window = new E01Window();
```

We initialize the window parameters:

```
window.init();
```

The window is centred on the screen:

```
window.setLocationRelativeTo(null);
```

Finally, we display the window:

```
window.setVisible(true);
```

3.1.1.2 Create a canvas

To obtain the best possible performance for the display, we opt for a display using a canvas. A canvas represents a rectangular area where you can draw. This approach makes it possible, in particular, to use the double buffering presented in the following section.

We enrich the previous example with this new feature (file "E02Canvas.java"). We add an attribute of type `java.awt.Canvas` with a predefined size:

```
private int canvasWidth = 800;
private int canvasHeight = 600;
private Canvas canvas;
```

Add a `createCanvas()` method to instantiate and set this pattern:

```java
public void createCanvas() {
    canvas = new Canvas();
    Dimension dim = new Dimension(canvasWidth,canvasHeight);
    canvas.setPreferredSize(dim);
    canvas.setMinimumSize(dim);
    canvas.setMaximumSize(dim);
    add(canvas);
    pack();
}
```

- The three methods `setXXXSize()` allow you to set a static canvas size.
- The `add()` method adds the canvas to the window.
- Finally, the `pack()` method adjusts the size of the window to contain the canvas. Its final size is that of the canvas plus the one for the window frame.

We add the canvas creation to the `main()` method:

```java
public static void main(String args[]) {
    E02Canvas window = new E02Canvas();
    window.init();
    window.createCanvas();
    window.setLocationRelativeTo(null);
    window.setVisible(true);
}
```

The result is a window with a canvas of 800 per 600 pixels:

3.1.1.3 Double buffering and main loop (Game Loop Pattern)

It is advisable to use canvas with a double buffering to display most efficiently. The
canvas is not visible on the screen, and its content is displayed when requested. This
low-level approach to the display allows you to draw in a non-visible buffer when a
second one is displayed. Then, when the first buffer is ready to be displayed, we
swap the two buffers: the first is displayed, and the second one is rendered. In doing
so, there is no flickering effect: the user does not see the rendering of successive
layers, only the final result. Besides, it allows parallelizing the processing: part of
the resources is used for rendering, while another part is used for display.

To obtain this display strategy, we add a new `render()` method:

```java
public void render() {
    BufferStrategy bs = canvas.getBufferStrategy();
    if (bs == null) {
        canvas.createBufferStrategy(2);
        return;
    }
    Graphics g = null;
    try {
        g = bs.getDrawGraphics();
        g.setColor(Color.black);
        g.fillRect(0,0,canvasWidth,canvasHeight);
        bs.show();
    }
    finally {
        if (g != null)
            g.dispose();
    }
}
```

This method performs the following operations. It checks that the canvas has
display buffers with the `getBufferStrategy()` method. If it is not the case, we
ask for its creation with 2 buffers with the `createBufferStrategy()` method, and
then we leave the method:

```java
BufferStrategy bs = canvas.getBufferStrategy();
if (bs == null) {
    canvas.createBufferStrategy(2);
    return;
}
```

To draw in the canvas, we go through the buffer strategy `bs`. This can return
a `Graphics` with the `getDrawGraphics()` method. This `Graphics` automatically
points to the buffer ready to be drawn. It is necessary to release this `Graphics`
at the end of the display whatever the circumstances, so the use of a `try` ...

`finally` block:

```java
Graphics g = null;
try {
    g = bs.getDrawGraphics();
    ... Draw in g ...
}
finally {
    if (g != null) {
        g.dispose();
    }
}
```

In the `try ... finally` block, we can draw in `Graphics`, as in the `paintComponent()` method of a `JComponent` Here, we draw a solid rectangle, to give a black background to the canvas:

```java
g.setColor(Color.black);
g.fillRect(0,0,canvasWidth,canvasHeight);
```

Finally, we call the `show()` method of the buffer to get the display. With a double buffer, this swaps the buffer to draw with the one to display:

```java
bs.show();
```

The `render()` method must be called regularly to update the display. To do this, we implement a new `run()` with a loop that calls it continuously:

```java
public void run() {
    while (running) {
        render();
    }
    dispose();
}
```

This method uses a new `running` boolean attribute set to `true`. As long as it has this value, the loop continues infinitely. Once passed to `false`, we leave the loop, then we ask for the destruction of the window with the `dispose()` method. This loop is at the heart of any video game: once embellished with other calls presented in this section, it is a pattern that does not have an "official" name, but can be called the *Game Loop Pattern*.

To pass the `running` attribute to `false`, and thus leave the game, we modify the closing behavior of the window in the `init()` method: instead of destroying the window, we pass `running` to `false`:

```java
public void init() {
    setTitle("Display and controls with AWT");
    setSize(200,200);
    setResizable(false);
    addWindowListener(new WindowAdapter() {
        public void windowClosing(WindowEvent we) {
            running = false;
        }
    });
}
```

Finally, all that remains is to call the `run()` method in the `main()` method to trigger the loop:

```java
public static void main(String args[]) {
    E03DoubleBuffer window = new E03DoubleBuffer();
    window.init();
    window.createCanvas();
    window.setLocationRelativeTo(null);
    window.setVisible(true);
    window.run();
}
```

The complete code for this example is in the file "E03DoubleBuffer.java". The result is an entirely black canvas:

3.1.1.4 Synchronization

The solution in the previous example performs a constant display, using all available resources. If we observe the use of the processor during its execution, we can see that it uses a full core. On the smallest machines, it can slow down the whole system. This expenditure of resources is useless: even on a small machine, many more images are drawn than displayed. Indeed, screens all have a maximum refresh rate: usually 60 frames per second. This frequency is a function of the sensitivity of the human eye, which hardly perceives the image changes at this frequency.

One solution is not to draw more frames per second than can display the screen. To do this, we modify the `run()` method to impose a pause between two drawings. The pause time is calculated to ensure a fixed number of frames per second. If we run the example "E04DisplaySync.java", the display is the same, but the CPU usage of the program is very low.

Here is the new `run()` method:

```java
public void run()
{
    int fps = 60;
    long nanoPerFrame = (long) (1000000000.0 / fps);
    long lastTime = System.nanoTime();
    while (running) {
        long nowTime = System.nanoTime();
        if ((nowTime-lastTime) < nanoPerFrame) {
            continue;
        }
        lastTime = nowTime;
        render();
        long elapsed = System.nanoTime() - lastTime;
        long milliSleep = (nanoPerFrame - elapsed) / 1000000;
        if ( milliSleep > 0) {
            try {
                Thread.sleep (milliSleep);
            } catch (InterruptedException ex) {
                ex.printStackTrace();
            }
        }
    }
    dispose();
}
```

Step by step, it does the following. We define the number of frames per second. Here, this number is 60, which is the most common case:

```
int fps = 60;
```

It is possible to determine the frequency of the user's screen with the `getLocalGraphicsEnvironment()` method of the `java.awt.GraphicsEnvironment` class.

The time available in nanosecond is then calculated to draw a new image:

```
long nanoPerFrame = (long) (1000000000.0 / fps);
```

As a reminder, it takes 1 billion nanoseconds to make a second, a 1 followed by 9 zeros = 1 000 000 000. If we divide this value by the number of frames per second, we deduce the time of an image. For 60 frames per second, this is about 16666666 nanoseconds or about 16.6 milliseconds. In other words: there is not much time to draw each image!

A variable is defined to store the last time the display was updated:

```
long lastTime = 0;
```

At the beginning of each loop, we measure the current time in nanoseconds. This "time" is the time elapsed since the start of the Java virtual machine: it is relevant for making time offset measurements, but not for working on the time of day:

```
long nowTime = System.nanoTime();
```

Then, we compute the elapsed time, the difference between the current time and the last update. If this time is less than the refresh time, we resume the loop at the beginning. In other words, as long as there has not been enough time since the beginning of the last display, we wait:

```
if ((nowTime-lastTime) < nanoPerFrame) {
    continue;
}
```

If enough time has passed, we update the last time to the current one:

```
lastTime = nowTime;
```

The rest of the loop is the display, the call to the `render()` method. Subsequently, if other operations must be performed synchronously with the screen, this is where we add them.

It is possible to stop the improvement of the `render()` method: we get a rendering at the desired frequency, in this example at 60 frames per second. However, the use of the processor remains very high: it spends most of its time at the beginning of the loop to measure the current time and compare it to the previous one. It is possible to pause the execution of the program with the `Thread.sleep()` method, to avoid this loss of resources. With this method, it is possible to release the processor for a predetermined period of time.

We add the call to this method at the end of the loop:

```java
long elapsed = System.nanoTime() - lastTime;
long milliSleep = (nanoPerFrame - elapsed) / 1000000;
if (milliSleep > 0) {
    try {
        Thread.sleep (milliSleep);
    } catch (InterruptedException ex) {
        ex.printStackTrace();
    }
}
```

It is worth noting that the pause time is not that of the refresh time. Indeed, the rendering takes a specific time: the required pause is at most, the difference between the refresh time and the time spent to draw. We compute the time spent drawing in the `elapsed` variable. Then, the difference between the refresh time and the rendering time is calculated in the `miliSleep` variable, converted into milliseconds. If this time is non-zero, `Thread.sleep()` is called with a time expressed in milliseconds.

With this new addition, the display is at 60 frames per second, and the application's CPU use is very low.

3.1.2 Display with tiles

The display of most two-dimensional games is with tiles. This approach makes it easy to create large worlds, but also to manage its properties. For example, for the Pacman game, the tiles are square and placed according to an orthogonal grid with the following set of tiles:

It is possible to display a level like this:

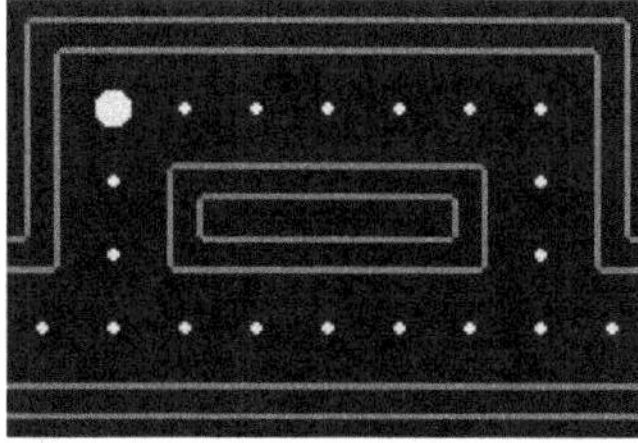

To obtain this result, copy one tile from the tileset for each position of the orthogonal grid. For example, for the first cell at the top left, copy the fifth tile of the second line:

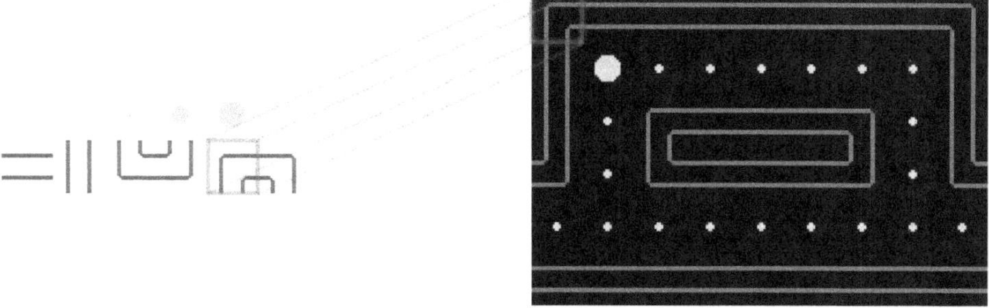

There are two other types of tiles: hexagonal and isometric. Hex tiles are staggered, and always have the same distance between adjacent tiles. Isometric tiles give the illusion of a three-dimensional world. For all these cases, the principles remain the same, and only a few parameters differ in the final solution.

3.1.2.1 Draw a world with tiles

Before you can display a level in tiles, we need two things: the tileset and the definition of a world according to this set. To create a tileset, you can recover an existing set: there are many free and royalty-free sets. You can also draw your own set. For that, any image editor does the trick. For example, the Gimp software can display a regular grid and draw in all the usual ways. Once the tileset is ready, we save it in an image whose format is lossless, such as gif or png. In addition, it is advisable to choose a square image whose size is a power of two: 64x64, 128x128, 256x256, etc. Indeed, many graphics cards prefer textures in this format. We place the tileset images in the "res" folder of the Java project.

Then, you have to design a world with this set. There are several free software to create it. In this book, we use "Tiled Map Editor". To download it, follow the instructions on the official website http://www.mapeditor.org/. Its default interface is as follows:

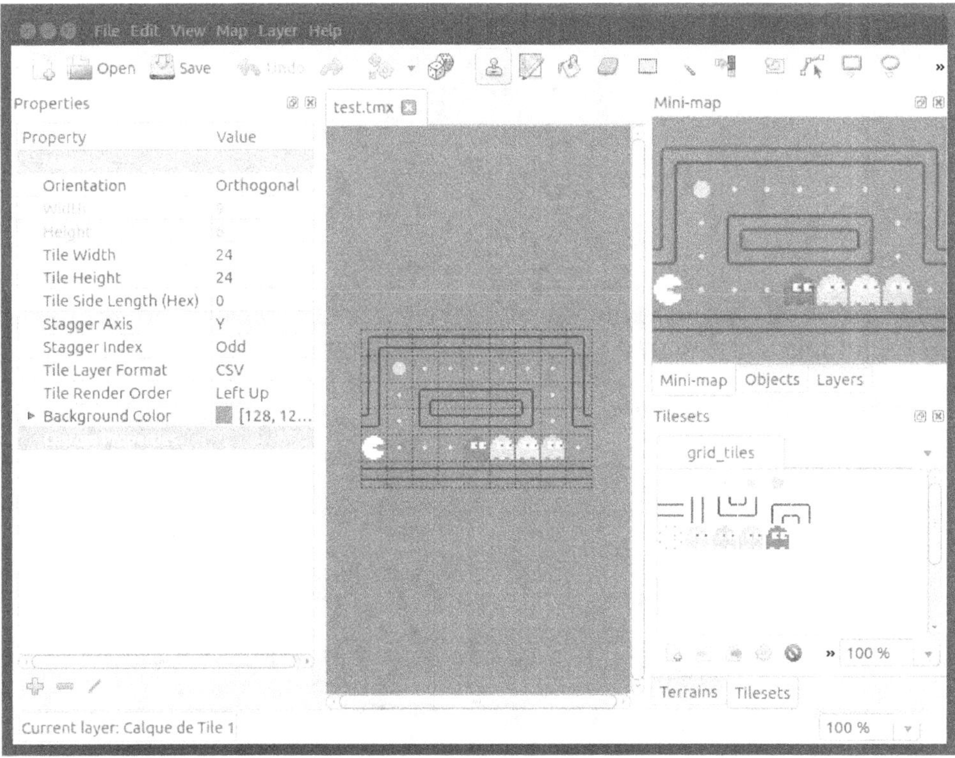

The left side has properties - in the above example, the properties of the world map are displayed. The central part allows modifying the map of the world. The upper right part is used to manage layers: tiled can manage the multilayer worlds. Finally, the bottom right shows the tileset currently in use.

The following steps can be followed to create a level:

→ Create a new map via the menu **File - New - New map ...** The following dialog appears:

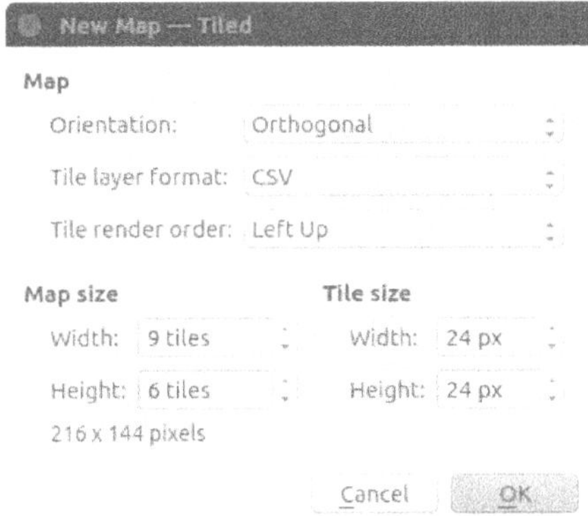

→ Choose the orientation of the map: orthogonal, isometric, or hexagonal.

→ For the **Tile Layer** Format, choose **CSV**.

→ For **Tile Render Order**, select **Top Left**. It is the default scanning order of screens.

→ For the size of the map, choose the size that corresponds to the world you want to create.

→ Finally, enter the **Tile Size** in the last part of the dialog. This setting depends on your tile game. In our example, the tiles are 24 pixels wide and 24 pixels high.

→ Once you have chosen all settings, click **Save As ....** If it does not exist, create a "res" folder in the root of your Java project. Save your map in this folder.

The tiled interface then takes the following form:

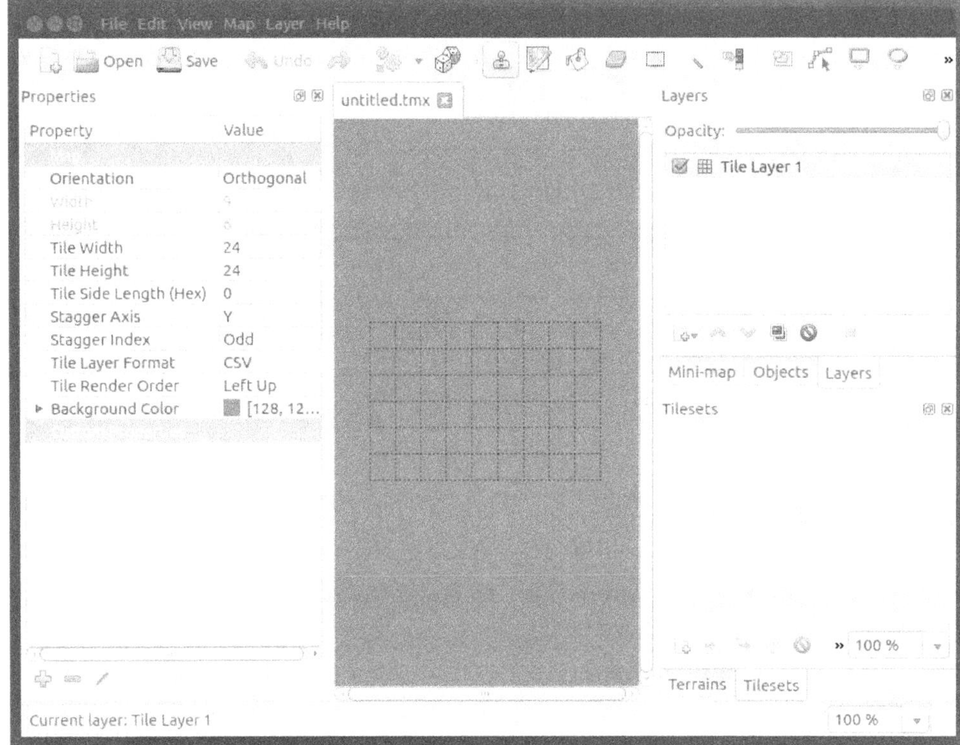

→ If the grid is not visible as in the screenshot above, use the menu **View - Show Grid**.

→ In the lower right corner, click the green "+" icon.

→ A new dialog appears: click on the **Browse...** button, then select the image that contains your tileset.

With these parameters, the following result was obtained for the example above:

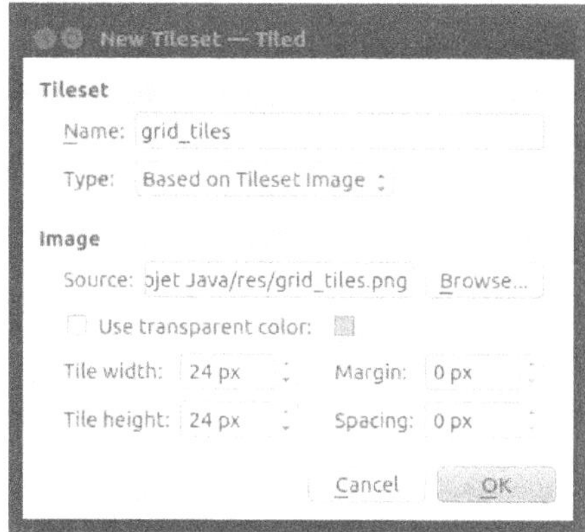

→ Click **OK**.

The interface then takes the following form:

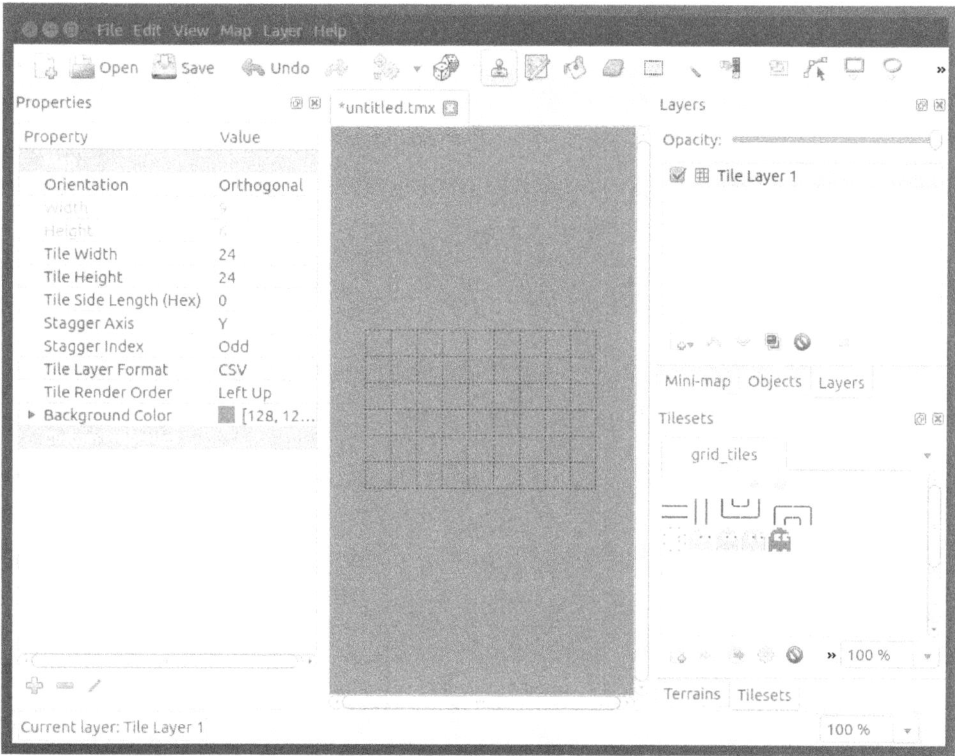

→ All you have to do is select an item in the tileset at the bottom right and click on the cells to modify. Save the world map once your level is ready.

3.1.2.2   Load and display an image

Adding a resource in a Java project

To be able to display a world with tiles, you must first load the image of the tileset. For that, it is advisable to integrate the image with the Java project: during the export of this one, images are added to the final .jar.

With Netbeans, define a resource folder, then any file in this folder is integrated into the project:

→ Right-click your Java project in the Project Explorer at the top left of the Netbeans interface.

→ This brings up the context menu, choose **Properties**.

→ The following dialog becomes visible:

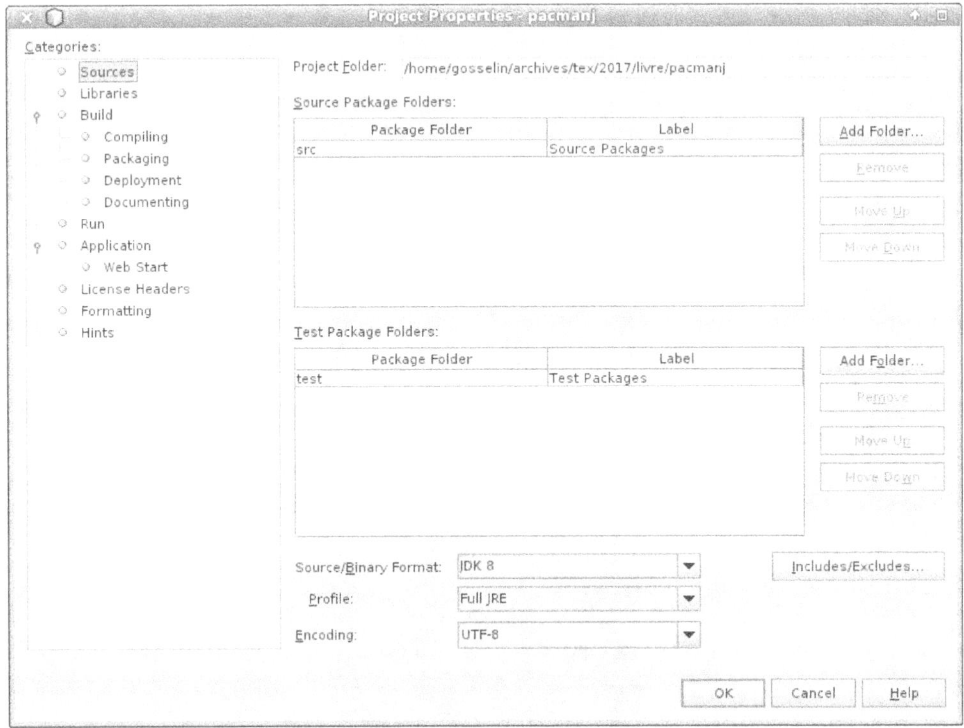

→ In the **Source Packages Folders** box, click the **Add Folder...** button.

→ Select the "res" folder in the root of your Java project. It is the folder where we saved the tileset images and the world map.

→ A new line in the **Source Packages Folders** table appears

→ In the **Label** column, in front of the "res" folder, enter a description of the "Resources" type. It is the name of the folder that contains your files for inclusion in the project.

→ Click **OK**.

Load and display an image

To load the image with the tileset, we add to the above example program a new method `loadTexture()`:

```java
public void loadTexture() throws IOException {
    ClassLoader classLoader =
        classLoader.getClass().getClassLoader()
    texture = ImageIO.read(
        classLoader.getResource("grid_tiles.png"));
}
```

This method calls the `ImageIO.read()` method of `javax.imageio` to load the file 'grid_tiles.png'. This file is an image of 256x256 pixels with tiles to display a level of Pacman. The following expression:

```java
ClassLoader classLoader = classLoader.getClass().getClassLoader()
classLoader.getResource("image file")
```

get the URL of a resource included in the Java project. Whatever the case, the URL is correct and the file is found.

We place the loaded image in a new `texture` attribute of `BufferedImage` type. We display it in the loop of the `run()` method, just after displaying the black rectangle:

```java
...
g = bs.getDrawGraphics();
g.setColor(Color.black);
g.fillRect(0,0,canvasWidth,canvasHeight);
g.drawImage(texture, 0, 0, null);
bs.show();
...
```

Finally, we call the `loadTexture()` method in the `main` method:

```java
public static void main(String args[]) {
    E05DrawImage window = new E05DrawImage();
    window.init();
    window.loadTexture();
    window.createCanvas();
    window.setLocationRelativeTo(null);
    window.setVisible(true);
```

```
    window.run();
}
```

This class is available in the "E05DrawImage.java" file in the "examples/chap03/awt" folder of the sample Java project.

3.1.2.3 Draw with tiles

We define new attributes to draw with a tileset:

```java
private int tileWidth = 24;
private int tileHeight = 24;
private int textureWidth;
private int textureHeight;
```

The attributes `tileWidth` and `tileHeight` define the width and height of a tile. In this example, they are predefined: it is not mandatory, we could load these values from a configuration file.

The `textureWidth` and `textureHeight` attributes store the number of tiles in width and height in the tile image. They are defined in the `loadTexture()` method:

```java
public void loadTexture() throws IOException {
    ClassLoader classLoader =
        classLoader.getClass().getClassLoader()
    texture = ImageIO.read(
        classLoader.getResource("grid_tiles.png")
    textureWidth = texture.getWidth()/tileWidth;
    textureHeight = texture.getHeight()/tileHeight;
}
```

In the example, the image is 256x256 pixels, and the tiles 24x24 pixels. So there is `textureWidth` = 10 by `textureHeight` = 10 tiles in this image. There is a slight loss in the image - a band of 16 pixels to the right and bottom of the image. This loss is nevertheless tolerable, knowing that many graphics cards do not natively manage textures whose size is not a power of 2.

The `render()` method is enriched to display the tile with Pacman, instead of the one in the previous example:

```java
int tileX = 0;
int tileY = 2;
int screenX = (canvasWidth - tileWidth)/2;
int screenY = (canvasHeight - tileHeight)/2;
g.drawImage(texture,screenX,screenY,screenX + tileWidth,
    screenY + tileHeight,tileX * tileWidth,tileY * tileHeight,
    tileX * tileWidth + tileWidth,tileY * tileHeight + tileHeight,
    null);
```

The `tileX` and `tileY` variables define the tile to display. In this example, we selected the Pacman tile at the beginning of the second row in the tileset. Changing these two variables allows you to choose any tile in the set.

The `screenX` and `screenY` variables define the coordinates of the tile on the screen. In this example, we want to draw it in the center of the canvas.

The `drawImage()` method has the following arguments:

- The first four arguments define the coordinates of the tile on the screen. It is not mandatory to form coordinates with exactly the same shape as the displayed tile. We can draw a tile smaller or larger, or turned in another direction by playing on these coordinates.
- The following four arguments define the coordinates of the tile in the tileset.
- The last argument allows us to propose a listener; in this example, this is not useful, hence the `null` value.

These modifications, available in the file "E06Tileset.java", offer the following result:

3.1.2.4   Draw a world in tiles

Now, the goal is to display a world (or level) with tiles. The following attributes are added to the class:

```
static final int levelWidth = 9;
static final int levelHeight = 6;
static final int[][] level = new int[][] {
    { 15,11,11,11,11,11,11,11,16 },{ 12,5,3,3,3,3,3,3,12 },
    { 12,3,15,11,11,11,16,3,12 },{ 14,3,13,11,11,11,14,3,13 },
    { 3,3,3,3,3,3,3,3,3 },{ 11,11,11,11,11,11,11,11,11 }
};
```

The `levelWidth` and `levelHeight` attributes define the width and height of the world. In this example, there are 9 tiles in width and 6 tiles in height.

The `level` attribute contains codes to define the tiles to draw. It is a two-dimensional array, such that `level[y][x]` is the tile code at coordinates *(x, y)*. The value of the codes is a function of the previously loaded tileset, which has 10 by 10 tiles of 24 by 24 pixels in an image of 256 by 256 pixels:

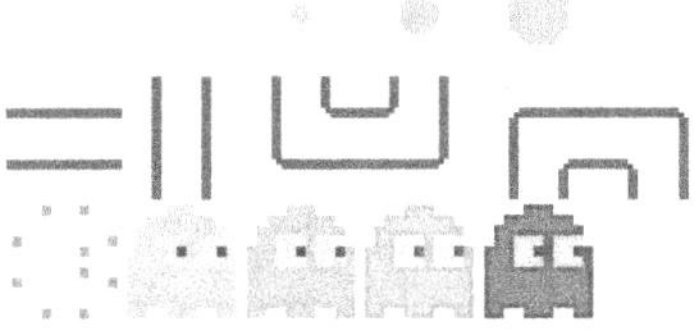

If you denote by `tileX` the column of a tile and `tileY` the row of a tile in the game, then its code is equal to `1 + tileX + tileY * 10`. The zero code is used to define the absence of tile. The first tile with a question mark has code 1. The next one, which represents empty space, has code 2. Then, the smallest gum has code 3.

The tile with a horizontal wall on the second row has the code 11, and the one with Pacman the code 21.

To define the values of `level` array, two solutions: either fill it directly in the Java file or use "Tiled Map Editor" presented previously. With the software, saving in CSV format, we can get the following world file:

```
<?xml version="1.0" encoding="UTF-8"?>
<map version="1.0" orientation="orthogonal"
 renderorder="left-up" width="9" height="6"
 tilewidth="24" tileheight="24" nextobjectid="1">
 <tileset firstgid="1" name="grid_tiles"
  tilewidth="24" tileheight="24" tilecount="100">
  <image source="grid_tiles.png"
   width="256" height="256"/>
 </tileset>
 <layer name="Layer 1" width="9" height="6">
  <data encoding="csv">
15,11,11,11,11,11,11,11,16,12,5,3,3,3,3,3,3,12,
12,3,15,11,11,11,16,3,12,12,3,13,11,11,11,14,3,12,
3,3,3,3,3,3,3,3,3,11,11,11,11,11,11,11,11,11
</data>
 </layer>
</map>
```

Simply copy and paste the codes between the <data encoding ="csv"> and </data> tags, and then add braces '{' and '}' at the beginning and at the end of each line. This approach is relevant for this case, to load larger levels, a procedure is presented in the next chapter.

The `createCanvas()` method is modified to fit the size of the canvas to that of the world:

```java
public void createCanvas() {
    canvasWidth = levelWidth * tileWidth;
    canvasHeight = levelHeight * tileHeight;
    ...
```

We add the drawing of the world in the `render()` method, between the drawing of the black background and that of the tile with Pacman:

```java
for (int j=0;j<levelHeight;j++) {
    for (int i=0;i<levelWidth;i++) {
        int tileIndex = level[j][i];
        if (tileIndex < 0)
            tileIndex = 0;
        int tileX = (tileIndex-1) % textureWidth;
        int tileY = (tileIndex-1) / textureHeight;
```

```
        if (tileY >= textureHeight) {
            tileX = 0;
            tileY = 0;
        }
        g.drawImage(texture,i * tileWidth,j * tileHeight,
            i * tileWidth + tileWidth,j * tileHeight + tileHeight,
            tileX * tileWidth,tileY * tileHeight,
            tileX * tileWidth + tileWidth,
            tileY * tileHeight + tileHeight,null);
    }
}
```

In this procedure, we go through all the cells of the `level` array to read the code of the tile:

```
int tileIndex = level[j][i];
```

If the code is invalid, replace it with the first tile - this avoids crashing the program unnecessarily:

```
if (tileIndex < 0)
    tileIndex = 0;
```

We compute the coordinates of a tile from its code. The calculation to achieve this is the opposite of the expression to get it:

```
int tileX = (tileIndex-1) % textureWidth;
int tileY = (tileIndex-1) / textureHeight;
```

We make sure that the tile is in the texture. In the opposite case, we display the first tile at the top left of the set:

```
if (tileY >= textureHeight) {
    tileX = 0;
    tileY = 0;
}
```

We draw the selected tile:

```
g.drawImage(texture,i * tileWidth, j * tileHeight,
    i * tileWidth + tileWidth,j * tileHeight + tileHeight,
    tileX * tileWidth, tileY * tileHeight,
    tileX * tileWidth + tileWidth,tileY * tileHeight + tileHeight,
    null);
```

The coordinates on the screen are functions of its position *(i, j)* in the world. We multiply the tileWidth and tileHeight by a tile to deduce its position in pixels.

By setting Pacman to the coordinates *(0,4)* in the world, the following result is obtained:

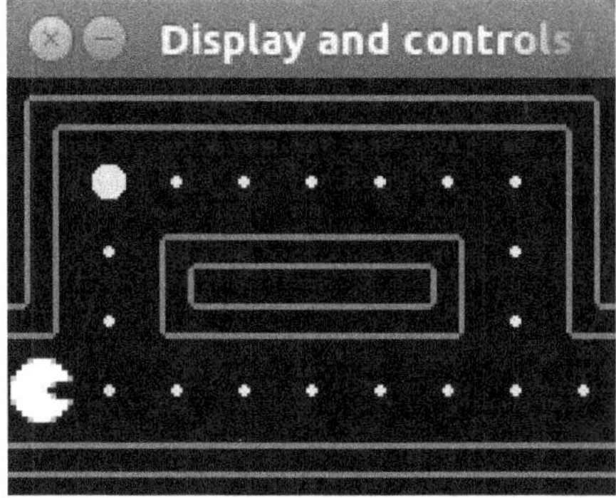

The complete code for this step is in the file "E07Level.java".

3.1.2.5 Animation with tiles

To animate the display, we add a new `lastUpdate` attribute and a new `update()` method:

```java
private long lastUpdate;
public void update() {
    long now = System.nanoTime();
    if ( (now - lastUpdate) < 1000000000/4)
        return;
    lastUpdate = now;
    for (int j=0;j<levelHeight;j++) {
        for (int i=0;i<levelWidth;i++) {
            int id = level[j][i];
            if (id == 5) level[j][i] = 4;
            else if (id == 4) level[j][i] = 5;
        }
    }
}
```

The function of the `update()` method is to modify the world. The `lastUpdate` attribute and the beginning of this method allow us to apply these changes periodically:

```java
long now = System.nanoTime();
if ( (now - lastUpdate) < 1000000000/4)
    return;
lastUpdate = now;
```

These lines compare the current time (now) with the time of the last update (lastUpdate). If this difference is less than a quarter of a second (250 milliseconds), we leave the method. Otherwise, the last update is set to the current time.

The following lines are free, and we can imagine any updates. In this example, we want to animate the display. To do this, we animate all the super gums. Since drawing is a function of the game state, if we modify the world, we also change the display. For super gums, there are two codes: 4 for the medium version and 5 for the large version. We go around everyone, if we meet a code 4, we turn it into 5, and vice versa:

```java
for (int j=0;j<levelHeight;j++) {
    for (int i=0;i<levelWidth;i++) {
        int id = level[j][i];
        if (id == 5) level[j][i] = 4;
        else if (id == 4) level[j][i] = 5;
    }
}
```

The update() method is invoked in the loop of the run() method, just before calling the render() method.

The result is visible with the file "E08Animation.java": the super gum at the top left is animated.

The way we change the world in this example does not matter. The important thing is the following principle, that is, the idea of changing the world, and then letting the rendered part take care of drawing those changes. In addition, there is no reason that all animations are at the same frequency (here 4 frames per second), or even to be regular in their modifications. We extend all these concepts in the last part of this chapter and the following ones.

3.1.3 Controls

3.1.3.1 AWT Controls (Observer Pattern)

AWT manages the keyboard and mouse controls with the *Observer Pattern*. This pattern allows one class to observe (or "listen") the behavior of another class. For example, a class may ask to see keys pressed or released in a window. When this is the case, the window informs (or notifies) the observer class of the changes.

It is generally composed of the following elements:

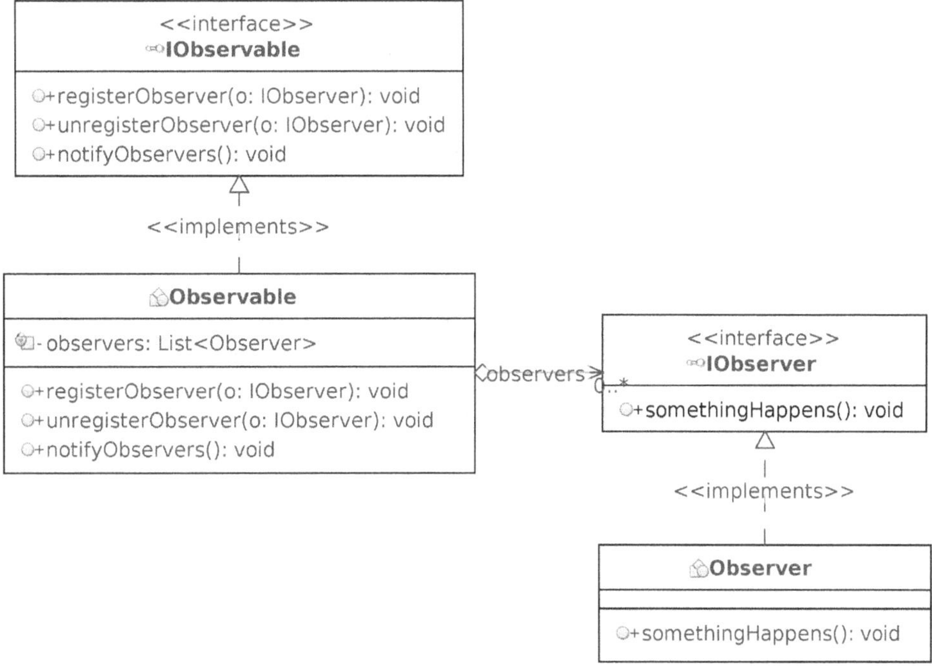

There are two parts: the part of the observable elements on the left, and that of the observer elements on the right. In each case, an interface defines the required functionalities. For the observable part, the `IObservable` interface defines three methods:

- The `registerObserver()` method, which adds a new observer.
- The `unregisterObserver()` method, which removes an observer.
- The `notifyObservers()` method, which informs observers.

Both methods of adding and removing observers are systematic. The notifications methods can be of various natures. In this example, the `notifyObservers()` method only informs that something has happened. It is quite possible to imagine other forms of notification, with or without arguments. For example, a `notifyObserversRepaint()` method can specify that the element is repaint. A `notifyObserversItemDeleted(Item e)` method can inform that an element is deleted, specifying the element concerned. These methods of notification are usually called by the observable class itself when it changes. For example, if there is a method of type `setValue(int x)` that modifies any attribute of the class, a notification method is called at the end of the method.

The `Observable` class is an example of implementing the `IObservable` interface. In this illustration, an observers list is used to memorize all observers. There are other solutions; for example, AWT uses an event queue, which allows you to choose the order and location of notifications.

In the observer part, on the right in the diagram, the `IObserver` interface defines the methods that receive the notifications. In this illustration, only the `somethingHappens()` method is offered and indicates that something has happened. It is quite possible to imagine other methods as needed. For example, an observer can be informed that the observed element is repaint with a `wasRepaint()` method. An observer can be notified of the deletion of an element with an `itemDeleted(Item e)` method.

The `IObservable` interface and its implementations should reflect the `IObserver` interface in its notifications. In general, a notification method is defined for each type of message. For example, for `KeyListener` we could have three methods:

- `void notifyObserversKeyTyped(KeyEvent event)`
- `void notifyObserversKeyReleased(KeyEvent event)`
- `void notifyObserversKeyPressed(KeyEvent event)`

The similarities between the `IObserver` interface and the notification methods of the `IObservable` interface do not have to form a perfect mirror. In some special cases, a notification method can perfectly call several methods of the observation interface.

The `Observer` class is an example of a class that implements the `IObserver` interface. It is free to react to the notifications of the observable as it sees fit.

3.1.3.2   Keyboard

For keyboard controls with AWT, it is necessary to create intermediate elements to have the necessary features for video games. Indeed, it is better - if not essential - to know the full state of the keyboard. In other words, you have to be able at any moment to know all the keys pressed. It is necessary, among other things, to handle the pressure of several keys at the same time. For example, to jump to the right with Mario, you need to press the right arrow and the jump button at the same time.

For the keyboard, AWT follows an observer pattern, with an observation interface formed by the following three methods:

- The `keyTyped (KeyEvent event)` method informs that a symbol was entered. The event argument contains information about this symbol.
- The `keyReleased (KeyEvent event)` method informs that a key was released. The event argument contains information about this key.
- The `keyPressed (KeyEvent event)` method informs that a key was pressed. The event argument contains information about this key.

In the class of the example, we define the following static subclass:

```java
private static class Keyboard implements KeyListener {
    private boolean[] keys;
    public Keyboard() {
        keys = new boolean[0x10000];
    }
    public boolean isKeyPressed(int keyCode) {
        if (keyCode >= keys.length)
            return false;
        return keys[keyCode];
    }
    public void keyTyped(KeyEvent e) {
    }
    public void keyPressed(KeyEvent e) {
        if (e.getKeyCode() < keys.length) {
            keys[e.getKeyCode()] = true;
        }
    }
    public void keyReleased(KeyEvent e) {
        if (e.getKeyCode() < keys.length) {
            keys[e.getKeyCode()] = false;
        }
    }
}
```

The role of this `Keyboard` class is to know at any time the state of any key on the keyboard, via the `isKeyPressed(int keyCode)` method. This method returns `true` if the `keyCode` key is pressed, `false` otherwise.

The `keys` attribute contains the pressed/released state of each key on the keyboard.

The `keyPressed()` and `keyReleased()` methods of the `java.awt.KeyListener` interface update the state of the `keys` array.

The `keyTyped()` method does nothing; there is no point in this example to recover the symbols typed on the keyboard.

We add a new `keyboard` attribute to the main class:

```
private Keyboard keyboard;
```

In the createCanvas() method, we initialize this attribute, and the canvas observes (or "listen") the keyboard:

```
keyboard = new Keyboard();
canvas.addKeyListener(keyboard);
```

At this stage of the modifications, it is possible to consult at any time the state of the keyboard via the keyboard attribute. To illustrate, we want to move Pacman with the arrow keys. We define two new attributes to memorize the position of Pacman:

```
private int pacmanX;
private int pacmanY;
```

Then, we add a new handleInputs() method to change the world according to controls:

```
public void handleInputs() {
    canvas.requestFocus();
    if (keyboard.isKeyPressed(KeyEvent.VK_RIGHT)) {
        pacmanX ++;
    }
    if (keyboard.isKeyPressed(KeyEvent.VK_LEFT)) {
        pacmanX --;
    }
    if (keyboard.isKeyPressed(KeyEvent.VK_DOWN)) {
        pacmanY ++;
    }
    if (keyboard.isKeyPressed(KeyEvent.VK_UP)) {
        pacmanY --;
    }
}
```

The first line ensures that the canvas always has focus. Otherwise, for example, if the window has the focus, keyboard events are not received by the canvas:

```
canvas.requestFocus();
```

The following lines change the Pacman coordinates according to the pressed keys. For example, if the right arrow is pressed, the horizontal coordinate of Pacman is increased:

```
if (keyboard.isKeyPressed(KeyEvent.VK_RIGHT)) {
    pacmanX ++;
}
```

The different keypress cases are not excluded: it is possible to press both the right and the bottom arrow, in which case the horizontal and the vertical Pacman coordinates are increased.

To allow the rendering to reflect the state of the game, we modify the part of the code that displays the Pacman tile. We draw the Pacman tile with the coordinates pacmanX, pacmanY:

```java
int tileX = 0;
int tileY = 2;
g.drawImage(texture,pacmanX,pacmanY,pacmanX + tileWidth,
    pacmanY + tileHeight,tileX * tileWidth,tileY * tileHeight,
    tileX * tileWidth + tileWidth,tileY * tileHeight + tileHeight,
    null);
```

All that remains is to add the call to the handleInputs() method in the main loop of the run() method, before the rendering call.

The result of these changes is to move Pacman with the arrow keys. The Java code is available in the file "E09Keyboard.java".

3.1.3.3 Mouse

The principle is very similar to that of the keyboard: we want to be able to know at any time the state of the mouse (position and buttons). AWT also use the Observer pattern for the mouse, divided into three interfaces: MouseListener for the buttons, MouseMotionListener for the position, and MouseWheelListener for the wheel. In this example, we only consider the position and buttons. We add a new static subclass that implements the interfaces:

```java
private static class Mouse
    implements MouseListener, MouseMotionListener {
    private boolean[] buttons;
    private int x;
    private int y;
    public Mouse() {
        buttons = new boolean[4];
    }
    public boolean isButtonPressed(int button) {
        if(button >= buttons.length)
            return false;
        return buttons[button];
    }
    public int getX() {
        return x;
    }
    public int getY() {
        return y;
```

```java
    }
    public void mouseClicked(MouseEvent e) {
    }
    public void mousePressed(MouseEvent e) {
        if (e.getButton() <= 3) {
            buttons[e.getButton()] = true;
        }
    }
    public void mouseReleased(MouseEvent e) {
        if (e.getButton() <= 3) {
            buttons[e.getButton()] = false;
        }
    }
    public void mouseEntered(MouseEvent e) {
    }
    public void mouseExited(MouseEvent e) {
    }
    public void mouseDragged(MouseEvent e) {
        x = e.getX();
        y = e.getY();
    }
    public void mouseMoved(MouseEvent e) {
        x = e.getX();
        y = e.getY();
    }
}
```

The `buttons`, `x` and `y` attributes memorize the state of the buttons and the position of the mouse. The methods `isButtonPressed()`, `getX()` and `getY()` allow to consult these states. The implementation of the methods `mousePressed()` and `mouseReleased()` allow modifying the state of the buttons, like what was done with the keyboard. The implementation of the `mouseDragged()` and `mouseMoved()` methods allows you to update the mouse position.

We add a new `mouse` attribute to the main class:

```java
private Mouse mouse;
```

We create the mouse handler and let it listen to canvas mouse events in the `createCanvas()` method:

```java
mouse = new Mouse();
canvas.addMouseListener(mouse);
canvas.addMouseMotionListener(mouse);
```

At this point, everything is ready to consult the status of the mouse at any time via the `mouse` attribute. For this example, we want to use the mouse to modify the tiles of the world: with a left-click, we erase a tile; with a right-click, we add a super gum. In addition, we want to see the tile that can be modified with a yellow frame.

We start by adding two attributes to store the tile currently under the mouse cursor:

```java
private int selectedTileX;
private int selectedTileY;
```

In the handleInputs() method, we define these attributes according to the position of the mouse. The pixel coordinates of the mouse position are divided by the size of the tiles. It allows to obtain the coordinates of the tile selected in the world, independently of the notions of control and display:

```java
selectedTileX = mouse.getX() / tileWidth;
selectedTileY = mouse.getY() / tileHeight;
```

In the render() method, we add the drawing of the tile that represents a yellow frame. The principle is the same as with the display of the tile with Pacman:

```java
int tileX = 5;
int tileY = 0;
g.drawImage(texture,selectedTileX * tileWidth,
    selectedTileY * tileHeight,
    selectedTileX * tileWidth + tileWidth,
    selectedTileY * tileHeight + tileHeight,tileX * tileWidth,
    tileY * tileHeight,tileX * tileWidth + tileWidth,
    tileY * tileHeight + tileHeight,null);
```

Thanks to this new code, moving the mouse makes a yellow frame appear under the cursor.

To change the world based on mouse clicks, we add a few lines in the handleInputs() method:

```java
if (selectedTileX >= 0 && selectedTileX < levelWidth
 && selectedTileY >= 0 && selectedTileY < levelHeight) {
    if (mouse.isButtonPressed(MouseEvent.BUTTON1)) {
        level[selectedTileY][selectedTileX] = 2;
    }
    if (mouse.isButtonPressed(MouseEvent.BUTTON3)) {
        level[selectedTileY][selectedTileX] = 5;
    }
}
```

If the coordinates of the selected tile are valid, we look at the mouse buttons. If the left button is pressed, place a space tile (code 2) at these coordinates. If the right button is pressed, we place a super gum (code 5).

The Java code for this example is available in the "E10Mouse.java" file.

3.1.4   Optimizing the display

This section introduces advanced notions that beginners can ignore.

3.1.4.1   Display performance

Measure the performance of the display

The AWT display with the previous strategy works in all situations. However, it may not always be the best. To be able to compare different display strategies, we start by adding ways to measure its performance. For the Java example program in this section, we add a new bench() method similar to run(). It will no longer limit the update time and measure the number of frames per second:

```java
public void bench()
{
    int count = 0;
    long begin = System.nanoTime();
    while (running) {
        handleInputs();
        update();
        render();
        count ++;
    }
    long end = System.nanoTime();
    double fps = count/((end-begin)/1000000000.0);
    System.out.println("Frames per second: "+fps);
    dispose();
}
```

With a laptop, the number of frames per second measured is about 3500. On a desktop computer, we measured a similar number of frames per second.

Enable OpenGL

It is possible to ask the Java virtual machine to enable OpenGL, by adding the
-Dsun.java2d.opengl=True option to its arguments. As a reminder, OpenGL is
an API that makes better use of the power of the graphics card of a computer. In
Netbeans, you can add this type of option in the project properties, category **Run**:

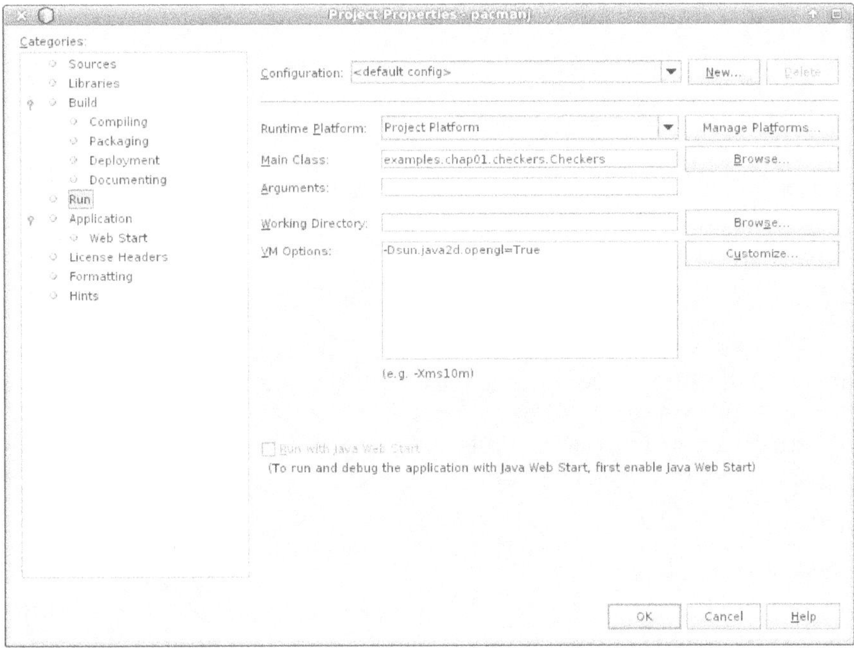

This option can be entered in the **VM Options** field.

With this option, and with the same laptop as before, we get about 9000 frames
per second. In this case, the gain is very appreciable. On the desktop computer,
we get about 150 frames per second. In this second case, OpenGL dramatically
reduces performance. It depends on the hardware configuration of the machine, as
well as the drivers used. It is also possible that this option crashes the java virtual
machine.

Use images compatible with the hardware

Another approach that improves the display speed with AWT is to use images
compatible with the hardware. If we want to create them, it is enough to convert
all the used images into a compatible format. To achieve this, we request a new
compatible image of the same size as the image to be converted, and then we draw
the image in the compatible image. For example, we can add the following lines in
the loadTexture() method:

```java
Graphics g = null;
try {
  BufferedImage compatibleTexture =
    getGraphicsConfiguration().createCompatibleImage(
      texture.getWidth(), texture.getHeight(),
      Transparency.TRANSLUCENT);
  g = compatibleTexture.createGraphics();
  g.drawImage(texture, 0, 0, null);
  texture = compatibleTexture;
}
finally {
  if (g != null) {
    g.dispose();
  }
}
```

The full Java code is available in the file "E12CompatibleImage.java".

With this change, the results may also vary depending on the hardware and software configuration of the computer being used. During tests, we sometimes observed an improvement, a loss, and in rare cases, errors (the displayed image is black). As the activation of OpenGL, it is advisable to use a launcher to allow the user to test the possible parameters.

3.1.4.2   Use a launcher

For use in the final version, it is advisable to make a launcher program. This program, written with the most portable features of Java, without option or special library, allows the user to activate the settings of his choice. For example, it can enable or disable the use of OpenGL. Then, the launcher starts the game in a new Java virtual machine with these parameters. If this new Java virtual machine crashes, the launcher can detect it and warn the user. He can then modify the parameters and attempt a new launch. Most current video games are launched in this way: it allows non-expert users to set up the game, but also to understand the problems and their solutions easily.

The sample file "E13Launcher.java" introduces a basic launcher. This one asks the user if he wants to activate OpenGL. If the user chooses to use it, he launches a new JVM with the option. If not, it launches a new JVM without the option:

```java
public static void main(String[] args)
{
    int selectedOption = JOptionPane.showConfirmDialog(null,
          "Launch with OpenGL ?","Launch settings",
          JOptionPane.YES_NO_OPTION);
    run("examples.chap03.awt.E11Bench",
```

```
        selectedOption == JOptionPane.YES_OPTION);
}
```

In this example, the `examples.chap03.awt.E11Bench` class is started - you can choose any other executable class in the Java project.

The `run()` method is used to launch a JVM with or without the option:

```java
public static boolean run(String className,
    boolean enableOpenGL) {
    try {
        ArrayList<String> argumentList = new ArrayList<String>();
        String javaHome = System.getProperty("java.home");
        argumentList.add(
          new File(javaHome, "bin/java").getPath());
        argumentList.add("-cp");
        argumentList.add(System.getProperty("java.class.path"));
        if (enableOpenGL) {
            argumentList.add("-Dsun.java2d.opengl=True");
        }
        argumentList.add(className);
        ProcessBuilder pb = new ProcessBuilder(argumentList);
        pb.directory(new File(System.getProperty("user.dir")));
        Process p = pb.start();
        StreamPrinter outputStream =
          new StreamPrinter(p.getInputStream());
        StreamPrinter inputStream =
          new StreamPrinter(p.getErrorStream());
        new Thread(outputStream).start();
        new Thread(inputStream).start();
        p.waitFor();
        return p.exitValue() == 0;
    } catch (IOException e) {
        e.printStackTrace();
        return false;
    } catch (InterruptedException e) {
        e.printStackTrace();
        return false;
    }
}
```

This method starts by creating a list of arguments to form a call to java:

```java
ArrayList<String> argumentList = new ArrayList<String>();
```

The first argument is the java binary, with its full path. It is in the "bin" folder of the main Java folder. The latter can be obtained with the environment variable "java.home":

```
String javaHome = System.getProperty("java.home");
argumentList.add(new File(javaHome, "bin/java").getPath());
```

The following two arguments define the classes to use - we take those of the Java project:

```
argumentList.add("-cp");
argumentList.add(System.getProperty("java.class.path"));
```

The following argument activates OpenGL. It is added if the user has chosen it:

```
if (enableOpenGL) {
  argumentList.add("-Dsun.java2d.opengl=True");
}
```

The last argument is the name of the Java executable class:

```
argumentList.add(className);
```

With these arguments, we launch a new Java virtual machine in the same folder as the current JVM:

```
ProcessBuilder pb = new ProcessBuilder(argumentList);
pb.directory(new File(System.getProperty("user.dir")));
Process p = pb.start();
```

The following lines are used to redirect the output streams of the new JVM to instances of a `StreamPrinter` class. This class, defined in the "E13Launcher.java" file, displays all the content it receives. The set allows you to see the messages sent by the new JVM, which can be very interesting to detect any errors. It is optional - the program works fine without it. The use of one thread per stream makes it possible to process these redirects in the background:

```
StreamPrinter outputStream =
    new StreamPrinter(p.getInputStream());
StreamPrinter inputStream =
    new StreamPrinter(p.getErrorStream());
new Thread(outputStream).start();
new Thread(inputStream).start();
```

The next line is just waiting for the new JVM to finish:

```
p.waitFor();
```

Then, we return `true` if the code returned by the new JVM is 0, `false` otherwise:

```
return p.exitValue() == 0;
```

All of these lines are framed by a `try ... catch` that intercepts the exceptions: if so, the `run()` method returns `false`, which is to know if the new JVM has failed.

This launcher is extremely simple and allows us to see the essential principles. For a complete launcher, you must add all the required options and parameters, and inform the user of the failure cases.

3.2   3D User Interface with LWJGL

This section can be ignored by novice readers.

This section introduces the basics of building a 3D game with version 3 of the *Lightweight Java Game Library (LWJGL)*. It is a low-level library based on OpenGL, a standard API compatible with all operating systems (Windows, Linux, Mac, Android ...). The approach proposed here is based on the use of vertex objects. It is more complex than approaches based on direct API calls for each element displayed. However, it is the only one that is truly relevant for the creation of a game; the second one quickly saturates when there are many elements.

The items in this section also allow you to use the library for a 2D display with OpenGL. This type of display is much smoother than with AWT and allows the use of many effects.

This section is not an exhaustive presentation of the 3D display: a complete book is required for this. As a result, many aspects are not detailed. The objective is to present the logic and the usual tools of this type of display, then to deduce good designs that allow us to make them interact with the other actors of the game.

The library is included in the Java project example, in its version for Windows. For other operating systems, you must modify the dependencies by replacing those for Windows with those available in one of the folders in the "lib" folder of the project. For example, the "lib/lwjgl-linux" folder contains the .jar for the Linux version.

3.2.1   Creating a window

Creating a simple window is much more complex than AWT, given the low-level aspect of the library. To achieve this, LWJGL uses the standard GLFW API linked to OpenGL. It allows you to manage all aspects of the interaction between the program and the operating system while providing access to OpenGL. This library is mainly used via static methods that always start with `glfw`, like a C program.

To create this window, a `Window` class is defined. It has three attributes:

- `windowHandle` to store the GLFW identifier of the window
- `windowWidth` and `windowHeight` for the width and height of the window

3.2.1.1 Initialization

We initialize the window in an `init()` method:

```java
private void init() {
```

We start by defining how the error messages are displayed. Here, these messages are displayed on the standard error stream (`System.err`):

```java
GLFWErrorCallback.createPrint(System.err).set();
```

The GLFW library is initialized with the `glfwInit()` method:

```java
if (!glfwInit()) {
    throw new IllegalStateException(
            "Error when initializing GLFW");
}
```

The following lines define different options: window not visible at creation, window not resizable, and definition of an API level for compatibility reasons:

```java
glfwDefaultWindowHints();
glfwWindowHint(GLFW_VISIBLE, GLFW_FALSE);
glfwWindowHint(GLFW_RESIZABLE, GLFW_FALSE);
glfwWindowHint(GLFW_CONTEXT_VERSION_MAJOR, 3);
glfwWindowHint(GLFW_CONTEXT_VERSION_MINOR, 2);
glfwWindowHint(GLFW_OPENGL_PROFILE,
    GLFW_OPENGL_CORE_PROFILE);
glfwWindowHint(GLFW_OPENGL_FORWARD_COMPAT,GL_TRUE);
```

The window is created with the `glfwCreateWindow()` method. It returns the handle that allows to control it:

```java
windowHandle = glfwCreateWindow(windowWidth, windowHeight,
    "Display and controls with LWJGL",NULL, NULL);
if (windowHandle == NULL) {
    throw new RuntimeException(
            "Error when creating the window");
}
```

The `glfwSetKeyCallback()` method is used to respond to a keyboard action. Here, in case the escape key is released, we ask to close the window:

```java
glfwSetKeyCallback(windowHandle,
    (window, key, scancode, action, mods) -> {
        if (key == GLFW_KEY_ESCAPE && action == GLFW_RELEASE) {
            glfwSetWindowShouldClose(window, true);
        }
    });
```

The following lines center the window on the screen. The `glfwGetVideoMode()` method returns video mode information, here the width `vidmode.width()` and the height `vidmode.height()` interest us:

```
GLFWVidMode vidmode = glfwGetVideoMode(
    glfwGetPrimaryMonitor());
glfwSetWindowPos(windowHandle,
    (vidmode.width() - windowWidth) / 2,
    (vidmode.height() - windowHeight) / 2);
```

The following call to the `glfwMakeContextCurrent()` method indicates that the current thread is the thread that handles OpenGL. It highlights the single-threaded character of OpenGL: in general, one and only one thread can interact with OpenGL:

```
glfwMakeContextCurrent(windowHandle);
```

As its name does not indicate, the `glfwSwapInterval()` method enables vertical synchronization (*vsync*). It implies that the display buffer inversion function waits so that the display is synchronized with the screen (usually at 60 frames per second):

```
glfwSwapInterval(1);
```

The window is displayed:

```
glfwShowWindow(windowHandle);
```

OpenGL must be initialized after the creation of the window, and before the use of its functions:

```
GL.createCapabilities();
```

The `glClearColor()` method is used to define the erase color of the display buffer, here black (red = 0, blue = 0 and green = 0) has been chosen. The last argument of the method is the level of transparency, often called alpha:

```
glClearColor(0.0f, 0.0f, 0.0f, 0.0f);
}
```

3.2.1.2 Execution and destruction:

Once the window is initialized, the display follows the double buffer rule. A loop is repeated as long as the window is not closed:

```
private void run() {
    while (!glfwWindowShouldClose(windowHandle)) {
```

The display buffers are reversed:

```
glfwSwapBuffers(windowHandle);
```

An event queue handles actions such as keypresses. These aspects are not automatic, and we must explicitly trigger their management with the `glfwPollEvents()` method:

```
glfwPollEvents();
```

It is at this point, for example, that the action defined with `glfwSetKeyCallback()` in the `init()` method can be called.

As a display, the `glClear()` method is called to clear the buffer. This one has several parts, the ones that are used in these examples are the visual part (GL_COLOR_BUFFER_BIT) and the part which manages the occultation (GL_DEPTH_BUFFER_BIT):

```
        glClear(GL_COLOR_BUFFER_BIT
              | GL_DEPTH_BUFFER_BIT);
    }
}
```

The destruction of the window and its elements is not automatic: it must be done explicitly:

```
private void dispose() {
    glfwFreeCallbacks(windowHandle);
    glfwDestroyWindow(windowHandle);
    glfwTerminate();
    glfwSetErrorCallback(null).free();
}
```

The window can be started from a `main()` function using the previous functions:

```
public static void main(String[] args) {
    Window window = new Window();
    window.init();
    window.run();
    window.dispose();
}
```

The code is present in the "examples/chap03/lwjgl01" folder of the sample Java project. The run has an empty window with black content.

3.2.2 Show a triangle

3.2.2.1 Display Pipeline

The data to display follow a long chain of processing (or *pipeline*), reproduced for each displayed frame. It is summarized by the following figure:

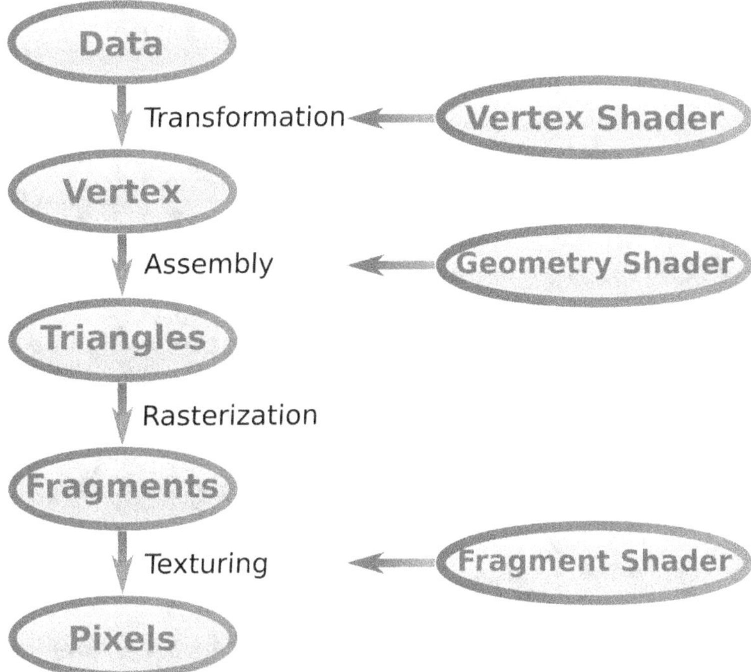

The initial data can take different forms, the simplest being a list of vertices that form the mesh of an object. In the following example, the simplest object is considered: a triangle formed by 3 vertices. Each vertex is a vector with three values: x, y, and z.

This data is provided to the graphics pipeline for the first transformation. This transformation can be very simple, namely, no transformation. It is also possible to make them undergo affine transformations, such as translation or rotation. In a perspective view, this is where it is applied. These transformations can be programmed via *vertex shaders*.

Once the vertex is produced, the next assembly step consists in producing the triangles that will form the faces of the objects. This step is usually automatic but can be programmed via *geometry shaders*. These allow, among other things, to generate new vertexes and new primitives on the fly.

The next step, called rasterization, transforms all triangles into fragments the size of a pixel. This step is not programmable.

The last texturing step allows assigning each fragment a color. This color can be fixed, or interpolated between two colors of vertex, or from a texture. These colorization choices are programmable via *fragment shaders*.

3.2.2.2   Pipeline to display a triangle

The goal here is to build a graphical pipeline that produces a centered triangle on the screen:

The code is present in the "examples/chap03/lwjgl02" folder of the sample Java project.

Shaders

A Renderer class is defined to handle the examples. It initializes the pipeline in the init() method:

```java
public void init() throws Exception {
```

It uses an instance of the Shader class, described later, which allows you to manage shader compilation and execution aspects:

```java
shader = new Shader();
```

A vertex shader is added to `shader`. This addition involves its compilation and validation:

```
String vertexShaderSource = ... shader code ... ;
shader.createVertexShader(vertexShaderSource);
```

The vertex shader code is as follows:

```
#version 330
layout (location=0) in vec3 vertex;
void main() {
  gl_Position = vec4(vertex, 1.0);
}
```

The processing of this shader is very simple: all three-dimensional input vectors are transformed into 4-dimensional vectors, adding the value 1.0 as the 4th value. As discussed below, vertexes are processed in 4 dimensions to facilitate the implementation of affine transformations.

The first line indicates the version of the code.

The second declares the input variable `vertex` of the 3-dimensional vector type. The expression `layout (location = 0)` indicates that this data is contained in the first Vertex Buffer Object (VBO), described below.

The `main()` function constructs a 4-dimensional vector by adding the value 1.0 to all vertex vectors. The result of this processing is placed in the `gl_Position` variable. This variable is set by default, and it is expected to contain the vertex result of the shader.

The following lines define the fragment shader:

```
String fragmentShaderSource = ... shader code ...
shader.createFragmentShader(fragmentShaderSource);
```

The code of the fragment shader is as follows:

```
#version 330
out vec4 color;
void main() {
  color = vec4(1.0, 1.0, 1.0, 1.0);
}
```

Its processing is very simple: assign the white color (red = 1.0, green = 1.0, blue = 1.0). The first line is also the version of the code. The second declares a `color` output variable of dimension 4. The `main()` function assigns the white color to this variable, as well as the opacity of 1.0. It does not affect because we did not enable the corresponding OpenGL options.

Once the shaders have been compiled and validated, you have to execute the link edition, like the usual programs:

```
shader.link();
```

Data

The rest of the method declares the data necessary for the representation of a triangle. It is necessary to have three vertices corresponding to the three edges of the triangle. The values of these vertices are placed one behind the other in an array:

```
float[] vertex = new float[]{
    0.0f, 0.5f, 0.0f,-0.5f, -0.5f, 0.0f,0.5f, -0.5f, 0.0f
};
```

These values are based on the fact that the area drawn in the window is according to the first two axes (x and y). The last axis z is the depth, the elements with the smallest z are drawn before those with larger values. In this example, the z value of the three vertices is 0: all vertices are in the same plane. Warning: There is no concept of perspective in this coordinate system. All values are between -1 and 1. Any value outside it is not displayed. Knowing this, the center of the window is (0,0). With the values chosen above, the triangle is drawn in the middle of the window.

The `vertex` array is converted to `java.nio.FloatBuffer` format: it is the one supported by LWJGL, for optimization reasons:

```
FloatBuffer vertexBuffer = null;
try {
    vertexBuffer = MemoryUtil.memAllocFloat(vertex.length);
    vertexBuffer.put(vertex).flip();
```

In more advanced cases, these `java.nio` format buffers are directly filled from a file containing the mesh. In this example, a native array `float[]` was used to enter the vertex of the triangle for readability.

This data must be copied into the memory of the graphics card for it to exploit. We must use a particular structure to perform this copy. It consists of two levels: a higher level called *Vertex Array Object (VAO)*, and a lower level *Vertex Buffer Object (VBO)*. VAOs contain several VBOs. A new VAO is created by the `glGenVertexArrays()` method, and its identifier is placed in the `vaoId` attribute:

```
vaoId = glGenVertexArrays();
```

Then, we move the OpenGL context on this VAO with the `glBindVertexArray()` method:

```
glBindVertexArray(vaoId);
```

The entire OpenGL API is based on a context principle: the nature of the requested operations depends on contextual parameters. In this example, the operations that modify a VAO concerns the one whose identifier is `vaoId`. It emphasizes the single-threaded and highly procedural nature of this API. When the mind is used to object-oriented programming, it can imagine expressions of the type `openglContext.glBindVertexArray(vaoId)`, where `openglContext` is an instance of an imaginary class that contains the parameters of the current context.

A VBO is created with the `glGenBuffers()` method, and attention is focused on it with the `glBindBuffer()` method:

```
vboId = glGenBuffers();
glBindBuffer(GL_ARRAY_BUFFER, vboId);
```

The `glBufferData()` method is used to copy the vertices into the memory of the graphics card. The VBO concerned by this operation is the one defined contextually:

```
glBufferData(GL_ARRAY_BUFFER, vertexBuffer,GL_STATIC_DRAW);
```

The last argument is a clue to allow OpenGL to do optimizations. In this case, `GL_STATIC_DRAW` was chosen, and means that the data is not changed and used for display.

The `glVertexAttribPointer()` method allows to give properties to the VBO within the VAO:

```
glVertexAttribPointer(0, 3, GL_FLOAT, false, 0, 0);
```

The first argument (0) is the index within the VAO. The vertex shader uses this value in the expression `layout (location = 0) in vec3 vertex`, which indicates through (`location = 0`) that the shader uses the VBO index 0 within the VAO.

The second argument (3) indicates the size of the vectors. In this example, the data are vertices of dimension 3.

The third argument (`GL_FLOAT`) indicates the type of values, in this case `float`.

The fourth argument (`false`) indicates whether the values should be normalized. This option only applies to entire data types.

The last two arguments (0, 0) are advanced settings that go beyond the scope of these presentations.

Once the operations are completed, the VBO and the VAO are freed from the context, using the same methods of assignment, but with null identifiers:

```
glBindBuffer(GL_ARRAY_BUFFER, 0);
glBindVertexArray(0);
```

In any case, the memory allocated for the transfer of data must be freed, no automatic process will do it:

```
} finally {
    if (vertexBuffer != null) {
        MemoryUtil.memFree(vertexBuffer);
    }
}
```

Destruction

The elements are not destroyed automatically: it must be done manually. The dispose() method of the class does this:

```
public void dispose() {
    if (shader != null) {
        shader.dispose();
    }
    glDisableVertexAttribArray(0);
    glBindBuffer(GL_ARRAY_BUFFER, 0);
    glDeleteBuffers(vboId);
    glBindVertexArray(0);
    glDeleteVertexArrays(vaoId);
}
```

Rendering

Previous operations are performed only once. Then, the information we placed in the graphic card allows rendering with few calls. We implement it in the render() method of the Renderer class, and starts by assigning the previous shaders to the context with the bind() method of the Shader class:

```
shader.bind();
```

The Shader class is presented in the next section.

The previously created VAO is also assigned to the context:

```
glBindVertexArray(vaoId);
```

The first element of the VAO, the VBO with the vertex of the triangle, is also assigned to the context:

```
glEnableVertexAttribArray(0);
```

The glDrawArrays() method can then be called, knowing that it uses VBO vertex and assigned shaders:

```
glDrawArrays(GL_TRIANGLES, 0, 3);
```

The first argument (GL_TRIANGLES) is the way vertex is interpreted. Here the most common case, triangles, is selected.

The next two arguments 0 and 3 are the index of the first vertex and their number.

Finally, all the elements are freed from the context:

```
glDisableVertexAttribArray(0);
glBindVertexArray(0);
shader.unbind();
```

⇒ Note: This procedure for programming the graphics card with operations and data is particularly complex, but worths it given the gains in terms of speed of display. Indeed, by programming the graphics card, few interactions are necessary to handle large volumes of data. With the present example, the same number of calls is necessary for a triangle as for a million.

3.2.2.3 Manage shaders

The Shader class contains operations around shaders. The main shader can group several sub-shaders: in this class, the main shader shaderId contains a vertex shader vertexShaderId and a fragment shader fragmentShaderId:

```
public class Shader {
    private final int shaderId;
    private int vertexShaderId;
    private int fragmentShaderId;
    public Shader() {
        shaderId = glCreateProgram();
        if (shaderId == 0) {
            throw new RuntimeException(
                "Error when creating the shader");
        }
    }
    protected int createShader(String code,int type) {
        int id = glCreateShader(type);
        if (id == 0) {
            throw new RuntimeException(
                "Error when creating the shader");
        }
        glShaderSource(id, code);
        glCompileShader(id);
        if (glGetShaderi(id,GL_COMPILE_STATUS) == 0) {
            throw new RuntimeException(
                "Error when compiling the shader");
        }
```

```java
        glAttachShader(shaderId, id);
        return id;
    }
    public void createVertexShader(String code) {
        vertexShaderId = createShader(code,GL_VERTEX_SHADER);
    }
    public void createFragmentShader(String code) {
        fragmentShaderId = createShader(code,
            GL_FRAGMENT_SHADER);
    }

    public void link() {
        glLinkProgram(shaderId);
        if (glGetProgrami(shaderId,GL_LINK_STATUS) == 0) {
            throw new RuntimeException(
                "Error when linking the shader");
        }
        if (vertexShaderId != 0) {
            glDetachShader(shaderId,vertexShaderId);
        }
        if (fragmentShaderId != 0) {
            glDetachShader(shaderId,fragmentShaderId);
        }
        glValidateProgram(shaderId);
        if (glGetProgrami(shaderId,GL_VALIDATE_STATUS) == 0) {
            throw new RuntimeException(
                "Error when validating  the shader");
        }
    }
    public void bind() {
        glUseProgram(shaderId);
    }
    public void unbind() {
        glUseProgram(0);
    }
    public void dispose() {
        unbind();
        if (shaderId != 0) {
            glDeleteProgram(shaderId);
        }
    }
}
```

3.2.3 Color and index

3.2.3.1 Color

Color data

To give several colors to a mesh, it is possible to use a buffer that contains the colors of each vertex. Each vertex then has the designated color, and then the interior of the triangles formed by the vertices have an interpolated color. For example, if the first sum of the preceding triangle has the red color, the second the green color, and the third the blue color, the following result is obtained:

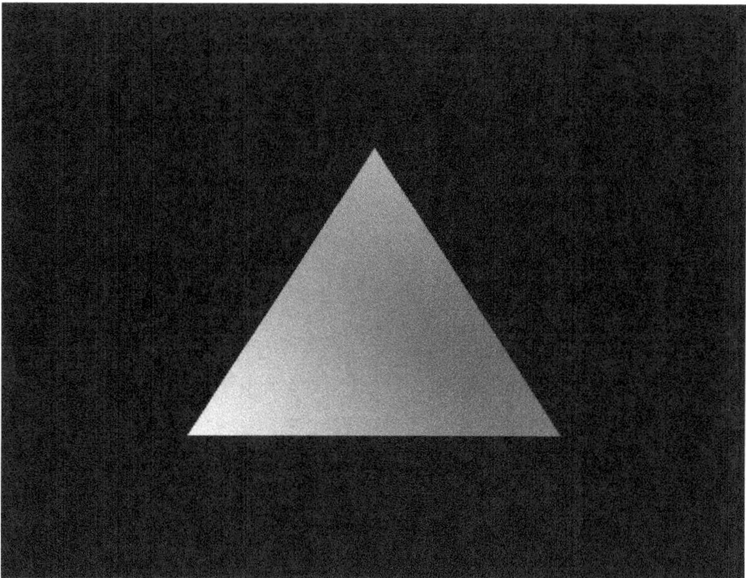

To assign these colors, the same buffer mechanism is used:

```
float[] colors = new float[]{
    1.0f, 0.0f, 0.0f,0.0f, 1.0f, 0.0f,0.0f, 0.0f, 1.0f,};
```

The colors are vectors of dimension 3, which gives a total of nine values, as for the table with the vertex of the triangle.

These data must be added to the declared VAO for the mesh. A second VBO is added to store the colors:

```
colorVboId = glGenBuffers();
colorBuffer = MemoryUtil.memAllocFloat(colors.length);
colorBuffer.put(colors).flip();
glBindBuffer(GL_ARRAY_BUFFER, colorVboId);
```

```
glBufferData(GL_ARRAY_BUFFER, colorBuffer,GL_STATIC_DRAW);
glVertexAttribPointer(1, 3, GL_FLOAT, false, 0, 0);
```

Apart from the copied data, the main difference is the index of this VBO: a value of 1 is assigned, via the first argument of the `glVertexAttribPointer()` method.

Shaders

Shaders must be modified to use color data. Concerning the vertex shader, a simple copy of the colors is applied:

```
#version 330
layout (location=0) in vec3 vertex;
layout (location=1) in vec3 inputColor;
                    out vec3 vertexColor;
void main() {
  gl_Position = vec4(vertex, 1.0);
  vertexColor = inputColor;
}
```

A new input variable `inputColor` is declared. It is a 3-dimensional vector (vec3) and the VBO index in the VAO is 1, as defined by the call to the `glVertexAttribPointer()` method.

A new output variable `vertexColor` is declared. It is also a vector of dimension 3. The process is a simple copy: `vertexColor = inputColor`.

The fragment shader is modified in the following way to use the colors:

```
#version 330
in vec3 vertexColor;
out vec4 color;
void main () {
  color = vec4 (vertexColor, 1.0);
}
```

We declare an input with `vertexColor`: it is the same as the output variable of the vertex shader, both are connected, and the fragment shader uses the data produced by the vertex shader thanks to this variable.

For processing, the white color (1.0,1.0,1.0) is replaced by the content of `vertexColor`.

Rendering

For the rendering, it is enough to assign to the context the second VBO (of index 1) of the VAO which contains the data colors:

```
shader.bind();
glBindVertexArray(vaoId);
glEnableVertexAttribArray(0);
glEnableVertexAttribArray(1);
glDrawArrays(GL_TRIANGLES, 0, 3);
glDisableVertexAttribArray(0);
glDisableVertexAttribArray(1);
glBindVertexArray(0);
shader.unbind();
```

One must not forget to free it from the context.

3.2.3.2 Index

Create an index

Complex meshes use the same vertex several times. For example, to draw a rectangle, you need two triangles:

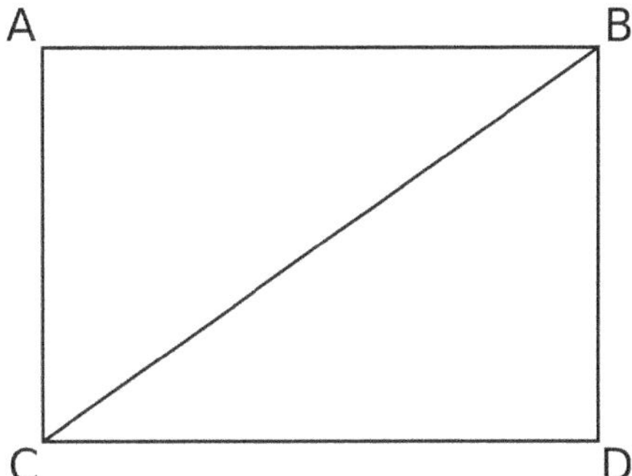

The first triangle is based on vertex A, B and C, and the second on vertex B, C, and D. So there are two vertices in common: B and C. Without indexing, it is necessary to define 6 vertex: 3 for the first triangle, and 3 for the second triangle. With indexing, it is possible to share vertices between several triangles, and thus reduce the memory footprint of the data. With large meshes, the gain is very important, knowing that a vertex can quickly be used by 6 triangles.

For a centered rectangle, you need four:

```
float[] vertex = new float[]{
    -0.5f,  0.5f, 0.0f, // Vertex A
     0.5f,  0.5f, 0.0f, // Vertex B
    -0.5f, -0.5f, 0.0f, // Vertex C
     0.5f, -0.5f, 0.0f, // Vertex D
};
```

An array of integers defines the different indexes, whose values correspond with the defined vertexes:

```java
int[] index = new int[]{
    0, 1, 2, // Triangle A, B, C
    1, 2, 3, // Triangle B, C, D
};
```

The index data joins the VAO:

```java
indexVboId = glGenBuffers();
indexBuffer = MemoryUtil.memAllocInt(index.length);
indexBuffer.put(index).flip();
glBindBuffer(GL_ELEMENT_ARRAY_BUFFER, indexVboId);
glBufferData(GL_ELEMENT_ARRAY_BUFFER, indexBuffer,
    GL_STATIC_DRAW);
```

In this case, there is no assignment to an index in the VAO: an index is considered to be a property of a `GL_ARRAY_BUFFER`, just like the properties defined by the `glVertexAttribPointer()` method. We must add the index of a vertex buffer just after declaring it.

Rendering

To use an index, use the `glDrawElements()` method instead of `glDrawArrays()`. This method has four arguments: the type of primitives (here `GL_TRIANGLES`), the number of vertexes, the type of index (here `GL_UNSIGNED_INT`) and finally the index of the first value to be considered in the index list (here 0):

```java
shader.bind();
glBindVertexArray(object.getVaoId());
glEnableVertexAttribArray(0);
glEnableVertexAttribArray(1);
glDrawElements(GL_TRIANGLES,4,GL_UNSIGNED_INT,0);
glDisableVertexAttribArray(0);
glDisableVertexAttribArray(1);
glBindVertexArray(0);
shader.unbind();
```


3.2.3.3   Example with the drawing of a disc

Indexing allows you to draw a disk with a minimum of vertices. We define a set of triangles where one edge is always a vertex in the center of the circle (here index 0). Then, we define the two other vertices of each triangle all around the center of the circle. In doing so, it is possible to draw a circle of n triangles with n + 1 vertex:

The following Java code is used to compute these values:

```java
int vertexCount = 11;
float[] vertex = new float[3 * vertexCount];
int[] index = new int[3 * (vertexCount - 1)];
vertex[0] = 0;
vertex[1] = 0;
vertex[2] = 0;
for (int i = 1; i < vertexCount; i++) {
    double ip = (2*Math.PI*(i-1))/(vertexCount-1);
    vertex[3 * i + 0] = (float)(0.5*Math.cos(ip));
    vertex[3 * i + 1] = (float)(0.5*Math.sin(ip));
    index[3 * (i - 1) + 0] = 0;
    index[3 * (i - 1) + 1] = i;
    index[3 * (i - 1) + 2] = i + 1;
}
index[3 * (vertexCount - 2) + 2] = 1;
```

With 11 vertices, the following result is obtained, also playing on the vertex colors:

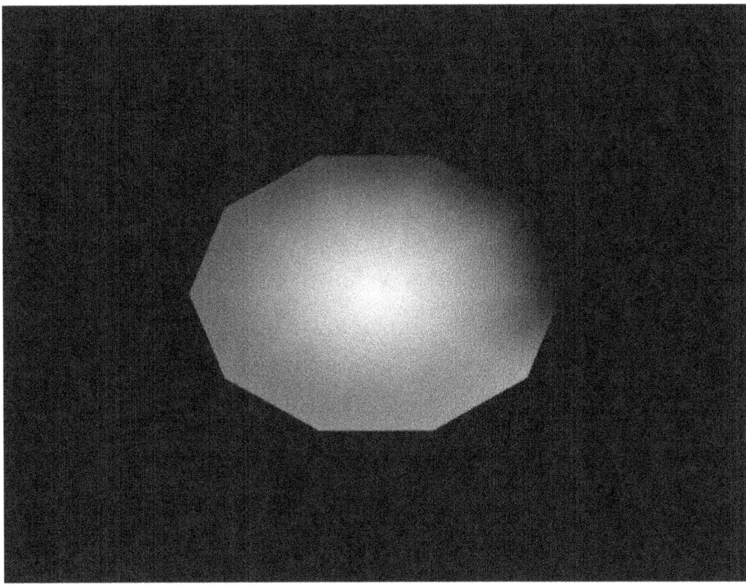

With more vertex, the angles disappear, and the circle looks perfect. In the above display, the circle looks flatten: this effect is because the window is not square. We correct this problem later with the perspective matrix.

The code is present in the "examples/chap03/lwjgl03" folder of the sample Java project. An `ObjectMesh` class is defined to handle aspects of VAO and VBO.

3.2.4 Perspective and controls

3.2.4.1 Perspective

The rendering in the previous examples does not include any notion of perspective. It's a simple 2D display with a notion of depth. To add perspective, you need to apply a transformation that projects the vertex to dimension 3 in the screen plane. This transform is available in the JOML library that accompanies LWJGL. It is necessary to define the angle of the field of view, the ratio width/height of the window (*aspect ratio*), the depth of the elements closest (*near z*) and that of the most distant elements (*far z*):

```
float fov = (float) Math.toRadians(60.0f);
float aspectRatio = ((float)windowWidth) / windowHeight;
float zNear = 0.01f;
float zFar = 1000.0f;
```

Then, the `perspective()` method of the JOML `Matrix4f` class gets the corresponding perspective transform:

```
projectionMatrix = new Matrix4f().perspective(
    fov, aspectRatio, zNear, zFar);
```

All the usual transformations in the world of computer graphics are matrices of dimension 4. Their application is very simple: it is enough to multiply the vertex to be transformed by this matrix, knowing that the vertex must have four dimensions. The mathematical role of this fourth dimension is not described here; we only need to know that it must be initialized with a value of 1.

The most efficient way to apply this transformation to all vertex is to use the vertex shader: the graphic card performs these multiplications infinitely faster than the processor. To do this, we add the multiplication with the projection matrix when calculating the output `gl_Position` of the vertex shader:

```
#version 330
layout (location=0) in vec3 vertex;
layout (location=1) in vec3 inputColor;
                    out vec3 vertexColor;
uniform mat4 projectionMatrix;
void main() {
  gl_Position = projectionMatrix * vec4(vertex, 1.0);
  vertexColor = inputColor;
}
```

The projection matrix is the same for all vertices: it is not necessary to place it in a VBO. This type of data can be declared in the shaders as *uniform variables*. We declare it just before the use of the shader during the rendering. In the example, this assignment is implemented in the `setUniformValue()` method of the Shader class:

```
shader.bind();
shader.setUniformValue("projectionMatrix",projectionMatrix);
... Usual rendering ...
shader.unbind();
```

The `setUniformValue()` method looks for the variable in the shader:

```
public void setUniformValue(String uniformName,
    Matrix4f matrix) {
    int uniformLocation =
        glGetUniformLocation(shaderId, uniformName);
    if (uniformLocation < 0) {
        throw new RuntimeException(
            "Invalid uniform variable "+uniformName);
    }
```

Then assigns its value:

```
    try (MemoryStack stack=MemoryStack.stackPush()){
        FloatBuffer fb = stack.mallocFloat(16);
        matrix.get(fb);
        glUniformMatrix4fv(uniformLocation, false, fb);
    }
}
```

The assignment also relies on `java.nio` buffers, such as `FloatBuffer`. In the previous examples, the heap was used because buffers were large. When the buffers are small, it is better to use the system stack, which can be done via the `MemoryStack` class.

The display obtained with the previous disk is then the following:

The disk is no longer flattened, the width/height ratio of the window is corrected. The code is present in the "examples/chap04/lwjgl04" folder of the sample Java project.

3.2.4.2   Camera

The ability to move around the 3D world allows you to reflect perspective better. To be able to move, a first approach consists in modifying the point of view of the window. However, this is not possible in OpenGL: the coordinates of the displayed area is always included in a cube of size 2 centered in (0,0,0). The solution giving the illusion of displacement is then to move the whole world.

Camera Class

The possible displacements are usual affine transformations: translations and rotations. These are available through the methods of the `Matrix4f` class of the JOML library. We define a `Camera` class to manage them. It contains the current position and viewing angles of this Camera:

```java
public class Camera {
    private final Vector3f position=new Vector3f();
    private final Vector3f rotation=new Vector3f();
```

Via the `getViewMatrix()` method, the camera makes it possible to produce the transformation that moves the world, giving the illusion of a point of view:

```java
public Matrix4f getViewMatrix() {
    Matrix4f viewMatrix = new Matrix4f().identity();
```

The movements considered are those common in video games: moving in all directions, and viewing angles corresponding to head movements. The plane (x, y) representing the area facing the observer (left / right and up / down), rotations on these two axes are applied:

```java
    viewMatrix.rotate(rotation.x,new Vector3f(1,0,0));
    viewMatrix.rotate(rotation.y,new Vector3f(0,1,0));
```

Then, the translation is applied according to the desired displacement. It is inverted, according to the trick of moving the world and not the observer:

```java
    viewMatrix.translate(-position.x,-position.y,-position.z);
    return viewMatrix;
}
```

The change of rotation, which increases the point of view in a given direction, is very simple:

```java
public void addRotation(float x, float y, float z) {
    rotation.x += x;
    rotation.y += y;
    rotation.z += z;
}
```

For the move, on the other hand, things are more complicated. Indeed, it is expected that the observer is moving relative to his point of view. If he looks on the right side of the world, the user expects him to move in that direction. Some trigonometry can find the necessary calculations to obtain this effect:

```java
public void addPosition(float x, float y, float z) {
  if ( z != 0 ) {
    position.x += (float)Math.sin(rotation.y)*(-z);
    position.z += (float)Math.cos(rotation.y)*z;
  }
  if ( x != 0) {
    position.x += (float)Math.cos(rotation.y)*x;
    position.z += (float)Math.sin(rotation.y)*x;
  }
  position.y += y;
}
```

Using the camera

The viewpoint matrix returned by the `getViewMatrix()` method of the `Camera` class is used in the vertex shader:

```
#version 330
layout (location=0) in vec3 vertex;
layout (location=1) in vec3 inputColor;
                     out vec3 vertexColor;
uniform mat4 projectionMatrix;
uniform mat4 viewMatrix;
void main() {
  gl_Position =
    projectionMatrix * viewMatrix * vec4(vertex,1.0);
  vertexColor = inputColor;
}
```

The value of the uniform variable `viewMatrix` is defined in the shader as for `projectionMatrix`.

All that remains is to activate occlusion management when opening the window:

```
glEnable(GL_DEPTH_TEST);
```

By defining the mesh of a cube and choosing a camera view angle highlighting this cube, the following result can be obtained:

It only remains to change the values of the camera to move.

3.2.4.3 Controls

GLFW provides the features needed to capture keyboard and mouse actions. These
are based on usual patterns, just like AWT.

Keyboard

A KeyboardHandler class is defined to handle keyboard actions. Its use is the same
as in the example with AWT, which is replaced by GLFW calls. This class extends
GLFWKeyCallback, which reacts to keyboard events via the invoke() method. With
each call of this one, the keys array is updated to memorize the state of the
keyboard:

```java
public class KeyboardHandler
    extends GLFWKeyCallback {
    public boolean[] keys = new boolean[0x10000];

    public KeyboardHandler(long windowHandle) {
        glfwSetKeyCallback(windowHandle,this);
    }
    public void invoke(long window, int key,
        int scancode, int action, int mods) {
        if (key < keys.length) {
            keys[key] = action != GLFW_RELEASE;
        }
    }
    public boolean isKeyPressed(int keyCode) {
        if (keyCode >= keys.length)
            return false;
        return keys[keyCode];
    }
}
```

Mouse

A Mouse class is defined to handle the mouse. It relies on two types of notifications:
moving the mouse, updating the coordinates (x, y), and pressing a button, which
updates the buttons array of buttons. In term of conventions, that of AWT is
preserved, namely: the left button has the index 0, the right button the index 2
and the central button the index 1:

```java
public class Mouse {
    private boolean[] buttons;
    private int x;
```

```java
    private int y;
    public Mouse(long windowHandle) {
        buttons = new boolean[4];

        glfwSetCursorPosCallback(windowHandle,
        (handle, xpos, ypos) -> {
            x = (int)xpos;
            y = (int)ypos;
        });
        glfwSetMouseButtonCallback(windowHandle,
        (handle, button, action, mode) -> {
            buttons[0] = button == GLFW_MOUSE_BUTTON_1
                && action == GLFW_PRESS;
            buttons[1] = button == GLFW_MOUSE_BUTTON_3
                && action == GLFW_PRESS;
            buttons[2] = button == GLFW_MOUSE_BUTTON_2
                && action == GLFW_PRESS;
        });
    }
    public boolean isButtonPressed(int button) {
        if (button >= buttons.length) {
            return false;
        }
        return buttons[button];
    }
    public int getX() {
        return x;
    }
    public int getY() {
        return y;
    }
}
```

Use

A `handleInputs()` method is added to the `Window` class. We call it in the loop of
the `run()` method. It uses the `keyboard` and `mouse` attributes, instances of the
classes defined above. The values of the camera are modified according to the
usual keys of 3D games:

```java
private int prevMouseX;
private int prevMouseY;
private void handleInputs()
{
```

```java
if (keyboard.isKeyPressed(GLFW_KEY_ESCAPE)) {
    glfwSetWindowShouldClose(windowHandle,true);
}
if (keyboard.isKeyPressed(GLFW_KEY_UP)
  || keyboard.isKeyPressed(GLFW_KEY_W)
  || keyboard.isKeyPressed(GLFW_KEY_Z)) {
    camera.addPosition(0, 0, -0.01f);
}
else if (keyboard.isKeyPressed(GLFW_KEY_DOWN)
      || keyboard.isKeyPressed(GLFW_KEY_S)) {
    camera.addPosition(0, 0, 0.01f);
}
if (keyboard.isKeyPressed(GLFW_KEY_LEFT)
  || keyboard.isKeyPressed(GLFW_KEY_Q)
  || keyboard.isKeyPressed(GLFW_KEY_A)) {
    camera.addPosition(-0.01f, 0, 0);
}
else if (keyboard.isKeyPressed(GLFW_KEY_RIGHT)
      || keyboard.isKeyPressed(GLFW_KEY_D)) {
    camera.addPosition(0.01f, 0, 0);
}
int mouseDiffX = mouse.getX() - prevMouseX;
int mouseDiffY = mouse.getY() - prevMouseY;
if (mouse.isButtonPressed(2)) {
    camera.addRotation(mouseDiffY * 0.005f,
        mouseDiffX * 0.005f,0);
}
prevMouseX = mouse.getX();
prevMouseY = mouse.getY();
}
```

The code is present in the "examples/chap05/lwjgl05" folder of the sample Java project. It is possible to go around the cube, reflecting the perspective effect.

3.2.5 Transformation and animations

3.2.5.1 Transform an object

The affine transformation operations with the 4-dimensional matrices also make it possible to modify a particular object, either to move it or to modify it. To illustrate it, a `position` attribute and a `rotation` attribute of `Vector3f` type are added to the `ObjectMesh` class, as well as a `scale` attribute. The purpose of these attributes is to allow the construction of a transformation matrix that groups all the changes: moving the object, rotating the object, and changing its size. This transformation matrix is computed by the `getTransformMatrix()` method of the `ObjectMesh` class:

```java
public Matrix4f getTransformMatrix() {
    Matrix4f transformMatrix = new Matrix4f().identity();
    transformMatrix.translate(position);
    transformMatrix.rotateX(rotation.x);
    transformMatrix.rotateY(rotation.y);
    transformMatrix.rotateZ(rotation.z);
    transformMatrix.scale(scale);
    return transformMatrix;
}
```

Rotation is counter-intuitive: is it relative to the center of the world, whatever the displacement of the object. If the center of the object is the center of the world, this rotation seems natural, the object revolving around itself. Defining an object in the center of the world is not a problem since it is possible to move it anywhere later. As a result, the rotation is first applied, and then the translation.

The transformation matrix is added to the vertex shader:

```glsl
#version 330
layout (location=0) in vec3 vertex;
layout (location=1) in vec3 inputColor;
                    out vec3 vertexColor;
uniform mat4 projectionMatrix;
uniform mat4 viewMatrix;
uniform mat4 transformMatrix;
void main() {
  gl_Position = projectionMatrix
              * viewMatrix
              * transformMatrix
              * vec4(vertex, 1.0);
  vertexColor = inputColor;
}
```

Depending on the case, it can be more interesting in terms of performance to precompute the product of `viewMatrix` and `transformMatrix` in Java, then to send the resulting matrix to the shader. If so, the transformation matrix must be recomputed and retransmitted to the shader for each object.

3.2.5.2   Animation

The cube of the example is animated by making it jump and turn on itself. The `update()` method of the `Window` class modifies the parameters of the cube transformation. It is called in the loop of the `run()` method of the `Window` class, forming with the management of the inputs and the rendering the Game Loop Pattern.

```java
private boolean translateUp;
private void update() {
    Vector3f position = object.getPosition();
    if (translateUp) {
        position.y += 0.01f;
        if (position.y >= 1.0f) {
            translateUp = false;
        }
    }
    else {
        position.y -= 0.01f;
        if (position.y <= 0.0f) {
            translateUp = true;
        }
    }
    object.setPosition(position);
    Vector3f rotation = object.getRotation();
    rotation.x += 0.01f;
    if (rotation.x > 2*Math.PI) {
        rotation.x = 0;
    }
    rotation.y += 0.01f;
    if (rotation.y > 2*Math.PI) {
        rotation.y = 0;
    }
    rotation.z += 0.01f;
    if (rotation.z > 2*Math.PI) {
        rotation.z = 0;
    }
    object.setRotation(rotation);
}
```

The code is present in the "examples/chap06/ lwjgl06" folder of the sample Java project.

3.2.6 Textures

3.2.6.1 Load a texture

A texture is loaded from an image file, here named `fileName`, as it was done previously:

```
ClassLoader loader = this.getClass().getClassLoader();
BufferedImage image = ImageIO.read(loader.getResource(fileName)
);
```

LWJGL requires an RGBA format, while the `BufferedImage` format is BGRA. Processing is applied to reverse the position of red and blue:

```
int width = image.getWidth();
int height = image.getHeight();
int[] bgrPixels = new int[width * height];
image.getRGB(0,0,width,height,bgrPixels,0,width);
int[] rgbPixels = new int[width * height];
for (int i=0;i<bgrPixels.length;i++) {
    int a = (bgrPixels[i] & 0xff000000) >> 24;
    int r = (bgrPixels[i] & 0x00ff0000) >> 16;
    int g = (bgrPixels[i] & 0x0000ff00) >> 8;
    int b =  bgrPixels[i] & 0x000000ff;
    rgbPixels[i] = a << 24 | b << 16 | g << 8 | r;
}
```

Loading a texture on the graphic card is also only possible from a `java.nio` buffer. The pixel array of the image is converted:

```
IntBuffer pixelsBuffer =
    BufferUtils.createIntBuffer(rgbPixels.length);
pixelsBuffer.put(rgbPixels);
pixelsBuffer.flip();
```

A new `textureId` texture identifier is obtained via the `glGenTextures()` method:

```
int textureId = glGenTextures();
```

This identifier is assigned to the context: the texture operations that follow concerns this texture:

```
glBindTexture(GL_TEXTURE_2D, textureId);
```

The following two calls indicate the nature of the interpolation between two pixels of the texture. With the `GL_NEAREST` parameter, interpolation is the simplest and fastest:

```
glTexParameteri(GL_TEXTURE_2D,
    GL_TEXTURE_MIN_FILTER, GL_NEAREST);
glTexParameteri(GL_TEXTURE_2D,
    GL_TEXTURE_MAG_FILTER, GL_NEAREST);
```

The `glTexImage2D()` method is used to transmit the texture data to the graphics card:

```
glTexImage2D(GL_TEXTURE_2D, 0, GL_RGBA,
    width, height, 0, GL_RGBA,GL_UNSIGNED_BYTE, pixelsBuffer);
```

3.2.6.2 Use texture

Shader

The textures are implemented in the fragment shader:

```
#version 330
in  vec2 vertexTextureCoords;
out vec4 color;
uniform sampler2D textureSampler;
void main() {
   color = texture(textureSampler, vertexTextureCoords);
}
```

The input variable `vertexTextureCoords` contains the coordinates in the texture for each vertex. It is produced by the vertex shader, who read it in a VBO. Each vertex is connected to a point in the texture: thus, the three vertices of each triangle correspond to three points in the texture. The triangle in the texture is thus projected on the triangle displayed on the screen.

The uniform variable `textureSampler` is used to indicate the texture in the graphic card. In this example, texture 0 is always used.

Processing in the `main()` function uses the `texture()` function, which calculates the color of the fragment by drawing the value in the texture, modulo the coordinates provided, and the interpolation rules.

Apply a texture on an object

The above settings are general; they must be set for each object to be textured. First, we have to calculate the coordinates of the texture on the object (a.k.a. *UV Map*). This fairly complex operation is well managed by most 3D drawing software, so it is better to use them. Then, you have to put these coordinates in a VBO. Since color data is no longer useful with texture, it is replaced by texture data when building an `ObjectMesh`:

```
textureVboId = glGenBuffers();
textureCoordsBuffer =
    MemoryUtil.memAllocFloat(textureCoords.length);
textureCoordsBuffer.put(textureCoords).flip();
glBindBuffer(GL_ARRAY_BUFFER, textureVboId);
glBufferData(GL_ARRAY_BUFFER, textureCoordsBuffer,
    GL_STATIC_DRAW);
glVertexAttribPointer(1, 2, GL_FLOAT, false, 0, 0);
```

Finally, when rendering in the render() method of the Renderer class, all you have to do is activate texture 0, and indicate with the glBindTexture() method the texture that is used :

```
shader.setUniformValue("textureSampler", 0);
glActiveTexture(GL_TEXTURE0);
glBindTexture(GL_TEXTURE_2D, object.getTextureId());
```

The code is present in the "examples/chap07/lwjgl07" folder of the sample Java project. The cube always jumps, and is decorated with an identical wall texture on all sides:

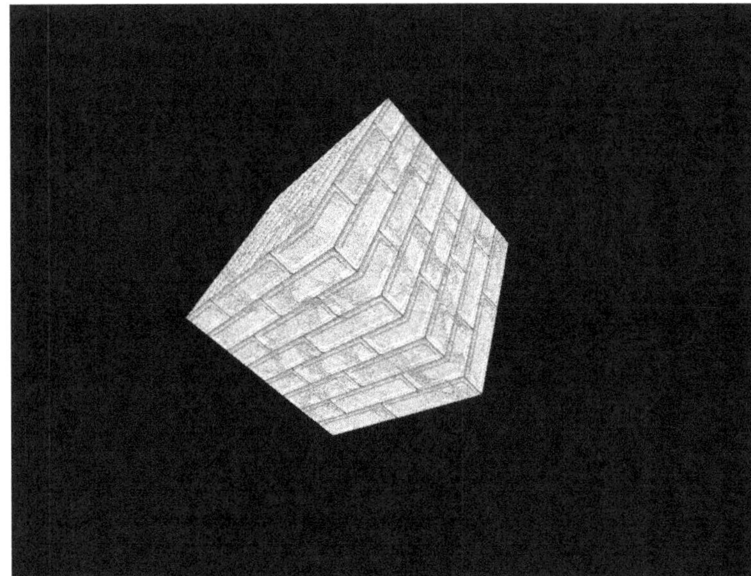

3.3   Software design

3.3.1   Abstraction of the user interface

The examples in the previous sections introduce the basics for displaying and controlling a video game. For the Pacman example game with the AWT library, everything has been placed in a single Java file, like "examples/chap03/awt/E10Mouse.java". This format is relevant to present basic concepts incrementally. However, for all the reasons given in the first chapter, continuing without a minimum of organization and design lead to an unmanageable project.

This section presents some techniques and associated patterns to organize a software solution better. More specifically, the goal is to separate the graphic library used from the rest of the game logic. We follow the golden rule of "divide and conquer" or "reduce problems to sub-problems". The problem, in this case, is the whole game, and we want to extract the sub-problem of the GUI from the rest. In the following sections, other sub-problems are extracted.

Features isolation is a difficult exercise. To better understand it, an incremental approach is followed: the functions are extracted one by one until the graphic library is completely separated. Once the operation is successful, it is worth noting that it is easy to change the graphic library without changing the logic of the game.

3.3.1.1   Facade Pattern

A first technique followed to obtain the desired result is to use the *Facade Pattern*. The purpose of this pattern is to provide a simplified version of the existing software interface (*API*). In our case, the complex API is the graphic library used, and the facade is the set of functionalities required by the game.

Basic facade

If we start from the example "examples/chap03/awt/E01Window.java" which displays a simple window in AWT, a facade that allows creating a window can take the following form:

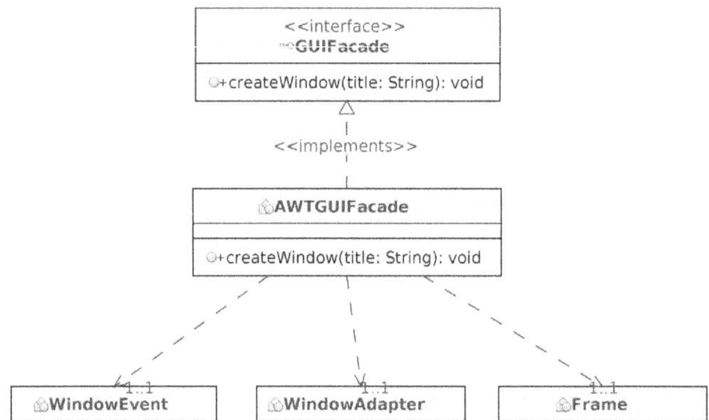

The GUIFacade interface defines the facade: there is a unique createWindow() method. The class AWTGUIFacade is an implementation of the facade. It uses three classes of AWT: Frame, WindowAdapter and WindowEvent. The user of the facade does not see the AWT classes, only the interface, and its implementation. Creating a window via this facade is simplified, for example:

```
GUIFacade gui = new AWTGUIFacade();
gui.createWindow("Graphic User Interface Facade");
```

The implementation of AWTGUIFacade is very simple from the initial code: we copy/paste the parts relating to the creation of a window:

```
public class AWTGUIFacade implements GUIFacade {
    private static class Window extends Frame {
        public void init(String title) {
            setTitle(title);
            setSize(200,200);
            setResizable(false);
            addWindowListener(new WindowAdapter() {
                public void windowClosing(WindowEvent we) {
                    dispose();
                }
            });
        }
    }
    public void createWindow(String title) {
        Window window = new Window();
        window.init(title);
        window.setLocationRelativeTo(null);
        window.setVisible(true);
    }
}
```

The result can be found in the "examples/chap03/awtfacade01" folder.

Facade with drawing capabilities

The next step is to form a facade capable of displaying a window where you can regularly draw, like the example "examples/chap03/awt/E04DisplaySync.java" which draws a black background in the window. To do this, we design a class AWTWindow that contains all aspects of the window and its display. Then, it is necessary to enrich the facade to be able to pilot this class. Keeping in mind that other features like the main loop must remain in the main part, the following diagram is proposed:

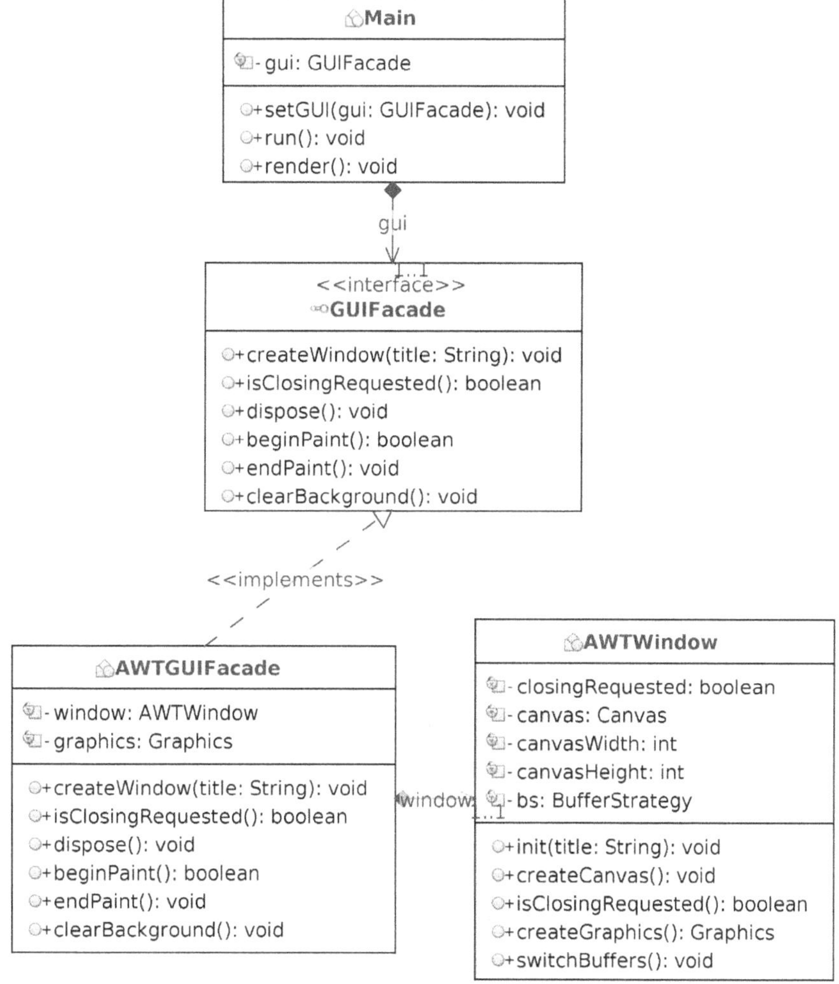

Within the AWTWindow class, we find all the attributes of the AWT library used in the code "examples/chap03/awt/E04DisplaySync.java". The same goes for some methods that are reproduced, such as init() and createCanvas().

The remaining methods allow the facade to control this class:

```java
public Graphics createGraphics() {
    bs = canvas.getBufferStrategy();
    if (bs == null) {
        canvas.createBufferStrategy(2);
        return null;
    }
    return bs.getDrawGraphics();
}
```

The `switchBuffer()` method tells the canvas to swap the display buffer with the rendering buffer:

```java
public void switchBuffers() {
    if (bs != null) {
        bs.show();
    }
}
```

The `AWTGUIFacade` class has a `window` attribute to drive the created window, as well as a `graphics` attribute for drawing. The first three methods allow a user of the facade to interact with the window: create it with `createWindow()`, be informed of a closing request with `isClosingRequested()`, and destroy it with `dispose()`.

The following methods allow drawing. First, the `beginPaint()` method allows you to get a `Graphics` to draw:

```java
public boolean beginPaint() {
    if (graphics != null) {
        graphics.dispose();
    }
    graphics = window.createGraphics();
    if (graphics == null) {
        return false;
    }
    return true;
}
```

The `endPaint()` method is used to display what has been drawn:

```java
public void endPaint() {
    if (graphics == null) {
        return;
    }
    graphics.dispose();
    graphics = null;
    window.switchBuffers();
}
```

These two methods are the beginning and the end of the `render()` method of the
initial code: once again, the work here is primarily organization.

The last method draws all the canvas in black:

```java
public void clearBackground() {
    if (graphics == null) {
        return;
    }
    graphics.setColor(Color.black);
    graphics.fillRect(0, 0,window.getCanvasWidth(),
        window.getCanvasHeight());
}
```

You can add other drawing methods, such as drawing a rectangle, a line, text, and
so on.

The `Main` class is the user of the facade: it has a `gui` attribute to interact with the
facade, then the same `run()` and `render()` methods. The content of these methods
is slightly modified: calls to the facade replace the ones to AWT. For example, for
the `render()` method:

```java
public void render() {
    if (!gui.beginPaint())
        return;
    try {
        gui.clearBackground();
    } finally {
        gui.endPaint();
    }
}
```

It is the same operation as in the initial code but passed through the facade.

Finally, the `main()` method that starts the program is also simplified. It is at this
level that the implantation of the facade is chosen. If another facade was available,
change this piece of code to switch from one to the other. All the rest of the code
is fully independent:

```java
public static void main(String args[]) {
    Pacman pacman = new Pacman();
    pacman.setGUI(new AWTGUIFacade());
    pacman.run();
}
```

The code of this facade can be found in the folder "examples/chap03/awtfacade02".

3.3.1.2 Layers and display (Factory Method Pattern)

In this section, we want to enrich the facade to allow drawing with tiles, like the example "chapters/chap03/awt/E07Level.java". It draws a world and the Pacman character with tiles:

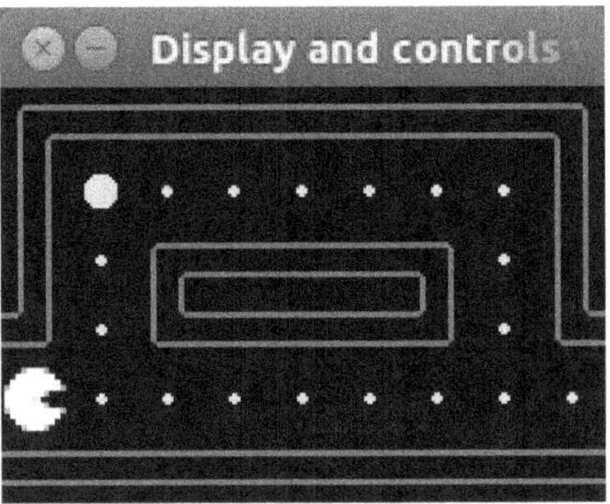

The previously followed approach also works in this case. We must add new methods to the facade, and possibly the methods that implement it.

Layers

In this section, we propose to take advantage of the framework offered by the facade to introduce more advanced features. In particular, we want to add a display mechanism based on layers. This approach divides the display into different planes, which are drawn in a specific order. In general, we use three layers: one for the background, one for the characters, and one for the information (lives, score, etc.):

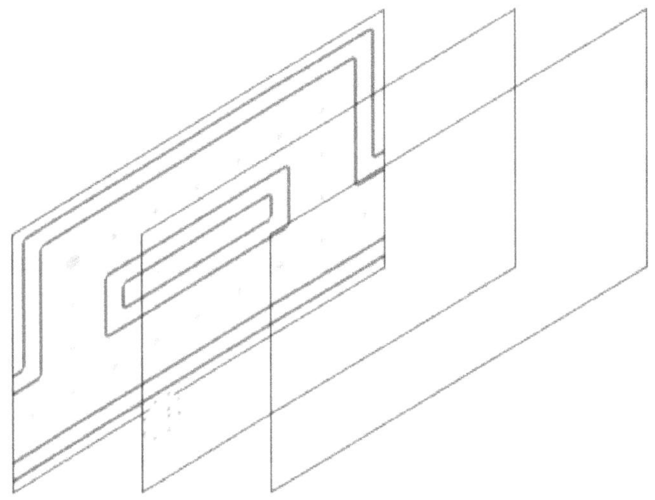

Factory Method Pattern

The first solution is to enrich the interface of the facade with a new batch of methods. Another easier solution is to use the *Factory Method Pattern*. It is mainly based on a method that returns a new instance of a particular interface:

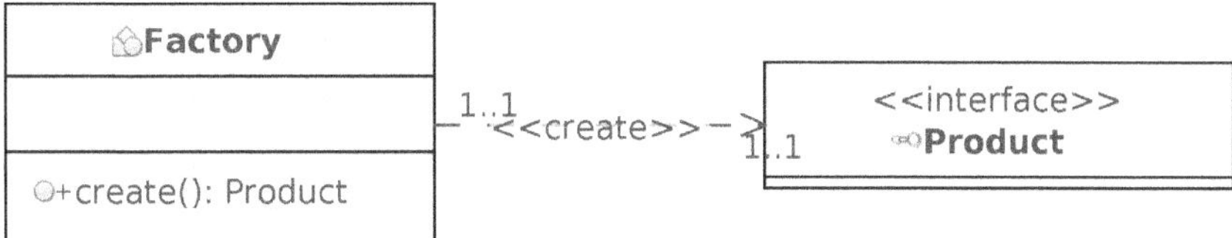

The `Factory` class has a `create()` method that returns an implementation of the `Product` interface. The instance returned is not necessarily always the same; it can depend on a context. For example, the `Factory` class can be an implementation of an interface that defines the `create()` method - as in the case of the front panel below. The creation method can also have arguments, which depend on the type of objects. Other elements can also intervene, like the current time, a configuration, the content of files, etc.

Facade with layer management

The Factory Method Pattern is used for the creation of layers by the facade. A `createLayer()` method is added to the `GUIFacade` interface and returns a new instance of a `Layer` interface dedicated to the management a layer:

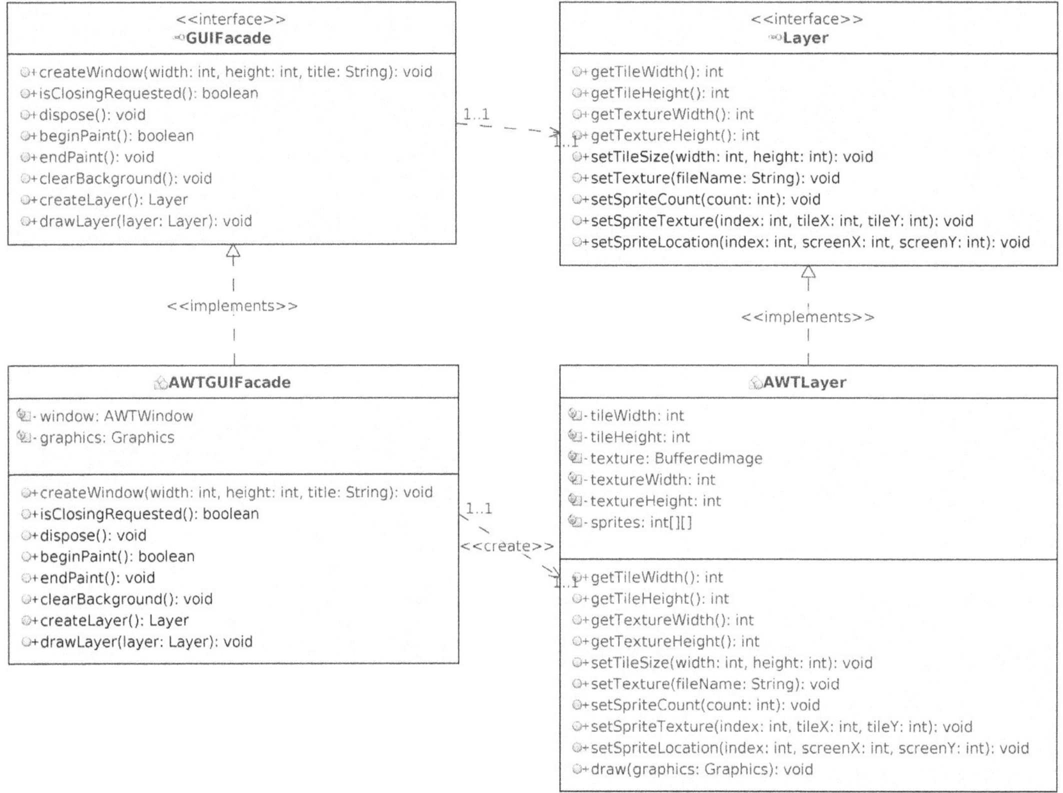

The instance returned by the `createLayer()` method of the `GUIFacade` interface depends on its implementation. In this example, if an instance of `AWTGUIFacade` is created, its method returns an instance of `AWTLayer`, which is a layer that works with the AWT library:

```java
public Layer createLayer() {
    return new AWTLayer();
}
```

If another graphical library is used, for example LWJGL, an instance of a `LWJGLGUIFacade` class is instantiated, and its `createLayer()` method returns an instance of a `LWJGLLayer` class. For the user of the facade, all these details are invisible: it requires an implementation of the `Layer` interface, without ever knowing - or having to know - its true nature.

Layers optimized for tile display

The first methods of the `Layer` interface are simple accessors. Then, the `setTileSize()` and `setTexture()` methods allow you to set the size of the tiles and load the tileset image. Their implementation is almost identical to what is done in "examples/chap03/awt/E07Level.java".

The `setSpriteXXXX()` methods, on the other hand, follow a different strategy from the one adopted in the initial code. The idea is to ask each layer to memorize the necessary information to draw a set of sprites. A sprite is defined by a tile chosen in the tileset, as well as a position on the screen. Multiple sprites can use the same tile for rendering, and/or multiple sprites can be displayed at the same location on the screen. This approach has several interesting properties:

- The definition of sprites to draw and their rendering are separated: it becomes possible to establish these definitions in a first step, then to render in a second step. Among other consequences, it is possible to parallelize the definition of sprites and their rendering, via mechanics presented in chapter 6.
- The definition of the sprites being memorized, it is not necessary to redefine them for each displayed image. Sprites that do not change, or very rarely, do not need to be continually defined. It is usually the case for decor elements, or elements of information, such as the number of lives. "Rarely" means something that occurs much less frequently than 60 times per second. Once per second can already be considered "rare".
- Graphic cards prefer to receive batches of drawing commands in a short time, rather than many commands spaced by pauses. Once again, these are display-scale considerations - 1 microsecond can be considered a "break" at this scale. This property is not very interesting with the AWT library, which does not offer a solution to draw lots of images (for now). However, for sufficiently low-level libraries like LWJGL, the gain in performance can be considerable.

AWTLayer class

To memorize the sprite definitions, the `AWTLayer` class uses a two-dimensional `int[][] sprites` array. The first dimension is the sprite index, and the second dimension always has four values: the (x, y) coordinates of the tile in the tileset, and the (x, y) coordinates on the screen. This array is initialized by the `setSpriteCount()` method, which defines the number of sprites in the layer:

```java
public void setSpriteCount(int count) {
    sprites = new int[count][4];
}
```

The `setSpriteTexture()` method allows you to define the coordinates (tileX,tileY) in the tileset of the sprite number index to draw. These coordinates are not in pixels, but according to the size of the tiles:

```java
public void setSpriteTexture(int index,int tileX, int tileY) {
    if (sprites == null) {
        throw new RuntimeException("Sprites are not defined");
    }
    if (index < 0 || index >= sprites.length) {
        throw new IllegalArgumentException(
            "Invalid sprite index "+index);
    }
    if (tileX < 0 || tileX >= textureWidth
     || tileY < 0 || tileY >= textureHeight) {
        throw new IllegalArgumentException(
            "Invalid tile coordinates "+tileX+","+tileY);
    }
    sprites[index][0] = tileX;
    sprites[index][1] = tileY;
}
```

The setSpriteLocation() method sets the display (screenX,screenY) coordinates of the sprite index:

```java
public void setSpriteLocation(int index,
    int screenX, int screenY) {
    if (sprites == null || index < 0 || index >= sprites.length)
        return;
    sprites[index][2] = screenX;
    sprites[index][3] = screenY;
}
```

All sprites are drawn in a Graphics by the draw() method of the layer:

```java
public void draw(Graphics graphics) {
    if (texture == null) {
        throw new RuntimeException("Texture not loaded");
    }
    if (sprites == null) {
        throw new RuntimeException("Sprites are not defined");
    }
    if (tileWidth == 0 || tileHeight == 0) {
        throw new RuntimeException("Tile size is not defined");
    }
    for (int i = 0; i < sprites.length; i++) {
        int tileX = sprites[i][0];
        int tileY = sprites[i][1];
        int screenX = sprites[i][2];
        int screenY = sprites[i][3];
        graphics.drawImage(texture,screenX,screenY,
            screenX + tileWidth,screenY + tileHeight,tileX * tileWidth,
```

```
                tileY * tileHeight,tileX * tileWidth + tileWidth,
                tileY * tileHeight + tileHeight,null);
    }
}
```

AWTGUIFacade class

The AWTGUIFacade class is also enriched with a drawLayer() method that uses its graphics to render a layer:

```
public void drawLayer(Layer layer) {
    if (graphics == null) {
        return;
    }
    if (layer == null) {
        throw new IllegalArgumentException("No layer");
    }
    if (!(layer instanceof AWTLayer)) {
        throw new IllegalArgumentException("Invalid layer type"
        );
    }
    AWTLayer awtLayer = (AWTLayer) layer;
    awtLayer.draw(graphics);
}
```

Using the facade with layer management

From a user's point of view this facade, here the `Main` class, the AWT library does not exist:

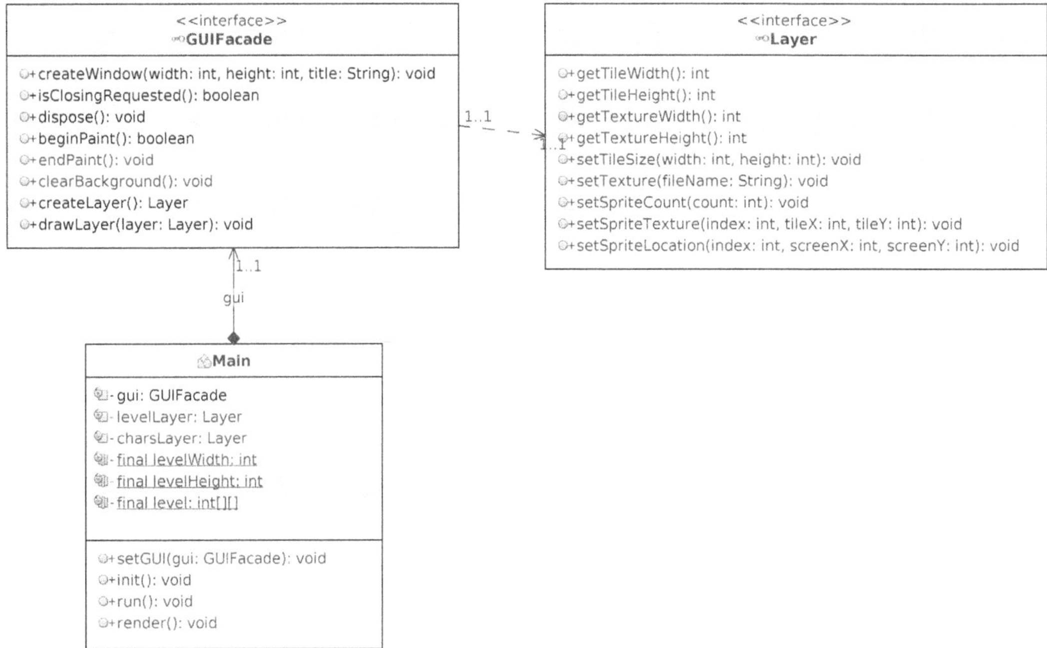

New attributes are added to the `Main` class: a `levelLayer` for the world, a `charsLayer` for the characters, and the definition of a level with the attributes `levelXXXX`.

The `init()` method produces different elements. It begins with the creation of the layer for the characters:

```java
public void init()
{
    charsLayer = gui.createLayer();
    charsLayer.setTileSize(24, 24);
    charsLayer.setTexture("chars_tiles.png");
    charsLayer.setSpriteCount(1);
    charsLayer.setSpriteTexture(0, 6, 1);
    charsLayer.setSpriteLocation(0,
        0 * charsLayer.getTileWidth(),4 * charsLayer.getTileHeight());
```

In this example, there is only one sprite, Pacman. Its tile is the 7th in the second row in the tileset, the coordinates (6,1). It is placed as on the screenshot above, with coordinates in pixels (0 * 24,4 * 24) on the screen.

The rest of the method defines the layer for the world:

```java
levelLayer = gui.createLayer();
levelLayer.setTileSize(24, 24);
levelLayer.setTexture("grid_tiles.png");
levelLayer.setSpriteCount(levelWidth * levelHeight);
for (int j = 0; j < levelHeight; j++) {
    for (int i = 0; i < levelWidth; i++) {
        int index = i + j * levelWidth;
        levelLayer.setSpriteLocation(index,
            i * levelLayer.getTileWidth(),
            j * levelLayer.getTileHeight());
        int tileIndex = level[j][i];
        if (tileIndex < 0)
            tileIndex = 0;
        int tileX = (tileIndex - 1)
            % levelLayer.getTextureHeight();
        int tileY = (tileIndex - 1)
            / levelLayer.getTextureHeight();
        if (tileY >= levelLayer.getTextureHeight()) {
            tileX = 0;
            tileY = 0;
        }
        levelLayer.setSpriteTexture(index, tileX, tileY);
    }
}
```

The number of sprites in this layer equals the total number of squares in the world, which is `levelWidth * levelHeight` cells. The position of each sprite is a function of its position in the world, multiplied by the size of the tiles. The sprite with coordinates *(i,j)* in the world is displayed at the coordinates (i * 24,j * 24). The texture of the sprites depends on the value in the `level` array: the computation performed is the same as that in the initial code.

Finally, the method ends with the creation of the window, whose size depends on the size of the world:

```java
gui.createWindow(levelWidth * levelLayer.getTileWidth(),
    levelHeight * levelLayer.getTileHeight(),"GUI Facade");
}
```

The `render()` method of the `Main` class is modified to show the two layers:

```java
public void render() {
    if (!gui.beginPaint())
        return;
    try {
        gui.clearBackground();
        gui.drawLayer(levelLayer);
        gui.drawLayer(charsLayer);
    } finally {
        gui.endPaint();
    }
}
```

The complete code is available in the folder "examples/chap03/awtfacade03".

3.3.1.3 Controls

Facade with controls

To add the keyboard and mouse controls to the facade, we follow the principles presented above. We also choose to separate them in interfaces specific to the keyboard and mouse:

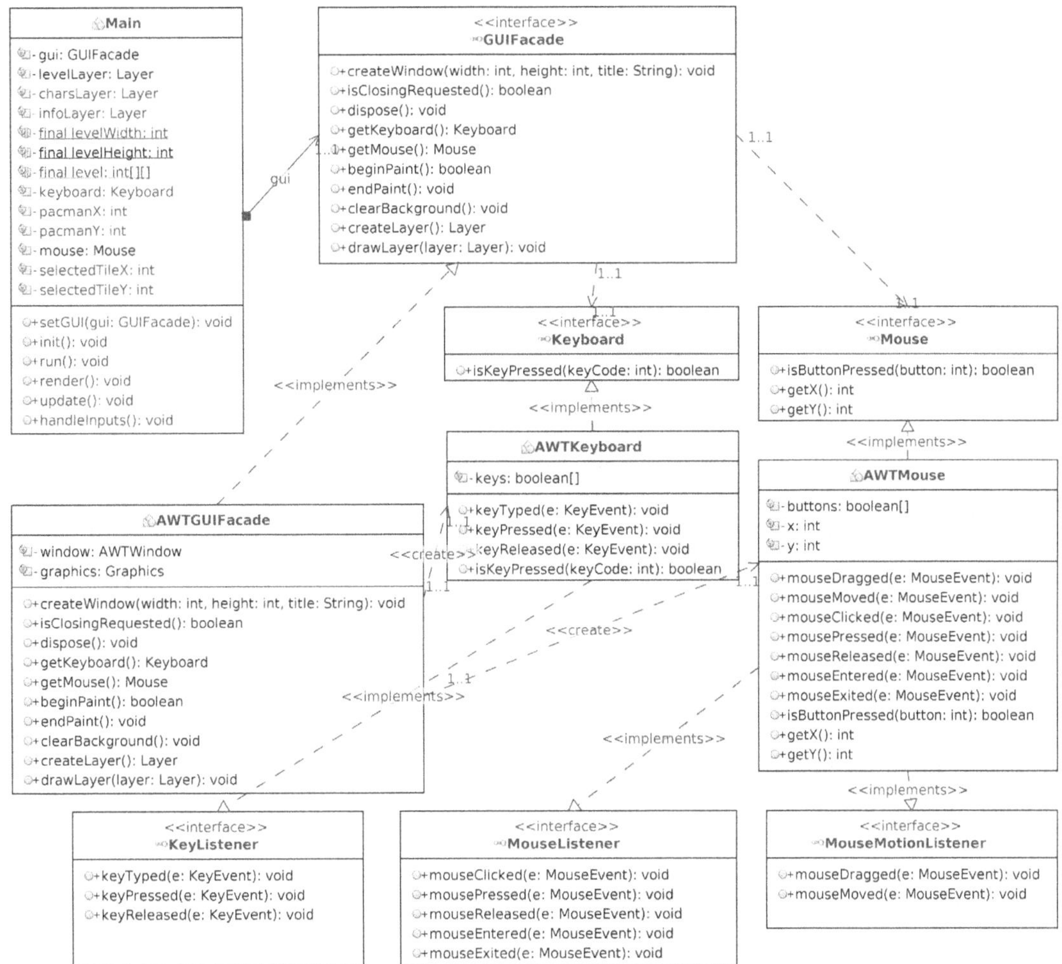

The Keyboard interface takes the isKeyPressed() method from the Keyboard sub-class of the example "examples/chap03/awt/E09Keyboard.java". Its implementation with the AWTKeyboard class is also taken from this example.

Using controls through the facade

Once again, from a front-end user's point of view, the AWT library and all associated classes do not exist. We can see how much the facade is much easier for the user:

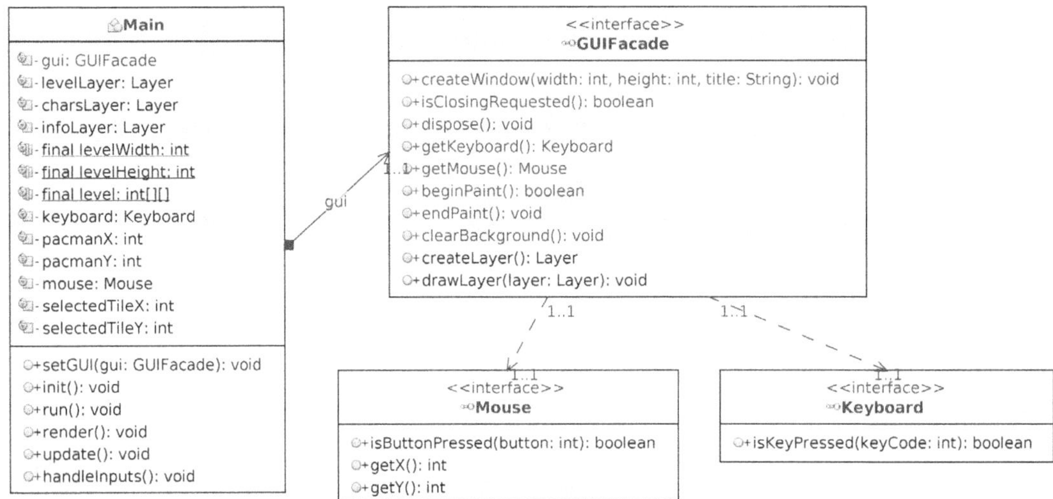

The `Main` class has new attributes and methods that are retrieved from the initial code and then adapted to the facade. A new `infoLayer` layer is initialized in the `init()` method. Its role is to display the yellow frame under the mouse cursor:

```java
infoLayer = gui.createLayer();
infoLayer.setTileSize(24, 24);
infoLayer.setTexture("grid_tiles.png");
infoLayer.setSpriteCount(1);
infoLayer.setSpriteTexture(0, 5, 0);
infoLayer.setSpriteLocation(0,0 * charsLayer.getTileWidth(),
    0 * charsLayer.getTileHeight());
```

The position of the yellow frame is initialized to *(0,0)*: we move it according to the mouse in the `update()` method.

The `init()` method also initializes the controls:

```java
keyboard = gui.getKeyboard();
mouse = gui.getMouse();
```

The `Main` class has two new methods: `handleInputs()` and `update()`. The role of the first is to manage the controls, and the second to change the world and the layers.

The `handleInputs()` method is the same as in 'examples/chap03/awt/E10Mouse.java', except for the use of `Keyboard` and `Mouse` interfaces of the facade.

The `update()` method continues to change the world to animate it, still at 4 frames per second:

```java
public void update() {
    long now = System.nanoTime();
    if ( (now - lastUpdate1) >= 1000000000/4) {
        lastUpdate1 = now;
        for (int j=0;j<levelHeight;j++) {
            for (int i=0;i<levelWidth;i++) {
                int id = level[j][i];
                if (id == 5) level[j][i] = 4;
                else if (id == 4) level[j][i] = 5;
            }
        }
    }
}
```

Then it updates the layers 12 times per second:

```java
    if ( (now - lastUpdate2) >= 1000000000/12) {
        lastUpdate2 = now ;
        for (int j = 0; j < levelHeight; j++) {
            for (int i = 0; i < levelWidth; i++) {
                int index = i + j * levelWidth;
                levelLayer.setSpriteLocation(index,
                    i * levelLayer.getTileWidth(),
                    j * levelLayer.getTileHeight());
                int tileIndex = level[j][i];
                if (tileIndex < 0)
                    tileIndex = 0;
                int tileX = (tileIndex - 1)
                    % levelLayer.getTextureHeight();
                int tileY = (tileIndex - 1)
                    / levelLayer.getTextureHeight();
                if (tileY >= levelLayer.getTextureHeight()) {
                    tileX = 0;
                    tileY = 0;
                }
                levelLayer.setSpriteTexture(index, tileX, tileY
                );
            }
        }
        charsLayer.setSpriteLocation(0,pacmanX, pacmanY);
        infoLayer.setSpriteLocation(0,
            selectedTileX*charsLayer.getTileWidth(),
            selectedTileY*charsLayer.getTileHeight());
    }
```

```
}
```

The `render()` method displays the new layer:

```java
public void render() {
    if (!gui.beginPaint())
        return;
    try {
        gui.clearBackground();
        gui.drawLayer(levelLayer);
        gui.drawLayer(charsLayer);
        gui.drawLayer(infoLayer);
    } finally {
        gui.endPaint();
    }
}
```

This example illustrates the ability of this approach to managing the display and evolution of the world independently. The world moves at different frequencies: at any time with controls, 4 times per second with animation, and 12 times per second for updating sprites.

The complete code is available in the folder "examples/chap03/awtfacade04".

3.3.2 Game modes

The goal of this section is to be able to navigate between different game modes, each with its data and the way it works. To illustrate this, the creation of a welcome screen and a menu to choose the game parameters are presented.

Before starting this presentation, all the features of the previous user interface facades are combined:

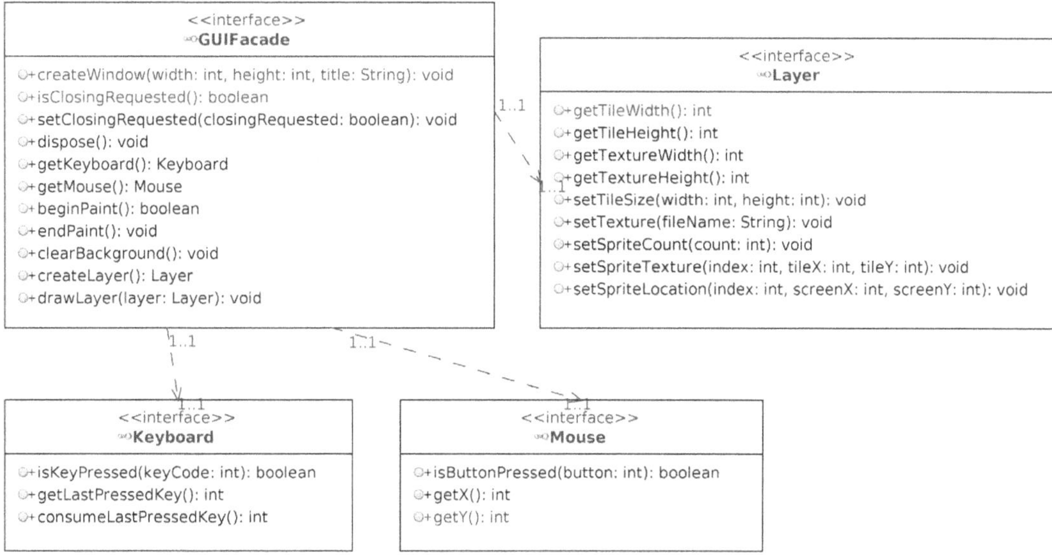

It provides display capability with tiles, and keyboard and mouse controls. In terms of code generation, all these classes are placed in the gui package.

The implementations with the AWT library of the functionalities of this interface are also gathered, and the code is generated in the gui.awt package.

3.3.2.1 Game mode abstraction (Template Pattern)

We begin by defining in an abstract way what forms a game mode. Since we follow the game loop pattern, the game runs around a main loop that regularly calls three methods, `handleInputs()`, `update()`, and `render()`. The *Template Pattern* can be followed to formalize this property.

Template Pattern

This pattern is based on three main actors:

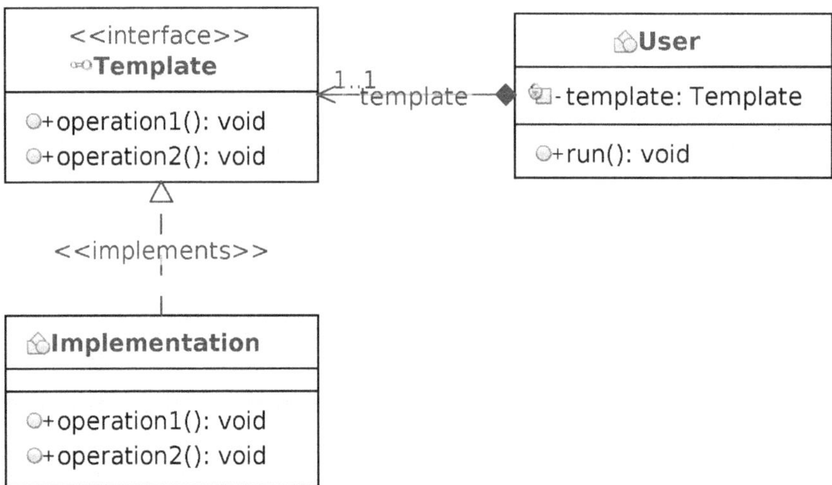

The `Template` interface defines the different operations of a process.

```
public void run() {
    operation1() ;
    operation2() ;
}
```

The user does not know the implementation of the methods of the template, only what they are supposed to produce. In this illustration, the user and the template interface are separated: it is also common to group them in the same abstract class. Finally, the `Implementation` class is one of many.

Definition of a game mode

The implementation of the pattern in the case of the video game can give the following result, knowing that we added the `init()` method for the initiation of the mode:

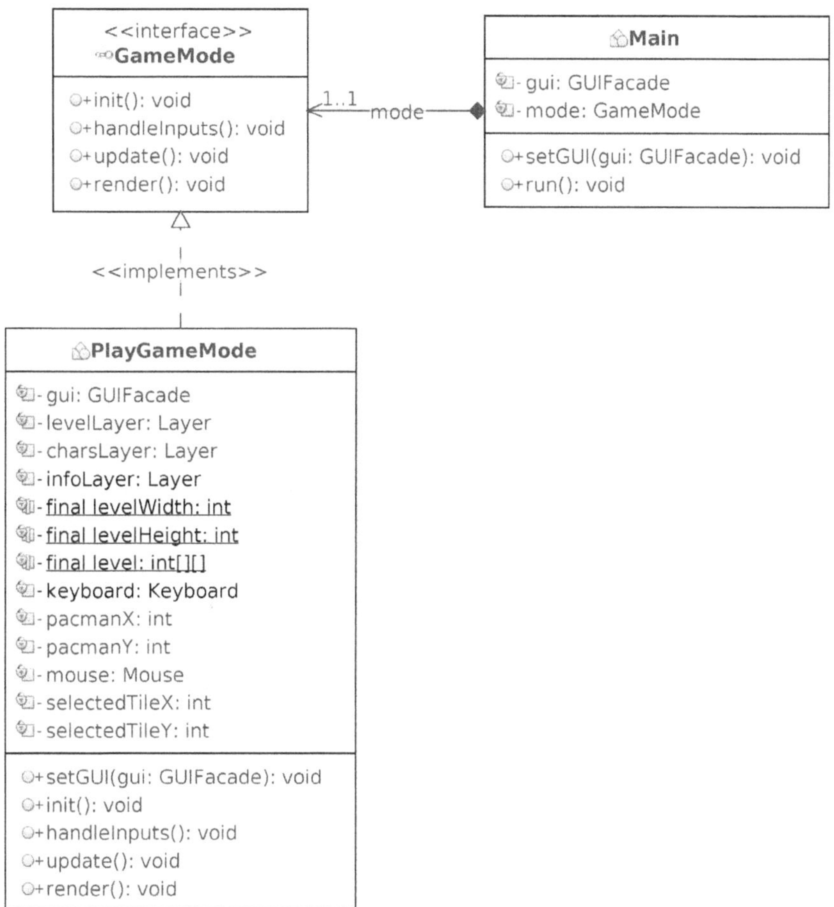

The user of the template is the `Main` class, through the `run()` method.

```java
public void run() {
    int fps = 60;
    long nanoPerFrame = (long) (1000000000.0 / fps);
    long lastTime = 0;
    while (!gui.isClosingRequested()) {
        long nowTime = System.nanoTime();
        if ((nowTime - lastTime) < nanoPerFrame) {
            continue;
```

```java
    }
    lastTime = nowTime;
    mode.handleInputs();
    mode.update();
    mode.render();
    long elapsed = System.nanoTime() - lastTime;
    long milliSleep = (nanoPerFrame - elapsed) / 1000000;
    if (milliSleep > 0) {
        try {
            Thread.sleep(milliSleep);
        } catch (InterruptedException ex) {
            ex.printStackTrace();
        }
    }
    }
    gui.dispose();
}
```

The implementation of this solution is a reorganization of the previous `Main` class, which has been divided into three parts: the `GameMode` interface, its `PlayGameMode` implementation, and what remains in the `Main` class.

The diagrams in this example are available in the "gamemodes00*.cdg" files in the "Class Diagrams/chap03" folder of the sample UML project. The code is present in the "examples/chap03/gamemodes00" folder of the sample Java project.

3.3.2.2 Change game mode (State Pattern)

In this section, we want to provide a presentation screen, followed by the game screen. To achieve this, we rely on the *State Pattern*.

State Pattern

The state pattern, in its simplest form, relies on an interface that defines the possible commands, and a context that memorizes and executes the current state:

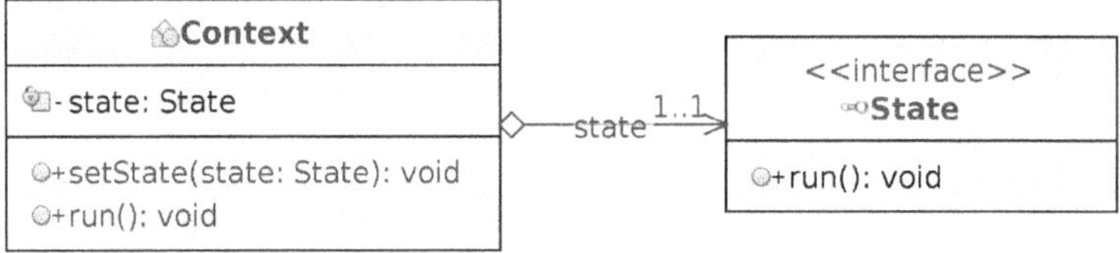

The methods of the `State` interface are free: here, there is only one `run()` method, but many other methods are possible.

The user of this pattern builds an implementation of the `State` interface, then asks via the `setState()` method to switch to the desired state. Finally, the user calls the `run()` method of the `Context` class to execute the operation corresponding to the current state.

When using this pattern, it is common to speak of states. However, in our case, this is confusing with the state of the game world presented in the first chapter. It is worth noting that the state of the game is part of a much more complex version of the state pattern, presented in the next chapter. To avoid the confusion between "game state with world data, characters, etc." and "general state of the game", we use in the rest of this book the term "game mode" to designate the general state of the game.

Example with Pacman

In our example of the Pacman game, the first two desired modes are:

- A welcome screen, which has just one image:

- The Pacman game:

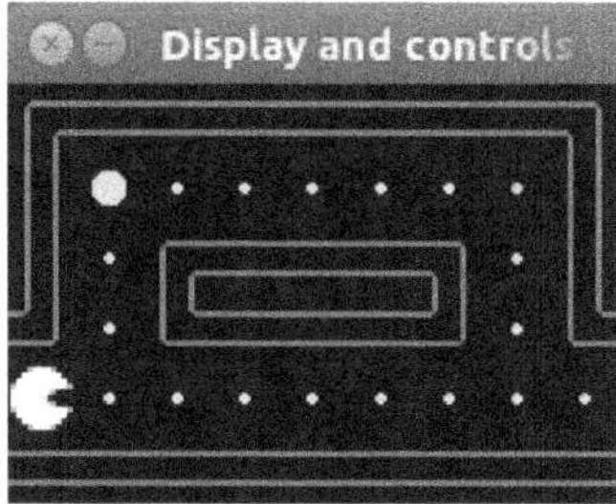

We implement the state pattern, with `Main` the context class, `GameMode` the state interface, and `WelcomeGameMode` and `PlayGameMode` state implementations:

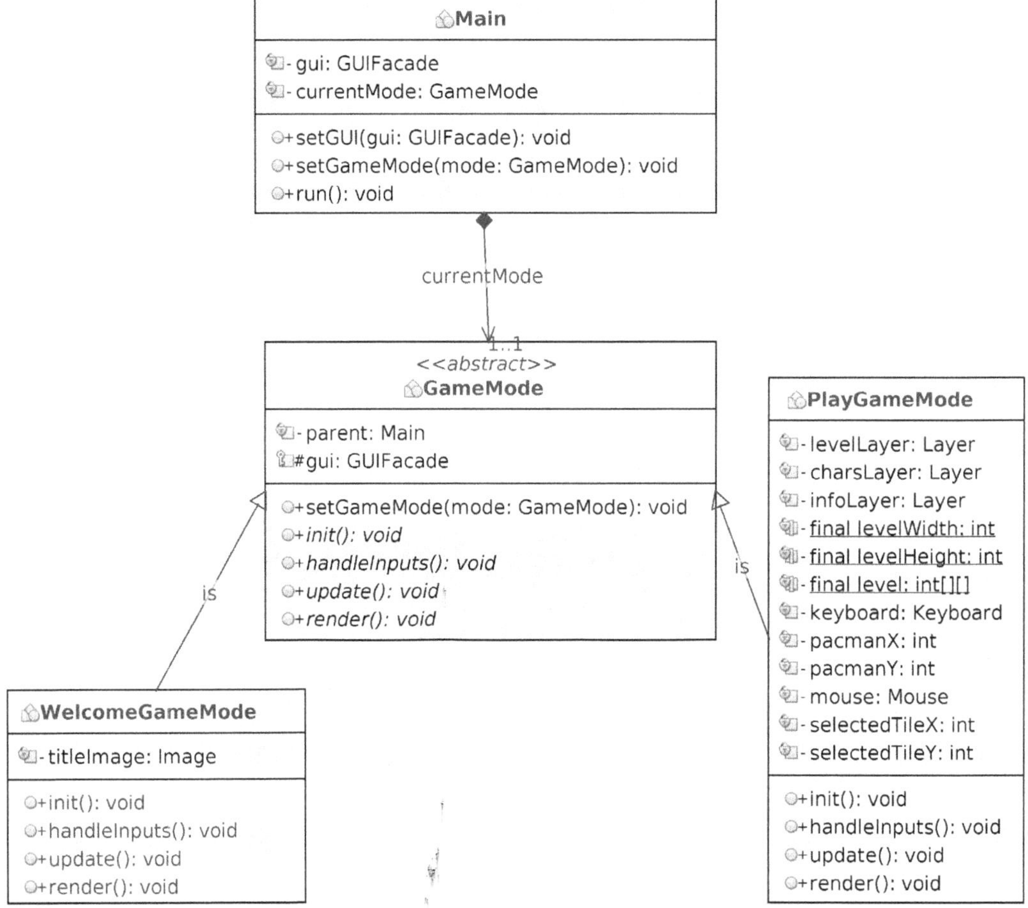

The `GameMode` class is an abstract class and combines both interface aspects with its abstract methods (italicized in the diagram), and features.

The abstract methods of the `GameMode` class are those of the Game Loop pattern. The `init()` method is called when switching to mode, and the other three by the `run()` method of the `Main` class. Switching from one mode to the other allows you to change the game's behavior completely. One could thus have two completely different games and switch from one to the other.

The `parent` attribute and the `setGameMode()` method of the `GameMode` class allows any mode to trigger a state change itself. It simply invokes the `setGameMode()` method of the parent:

```java
public void setGameMode(GameMode mode) {
```

```
    parent.setGameMode(mode);
}
```

The setGameMode() method of the Main class initializes the new mode, and updates the currrentMode attribute:

```java
public synchronized void setGameMode(GameMode mode){
    try {
        mode.setParent(this);
        mode.setGUI(gui);
        mode.init();
        this.currentMode = mode;
    }
    catch(Exception ex) {
        ex.printStackTrace();
        JOptionPane.showMessageDialog(null,
            ex.getMessage(),"Error",JOptionPane.ERROR_MESSAGE);
    }
}
```

The method must be synchronized: competing requests for mode changes would result in indeterminate behavior.

The run() method of the Main class invokes the three methods of the Game Loop pattern:

```java
public void run() {
    int fps = 60;
    long nanoPerFrame = (long) (1000000000.0 / fps);
    long lastTime = 0;
    while (!gui.isClosingRequested()) {
        long nowTime = System.nanoTime();
        if ((nowTime - lastTime) < nanoPerFrame) {
            continue;
        }
        lastTime = nowTime;
        synchronized(this) {
            currentMode.handleInputs();
            currentMode.update();
            currentMode.render();
        }
        long elapsed = System.nanoTime() - lastTime;
        long milliSleep = (nanoPerFrame - elapsed) / 1000000;
        if (milliSleep > 0) {
            try {
                Thread.sleep(milliSleep);
            } catch (InterruptedException ex) {
```

```
            ex.printStackTrace();
        }
    }
}
gui.dispose();
}
```

All the calls - all three together - are synchronized: a change of mode in the middle of this cycle could be disastrous.

Implementation of the game mode

The mode with the Pacman game in an elementary state is implemented in the `PlayGameMode` class. The only noticeable difference with the example at the end of the previous section is the management of the escape key, which switches to the welcome mode:

```
public void handleInputs() {
    switch(keyboard.getLastPressedKey()) {
        case KeyEvent.VK_ESCAPE:
            keyboard.consumeLastPressedKey();
            setGameMode(new WelcomeGameMode());
            return;
    }
    ...
```

This management uses two new methods of the facade, via the `Keyboard` interface. The `getLastPressedKey()` method returns the last key passed from a 'relaxed' state to 'pressed'. The `consumeLastPressedKey()` method consumes this key and removes it from the history. This approach makes it possible to manage the case of a simple pressure, without repetition. It is a simplified case of Exercise 3.3.3: Detect key sequences.

Implantation of the welcome mode

For the welcome mode, new features are added to the facade to display images:

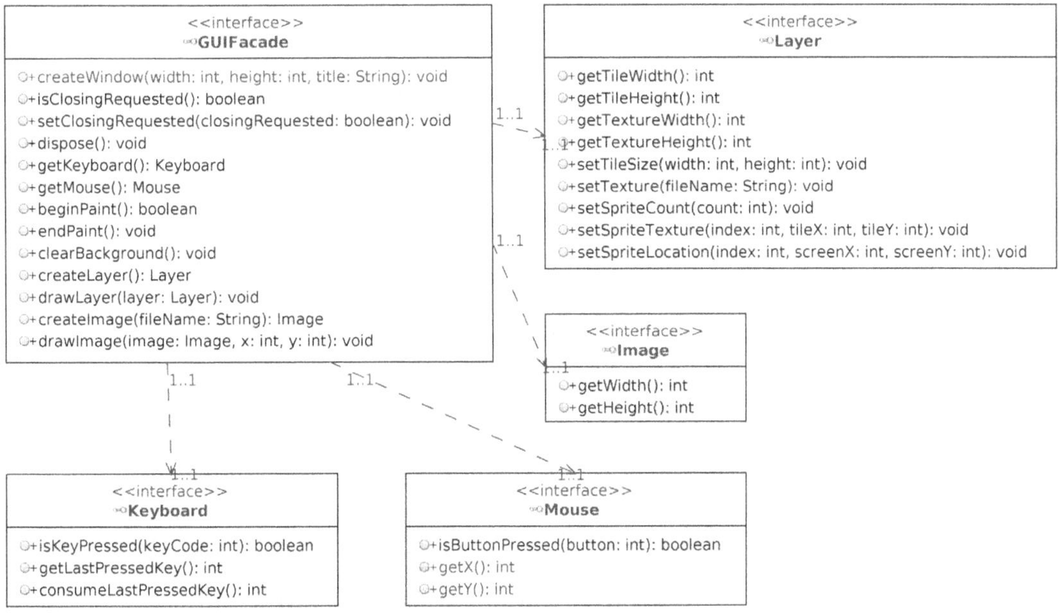

The principle is the same as Exercise 3.3.2.

The welcome mode of the `WelcomeGameMode` class is initialized with the `init()` method:

```java
public void init() {
    titleImage = gui.createImage("pacman_title.png");
    gui.createWindow(windowWidth, windowHeight, "Pacman");
}
```

The `titleImage` image is loaded from the file 'pacman_title.png'. A window is created with the `createWindow()` method of the facade.

For control management, this mode leaves the application if you press the escape key, and switches to the game mode if you press the space key or the enter key:

```java
public void handleInputs() {
    Keyboard keyboard = gui.getKeyboard();
    switch(keyboard.getLastPressedKey()) {
        case KeyEvent.VK_ESCAPE:
            gui.setClosingRequested(true);
            return;
        case KeyEvent.VK_SPACE:
```

```
        case KeyEvent.VK_ENTER:
            keyboard.consumeLastPressedKey();
            setGameMode(new PlayGameMode());
            return;
    }
}
```

The display uses the `titleImage` image with the `drawImage()` method of the facade:

```
public void render() {
    if (!gui.beginPaint())
        return;
    try {
        gui.clearBackground();
        gui.drawImage(titleImage,
            (windowWidth-titleImage.getWidth())/2,
            (windowHeight-titleImage.getHeight())/2);
    } finally {
        gui.endPaint();
    }
}
```

The diagrams in this example are available in the gamemodes01*.cdg files in the "Class Diagrams/chap03" folder of the sample UML project. The code is present in the "examples/chap03/gamemodes01" folder of the sample Java project.

3.3.2.3   Create a menu

We now want to add a new mode that includes a menu with three possibilities:

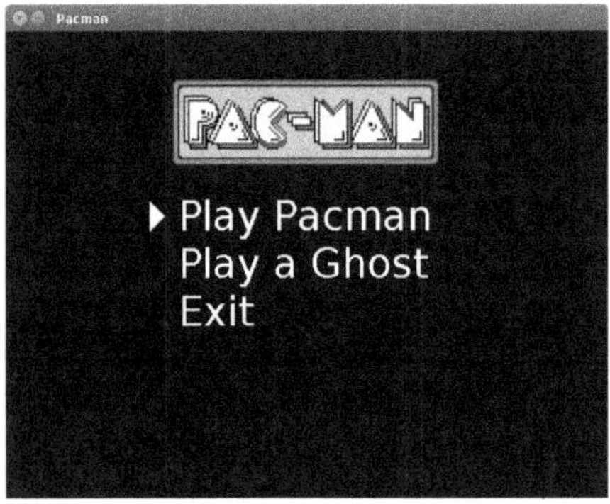

To do this, we add a new class `MainMenuGameMode`:

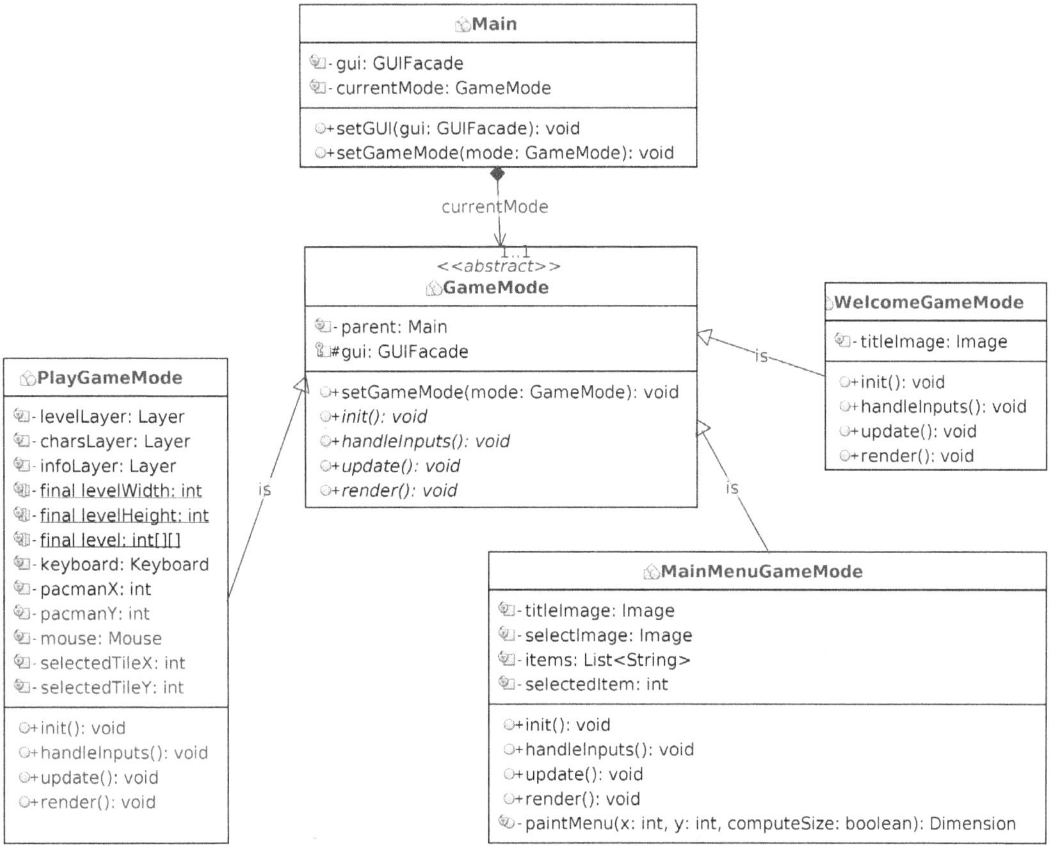

The `MainMenuGameMode` class has the following attributes:

- `titleImage` attribute: the image displayed above the menu;
- `selectImage` attribute: the image of a white triangle to designate the currently selected element;
- `items` attribute: the list of menu items;
- `selectedItem` attribute: the currently selected menu item.

The `MainMenuGameMode` constructor initializes the menu items:

```java
public MainMenuGameMode() {
    items.add("Play Pacman");
    items.add("Play a ghost");
    items.add("Exit");
}
```

The `init()` method loads the images and creates the window:

```java
public void init() {
  titleImage = gui.createImage("pacman_title.png");
  selectImage = gui.createImage("select.png");
  gui.createWindow(windowWidth, windowHeight, "Pacman");
}
```

The `handleInputs()` method closes the application with the escape key, and modifies the selected element with the up and down arrows:

```java
public void handleInputs() {
    Keyboard keyboard = gui.getKeyboard();
    switch(keyboard.getLastPressedKey()) {
        case KeyEvent.VK_ESCAPE:
            keyboard.consumeLastPressedKey();
            gui.setClosingRequested(true);
            return;
        case KeyEvent.VK_UP:
            keyboard.consumeLastPressedKey();
            if (selectedItem > 0) {
                selectedItem --;
            }
            return;
        case KeyEvent.VK_DOWN:
            keyboard.consumeLastPressedKey();
            if (selectedItem < items.size()-1) {
                selectedItem ++;
            }
            return;
```

Then, if you press the enter or space key, an operation is executed based on the selected element:

```java
        case KeyEvent.VK_SPACE:
        case KeyEvent.VK_ENTER:
            keyboard.consumeLastPressedKey();
            switch(selectedItem) {
              case 0:
                  setGameMode(new PlayGameMode());
                  break;
              case 1:
                  JOptionPane.showMessageDialog(null,
                      "Under construction !", "Error",
                      JOptionPane.ERROR_MESSAGE);
                  break;
              case 2:
                  gui.setClosingRequested(true);
                  break;
```

```
        }
        return;
    }
}
```

For the item "Play Pacman", we go into gaming mode. For the item "Play a ghost", the message "Under construction !" is displayed. Finally, the last element leaves the application.

The `render()` method draws the image and the menu in a centered way:

```
gui.clearBackground();
gui.drawImage(titleImage,(windowWidth-titleImage.getWidth())/2,
    50);
gui.setColor(Color.white);
gui.setTextSize(selectImage.getHeight());
Dimension menuSize = paintMenu(0,0,true);
paintMenu((windowWidth-menuSize.width)/2,
    (windowHeight-menuSize.height)/2,false);
```

The `setColor()` and `setTextSize()` methods are new methods of the façade. They set the color and size in pixels of the text to draw.

The `paintMenu()` method calculates the size of the menu if its last argument is `true`, and draw it if it is `false`:

```
private Dimension paintMenu(int x,int y,boolean computeSize) {
    int menuWidth = 0;
    int menuHeight = 0;
    for (int i=0;i<items.size();i++) {
        String text = items.get(i);
        Dimension textSize = gui.getTextMetrics(text);
        if (!computeSize) {
            gui.drawText(text, x, y,
                textSize.width, textSize.height);
            if (i == selectedItem) {
                gui.drawImage(selectImage,
                    x-selectImage.getWidth(), y);
            }
        }
        y += textSize.height;
        menuHeight += textSize.height;
        if (textSize.width > menuWidth) {
            menuWidth = textSize.width;
        }
    }
    return new Dimension(menuWidth,menuHeight);
}
```

This method uses two new methods of the facade:

- `getTextMetrics()` method, which returns the size of a text when drawn;
- `drawText()` method, which draws a text in a box;
- The implementation of these new features is an extension of the Exercise 3.3.1: Display text with the facade.

The diagrams in this example are available in the gamemodes02*.cdg files in the "Class Diagrams/chap03" folder of the sample UML project. The code is present in the "examples/chap03/gamemodes02" folder of the sample Java project.

3.3.2.4 Cache fonts (Flyweight Pattern)

A simple implementation of the text rendering methods used for the menu quickly leads to the creation of a large number of fonts. For example, the `setTextSize()` method should instantiate a large number of fonts to find the one that allows you to have the right pixel size. This approach is needed with the AWT library, which produces only inch-sized fonts related to the screen size:

```java
public void setTextSize(int size) {
    if (graphics == null)
        return;
    for (int i=2*size;i>=4;i--) {
        Font font = new Font("Arial",Font.PLAIN,i);
        graphics.setFont(font);
        FontMetrics fm = graphics.getFontMetrics();
        if (fm.getHeight() < size) {
            break;
        }
    }
}
```

In subsequent chapters, it is necessary to make many calls to this method. It can also be the case for other video games. Knowing that these calls are repeated 60 times per second for most screens, we quickly arrive at an unnecessary loss of resources. The repeated creation of the same objects consumes processor time and uses memory. In addition, the destruction of these many objects unnecessarily uses the garbage collector.

Other libraries may not be suffering from this problem, or when these lines are read, AWT may be able to create a pixel-sized font. In any case, this makes it possible to present a very effective trick to solve this type of situation: use the *Flyweight Pattern* to pool the creation of identical objects.

Flyweight pattern

The Flyweight pattern allows you to get instances of a particular interface (or a super class):

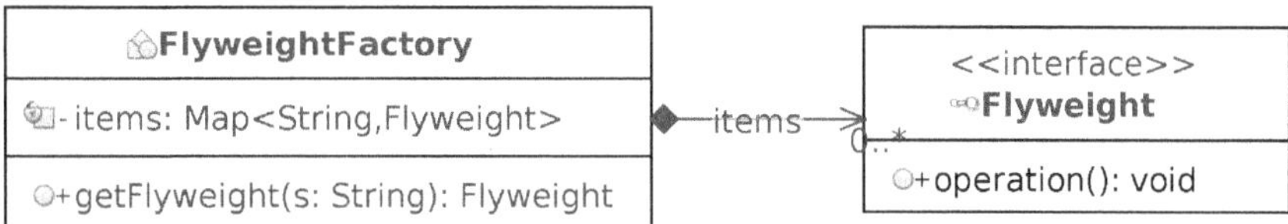

The `Flyweight` interface defines the type of object managed by the pattern. The `FlyweightFactory` class is used to obtain an instance that implements this interface. It is similar to the Factory Method pattern; however there is a fundamental difference: the objects returned by the pattern are not editable. No element in their interface should allow modifying their contents, or if it is the case, it is necessary to inform the user that the objects returned can not be modified. This property is used to memorize all the objects already created, and to return the memorized objects when the parameters are the same.

```
FlyweightFactory factory = new FlyweightFactory();
Flyweight item1 = factory.getFlyweight("apple");
Flyweight item2 = factory.getFlyweight("apple");
```

The first call to `getFlyweight()` builds a new instance of a Flyweight with the "apple" parameter. On the second call, however, no object is made, and the same instance is returned. In the end, the `item1` and `item2` variables are identical and reference the same object. If we ask a large number of times for objects with the same parameters, few objects are made, even if we have the illusion of having manufactured many objects.

Mutualize fonts

To apply this pattern to the font, we define a new class `AWTFonts`:

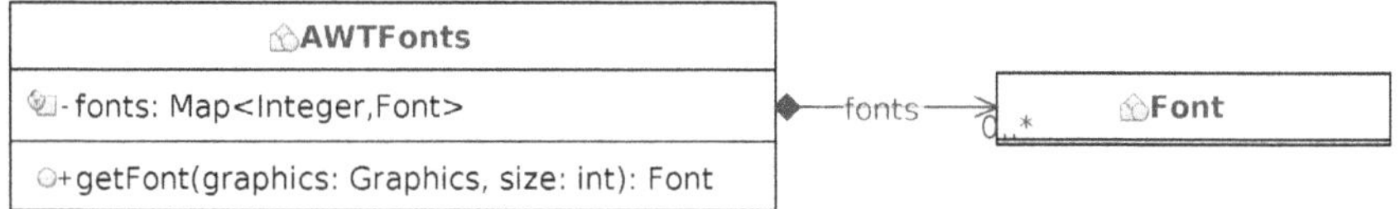

The `getFont()` method is used to obtain a font of a given pixel size:

```
public Font getFont(Graphics graphics,int size) {
    Font font = fonts.get(size);
    if (font == null) {
        Font oldFont = graphics.getFont();
```

```java
        for (int i=2*size;i>=4;i--) {
            font = new Font("Arial",Font.PLAIN,i);
            graphics.setFont(font);
            FontMetrics fm = graphics.getFontMetrics();
            if (fm.getHeight() < size) {
                break;
            }
        }
        fonts.put(size,font);
        graphics.setFont(oldFont);
    }
    return font;
}
```

The method starts by looking if the `fonts` associative array contains a font for `size`: if it is the case, there is nothing to do, return the found font. In the opposite case, we build the font, memorize it in the associative array, then return it.

To benefit from this feature, create an instance of **AWFonts**, for example in the class of the facade, and then modify the `setTextSize()` method:

```java
public void setTextSize(int size) {
    if (graphics == null)
        return;
    graphics.setFont(fonts.getFont(graphics,size));
}
```

This method requests the desired font from the factory `fonts`.

The diagrams in this example are available in the gamemodes03*.cdg files in the "Class Diagrams/chap03" folder of the sample UML project. The code is present in the "examples/chap03/gamemodes03" folder of the sample Java project.

3.3.2.5 Make a menu sequence (State Pattern)

We now want to add sub-menus and be able to return to a previous menu. To illustrate, the following menu sequence is added to the Pacman game:

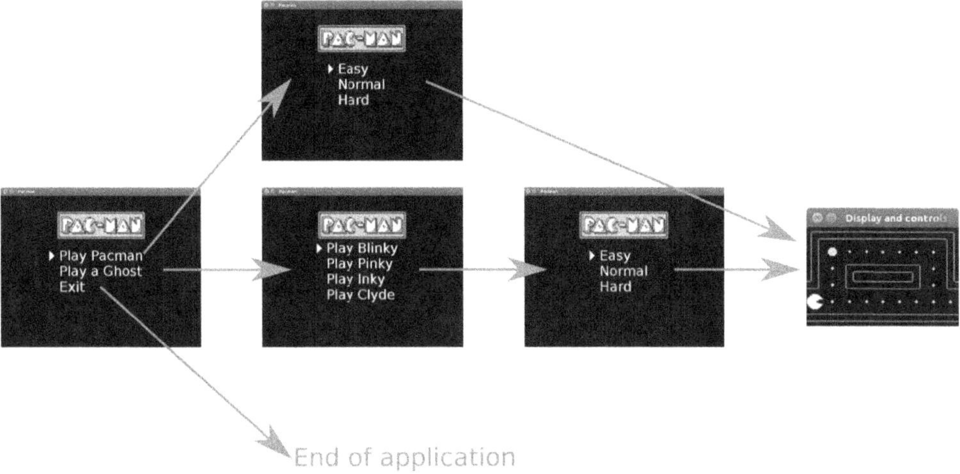

To be able to define several menus easily, an abstract class `MenuGameMode`, child of `GameMode`, is added: it allows to create menus by defining child classes:

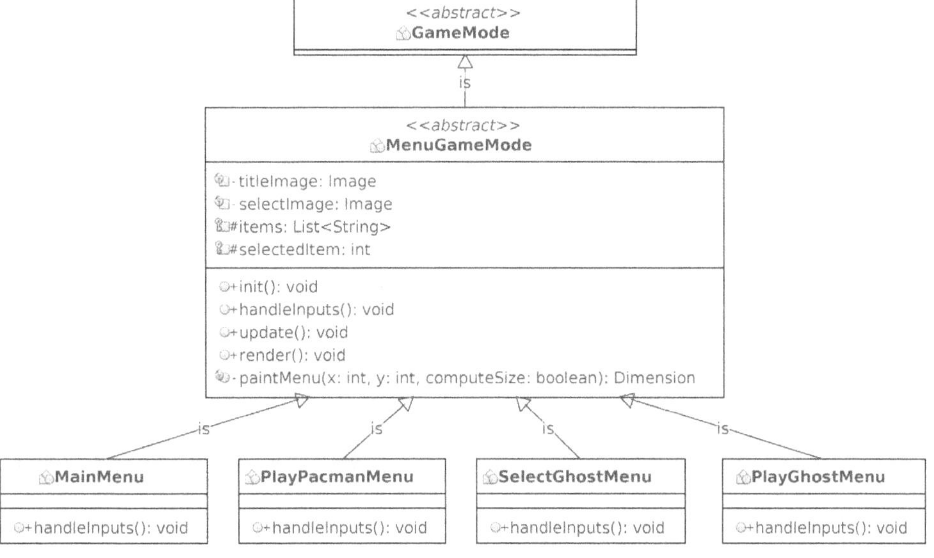

The `MenuGameMode` class is almost identical to the previous `MainMenuGameMode` class. Only the definition of the menu items has been removed, as well as the actions to be performed when an item is selected. Each child class defines its elements and the actions to perform.

To move in the menus, we rely on the state pattern, enriching it with more advanced features. The `setGameMode()` method of the `Main` class still allows you to change the game mode. However, it also stores the previous mode with a `gameModes` linked list:

```java
public synchronized void setGameMode(GameMode mode){
    try {
        gameModes.push(mode);
        mode.setParent(this);
        mode.setGUI(gui);
        mode.init();
        this.currentMode = mode;
    }
    catch(Exception ex) {
        ex.printStackTrace();
        JOptionPane.showMessageDialog(null,
            ex.getMessage(),"Error",JOptionPane.ERROR_MESSAGE);
    }
}
```

A new method `setPreviousGameMode()` returns to the previous mode:

```java
public synchronized void setPreviousGameMode() {
    if (!gameModes.isEmpty()) {
        gameModes.pop();
    }
    if (gameModes.isEmpty()) {
        gui.setClosingRequested(true);
    }
    else {
        setGameMode(gameModes.pop());
    }
}
```

In this illustration, we are only interested in returning to the previous game mode. With this type of pattern, it is also possible to go back further. It is also possible to pause a mode, navigate through a set of modes, and return to the initial mode. It can be the case if you want to display a menu and its submenus during a game.

The diagrams in this example are available in the gamemodes04*.cdg files in the "Class Diagrams/chap03" folder of the sample UML project. The code is present in the "examples/chap03/gamemodes04" folder of the sample Java project.

The choices made in the menus are not yet taken into account: these aspects are discussed in the next chapter.

3.3.3   Exercices

3.3.3.1   Exercise 3.3.1: Displaying text with the facade

Create or enrich a facade that displays a centered message, for example with a method:

```
void drawString(String text,int x,int y,int width,int height);
```

Using this method on the entire display surface, we can obtain a result of the type:

To implement this facade, it is possible to start from scratch, or from the "Class Diagrams/chap03/awtfacade02.cdg" diagram of the UML sample project, and/or code in the "examples/chap03/awtfacade02" folder of the Java sample project.

3.3.3.2   Exercise 3.3.2: Display an image with the facade

Create or enrich a facade that displays an image. We want to follow a mechanism similar to that of the layers, with the Factory Method pattern. The facade makes it possible to create images from the name of a file. Then, these images can be drawn when the user wishes.

To test this feature, we can display the image "pacman_title.png" available in the resources of the Java sample project:

To implement this facade, it is possible to start from scratch, or from the "Class Diagrams/chap03/awtfacade02.cdg" diagram of the UML sample project, and/or code in the "examples/chap03/awtfacade02" folder of the Java sample project.

3.3.3.3   Exercise 3.3.3: Detecting key sequences

One wants to enrich a facade to be able to detect particular sequences of keys. It is often used in fighting games, where you have to chain a specific sequence of keys to trigger a special attack.

To achieve this, we want the facade to offer all the keyboard events that occurred in the last seconds. With this list, it becomes possible to search for sequences of interest and then act accordingly.

To test this feature, you want to display the following information in a window:

- A message that indicates whether the right arrow is currently pressed or released;
- A message that indicates whether the up arrow is currently pressed or released;
- A message that indicates whether the input key is currently pressed or released.

In addition, we want to display the state of different "combos". To pass from a state of inactive to active and vice-versa, it is necessary in each case to realize a precise sequence of keys. We are interested in three sequences: for each one of them, we display a message indicating the state of the corresponding combo. Sequences are:

- Right arrow pressed, released
- Up arrow pressed, released, Enter key pressed, released
- Right arrow pressed, Up arrow pressed, Enter key pressed

Finally, you want to display the status of the keyboard event list.

A possible display is the following one:

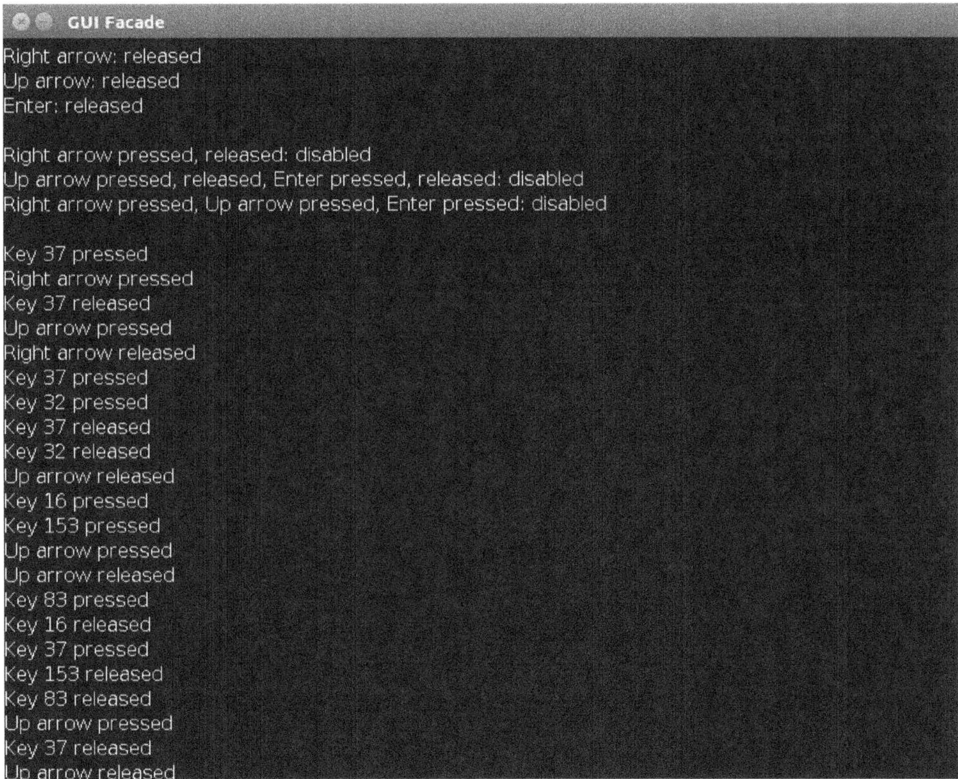

If the instructions are not clear, you can run the solution in the "examples/chap03/keybuffer" folder.

To make this facade, it is possible to start from scratch, or from the "Class Diagrams/chap03/awtfacade02.cdg" diagram of the UML sample project, and/or code in the "examples/chap03/awtfacade02" folder of the sample project Java.

3.4   Video Game Development: User Interface

→ Select the graphic library:

The choice depends in the first place on the nature of your graphics: if you have opted for 3D, a library like LWJGL is imperative. For beginners, it's best to start with a 2D game. For this, the AWT library is very suitable, even if its performance is not optimal. Besides, there is a good chance that you can reuse much of the sample code presented in this chapter. Remember that you can change later the graphic library if you have a good facade. For example, start with a facade layout with AWT, then when you have gained skills, implement a version with a better library like LWJGL. If your facade is well thought out, you will not have to modify your game.

→ Identify the graphic elements:

The first elements to identify are naturally the objects of the game itself, such as tiles or textures. Then you have to think of everything that makes the user interface, such as text, icons, decorative frames, etc. When the list of these elements begins to be complete, it is necessary to find or create the corresponding 3D images or meshes. Finally, it is also necessary to define the nature of the possible interactions with the controls of the game.

→ Design your facade for the user interface:

Even if you program alone and with a single graphics library, it is strongly recommended to make a facade between your game and the graphic library. As presented throughout this book, the success of a complex application lies primarily in the ability to divide the problems into much simpler subproblems. Considering the use of the facade, you only have to focus on the organizational aspects of the graphic elements, with no concerns for low-level graphics aspects. Concerning facade implementation, you can focus entirely on the API of the library without having to worry about the overall graphic organization of the game. For example, if you want to display text:

- On the user side of a text display method, one focuses only on the texts to be displayed and their locations on the screen.
- On the developer side of this method, we focus on the calls to the graphics library chosen, without having to worry about the texts and their real locations.

Designing a good facade for your game is hard work: do not hesitate to spend a lot of time, especially for its definition. This step does not rely on any programming: it comes after when the facade is well defined.

→ Tests :

For user interface aspects, it is difficult to automate tests as it was done previously for the game state. One can imagine to record a sequence of actions with the keyboard and/or the mouse with dedicated software, then to replay the record while checking that the behavior is the expected one.

3.5   Exercise Solutions

3.5.1   Exercise 3.3.1: Display text with the facade

Concerning the facade interface, add the proposed drawString() method to the GUIFacade interface.

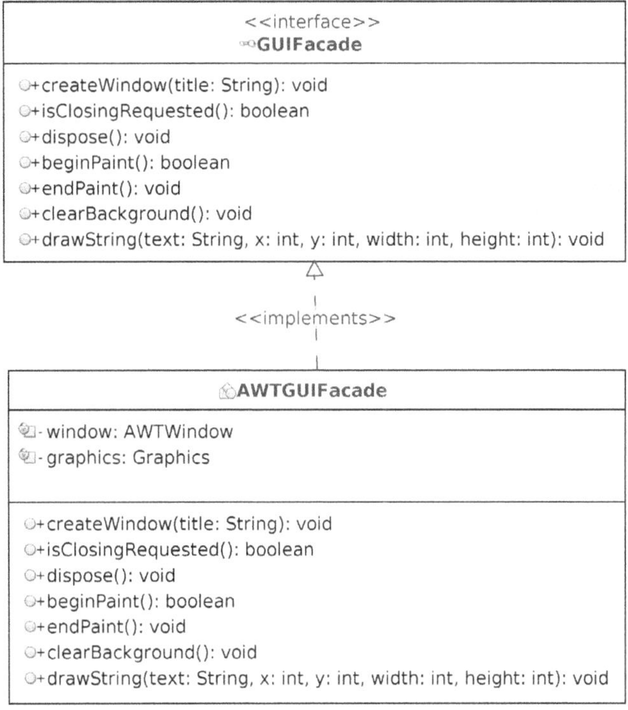

For implementation in AWT, a version that has a Graphics is sufficient, for example:

```java
public void drawString(String text,int x, int y,
    int width, int height) {
    graphics.setFont(new Font("Arial",Font.PLAIN,44));
    graphics.setColor(Color.white);
    FontMetrics fm = graphics.getFontMetrics();
    int textWidth = fm.stringWidth(text);
    int textHeight = fm.getHeight();
    graphics.drawString(text,x + (width-textWidth)/2,
```

```
        y + (height-textHeight)/2);
}
```

This method uses the AWT library's usual tools, including `FontMetrics`, to calculate the rendering size of a string.

To display centered text, this new method is used between calls to `beginPaint()` and `endPaint()` of the facade:

```java
public void render() {
    if (!gui.beginPaint())
        return;
    try {
        gui.clearBackground();
        gui.drawString("Welcome", 0, 0, 800, 600);
    } finally {
        gui.endPaint();
    }
}
```

A complete sample code is available in the "examples/chap03/facadetext" folder of the Java sample project.

3.5.2   Exercise 3.3.2: Display an image with the facade

The following facade meets the specifications:

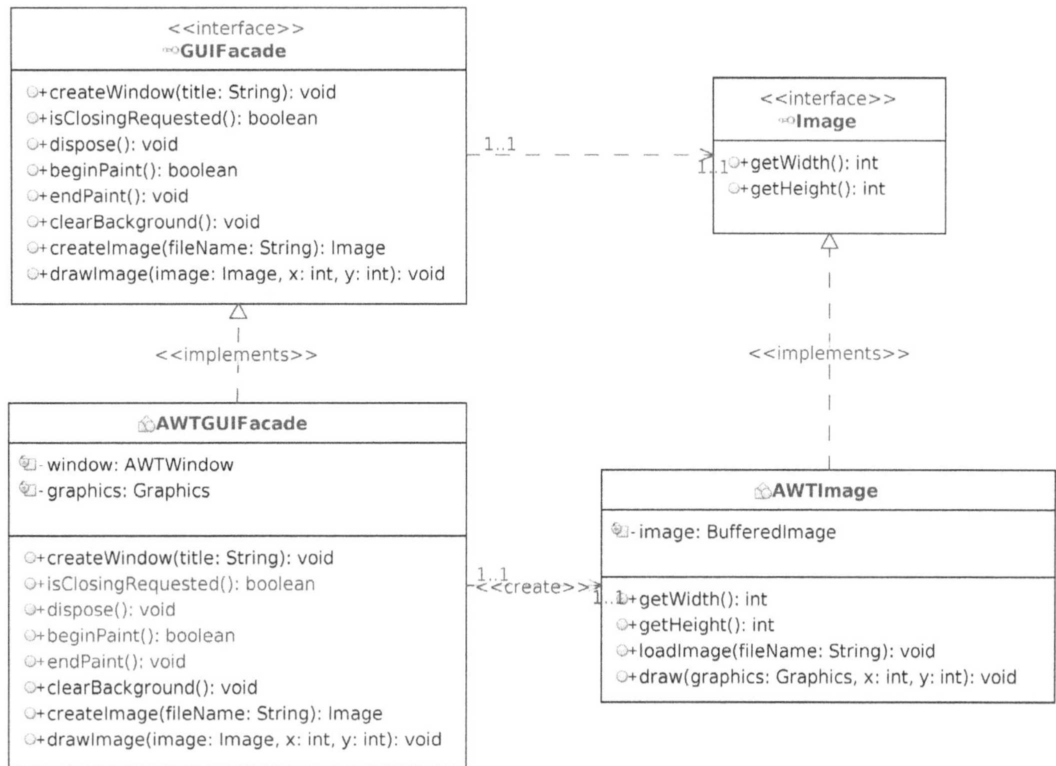

The new `Image` interface allows you to manipulate an image loaded by the `createImage()` method of the facade:

```java
public Image createImage(String fileName) {
    AWTImage image = new AWTImage();
    image.loadImage(fileName);
    return image;
}
```

This method calls the `loadImage()` method of the `AWTImage` class:

```java
public void loadImage(String fileName) {
    try {
        image = ImageIO.read(this.getClass()
            .getClassLoader().getResource(fileName));
    } catch (IOException ex) {
        throw new RuntimeException(
```

```
                      "Error when reading "+fileName);
    }
}
```

The drawing part starts with the `drawImage()` method of the facade:

```java
public void drawImage(Image image,int x,int y) {
    if (graphics == null) {
        return;
    }
    if (image == null) {
        throw new IllegalArgumentException("No image");
    }
    if (!(image instanceof AWTImage)) {
        throw new IllegalArgumentException("Invalid image type"
        );
    }
    AWTImage awtImage = (AWTImage) image;
    awtImage.draw(graphics,x,y);
}
```

This one calls the `draw()` method of the `AWTImage` class:

```java
public void draw(Graphics graphics,int x,int y) {
    graphics.drawImage(image, x, y, null);
}
```

A complete sample code is available in the "examples/chap03/facadeimage" folder
of the Java sample project.

3.5.3   Exercise 3.3.3: Detecting key sequences

A solution facade can be:

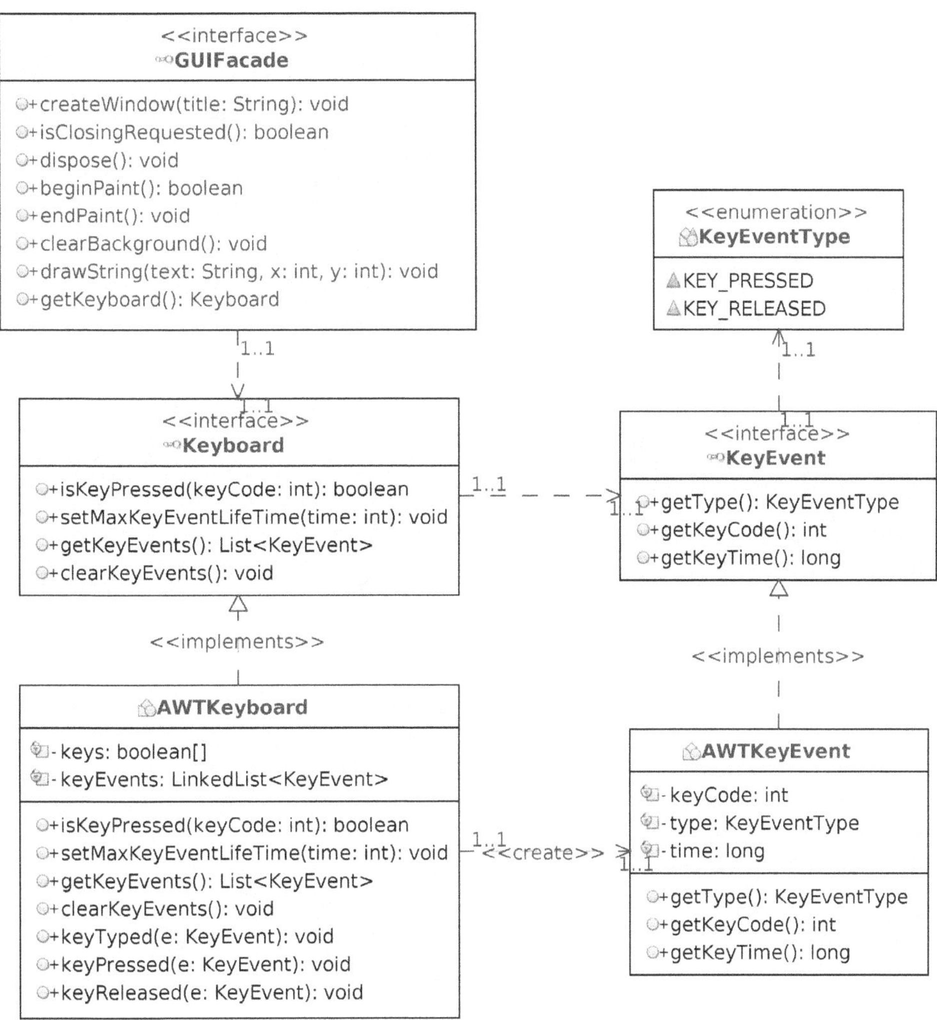

The list of keyboard events is obtained thanks to the getKeyEvents() method of
the Keyboard interface and implemented in the AWTKeyboard class:

```
public List<KeyEvent> getKeyEvents() {
    long now = System.nanoTime();
    Iterator<KeyEvent> iterator = keyEvents.iterator();
    while (iterator.hasNext()) {
        KeyEvent event = iterator.next();
        if ( (now - event.getKeyTime()) >
```

```
                maxKeyEventLifeTime ) {
            iterator.remove();
        }
    }
    return new ArrayList<KeyEvent>(keyEvents);
}
```

In this method, we start by eliminating old events. The notion of old time is defined by the maxKeyEventLifeTime attribute, which is defined by the setMaxKeyEventLifeTime() method. A copy of the list of events is then returned: returning the list itself is too risky since it can be modified at any time by the notification of new key events.

The facade is also enriched with a KeyEvent interface that defines an abstract keyboard event. It returns the type of events with the getType() method, the code of the key with the getKeyCode() method, and the time of the event with the getKeyTime() method. The event types are defined in the KeyEventType enumeration.

The event list is populated during keyboard notifications, for example, with the keyPressed() method of the java.util.KeyListener interface:

```
public void keyPressed(java.awt.event.KeyEvent e) {
    keys[e.getKeyCode()] = true;
    keyEvents.add(new AWTKeyEvent(e.getKeyCode(),
            KeyEventType.KEY_PRESSED,System.nanoTime()));
}
```

As a unit and a time reference, System.nanoTime() is used here.

For display, we have enriched the facade with a method drawString() which draws a message at coordinates x,y. The messages displayed on the screen are functions of boolean attributes added in the main class: according to their value, one message is displayed rather than another.

For the first three messages, which display the state of a key, the corresponding attribute is updated according to the isKeyPressed() method of the Keyboard interface. For example, for the right arrow:

```
rightArrow = keyboard.isKeyPressed(
    java.awt.event.KeyEvent.VK_RIGHT);
```

For the next three messages, we run a search for a desired sequence in the event list. For example, for the first case, "right arrow pressed, then released":

```
List<KeyEvent> keyEvents = keyboard.getKeyEvents();
for (int i=0;i<keyEvents.size();i++) {
    if (i+1 < keyEvents.size()
      && (keyEvents.get(i+0).getKeyCode()
          == java.awt.event.KeyEvent.VK_RIGHT)
```

```
            && (keyEvents.get(i+0).getType()
                == KeyEventType.KEY_PRESSED)
            && (keyEvents.get(i+1).getKeyCode()
                == java.awt.event.KeyEvent.VK_RIGHT)
            && (keyEvents.get(i+1).getType()
                == KeyEventType.KEY_RELEASED)) {
            combo1 = !combo1;
            keyboard.clearKeyEvents();
            break;
        }
    }
}
```

The sequence can appear at any level of the list: so we try from the first position (i
= 0), then from the second (i = 1), and so on. If the sequence is found, we switch
the corresponding boolean attribute (here `combo1`), which modifies the display
accordingly. In addition, we empty the list of events with the `clearKeyEvents()`
method, so that we do not detect the same occurrence of a sequence more than
once.

The other cases are similar and can be found in the "examples/chap03/keybuffer"
solution of the Java example project.

4.1 General approach

4.1.1 Presentation

As quickly presented in Chapter 1, the general approach followed in this book is a modified version of the Model-View-Controller (MVC) approach:

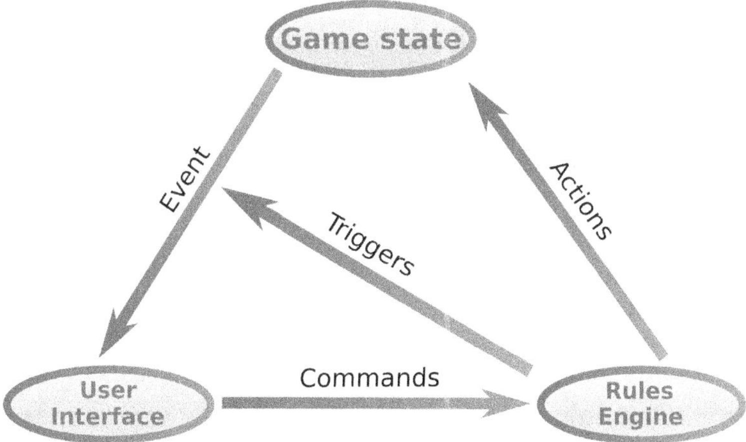

As a model, we find the state of the game, presented in Chapter 2. Unlike the MVC approach, the game state in the proposed approach is only a storage location: the only available modifications are basic setters. In the example of the Pacman game presented so far, the attributes of the `PlayGameMode` class form the game state. For example, the `level` attribute contains the cells of the world. As a view, we find the user interface presented in Chapter 3. Finally, as a controller, we find the rules engine, embodied by the `update()` method in the Pacman game example. Unlike the MVC approach, it is the rule engine that validates changes in the state of the game.

Concerning the interaction between these three actors, the major difference lies in the passive nature of the game state. When the user acts, such as pressing a key or selecting an item in a menu, the user interface produces a command, such as "move the character to the right." This command is sent to the rules engine, which deduces the actions needed to modify the state, for example, to change the character's x coordinates. Besides, the rule engine triggers the sending of events indicating state changes - it is not the state that transparently indicates that it has changed. When the user interface receives the event, it modifies its rendering data accordingly, and for example, it modifies the x coordinate of the character's sprite.

4.1.2 Motivation

This approach is the result of constraints specific to video games, and to any application whose display requires the same constraints. Indeed, the user interface, on the one hand, and the state of the game and the game engine on the other, evolve in two "parallel" universes:

- The user interface must provide high-speed rendering, typically at 60 frames per second. Aesthetics motivate this constraint, on the contrary to office applications that usually ignore it;
- The state of the game evolves at a slower speed, regularly or irregularly. The first reason for this constraint is simply that not all screens work at the same refresh rate. It would be strange to watch a game whose evolution is faster on a screen at 144Hz than on a screen at 60Hz. It is also motivated by aspects of computational resources, especially when one wishes to include advanced artificial intelligence. Finally, the management of the multiplayer game requires it, and networks can not operate at frequencies as high as the refresh of a screen.

To manage these aspects, one must be able to operate the two entities independently. Communication should take place only briefly at key moments in the game cycle. Between these moments, everyone must evolve independently:

- When the rules engine changes the game state, the user interface should not be interrupted. It must be able to offer a consistent display until the state of the game is available for viewing. For example, in the GUI facade presented

earlier, that's why layers have their list of sprites. They are disconnected from the state of the game and can be drawn without consulting the data of the game state.
- When the user interface produces a command, for example, as a result of a pressed key, it can not be consumed if the rules engine is changing the state. We must find solutions to postpone this consumption.

The purpose of this chapter is to present different approaches and associated design patterns to meet these requirements. Section 2 focuses on the separation between game state and rendering in the user interface. Section 3 presents the rules engine and its interaction with the other two actors. Finally, section 4 presents several features that can be easily added thanks to the proposed approach. Indeed, if it meets the constraints presented above, it also offers other very interesting benefits.

⇒ Note: The general approach followed in this book is not the only solution to every conceivable problem. It is perfectly suited to a large number of cases, partially answers the problems raised by others, and is irrelevant in some cases. Once again, the primary goal of this book is to train the mind in software design techniques, primarily using design patterns. The example of this approach has many pedagogical interests and helps you to create new approaches. For the video game developed while reading this book, beginners are invited to reproduce it, and the most experienced should use it as an inspiration to design their solution.

4.2   Synchronization between state and user interface

The purpose of this section is to synchronize the game state data, as designed in Chapter 2, with the user interface presented in Chapter 3.

Before starting, here is a summary of the elements designed so far, with a little reorganization. First, the main classes are kept in the main package, and separated from the menu classes:

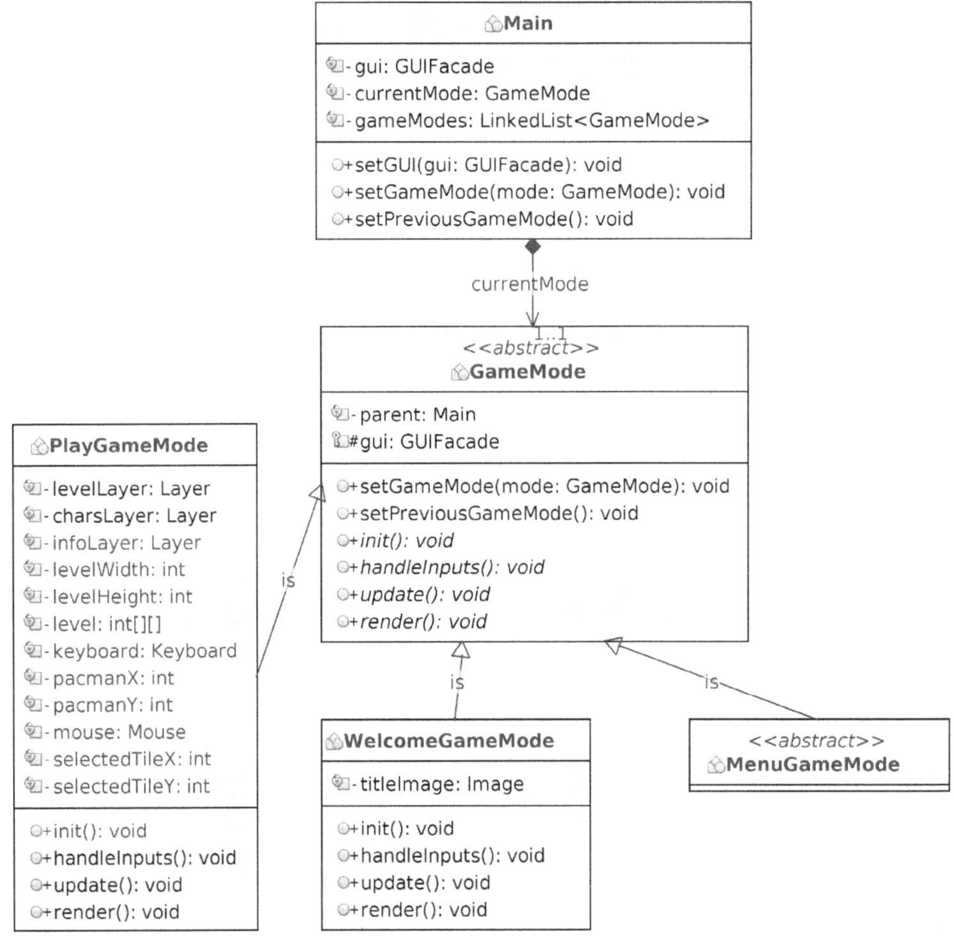

All menu classes are placed in the `menu` package:

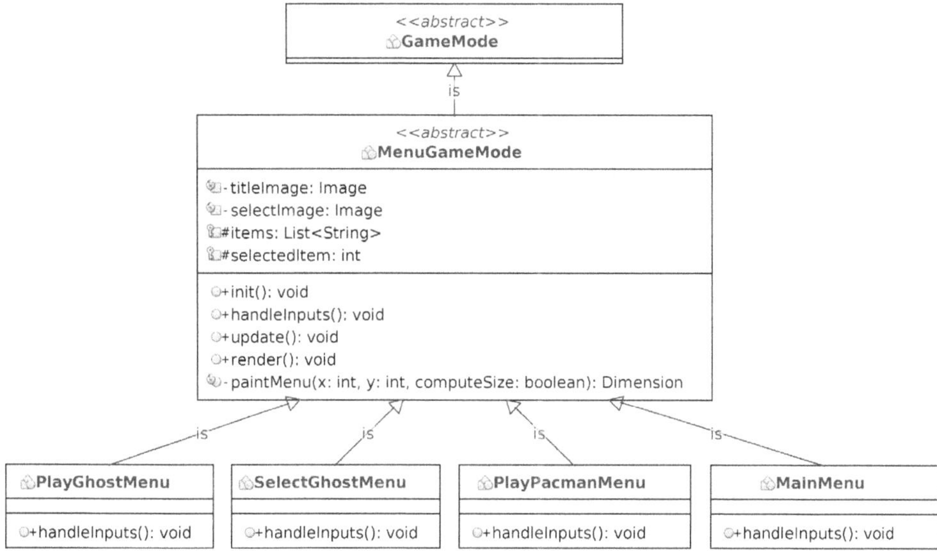

The facade for the user interface is kept, and placed in the `gui` package:

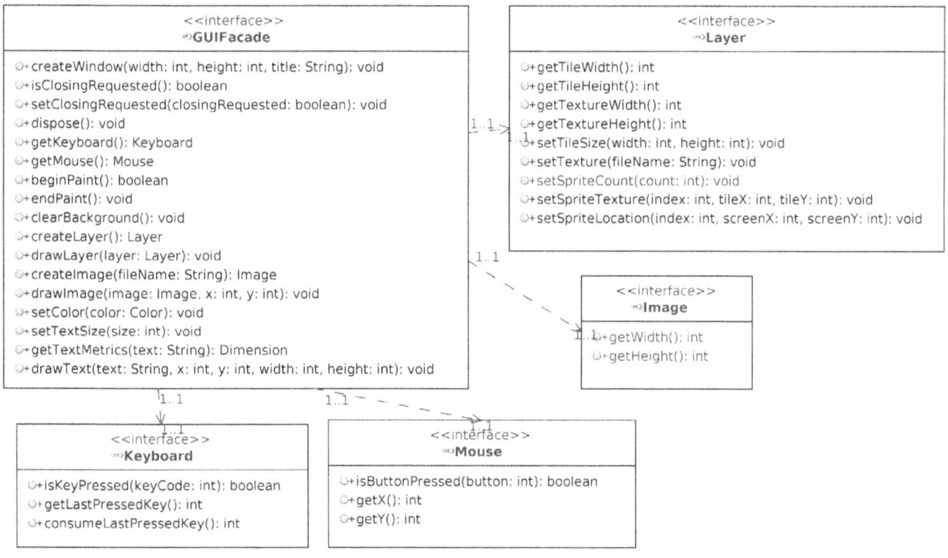

The implementation with the AWT library is also preserved, and placed in the `gui.awt` package. It is possible to use another implementation - all the following does not depend on a particular implementation, as long as the new features of the facade are added.

The state of the Pacman game, presented in Chapter 2, is reorganized into two parts: a first part with the containers, placed in the `state` package (here without the `WorldIterator` class for clarity):

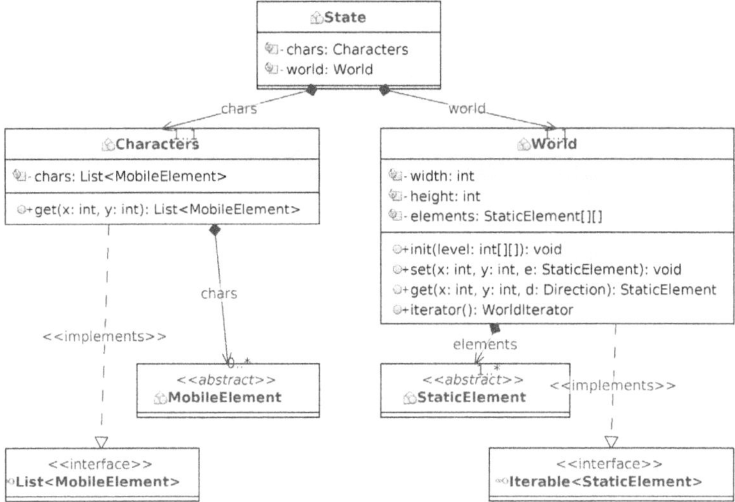

The second part with the elements is placed in the `state.element` package:

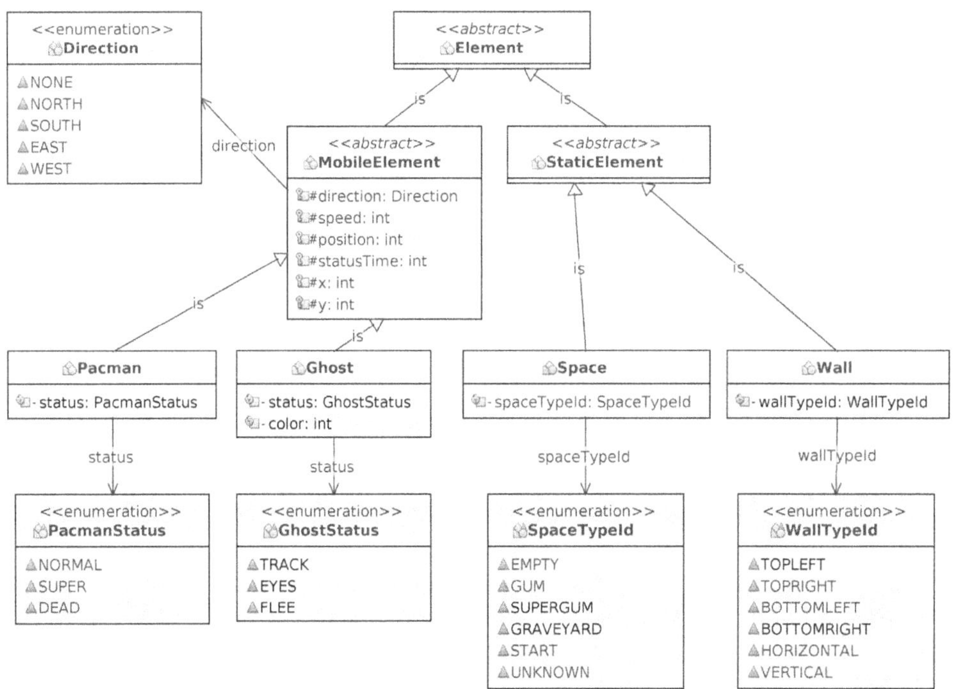

4.2.1 Render a view of the game state

4.2.1.1 Initialize the world (Abstract Factory Pattern)

To render a state of the game, we must fill it with data that represents a level of
Pacman. In the examples in Chapter 3, a simple native array was used:

```
static final int[][] level = new int[][] {
    { 15,11,11,11,11,11,11,11,16 },{ 12,5,3,3,3,3,3,3,12 },
    { 12,3,15,11,11,11,16,3,12 },{ 14,3,13,11,11,11,14,3,13 },
    { 3,3,3,3,3,3,3,3,3 },{ 11,11,11,11,11,11,11,11,11 }
};
```

This array is very good for presenting the display, but does not have all the advantages of a state like the one designed in Chapter 2. The goal now is to use
it to initialize the world's data. We have to build instances of the `Element` class
according to the different codes. For example, for code 15, we want to make an
instance of the `Wall` class with the `WallTypeId.TOPLEFT` type. A naive solution is to
program a large `switch ... case`. In this section, a richer approach is proposed,
based on the *Abstract Factory Pattern*.

Abstract Factory Pattern

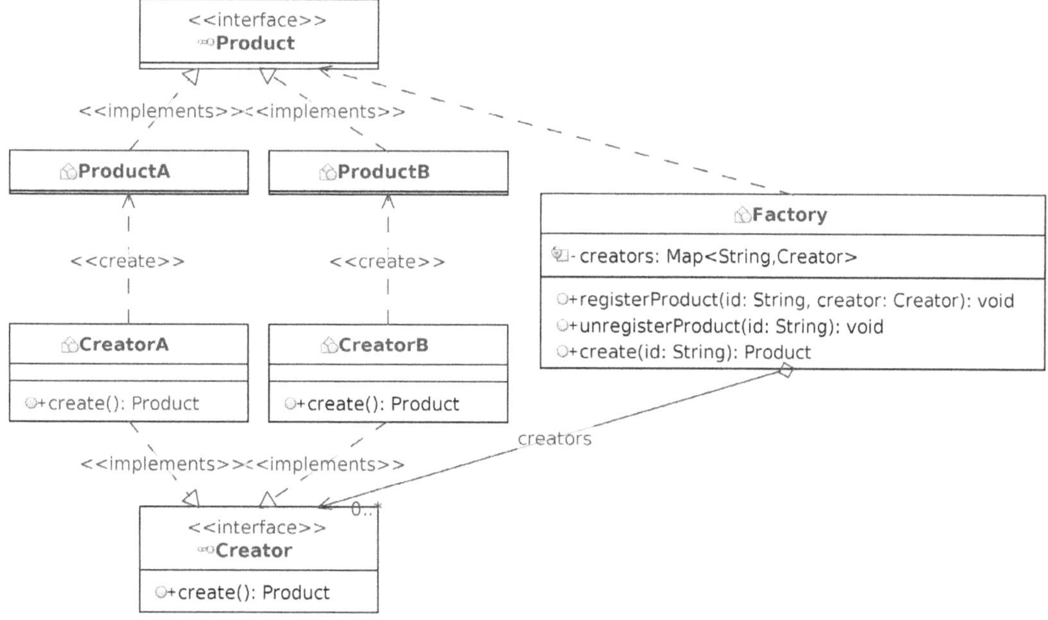

- The `Product` interface defines the objects that you want to make. In the illustration above, there are two implementations: `ProductA` and `ProductB`.
- The `Creator` interface is used to define classes that can build `Product` implementations. For example, the `CreatorA` class makes an instance of `ProductA` with the `create()` method. We present the simplest case here: there are no arguments to the `create()` methods. It is possible to propose methods of creation with arguments.
- The `Factory` class is the `Product` factory. There are several ways to define and implement it - here, the most common case is presented. The goal of this factory is to be able to build a product based on an identifier. In this example, the identifier is a string (`String`). Other types are possible, as well as any form of setting or context that influence the nature of the created object. All associations between an identifier and a product creator are stored in the `creators` attribute. The class has the following methods:
    - `registerProduct()` method: allows to define an association between an identifier and a product to be manufactured;
    - `unregisterProduct()` method: deletes an existing association;
    - `create()` method: returns a new product based on an identifier. This method must be consistent with that of the `Creator` interface.

Here is an example that illustrates the use of this factory:

```
Factory factory = new Factory();
factory.registerProduct("A", new CreatorA());
factory.registerProduct("B", new CreatorB());
factory.create("A").show();
factory.create("B").show();
```

Line 2 adds the association between the string "A" and the creation of `ProductA`. Similarly, line 3 adds the association between the string "B" and the creation of `ProductB`.

Line 4 makes a product using the string "A", then invokes the `show()` method of the newly created product. Line 5 does the same with string "B".

Knowing that the `show()` method of the `ProductA` class displays `Product A`, and that `ProductB` displays `Product B`, the following is displayed:

```
Product A
Product B
```

The first advantage of this pattern lies in the separation of the different features:

- The way a product is made is implemented in a specific class. For example, the `CreatorA` class creates `ProductA` objects;
- The associations between the identifiers and the creators are chosen by the user of the factory;
- A factory is interchangeable: a user can instantiate different factories, and switch from one to another to modify the behavior of the application.

Build Elements for Pacman's World

The pattern is applied to the creation of implementations of the `Element` class, knowing that the identifiers are integers (like those in the `level` array):

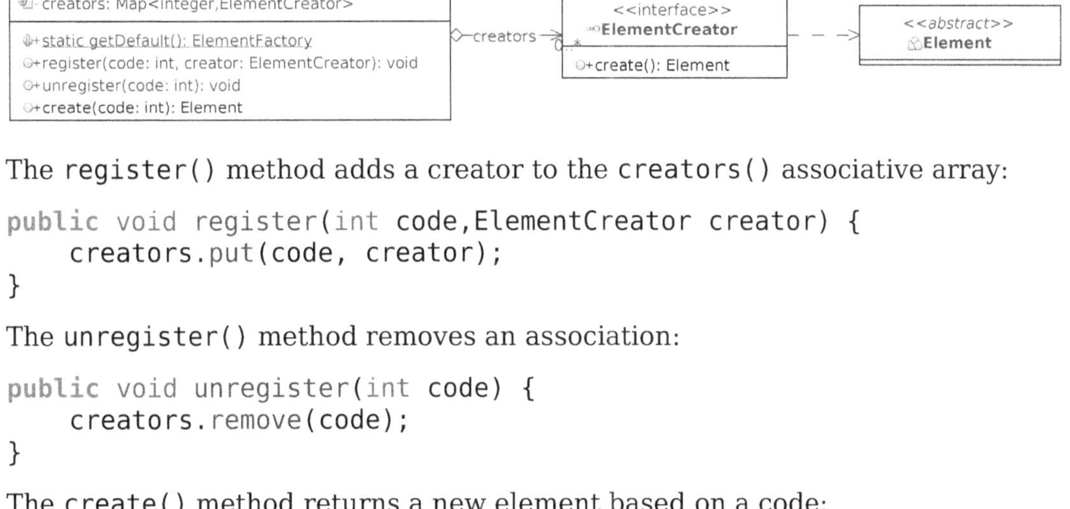

The `register()` method adds a creator to the `creators()` associative array:

```java
public void register(int code,ElementCreator creator) {
    creators.put(code, creator);
}
```

The `unregister()` method removes an association:

```java
public void unregister(int code) {
    creators.remove(code);
}
```

The `create()` method returns a new element based on a code:

```java
public Element create(int code) {
    ElementCreator creator = creators.get(code);
    if (creator != null) {
        return creator.create();
    }
    creator = creators.get(0);
    if (creator != null) {
        return creator.create();
    }
    throw new RuntimeException("Code not found");
}
```

If the creator of a code does not exist, the method returns code creator 0. Subsequently, we associate code 0 to the tile with a question mark. In doing so, if ever a bad code is introduced in a level, we avoid hanging the application and present the unknown tiles with the question mark. In the case where this code 0 is not associated, we are forced to throw an exception.

The static method `getDefault()` returns a default factory. It is not mandatory, and it is quite possible to create factories and their associations outside the `Factory` class. To add a creative class that implements the `ElementCreator` interface, we define a class on the fly for each code:

```java
public static ElementFactory getDefault() {
    ElementFactory factory = new ElementFactory();
    factory.register(0, new ElementCreator() {
        @Override
        public Element create() {
            return new Space(SpaceTypeId.UNKNOWN);
        }
    });
    factory.register(1, new ElementCreator() {
        @Override
        public Element create() {
            return new Space(SpaceTypeId.UNKNOWN);
        }
    });
    ... association of all codes ...
}
```

To exploit this factory, we add to the `World` class of the state a new `factory` attribute. The `factory` attribute is defined by a setter method.

A new `init()` method is also added:

```java
private ElementFactory factory;
public void init(int[][] level) {
  for (int y=0;y<height;y++) {
    for (int x=0;x<width;x++) {
      Element element = factory.create(level[y][x]);
      elements[x][y] = (StaticElement)element;
    }
  }
}
```

This method uses a native 2D array with the codes of the world, for example, the `level` array previously used. For each value in this array, the factory is used to produce the corresponding elements. It is worth noting that this procedure takes place without ever having to know the association between a code and an element.

To initialize the world is then very simple:

```java
World world = new World(9,6);
world.setFactory(ElementFactory.getDefault());
world.init(level);
```


4.2.1.2   Define the tileset (Flyweight Pattern)

Now that the state of the game is provided with data, you have to be able to choose a tile for each element. In the simple approach, we use a trick: there is a correspondence between the code and the position in the tileset. This trick is quite dangerous since it links the image of the tileset and the code that represents an element. If a graphic designer ever chooses to move or modify a tile in the tileset, the interpretation of the corresponding code must also be changed. Moreover, it assumes that there is always a perfect match (or bijection) between a tile and an element, which is not the case with animations.

Interface definition tile set

To provide access to information about a tileset, we define a `Tile` class that contains the information required to define a tile, and a `TileSet` interface that defines the tileset:

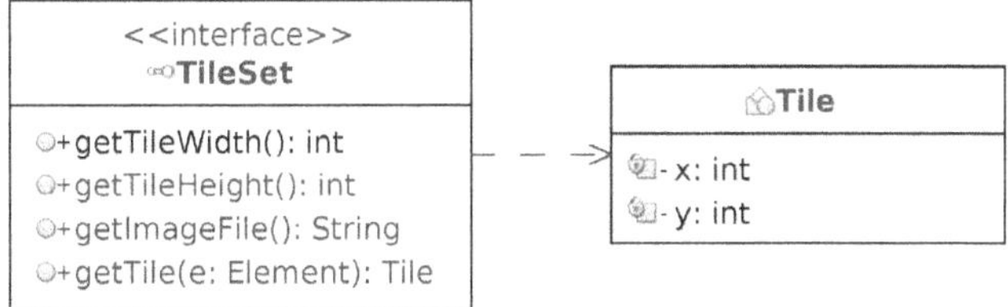

The `TileSet` interface contains the following methods:

- `getTileWidth()` and `getTileHeight()` methods: return the width and the height of a tile
- `getImageFile()` method: returns the name of the image file with the tile set
- `getTile()` method: returns the definition of a tile, as an instance of `Tile`, based on an element

This approach of abstracting the definition of a tileset is, once again, to divide the problems into subproblems. On the one hand, there is the one that implements the `TileSet` interface, and which focuses on its properties without having to know the levels to drawn. On the other hand, the user of these implementations focuses on the levels to draw without having to know the image to use or the positions of the tiles.

This approach can also be used to allow players to easily mod the game's graphics. For example, we can add a new method that loads a configuration file. This file contains the name of the image file and the definition of the tiles. An implementation of the `TileSet` interface loads and restores this information. It is also possible to mix predefined tile sets directly into the code, and tilesets defined by a configuration file. For the rendered part of the game, all this mechanics is transparent: there is nothing to modify in the drawing procedures, whatever the complexity.

Definition of the tileset for the world

We implement the interface above with the `GridTileSet` class to define the tileset for the world. The first three methods of the interface return the associated information: the tiles are 24 x 24 pixels, and the image is "grid_tiles.png":

```
public int getTileWidth() {
    return 24;
}
public int getTileHeight() {
    return 24;
}
public String getImageFile() {
    return "grid_tiles.png";
}
```

For the `getTile()` method, we use the Flyweight Pattern. Indeed, the definition of a tile has no reason to be modified by the user of the definitions: a tile for the horizontal wall is always at the same position in the image of the tileset. To implement this, we add two attributes to the `GridTileSet` class:

```
private Tile[] wallTiles;
private Tile[] spaceTiles;
```

The purpose of these tables is to memorize the tiles for walls and the tiles for spaces. They are initialized in the class constructor:

```
public GridTileSet() {
    wallTiles = new Tile[6];
    wallTiles[0] = new Tile(4,1);
    wallTiles[1] = new Tile(5,1);
    wallTiles[2] = new Tile(2,1);
    wallTiles[3] = new Tile(3,1);
    wallTiles[4] = new Tile(0,1);
    wallTiles[5] = new Tile(1,1);
    spaceTiles = new Tile[6];
    spaceTiles[0] = new Tile(0,0);
    spaceTiles[1] = new Tile(1,0);
    spaceTiles[2] = new Tile(2,0);
    spaceTiles[3] = new Tile(4,0);
    spaceTiles[4] = new Tile(1,0);
    spaceTiles[5] = new Tile(1,0);
}
```

With these definitions, for example, the horizontal wall tile is placed in `wallTiles[4]` and indicates that it is the first tile (0) of the second row (1) in the tile image.

This makes it possible to implement the getTile() method, which returns the definition of a tile according to an element. For example, if the e element is an instance of the Wall class, we convert the wall type to a numeric value using the getCode() method of the enumeration WallTypeId. Then we return the definition of the tile in the wallTiles array:

```java
public Tile getTile(Element e) {
    if (e instanceof Wall) {
        Wall wall = (Wall)e;
        int code = wall.getWallTypeId().getCode();
        if (code < wallTiles.length) {
            return wallTiles[code];
        }
    }
```

Similarly, if the e element is an instance of Space:

```java
    if (e instanceof Space) {
        Space space = (Space)e;
        int code = space.getSpaceTypeId().getCode();
        if (code < spaceTiles.length) {
            return spaceTiles[code];
        }
    }
```

By default, we return the very first tile of spaces - assuming that it contains a question mark:

```java
    return spaceTiles[0];
}
```

This method follows the Flyweight Pattern. It does not make a new instance of Tile on every call, which saves resources.

⇒ Note: It is possible to add attributes, constructors, and methods to enumerations in Java - this is a little known and quite valid practice. For example, to obtain a correspondence between the identifier of a wall and its code, we use the following implementation:

```java
public enum WallTypeId {
    TOPLEFT(0),TOPRIGHT(1),BOTTOMLEFT(2),BOTTOMRIGHT(3),
    HORIZONTAL(4),VERTICAL(5);

    private final int code;
    WallTypeId(int code) {
        this.code = code;
    }

    public int getCode() {
```

```
        return code;
    }
}
```

4.2.1.3   Draw the world contained in the game state

With the added features in the previous two sections, it becomes possible to draw.
We modify the PlayGameMode class, replacing all the attributes describing the world
with a simple reference to the game state, represented by the State class:

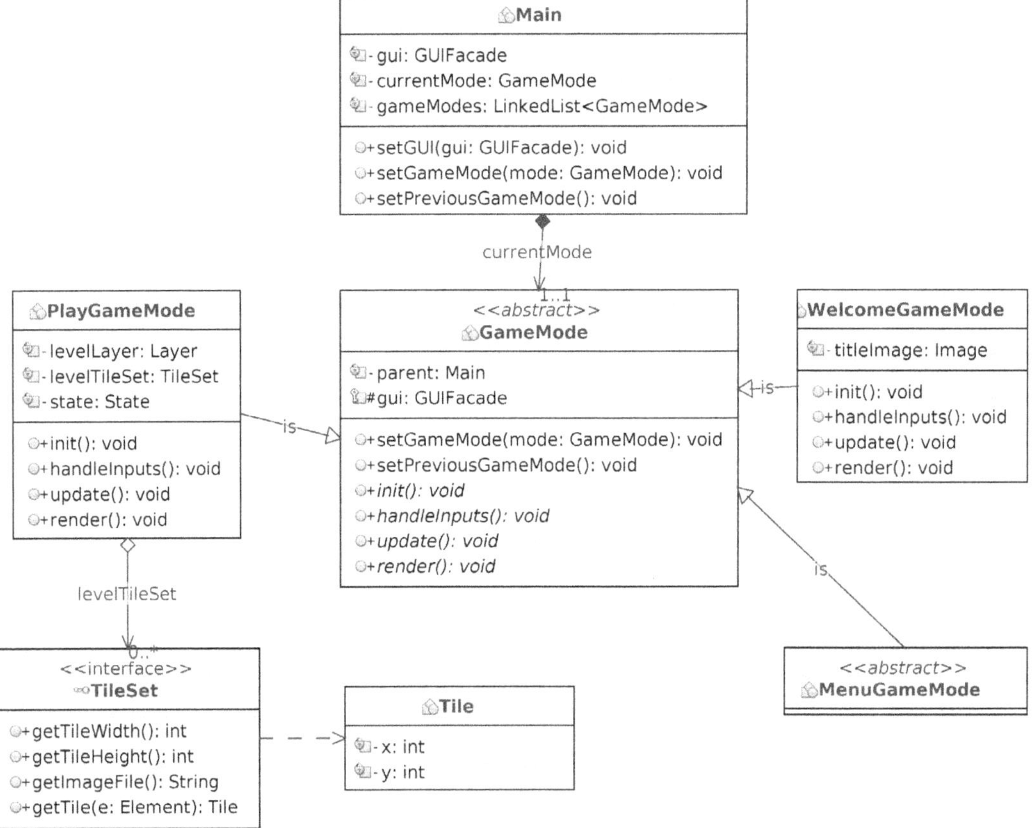

In the `PlayGameMode` constructor, we build a new world. We initialize it from a 2D level array:

```
public PlayGameMode() {
    World world = new World(9,6);
    world.setFactory(ElementFactory.getDefault());
    world.init(level);
```

Then, we create a state with this new world:

```
    state = new State();
    state.setWorld(world);
}
```

To test the drawing, we initialize the `levelLayer` with the elements of the game state. We start by building a definition of the tileset for the world:

```
public void init()
{
    levelTileSet = new GridTileSet();
```

Then, we make a layer for the world using the information from the tileset. The information previously statically placed in the code now depends on the object referenced by `levelTileSet`:

```
    levelLayer = gui.createLayer();
    levelLayer.setTileSize(levelTileSet.getTileWidth(),
        levelTileSet.getTileHeight());
    levelLayer.setTexture(levelTileSet.getImageFile());
```

The number of sprites in the layer is equal to the number of cells in the world:

```
    World world = state.getWorld();
    levelLayer.setSpriteCount(
        world.getWidth() * world.getHeight());
```

For the sprite positions, there are no changes. For the position of the tiles, we use the `getTile()` method of `levelTileSet`. The simple call to this method replaces the set of *ad hoc* calculations from the previous version. In addition, whatever strategy is followed to find the tile corresponding to an element, this part remains unchanged:

```
    for (int j = 0; j < world.getHeight(); j++) {
      for (int i = 0; i < world.getWidth(); i++) {
        int i = i + j * world.getWidth();
        levelLayer.setSpriteLocation(i,
          i * levelLayer.getTileWidth(),j * levelLayer.getTileHeight()
        );
        Element element = world.get(i, j, Direction.NONE);
        Tile tile = levelTileSet.getTile(element);
```

```
        levelLayer.setSpriteTexture(i,tile.getX(),tile.getY());
    }
}
```

The method ends with the creation of a window of the size of the drawn world:

```
gui.createWindow(world.getWidth()*levelLayer.getTileWidth(),
    world.getHeight()*levelLayer.getTileHeight(),
    "State and GUI Synchronization");
}
```

Once the program is launched, the world is visible on the screen:

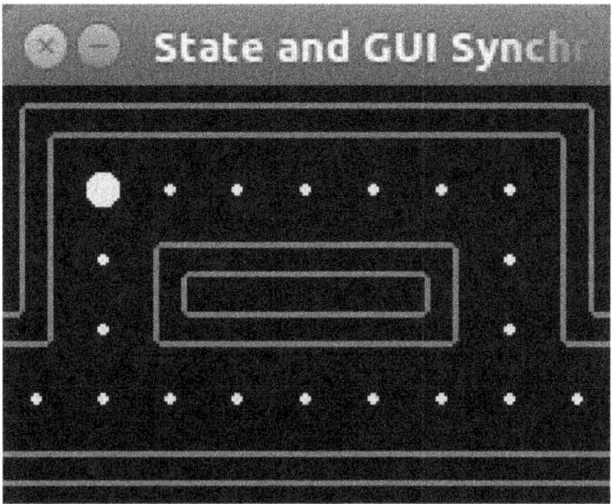

The diagrams in this example are available in the "Class Diagrams/chap04/draw01" folder of the sample UML project. The code is present in the "examples/chap04/draw01" folder of the sample Java project.

4.2.2 Displacement and Animations

4.2.2.1 Moving characters

A simple approach to movement management, as in the previous version of the Pacman game example, is to create attributes to memorize the position of the characters. These attributes are then immediately modified by the `handleInputs()` method of the Game Loop Pattern when an arrow is pressed.

With an approach with well-separated entities, the state of the game contains these positions. Besides, it is necessary to separate as much as possible the different components: the keyboard controls, the state of the game and the rendering. It is not desirable to immediately change positions in the game state when a key is pressed. Indeed, the evolution of the state of the game has its own pace, for example, 12 times per second in the example of the game Pacman. This rhythm is not necessarily that of changes in the state of the keyboard, so we must find a solution to manage these two aspects.

The possible solutions depend on the nature of the game developed and how the characters are moved. For the Pacman game, the characters are constantly heading in a given direction - provided they have direction. For example, if a character looks to the right, he moves continuously in that direction, as long as possible, even if no keys are pressed. This property can be used to separate the keyboard state from moving characters. For example, if the right arrow is detected as pressed in the `handleInputs()` method, the `direction` attribute of Pacman is immediately set to `Direction.EAST`. Then, at the next update of the game state in the `update()` method, the character's x coordinate is increased. In doing so, the movement of the characters is always in step with the changes of state of the game, and the changes of state of the keyboard can follow their tempo. For example, if between two updates, the left arrow is pressed and released, and the right arrow is pressed, then the character move to the right. Status changes of the left arrow are then nonexistent in this scenario.

⇒ Note that this kind of characters' movements is quite usual in video games. For instance, it is usual to click on a target position to order a character movement. The target position is similar to Pacman direction. The input handler can immediately set it, and later the rules engine performs the actual movements according to the target position.

Keyboard status management

The `handleInputs()` method is enriched to react to the state of the keyboard arrows. It starts with the acquisition of the d direction and the `pos` position of Pacman:

```java
public void handleInputs() {
    Keyboard keyboard = gui.getKeyboard();
    ... Escape key handling ...
    Characters chars = state.getChars();
    MobileElement me = chars.get(0);
    int pos = me.getPosition();
    Direction d = me.getDirection();
```

The value of `pos` is Pacman's position between two cells in the world. If it is zero, Pacman is exactly on a cell. Also, a character can only change direction if he is exactly on a cell, or if he wants to turn back. Knowing that, when the right key is pressed, and if the position is 0 or the current direction opposite, the direction of Pacman becomes `Direction.EAST`:

```java
    if (keyboard.isKeyPressed(KeyEvent.VK_RIGHT)) {
        if (pos == 0 || d == Direction.WEST) {
            me.setDirection(Direction.EAST);
        }
    }
```

The same reasoning is followed for the other three directions.

Movements in the Pacman game

The movement mechanics for the Pacman example game was chosen to minimize the number of possible coordinates in the world. This property brings several advantages, such as simplified management of collisions. The goal is to consider the characters as being on a world cell at coordinates (x, y), while smoothing this constraint with an intermediate position between two cells. Without the intermediate position, the characters would suddenly pass from one cell to another in their movements. In addition, it allows adjusting the speed with very accurate discrete states. To do this, we consider that a character moves from one cell to another when its intermediate position is equal to its speed.

For example, if the speed of Pacman is 2, the displacement corresponding to an entire cell is as follows:

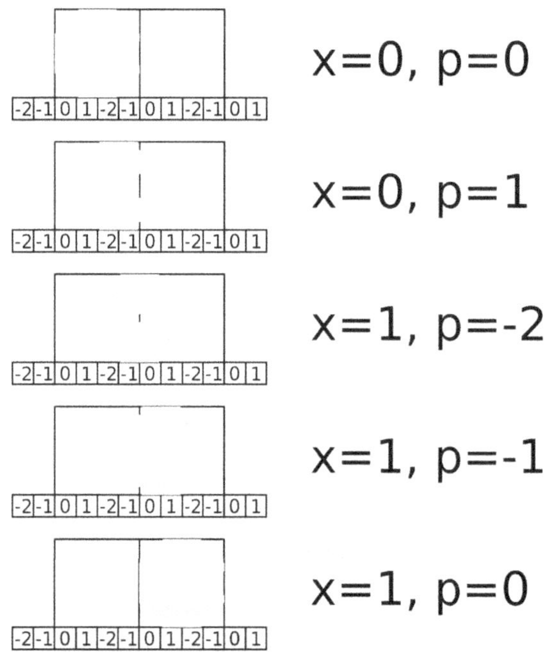

1. At startup, Pacman is on the cell at coordinate $x = 0$ and position $p = 0$;
2. After updating the state, the position is incremented and is 1. It is lower than the speed, Pacman is still on the cell $x = 0$;
3. After a second update of the state, the incremented position becomes equal to the speed 2. Pacman then crossed half of the cell: it is passed to the next cell of coordinates $x = 1$. The position takes the value -2, the opposite of the

speed. This comes down to saying that Pacman is halfway through the cell x = 1 on his left;
4. After a third update of the state, the position is incremented;
5. Finally, after a fourth update of the state, the position is incremented and takes the value 0. Pacman is then considered exactly on this cell.

This principle can be repeated on the following cells to the right, but also in all other directions.

⇒ Note: This mechanic can be used for all games whose characters move from one cell to another. It can be extended to diagonal movements, and is particularly interesting for hexagonal tile games since the distance between two adjacent cells is always the same. It can also be extended to three-dimensional worlds. Finally, it can be a source of inspiration for other mechanics. The main idea is finding a way to minimize the possible states while giving the illusion of a continuous world.

Update the state of the game

To update the state of the game, we start by ensuring that a twelfth of a second has elapsed, then we get the coordinates of Pacman:

```java
private long lastUpdate;
public void update() {
    long now = System.nanoTime();
    if ( (now - lastUpdate) >= 1000000000/12)
    {
        lastUpdate = now;
        World world = state.getWorld();
        Characters chars = state.getChars();
        MobileElement me = chars.get(0);
        Direction d = me.getDirection() ;
        int pos = me.getPosition();
        int x = me.getX();
        int y = me.getY();
```

It follows processing according to Pacman's direction. For the case Direction.EAST, the position pos is incremented:

```java
        switch(d) {
            case EAST:
                pos ++;
                if (pos == me.getSpeed()) {
                    x ++;
                    pos = -me.getSpeed();
                    if (x >= world.getWidth())
                        x = 0;
```

```
        }
    break;
```

If this position is equal to the speed of the character, it means that it has reached half the current cell *(x, y)*. We increment x, and the position pos takes as value the opposite of the speed of the character. The following test brings the character to the left if he leaves the world.

The other directions are managed similarly.

Pacman drawing according to the state

The Pacman drawing is done in the render() method. This rendering uses game state data to modify the charsLayer character layer:

```java
public void render() {
    Characters chars = state.getChars();
    MobileElement me = chars.get(0);
    int x = me.getX() * charsLayer.getTileWidth();
    int y = me.getY() * charsLayer.getTileHeight();
    Direction d = me.getDirection();
    if (d == Direction.EAST || d == Direction.WEST){
        x += (charsTileSet.getTileWidth()
            * me.getPosition()) / (2*me.getSpeed());
    }
    else if (d == Direction.NORTH || d == Direction.SOUTH) {
        y += (charsTileSet.getTileHeight()
            * me.getPosition()) / (2*me.getSpeed());
    }
    charsLayer.setSpriteLocation(i, x, y);
    Tile tile = charsTileSet.getTile(me);
    charsLayer.setSpriteTexture(i,tile.getX(), tile.getY());

    ... Layers rendering ...
}
```

The drawing coordinates of a character depend on the coordinates of its cell, as well as the intermediate position between two cells. We start by calculating the coordinate in pixels of the cell, for example, the coordinate x is equal to the coordinate of the cell me.getX() multiplied by the width in pixel of a cell:

```java
int x = me.getX() * charsLayer.getTileWidth();
```

Then, if Pacman looks to the right (Direction.EAST), the coordinate x is shifted to the right according to the ratio between the intermediate position me.getPosition() and the number of intermediate positions required for browse an entire cell, e.g., 2*me.getSpeed():

```
x += (charsTileSet.getTileWidth()
   * me.getPosition()) / (2*me.getSpeed());
```

This processing is a proportional rule:

Cell width (pixels)	2 x Character speed
Coordinate x	Intermediate position

Initialization of characters in the state

To initialize the characters at the start of the game, we also use the *level* array with
a modification: codes are used to represent the position of the characters at the
beginning of the game. For Pacman, the code is 21, and for ghosts from 22 to 25:

```
static final int[][] level = new int[][] {
    { 15,11,11,11,11,11,11,11,16 },{ 12,5,3,3,3,3,3,3,12 },
    { 12,3,15,11,11,11,16,3,12 },{ 14,3,13,11,11,11,14,3,13 },
    { 21,3,3,3,25,24,22,23,3 },{ 11,11,11,11,11,11,11,11,11 }
};
```

This trick also allows you to use a tile editor like "Tiled Map Editor" to easily
place the characters. The interpretation of these codes is different for the world
initialization method (World class) and for the characters (Characters class). For
the world, these codes are translated: for the code of Pacman, we place a space
cell with the starting position (SpaceTypeId.START). For ghost codes, we place a
space cell with a cemetery (SpaceTypeId.GRAVEYARD). It allows you to memorize
the starting position of Pacman and the place of resurrection of ghosts. For the
characters, the level is searched to find character codes. Depending on the case,
we add the character corresponding to the list:

```
public void init(int[][] level) {
    chars.clear();
    chars.add(new Pacman());
    for (int y=0;y<level.length;y++) {
        for (int x=0;x<level[y].length;x++) {
            int code = level[y][x];
            if (code == 21) {
                chars.get(0).setX(x);
                chars.get(0).setY(y);
            }
            else if (code >= 22 && code <= 25) {
                Ghost ghost = new Ghost(code-22);
                ghost.setX(x);
                ghost.setY(y);
                chars.add(ghost);
```

```
            }
         }
      }
}
```

⇒ Note: It is also possible to perform the same initialization with 2 separate arrays. Besides, with the "Tiled Map Editor" software, it is possible to define worlds with several layers and associated tilesets.

The diagrams in this example are available in the "Class Diagrams/chap04/draw02" folder of the sample UML project. The code is present in the "examples/chap04/draw02" folder of the sample Java project. This code also manages and draws all the characters. Also, the keys *F1* to *F5* allow us to choose the character to direct. Once all the characters have a direction, they are moving:

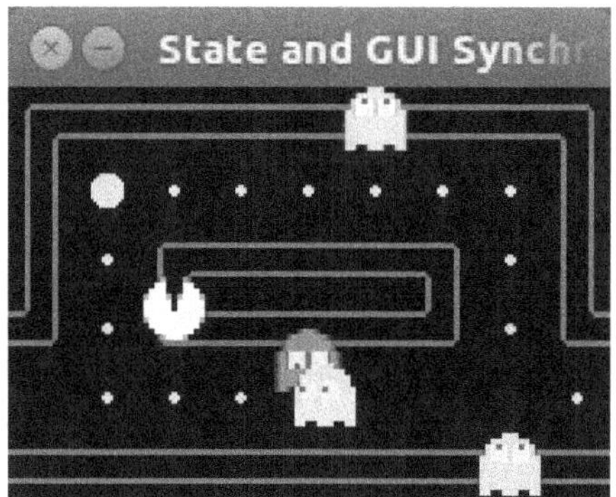

4.2.2.2 Animations (Composite Pattern)

Now, the goal is to restore the animations while using data from the state of the game. A first approach is to define a new class for animated tiles, then adapt the code to deal with either a static tile or the case of an animated tile. An interesting approach is to use the *Composite Pattern*: this one allows us to process a single element and a set of these elements indifferently. In doing so, only one class or interface is required for rendering, and there is no need to discuss between different tile cases.

The Composite pattern can be as follows:

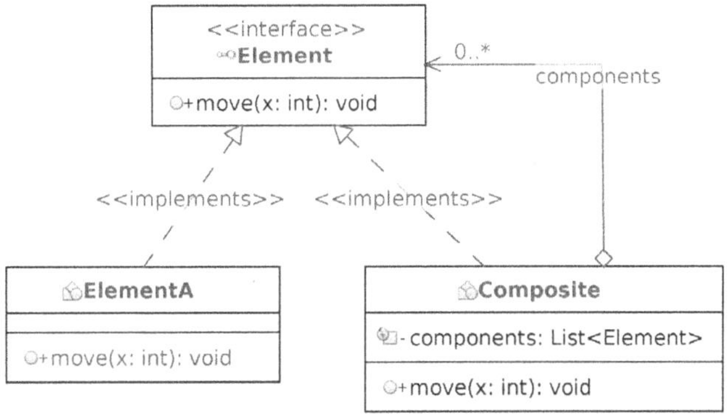

The `Element` interface represents possible interactions with the objects that one wishes to manipulate. In this example, there is a `move()` method that moves the element to a x position. The `ElementA` class is one of many implementations of the `Element` interface. The `Composite` class is a container of `Element`. In this illustration, the `components` attribute plays this role as a list - any other type of container is valid. The implementation of `Composite` class methods acts as if they were a simple element. For example, the `move()` `Composite` method moves all contained elements to the same position:

```java
public void move(int x) {
    for (Element e : composants) {
        e.move(x);
    }
}
```

The most common use of this pattern is in office software forms. Indeed, when moving a window with the mouse, the system only asks the window to change its position. It does not handle the fact that the window is a set of labels and buttons that each have their position. It is the window, as a composite element, that transmits the new coordinates to all its elements. We can also repeat this principle according to a hierarchy: a composite can contain composites.

Implementation for the tiles

We first separate rendering aspects in a `render` package for clarity, then we transform the `Tile` class into an interface:

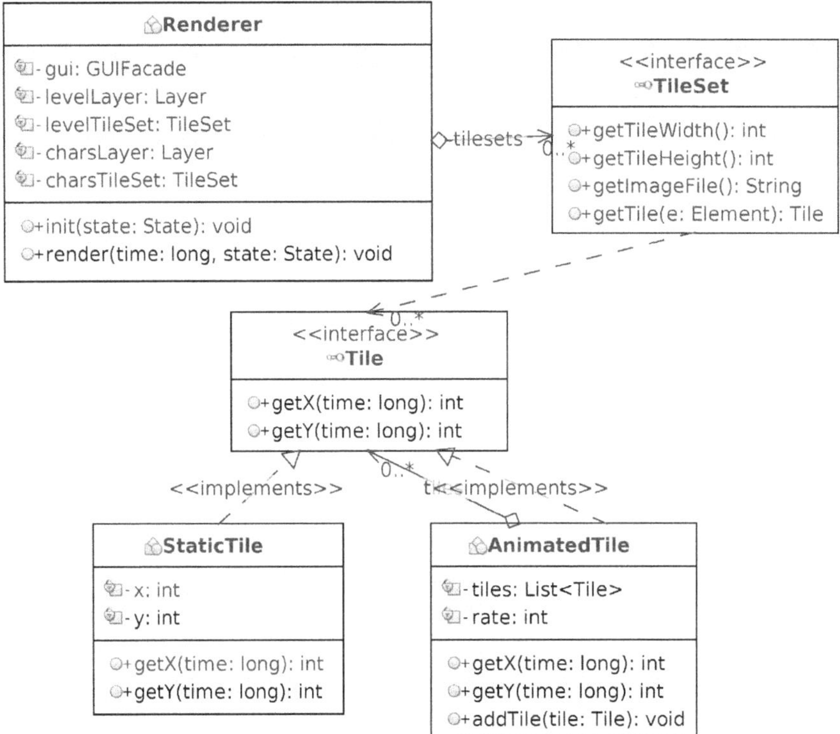

This approach allows to propose both static and animated tiles. Thus, its users do not have to worry about the exact nature of these tiles. Specifically, the `Tile` interface offers two `getX()` and `getY()` with a `time` argument. The returned coordinates depend on the current "time", which allows proposing tile coordinates that change regularly.

For the implementation of the `StaticTile` class, both methods always return the value of the `x` and `y` attributes. The `AnimatedTile` class has a `tiles` attribute that contains the list of tiles in an animation. It also has a `rate` attribute that sets the number of tile changes per second. Its methods compute the coordinates of the tile according to the current `time` and this `rate`. For example for the coordinates x:

```java
public int getX(long time) {
    time *= rate; time /= 1000000000;
    int i = (int)(time % tiles.size());
    return tiles.get(i).getX(time);
}
```

⇒ Note: In this implementation, the i of a tile in `tiles` is computed according to time. Then, the `getX()` method of this selected tile is called with the current `time`. In most cases, this selected tile is static: the `time` argument is ignored. Note that it is possible to place animated tiles in animated tiles and thus make combinations of animations.

Defining animations in tile set

The definition of animated tiles is very simple. For example, in the `CharsTileSet` class, the code for the Pacman character who looks to the right:

```
pacmanTiles[3] = new Tile(6,1);
```

is replaced by the following:

```
AnimatedTile animatedTile = new AnimatedTile(6);
animatedTile.addTile(new StaticTile(4,1));
animatedTile.addTile(new StaticTile(6,1));
animatedTile.addTile(new StaticTile(3,3));
animatedTile.addTile(new StaticTile(6,1));
pacmanTiles[3] = animatedTile;
```

Using animated tiles

The use of animated tiles is even easier. Just proceed as before, with the difference that the `getTile()` method of a tileset is called with the current "time" (here contained in the `time` variable):

```
World world = state.getWorld();
for (int j = 0; j < world.getHeight(); j++) {
    for (int i = 0; i < world.getWidth(); i++) {
        int i = i + j * world.getWidth();
        Element element = world.get(i, j, Direction.NONE);
        Tile tile = levelTileSet.getTile(element);
        levelLayer.setSpriteTexture(i,
            tile.getX(time),tile.getY(time));
    }
}
```

To see the animations with the current implementation, it is necessary to update the sprites for all the images to be displayed, within the `render()` method of the Game Loop pattern.

The diagrams in this example are available in the "Class Diagrams/chap04/draw03" folder of the sample UML project. The code is present in the "examples/chap04/draw03" folder of the sample Java project. This code also includes all the rendering code displacement in the Renderer class.

4.2.3 Separate state and rendering

4.2.3.1 Make independent animations (Observer Pattern)

The design in its current implementation suffers from a big defect: the rendering draws using the data in the game state at the refresh rate of the screen. It implies that the game state can not be changed during the rendering, and prohibits taking advantage of a slower update for further processing. It also prohibits parallel processing by multiple cores of the processor.

Renderer with independent animations

One solution is to reproduce for the animations what was done for the layers and the static tiles, using rendering data independent from game state data. To achieve this, we define two new LayerElement and Animation classes, and a new animations attribute in the Renderer class:

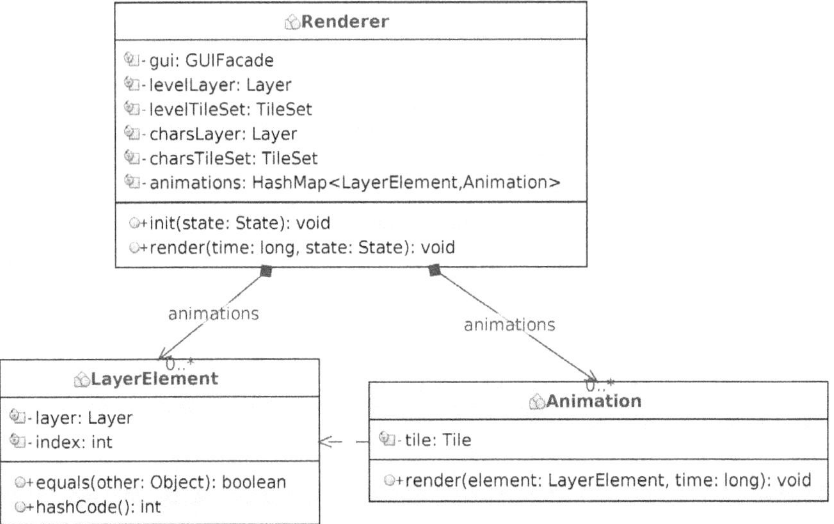

The animations attribute is an associative array that, to a specific tile within a layer, matches an animation. It makes it possible to list the animated tiles, but also to quickly find those who are already listed.

The purpose of the LayerElement class is to identify a layer and a tile within that layer. The equals() and hashCode() methods are implemented to allow this class to be used as a key in an associative array by hash function:

```java
public boolean equals(Object other) {
    if (other == null)
        return false;
    if (!(other instanceof LayerElement))
        return false;
    LayerElement element = (LayerElement)other;
    if (this.layer != element.layer)
        return false;
    if  (this.i != element.i)
        return false;
    return true;
}
public int hashCode() {
    return layer.hashCode() + i;
}
```

The Animation class aims to store a tile with the `tile` attribute, and then draw it with the `render()` method:

```java
public void render(LayerElement element,long time) {
    Layer layer = element.getLayer();
    int i = element.getIndex();
    layer.setSpriteTexture(i,tile.getX(time),tile.getY(time));
}
```

Once the `animations` array of the Renderer class is filled with the animated tiles, simply replace in the `render()` method the code using the game state with the following one:

```java
for (Map.Entry<LayerElement, Animation> entry :
    animations.entrySet()) {
    LayerElement element = entry.getKey();
    Animation animation = entry.getValue();
    animation.render(element,time);
}
```

With this approach, the complete rendering, animations included, does not depend anymore on the state of the game: the latter can be modified freely without impacting the display.

Updating the list of animations (Observer Pattern)

The list of animations in the Renderer class can be changed at the end of each game state update by browsing through all of its data. For games whose state is very large, this can lead to a very high consumption of resources. To overcome this problem, the Observer Pattern can be used. Unlike the case in the previous chapter, the observed part is implemented.

The idea is to consider the state of the game as an observed element, and the rendering engine as an observer element. A new `StateObserver` interface is defined with the methods corresponding to the notifications. The `State` class has a new `observers` attribute with the list of its observers, as well as the pattern methods:

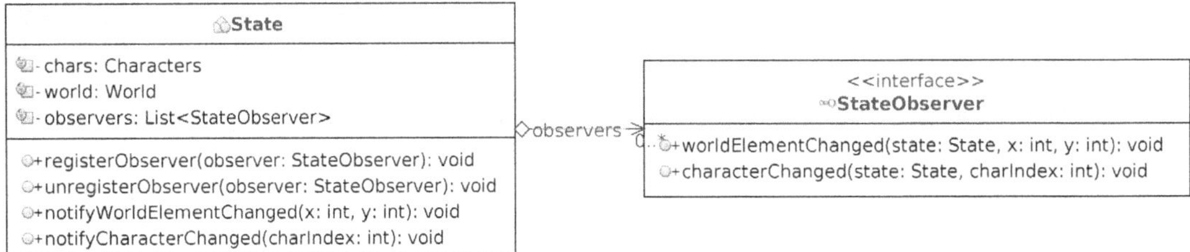

For notifications two methods have been defined:

- The `worldElementChanged()` method, which notifies the change of an element of the world at the coordinates *(x,y)*;
- The `characterChanged()` method, which notifies the change of a character.

The `registerObserver()` and `unregisterObserver()` methods add and remove an observer:

```java
public void registerObserver(StateObserver obs) {
    observers.add(obs);
}
public void unregisterObserver(StateObserver obs) {
    observers.remove(obs);
}
```

The `notifyWorldElementChanged()` and `notifyCharacterChanged()` methods pass their respective notifications to all observers:

```java
public void notifyWorldElementChanged(int x,int y) {
    for (StateObserver observer : observers) {
        observer.worldElementChanged(this, x, y);
    }
}
public void notifyCharacterChanged(int charIndex) {
    for (StateObserver observer : observers) {
        observer.characterChanged(this, charIndex);
    }
}
```

Rendering with Observer pattern

The Renderer class implements the StateObserver interface to react to notifications:

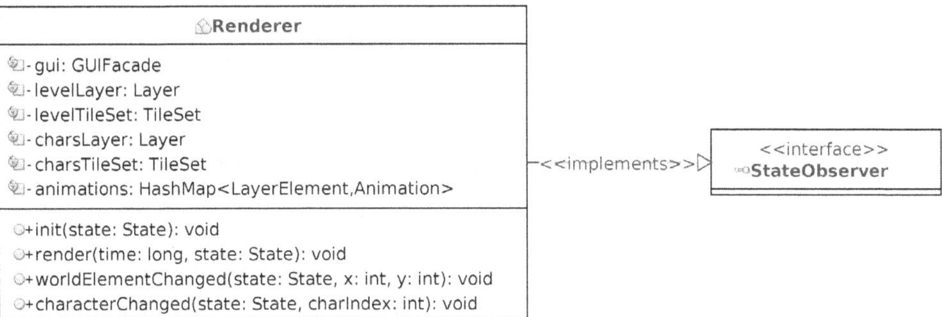

The worldElementChanged() method starts by retrieving the element in the cell *(x, y)* of the world:

```
public void worldElementChanged(State state,int x, int y) {
    World world = state.getWorld();
    int i = x + y * world.getWidth();
    StaticElement se = world.get(x, y, Direction.NONE);
```

Then, we use the definition of the tileset levelTileSet to get the corresponding tile.

```
    Tile tile = levelTileSet.getTile(se);
```

There are two possibilities: either the tile is static, or it is animated. For the static case, it is enough to modify the texture:

```
    if (tile instanceof StaticTile) {
        levelLayer.setSpriteTexture(i,tile.getX(0),tile.getY(0)
        );
```

Besides, if the tile in the layer was previously in the list of animated tiles, it is removed:

```
        LayerElement element = new LayerElement(levelLayer,i);
        animations.remove(element);
    }
```

For the case of an animated tile, we add a new instance of the Animation class in the list of animated tiles:

```
    else {
        LayerElement element = new LayerElement(levelLayer,i);
        Animation animation = animations.get(element);
        if (animation == null) {
```

```java
        animation = new Animation();
        animations.put(element,animation);
    }
    animation.setTile(tile);
    }
}
```

For the `characterChanged()` method, we also start by finding the selected character, and then we add its animated tile in the list of animated tiles:

```java
public void characterChanged(State state,int charIndex) {
    Characters chars = state.getChars();
    MobileElement me = chars.get(charIndex);
    Tile tile = charsTileSet.getTile(me);
    LayerElement element =
        new LayerElement(charsLayer,charIndex);
    Animation animation = animations.get(element);
    if (animation == null) {
        animation = new Animation();
        animations.put(element,animation);
    }
    animation.setTile(tile);
```

The rest of the method focuses on the position of the tile of the character who, unlike the elements of the world, is not static. The computation is the same as the one previously done in the `render()` method. The difference lies in the timing of this computation: in this case, it is done during the notification:

```java
    Direction d = me.getDirection();
    int x = me.getX() * charsLayer.getTileWidth();
    int y = me.getY() * charsLayer.getTileHeight();
    if (d == Direction.EAST || d == Direction.WEST) {
        x += (charsTileSet.getTileWidth()
            * me.getPosition()) / (2*me.getSpeed());
    }
    else if (d == Direction.NORTH || d == Direction.SOUTH) {
        y += (charsTileSet.getTileHeight()
            * me.getPosition()) / (2*me.getSpeed());
    }
    charsLayer.setSpriteLocation(charIndex, x, y);
}
```

Triggering notifications

The only thing left now is to choose when to trigger notifications. The most common approach is to ask the observed to trigger these notifications. It can be very convenient for the user but can lead to unnecessary notifications. For example, if a notification is generated for each state mutator (*setter*), the same notification may be triggered several times. For example, in the `update()` method of the Game Loop pattern, we update the position and coordinates of a character:

```
me.setPosition(pos);
me.setX(x);
me.setY(y);
```

If each setter triggers a notification, then three identical notifications are sent. It is why a user notification of the observed class is chosen here. For example, once a character is fully modified for the current epoch, only one notification is triggered manually:

```
state.notifyCharacterChanged(i);
```

The `update()` method is identical to the previous one, except for this new line.

The diagrams in this example are available in the "Class Diagrams/chap04/draw04" folder of the sample UML project.   The code is present in the "examples/chap04/draw04" folder of the sample Java project.

4.2.3.2 Interpolate displacements

This section introduces advanced notions that beginners can ignore.

The previous solution allows us to get animations with a free refresh rate. It is not the case for the movement of the characters, who remain at the frequency of updating the state of the game. To get smooth motion at the refresh rate of the screen, one solution is to interpolate the position of the moving elements between two status updates.

For example, in online role-playing games, when you play a magician who throws a fireball, you see on the screen a beautiful ball of fire that moves with perfect fluidity towards its target. In fact, at the level of the state of the game, and more specifically on the side of the game server, the fireball is not moved so smoothly. In many cases, there is not even an intermediate step. For the server, the fireball is at the magician's location when it's launched, and after several state updates, it's on target. Specifically, when the magician launches the fireball on a target at time t, the server receives and validates that command. It deduces that, depending on the distance to the target and the speed of the fireball, it will arrive at its destination at time $t + dt$. Once reached the time $t + dt$, if the target still exists and validates conditions, it suffers the effects of the fireball. The conditions to validate depend on the cases: if it's magic, then the fireball follows the targets like a homing missile. In the case where the fireball must advance in a straight line, the server can check if, at the time of impact, the fireball is still in the direction of the target. Other cases can also be imagined, depending on the nature of the rules of the game.

Whatever the situation, the visible trajectory is a pure illusion, and can offer a pleasant visual experience, while meeting the constraints of latency and updates of the state of the game.

Interpolated rendering of displacements

To illustrate this approach, the movements of Pacman characters are interpolated between two updates. We add new arguments to the render() method of the Animation class, and we set a MobileAnimation class to handle interpolation:

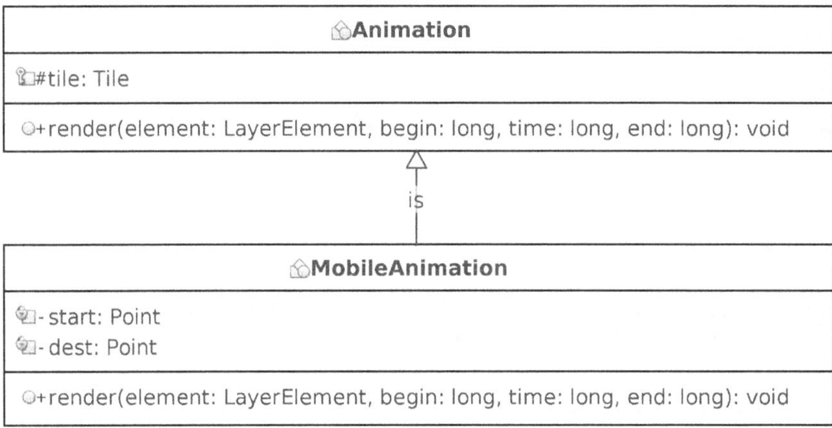

The goal of the render() method of the MobileAnimation class is to draw a tile between start coordinates at begin time and destination coordinates at end time:

```
public void render(LayerElement element,
    long begin, long time, long end) {
    super.render(element,begin,time,end);
    double step = time - begin;
    step /= end - begin;
    int dx = (int) ((dest.x - start.x) * step);
    int dy = (int) ((dest.y - start.y) * step);
    Layer layer = element.getLayer();
    int i = element.getIndex();
    layer.setSpriteLocation(i, start.x+dx, start.y+dy);
}
```

The method starts by calling the parent class to update the sprite's texture:

```
super.render(element,begin,time,end);
```

Then, it computes the coordinate shift (dx,dy) in the direction between the starting coordinates (start.x,start.y) and the ending coordinates (dest.x,dest.y). The offset amount, stored in the `step` variable, is the ratio between the time elapsed since the beginning of the move (`time - begin`) and the total time of the move (`end - begin`):

```
double step = time - begin;
step /= end - begin;
int dx = (int) ((dest.x - start.x) * step);
int dy = (int) ((dest.y - start.y) * step);
```

Finally, the coordinates of the tile in the layer are updated:

```
Layer layer = element.getLayer();
int i = element.getIndex();
layer.setSpriteLocation(i, start.x+dx, start.y+dy);
```

Computation of initial and final coordinates of a displacement

To exploit this new feature, the animation part in the `characterChanged()` method of the `Renderer` class is updated. We start with the simple case where there is no direction. For this one, the starting and ending position of the movement is the same, namely the current position of the character:

```
Direction d = me.getDirection();
if (d == Direction.NONE) {
    int x = me.getX() * charsLayer.getTileWidth();
    int y = me.getY() * charsLayer.getTileHeight();
    animation.setStart(new Point(x,y));
    animation.setDest(new Point(x,y));
}
```

Then, for cases where the character has a direction, we start by calculating the destination coordinates. The calculation is the same as the one used until now:

```
else {
    int x = me.getX() * charsLayer.getTileWidth();
    int y = me.getY() * charsLayer.getTileHeight();
    if (d == Direction.EAST || d == Direction.WEST) {
        x += (charsTileSet.getTileWidth()
            * me.getPosition()) / (2*me.getSpeed());
    }
    else if (d == Direction.NORTH || d == Direction.SOUTH) {
        y += (charsTileSet.getTileHeight()
            * me.getPosition()) / (2*me.getSpeed());
    }
    animation.setDest(new Point(x,y));
```

For start coordinates, we use the current coordinates of sprite on the screen. Another solution is to use the coordinates of the previous state. This other solution is not interesting, since it is necessary to calculate or save the coordinates of the previous state, and this can result in some cases of small jumps in the display. With the current display coordinates as a starting point, we get smooth moves. To get these coordinates, a `getSpriteLocation()` convenience method has been added to the facade:

```java
Point displayLocation =
    charsLayer.getSpriteLocation(charIndex);
```

The following code section is specific to Pacman, and games whose scenery repeats itself to infinity. Indeed, if a character arrives for example on the far right of the world, he is immediately "teleported" on the other side. Without special processing for this case, we would observe the characters move at full speed from one side to the other:

```java
World world = state.getWorld();
int worldWidth = world.getWidth()
                * charsTileSet.getTileWidth();
if (Math.abs(displayLocation.x-x)
    > charsTileSet.getTileWidth() ) {
    if (displayLocation.x < 0)
        displayLocation.x += worldWidth;
    else
        displayLocation.x -= worldWidth;
}
int worldHeight = world.getHeight()
                * charsTileSet.getTileHeight();
if (Math.abs(displayLocation.y-y)
    > charsTileSet.getTileHeight() ) {
    if (displayLocation.y < 0)
        displayLocation.y += worldHeight;
    else
        displayLocation.y -= worldHeight;
}
```

Finally, we transmit the starting position to the animation:

```java
animation.setStart(displayLocation);
}
```

Rendering

To invoke the rendering of the scene, it is necessary to define a notion of time for the beginning and the end of the movements. The "time" of the last update is stored in a `beginEpoch` attribute, and the end computed with the duration of an update (or epoch) of the game state. We increment an `epoch` attribute in the `State` class after each update to determine the "time" of the game state:

```java
private int lastEpoch = -1;
private long beginEpoch = 0;
public void render(long time) {
    if (state.getEpoch() != lastEpoch) {
        lastEpoch = state.getEpoch();
        beginEpoch = System.nanoTime();
    }
    renderer.render(beginEpoch,time,
        beginEpoch+state.getEpochDuration(),state);
}
```

These computations are not optimal for perfect synchronization - as for many other points in the current code. A more precise approach is presented in the next chapter.

The diagrams in this example are available in the "Class Diagrams/chap04/draw05" folder of the sample UML project. The code is present in the "examples/chap04/draw05" folder of the sample Java project. In the version of this code, the frequency of updating the state of the game is voluntarily very low (2 per second), to allow us to see the effects of the interpolation.

4.2.4 Exercices

4.2.4.1 Exercise 2.4.1: Build a galaxy

The goal of this exercise is to build a galaxy with its systems and planets from a text representation, such as a `String` array:

```java
public static String[] data = {
    "System", "Alpha","Habitable", "Alpha1","Gaseous", "Alpha2",
        "End","System", "Beta","Gaseous", "Beta1",
        "Gaseous", "Beta2","Gaseous", "Beta3","End",
    "System", "Gamma","Habitable", "Gamma1","End","End"
};
```

The shape of the galaxy is that of the previous exercise in **Chapter 2**. It is possible to start from the solution classes of this exercise in the `examples.chap02.stellaris` package.

→ Propose a solution that does not depend on the different possible types of planets. It must be possible to add new types of planets during program execution.

4.2.4.2 Exercise 2.4.2: Move an army

The goal here is to be able to move an entire army of units. We assume that there is a hierarchy of classes to represent the units. For this exercise, one or two types of units are sufficient. The only feature of these units considered here is the position (x, y) of these units, as well as a method that moves these units in one direction.

→ Propose a solution with groups of units, able to move all the units they contain. These groups must be able to be handled as if they were a single unit, and must be able to contain subgroups.

4.2.5 Video game development: state rendering

→ Fill in your game state with test data:

To be able to test the rendering of a game state, you need a state with data. The nature of this data depends on your game. It may be necessary to create multiple datasets. These game states do not necessarily correspond to played states. For example, to test the display of all possible tiles or all possible characters, it is necessary to create a state of the game that presents all these possibilities. Carefully record these states.

→ Design a rendering independent of game state data:

This work corresponds to the one followed in the Pacman game example with layers: they have a list of sprites disconnected from the state. Same for animations or displacements. In the final solution, these representations are updated with the game state data. During the development process, and in some cases, it is possible to test these representations without data from the state. Just like other validation elements, carefully record this code, even if it is not used in the final version of the game.

→ Design the data conversion from state to rendering representations:

The exercise is similar to the one done to defines tiles in the Pacman game. This one is extended for the case of animations. The nature of the tools depends on the nature of your state and your rendering representations. For example, if your game display is three-dimensional, an element of the state should lead to the creation of 3D meshes in your rendering engine. If these processes are quite complex, it is also advisable to produce carefully recorded validation tests.

→ Synchronize state and rendering:

Once you have the elements allowing the conversion of data from the state to the rendering, it only remains to orchestrate it respecting the independence of each component. It is at this level that the Observer pattern is able to play its role. For validation tests, it is quite difficult to automate them, since they rely on the feeling of fluidity felt when watching the game running.

→ Bonus: add primary controls and moves

This step is not essential at this stage of development and can be impossible or unnecessarily complex for some games in the absence of a rules engine (presented in the next section). If it is feasible, you can add some controls to test the displacement of the characters. For the more experienced readers, it is also possible to test the interpolation of displacements.

4.3 Game rules

4.3.1 Define the rules of the game

Now that the game state and rendering engine are connected, all we have to do is design a rules engine, and then connect it to form a complete solution. Before starting the design of this engine, it is strongly recommended, as for the state, to put on paper the different rules of the game. This step could have been done at the same time as the definition of the state - it is proposed later in this book to avoid introducing too many notions from the beginning.

Ideally, this description of the rules must be precise, without being too much like an algorithm. Very important choices are made at this level; it is very important to take the time to think. About the form, the mechanics linked to the commands must appear. For example, the type of order that can give a player or an AI. It can be the command of moving a character or changing the properties of a building, etc. Be careful; the origin of these commands is not of interest here. For example, the fact that you have to press a key or click in a specific place is not considered in this step. We ignore these origins, and we assume that these commands are produced from the user interface, an AI or the network.

Some events have no external origin. For example, in a game with gold mines, gold is added to the treasure at the end of each turn. This operation is not necessarily triggered by the user, who does not necessarily need to click on each mine to harvest the mined gold. For these cases, we consider passive commands, triggered systematically at each update of the game, without the intervention of a player or an AI. The relevance of this category of command can be questioned. Indeed, it may seem easier to perform all passive operations via calls to methods. However, with such an approach, you lose control of the flow of changes, as well as the functionality that results from a command-based approach, such as rolling back or recording a *replay*. Besides, by dividing the modifications into different classes, we gain once again in clarity and independence between components. With passive commands, we control on one side the command and the calls, and on the other, the nature of the modifications.

A textual description usually describes well these rules and commands. To be more precise, there are solutions in the UML world, such as activity diagrams. They allow to describe visually and very precisely a succession of actions, with or without conditions.

This book is not about game design, and in case a game with complex rules is developed, it is advisable to learn about the subject. For the simplest games, a naive approach is enough. In all cases, it is imperative to go through this step before starting the software design and programming, at the risk of having to rewrite everything if the rules have not been a minimum thought in advance!

4.3.2　Example of rules definitions

This section presents an example of rules definitions for the Pacman game.

4.3.2.1　Global clock

The changes of state follow a global clock: regularly, the current state is updated automatically. There is no notion of an intermediate state. These changes are calibrated on time it takes for a mobile element at maximum speed to move from one cell to another. As a result, all movements have a velocity that depends on this unitary time element.

4.3.2.2　External changes

External changes are caused by external commands, such as keypress or network packets:

- Initialize the world: the state is initialized with a default world
- Load a level: the state is initialized with a world described in a file
- Define the direction of a character: the direction of a character is changed. This change is only accepted if the movement is possible. For ghosts, turning around is forbidden, to get control of ghosts by humans more fun. This command does not move the character.

4.3.2.3　Autonomous changes

The following commands are considered:

- Move a character: if the character's direction exists, and there is no wall, then the character is moved in his direction. To do this, it increments (or decrements) its position. If this is equal to the speed of the character, we modify the corresponding coordinates, and we bring the position to the opposite value. If the character comes out of the screen, we move it to the opposite side, thus giving the illusion that the world is infinitely folded back on itself.
- Watch if Pacman can eat a gum: if it is the case, the gum is transformed into an empty space, and the gum counter is decremented. If the gum is a super gum, then Pacman takes super status, and all ghosts in hunting status go into fleeing status. The status time of all characters switches to a value defined in the state (default 100).
- Manage collisions: Pacman's coordinates are compared to the coordinates of each ghost (position is ignored). If there is collision, different cases are possible:
    - If the ghost is in "eyes" status, nothing happens.
    - If the ghost is in "fleeing" status, it goes into eye status, and its status time is reduced to 0.
    - If the ghost is in hunting status, Pacman goes into dead status. The ghost status time changes to 0, and the Pacman status time is calibrated to the time of the death animation.
- Update a character's status times: If the character status time is greater than 0, it is decremented. If it goes to 0, different cases are possible:
    - If the character is Pacman, and Pacman is in super status, then Pacman goes into normal status.
    - If the character is a ghost, and the ghost is in fleeing status, then the ghost goes into hunting status.
- Resurrection of a ghost: If the coordinates of a ghost in eye status are on a graveyard, then its status becomes a hunt and its status time changes to 0.

These autonomous changes are applied to each creation or update of the game state after external changes. They are executed in the following order:

1. Move Pacman
2. Watch if Pacman can eat a gum
3. Manage collisions
4. Update Pacman status time
5. For each ghost: move, update status time, and resurrect if possible
6. Manage collisions

Collision management is repeated before and after moving ghosts: this avoids the cases where each character moves from one cell to another at the same time.

4.3.2.4 Game over

The game ends if:

- The gum counter goes to 0
- Pacman is in dead status, and his status time is 0

4.3.3 Apply the rules (Command Pattern)

4.3.3.1 Command Pattern

To transform the user's actions into a state change, we use the *Command Pattern*. The main idea behind this pattern is to separate the origin of the modifications from their implementation. For example, in the Pacman game, if a user presses the right arrow on the keyboard, the position of the Pacman character in the game state is not directly changed. A command is first produced, and more precisely, a command that indicates that we want to change the direction of the Pacman character to the right. Then, at the moment chosen by a rules engine, the modification of the character is implemented.

This type of approach allows, once again, to divide and conquer: on the one hand, the user interface manages the various controls and the associated orders; on the other hand, the rules engine receives and processes formal commands. The pattern also offers other benefits. For example, commands can be produced by a source other than the user interface, such as an artificial intelligence or network packets. In any case, the rules engine works in the same way, whatever the origin of the commands. Another advantage is scheduling changes. Indeed, the commands can be executed later, or executed in another order than that of their creation.

There are several ways to implement these principles; here is the most common:

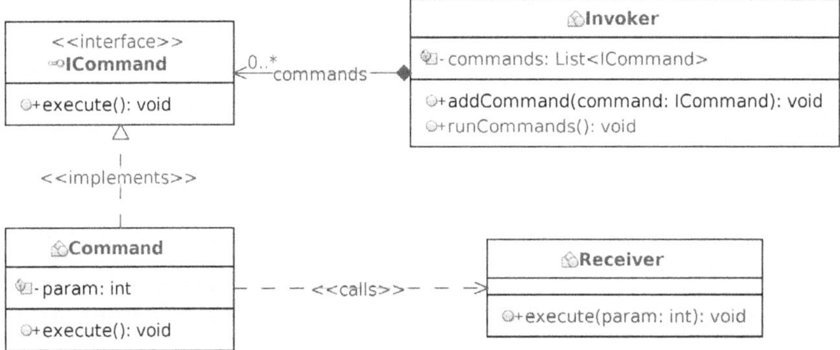

The first salient features of the pattern are the `ICommand` interface and its different implementations, for example, here the `Command` class. The interface defines how a command can be executed. In the most usual case, it's a simple method without arguments, like the `execute()` method above. Then, the primary role of the implementations of this interface is to contain the elements relating to a command.

For example, when moving a character into a game, you can find a way to identify the character and the direction or destination coordinates. In a building game, one can imagine a command whose attributes are the building to be built and its location.

Through the methods of the interface, as here the `execute()` method, it is possible to request the execution of a command. In the simplest case, changes can be made directly by the command class. In more advanced cases, this task is dedicated to a third party, represented by the `Receiver` class in the diagram above. The idea behind this division is to separate the information (the command) from the processing (the receiver). There may be more than one receiving class, especially when tasks are complex or numerous.

The last element is the summoner, represented by the `Invoker` class in the diagram. This one has two roles: memorize commands and execute them. In the example above, the commands are stored in the `commands` list, but other types of containers can be used. The invoker is controlled by a client who, when he wants to add a command, uses the `addCommand()` method. Then, when the client deems it necessary, the `runCommands()` method executes all the stored commands and then deletes them.

4.3.3.2 Initialize the game with a command

To present a first illustration of the command pattern, the Pacman example game is modified. We start by creating a new `Rules` class in a new `rules` package as an invoker:

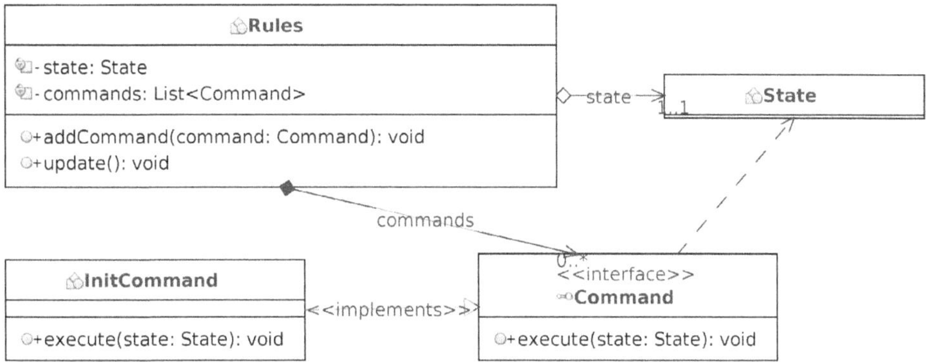

The `Rules` class is similar to the `Invoker` class in the previous diagram, to which a `state` attribute is added. This attribute allows continuous access to the game state. The `Command` interface has an `execute()` method with a `state` argument: the idea is to start with the simplest case of the Command pattern, where the commands directly modify the data.

A single `InitCommand` command is presented. Its role is to initialize the state with a default world, as has been the case so far:

```java
public class InitCommand implements Command {
    static final int[][] level = new int[][] {
        { 15,11,11,11,11,11,11,11,16 },{ 12,5,3,3,3,3,3,3,12 },
        { 12,3,15,11,11,11,16,3,12 },
        { 14,3,13,11,11,11,14,3,13 },{ 21,3,3,3,25,24,22,23,3 },
        { 11,11,11,11,11,11,11,11,11 }
    };
    public void execute(State state) {
        World world = new World(9,6);
        world.setFactory(ElementFactory.getDefault());
        world.init(level);

        Characters chars = new Characters();
        chars.init(level);

        state.setWorld(world);
        state.setChars(chars);
        state.notityStateChanged();
    }
}
```

The initialization operations, previously present in the `PlayGameMode` class, have been moved to this class.

A `rules` attribute is added to the `PlayGameMode` class: it has only three main attributes: game state, rendering engine, and rules engine:

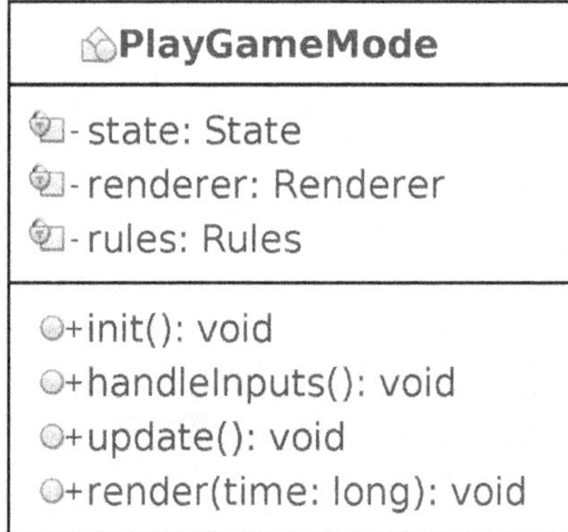

The `PlayGameMode` class is also simplified: there is no more constructor, and the `init()` method is reduced to the following operations:

```java
public void init()
```

```
{
    state = new State();
    renderer = new Renderer(gui);
    state.registerObserver(renderer);
    rules = new Rules(state);
    rules.addCommand(new InitCommand());
    rules.update();
}
```

As far as initialization is concerned, the `PlayGameMode` class is now limited to a series of calls to creation methods. The other actors manage all the internal mechanics.

To use the pattern, an `InitCommand` command is built when the backspace key is pressed. This operation is added to the list of key presses in the `handleInputs()` method:

```
case KeyEvent.VK_BACK_SPACE:
    rules.addCommand(new InitCommand());
    break;
```

Finally, the commands are executed through the call of the `update` method of the `Rules` class, at the end of the update of the state in the `update()` method of the `PlayGameMode` class.

These changes lead to similar behavior of the game Pacman, except the backspace key, which allows resetting the state of the game.

The diagrams in this example are available in the "Class Diagrams/chap04/command01" folder of the sample UML project. The code is present in the "examples/chap04/command01" folder of the sample Java project.

4.3.3.3 Move characters with commands

We are now interested in moving the characters. We consider two commands: the first modifies the direction of a character, and the second moves a character:

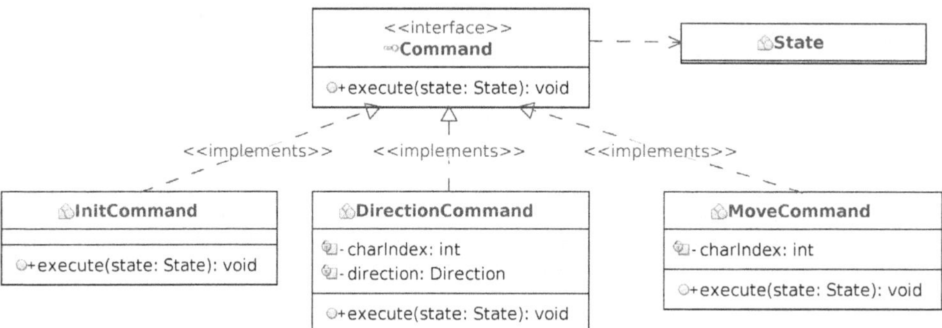

Direction command

The `DirectionCommand` class contains two pieces of information: the character's `charIndex` and the new `direction`. This command is made by the user interface when an arrow is pressed within the `handleInputs()` method of the `PlayGameMode` class:

```java
if (keyboard.isKeyPressed(KeyEvent.VK_RIGHT)) {
  rules.addCommand(currentChar,
    new DirectionCommand(currentChar,Direction.EAST));
}
if (keyboard.isKeyPressed(KeyEvent.VK_LEFT)) {
  rules.addCommand(currentChar,
    new DirectionCommand(currentChar,Direction.WEST));
}
if (keyboard.isKeyPressed(KeyEvent.VK_DOWN)) {
  rules.addCommand(currentChar,
   new DirectionCommand(currentChar,Direction.SOUTH));
}
if (keyboard.isKeyPressed(KeyEvent.VK_UP)) {
  rules.addCommand(currentChar,
   new DirectionCommand(currentChar,Direction.NORTH));
}
```

The `currentChar` attribute is the character currently controlled by the user interface. The `addCommand()` method of the `Rules` class has a new argument, here with the `currentChar` value, shown below.

The execution of the direction command begins by retrieving a reference to
the concerned character in a me variable, as well as its direction in a variable
currentDirection:

```java
public void execute(State state) {
    Characters chars = state.getChars();
    if (charIndex >= chars.size()) {
        Logger.getLogger("rules").log(
            Level.WARNING,"No Character "+charIndex);
        return;
    }
    MobileElement me = chars.get(charIndex);
    Direction currentDirection = me.getDirection();
```

If ever the character whose direction is to be changed does not exist,
e.g. if charIndex >= chars.size(), it is better not to throw an exception.
On the contrary, a message is added to the program log via the standard
java.util.logging.Logger library system or any other system.

It highlights an important point: commands are not necessarily always valid. For
example, an invalid command may be an impossible move or any operation that
does not respect the game rules. Another cause may be a bug in the user interface,
which produces a command with parameters that make no sense, such as asking
to move a character that does not exist. Finally, a player who tries to cheat
produces commands that do not respect the rules. In the case of a command whose
parameters are not supposed to be produced by a trusted third party, it is advisable
to note the error in the program log. The study of the program log makes it possible
to identify possible bugs without interrupting the user's experience.

The rest of the method looks if the character is a ghost (charIndex != 0) and if
the requested direction is the opposite of the current direction, or in other words, if
we want to make a ghost turn around. We consider that the player can request this
type of displacement, and if it is, it is just ignored: we leave the method without
adding a message to the log:

```java
    if (charIndex != 0
      && currentDirection.isOppositeOf(direction))
        return;
```

The isOppositeOf() method of the Direction enumeration is a convenience
method for returning true if one direction is the opposite of another.

The end of the method changes the direction of the character if it is exactly on a square (pos == 0) and the cell in the new direction is a space
(world.get(x, y, direction) instanceof Space), or if you want to turn back
(currentDirection.isOppositeOf(direction)):

```java
    int pos = me.getPosition();
    int x = me.getX();
```

```
    int y = me.getY();
    World world = state.getWorld();
    if ((pos == 0 && world.get(x, y, direction) instanceof Space)
     || currentDirection.isOppositeOf(direction)) {
        me.setDirection(direction);
    }
}
```

Move command

The direction command does not change the position of a character. We modify it with the `MoveCommand` class. This command is a passive command, which is added and executed systematically every time the state is updated. Two points motivate this approach. The first motivation is related to the fact that a character in the Pacman game can not stop and must stay in motion. Thus, even if the user stops pressing an arrow and therefore no longer creates commands, the character must continue to move. This property is quite usual; for example, it is common to click at a place where a character must go. Once the click is complete, the character moves alone without having to hold down a key or button continuously. The second motivation is related to the scheduling of the execution of commands. Indeed, it is very simple and robust to ensure that operations always take place in the same order rather than in an undetermined order. In the case of the Pacman game, we choose to move Pacman first, then the first ghost, then the second, and so on. In the `update()` method of the `PlayGameMode` class, we systematically add these commands:

```
Characters chars = state.getChars();
for (int i=0;i<chars.size();i++) {
    rules.addCommand(100+i,new MoveCommand(i));
}
```

The order of execution of the commands is not defined by the order in which they are added but by the value of the first argument of the `addCommand()` method, which can be named priority. The `update()` method of the `Rules` class executes commands from the lowest priority value to the largest. In the above example, the Pacman move command has priority 100, then the first ghost 101, and so on.

Executing the move command starts by checking that the character exists, and retrieves the information that concerns him in various variables:

```
public void execute(State state) {
    World world = state.getWorld();
    Characters chars = state.getChars();
    if (charIndex >= chars.size()) {
        Logger.getLogger("rules").log(
            Level.WARNING,"No character "+charIndex);
```

```
        return;
    }
    MobileElement me = chars.get(charIndex);
    int pos = me.getPosition();
    int x = me.getX();
    int y = me.getY();
    Direction direction = me.getDirection();
```

If the position is zero, the character is exactly on a cell. There are two possibilities: either the cell in its direction is a space, in which case we can continue. In the opposite case, we leave the method and the character no longer advances:

```
    if (pos == 0) {
        if (!(world.get(x, y, direction)
              instanceof Space)) {
            state.notifyCharacterChanged(charIndex);
            return;
        }
    }
```

The rest of the method is the computation of the movement of the character, as has already been done in the previous examples:

```
    switch(direction) {
        case EAST:
            pos ++;
            if (pos == me.getSpeed()) {
                pos = -me.getSpeed();
                x ++;
                if (x >= world.getWidth())
                    x = 0;
            }
            break;
        ... other directions ...
    }
```

Finally, the character's coordinates are updated, and the state notifies observers that the character has changed:

```
    me.setPosition(pos);
    me.setX(x);
    me.setY(y);
    state.notifyCharacterChanged(charIndex);
}
```

Rules engine with priority management

The Rules class is modified to handle the priorities of the commands. The commands are first stored in a binary tree associative array (java.util.TreeMap):

```java
public class Rules {
    private State state;
    private TreeMap<Integer,Command> commands = new TreeMap();
```

This type of array always orders the elements according to the keys. Here, the keys are integers, so if we iterate the array, it is always from the smallest integer to the largest.

The update() method is modified with an additional priority argument:

```java
public void addCommand(int priority,Command c) {
    commands.put(priority,c);
}
```

It is worth noting that associative arrays only tolerate one element per key. As a result, if you add two commands with the same priority, only the last one is retained. It avoids duplicates. For example, if the user very quickly presses the right arrow several times, even if the "Go to right" command is added several times, only one is retained.

The update() method runs through all the array elements (commands.values()). The order is that of the keys, from the smallest to the largest:

```java
public void update() {
    for (Command command : commands.values()) {
        command.execute(state);
    }
    commands.clear();
    state.incEpoch();
}
```

The diagrams in this example are available in the "Class Diagrams/chap04/command02" folder of the sample UML project. The code is present in the "examples/chap04/command02" folder of the sample Java project.

4.3.3.4 Implement all the rules

In this section, all the commands that form the Pacman game rules are implemented, as described in the section **Example of rules definitions**. All are not detailed; only those that are of educational interest are put forward. All diagrams in this example are available in the "Class Diagrams/chap04/command03" folder of the sample UML project. The code is present in the "examples/chap04/command03" folder of the sample Java project. This sample code shows the Pacman game with all its rules, playable by Pacman or by a ghost.

Adding passive commands

The `update()` method of the `PlayGameMode` class adds passive commands before updating the state:

```java
private long lastUpdate;
public void update() {
    long now = System.nanoTime();
    if ((now-lastUpdate)>=state.getEpochDuration())
    {
        lastUpdate = now;
        rules.addCommand(100, new MoveCommand(0));
        rules.addCommand(200,new UpdateStatusCommand(0));
        rules.addCommand(300, new GumsCommand());
        rules.addCommand(400,new CollisionsCommand());
        Characters chars = state.getChars();
        for (int i=1;i<chars.size();i++){
            rules.addCommand(500+i,new MoveCommand(i));
            rules.addCommand(600+i,new UpdateStatusCommand(i));
            rules.addCommand(700+i,new ResurrectionCommand(i));
        }
        rules.addCommand(800,new CollisionsCommand());
        rules.update();
```

The execution order is as defined in the rules of Pacman. If there are any problems related to the order of executions of the commands, it is enough to modify the values of the priorities. The command `CollisionsCommand`, which looks if Pacman encounters a ghost, is added twice: once before moving the ghosts, plus once after. It is a trick that avoids the particular case where two characters cross at the same state update. It presents another interest of the command pattern: we can repeat the same operations and in any order.

The end of the method manages the end of the game. If all the gums are eaten, it's the victory:

```java
        if (state.getGumCount() == 0) {
            setGameMode(new GameOverMode("Victory !"));
        }
```

If Pacman is dead (`pacman.getStatus () == PacmanStatus.DEAD`) and the life-to-death time is over (`pacman.getStatusTime () == 0`), then the game is lost:

```java
        Pacman pacman = chars.getPacman();
        if (pacman != null
```

```
            && pacman.getStatus() == PacmanStatus.DEAD
            && pacman.getStatusTime() == 0) {
         setGameMode(new GameOverMode("You lost !!"));
      }
   }
}
```

Synchronization between game time and animations

Until now, character animations are uncorrelated with the update speed of the state. For example, Pacman opens and closes the mouth at a free frequency. For the death of Pacman, on the other hand, it is necessary to synchronize the animation of death with the state of the game. It must start when Pacman is hit by a ghost and stop when Pacman is dead.

To achieve this result, we use the `statusTime` attribute of the `Pacman` class. First, when a collision between Pacman in normal status and a ghost in hunting status is detected, Pacman is set to dead status, and the status time is set to a non-zero value. The value must be correlated with the animation time. In this example, the animation lasts 12 epochs:

```
pacman.setStatus(PacmanStatus.DEAD);
pacman.setStatusTime(12);
```

Then, in the `CharsTileSet` class, `adyingTiles` attribute is added with the tiles of a Pacman animation going from life to death. The simplest case was chosen: an animation in 12 images, the number of epochs.

The `getTile()` method of the `CharsTileSet` class is enriched to handle the Pacman case in a dead state. If this case is detected, the i of the tile in the `dyingTiles` array is calculated. It is a function of Pacman's status time, which is decremented at each epoch:

```
public Tile getTile(Element e) {
    if (e instanceof Pacman) {
        Pacman pacman = (Pacman)e;
        if (pacman.getStatus()==PacmanStatus.DEAD) {
            int i = dyingTiles.length
                    - pacman.getStatusTime();
            if (i >= dyingTiles.length)
                i = dyingTiles.length - 1;
            if (i < 0) i = 0;
            return dyingTiles[i];
        }
    ... other cases ...
}
```

This type of synchronization is the simplest. It is quite possible to make animations that start and end at well-defined game times while having different frequencies from those of updating the state. For that, it is necessary to reproduce what was done for the interpolation of the displacements, but by interpolating here the steps of the animation.

4.3.4 Do and undo

The previous solution, which features the Command pattern in its simplest version, makes it possible to design robust and scalable solutions. In the case where advanced features are required, such as advanced artificial intelligence or the ability to quickly rewind into a replay, the ability to undo commands can be very interesting. To achieve this, there are several approaches.

4.3.4.1 Undo with the Memento Pattern

Memento Pattern

The simplest approach is to combine the *Memento Pattern* with the Command pattern. The Memento pattern has three main actors; here is a possible combination:

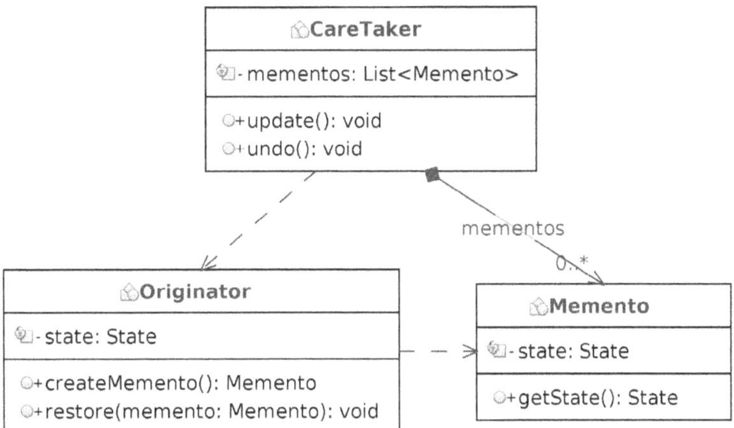

The `CareTaker` class is the element that drives the whole thing. A user can request to change the data, for example by calling an `update()` method. A user can also ask to go back, for example by calling an `undo()` method. There are many other possibilities, for instance: return to the very beginning; redo what was undone; go directly to a specific previous step; etc.

To provide its services, the `CareTaker` class uses an `Originator` class that contains the data, represented in the diagram above by the `state` attribute. Any other form of data representation is possible. The `Originator` class also has methods for making Memento, like the `createMemento()` method.

The `Memento` class must contain all the information needed to reproduce any dataset. The simplest way, which is shown in the diagram above, is to hold a complete copy of the data. Be careful, it must be a complete copy, or deep copy of the data, and not a reference! Otherwise, changing the current data also changes the data referenced by the other `Memento`.

The `CareTaker` class uses the `createMemento()` method to restore the current state. These mementos can be memorized, for example, in a list like in the diagram above - other solutions are quite viable, as long as the class fulfills its role.

Finally, the `Originator` class must have methods to restore data from a Memento, like the `restore()` method. In the solution above, copy the state of the memento in the current state. In other cases, where the memento memorizes the data in a more complex way, it is common to ask the memento to perform a data recovery task. For these cases, it is also possible to define a `Memento` interface, then different implementations functions of the nature of the data.

For example, if the data can take very different forms, you can create a `Memento` layout for each data shape, then call a `restore(Originator originator)` method from the interface. Whatever the situation, the idea is that the originator contains the data and controls the creation and implementation of the mementos, while the mementos manage the storage of the possible data and their recovery.

Command and Memento patterns

Command and Memento patterns can be combined in a variety of ways, including:

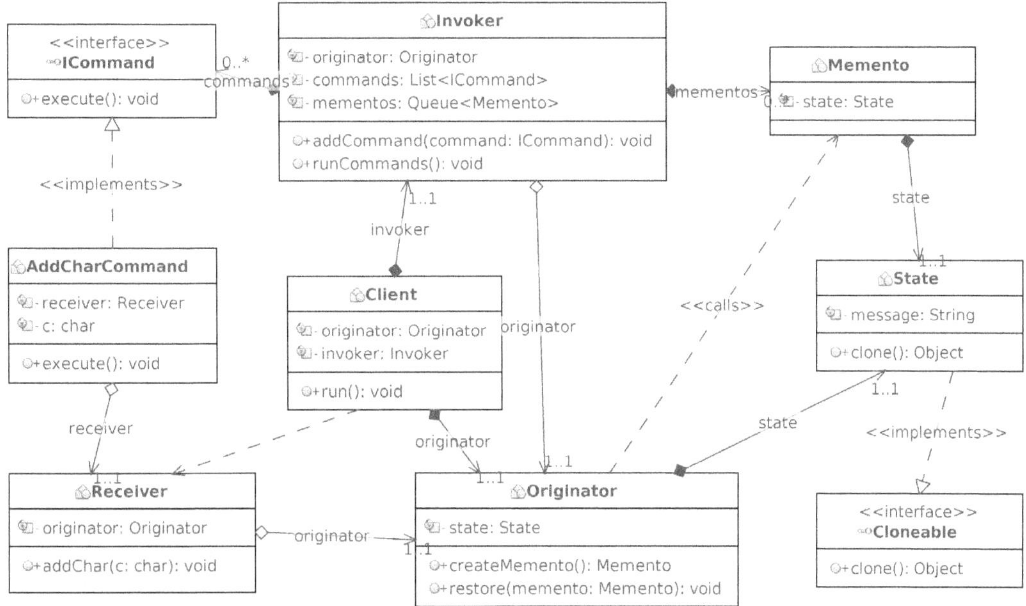

We find all the elements of the pattern Command: interface `ICommand` and an implementation `AddCharCommand`, the `Invoker` class, and the `Receiver` class. Regarding the Memento pattern, the `Invoker` class acts as `CareTaker`, then we find the `Memento` class and the `Originator` class.

Using the double pattern

The `Client` class represents a dual pattern user. Its purpose is to manipulate data represented by a `State` class, namely a message. The goal in this example is to add characters to the message and then cancel those additions. The `Client` class does not modify the data directly but adds and then requests the execution of commands to the `Invoker` class. For example, an implementation of the run() method of the `Client` class can be:

```
origin = new Originator();
invoke = new Invoker(origin);
Receiver receive = new Receiver(origin);
System.out.println(origin.getState().getMessage());
invoke.addCommand(new AddCharCommand(receive,'a'));
invoke.addCommand(new AddCharCommand(receive,'b'));
```

```
invoke.runCommands();
System.out.println(origin.getState().getMessage());
invoke.addCommand(new AddCharCommand(receive,'c'));
invoke.runCommands();
System.out.println(origin.getState().getMessage());
invoke.rollback();
System.out.println(origin.getState().getMessage());
invoke.rollback();
System.out.println(origin.getState().getMessage());
```

Its execution gives the following result:

```
ab
abc
ab
```

The first and last lines are empty: at the beginning, the message is empty. Then after two updates and two rollbacks, the message is empty again. The idea in this implementation is to find a state of the data before an update. Thus, there are two commands during the first update, and its cancellation corresponds to undoing these two commands.

Invoker class

The aim of the class Invoker is to receive, execute, and cancel commands. It does not manage the storage of data, nor the creation and application of mementos, it has a reference to an Originator which deals with these aspects:

```
public class Invoker {
    private Originator originator;
```

On the other hand, it memorizes the mementos, in this example in a stack:

```
    private Queue<Memento> mementos =
        Collections.asLifoQueue(new ArrayDeque());
```

Finally, it keeps the next commands in an array:

```
    private List<ICommand> commands=new ArrayList();
```

Adding commands is unchanged from the Command pattern:

```
    public void addCommand(ICommand command) {
        commands.add(command);
    }
```

However, the execution of the commands is a little different, since one begins by adding a memento to the stack of the mementos:

```java
public void runCommands() {
    mementos.add(originator.createMemento());
    for(ICommand command : commands) {
        command.execute();
    }
    commands.clear();
}
```

Creating the memento to restore the previous state is handled by the `Originator` class with the `createMemento()` method.

The rollback is very simple: we get the memento on the top of the stack, then we ask the originator to apply it:

```java
public void rollback() {
    Memento memento = mementos.poll();
    originator.restore(memento);
}
}
```

It's worth noting that the `Invoker` class does not depend on the data or how to manipulate it. The above implementation may be suitable for many cases, as long as we only need simple backtracking.

Originator class

The `Originator` class has three roles: to reference the data, to create mementos and to apply them. It does not have to contain this data: it is the role of the `State` class. It has a reference to the data:

```java
public class Originator {
    private State state = new State();
```

The creation of Memento, in this example, is based on a complete copy of the state:

```java
public Memento createMemento() {
    return new Memento((State)state.clone());
}
```

In the same way, to restore a state, the state contained in the memento is copied to the current state:

```java
public void restore(Memento memento) {
    state = (State)memento.getState().clone();
}
}
```

State class

To obtain a complete copy, the `State` class implements the `Cloneable` interface of the Java language. It involves creating a `clone()` method that returns a copy of the instance. Since there are no containers in this `State` class example, just call the `clone()` method of the`Object`class with the `super.clone()` expression to get a complete clone:

```java
public class State implements Cloneable {
    private String message = "";
    protected Object clone() {
        try {
            return super.clone();
        } catch (CloneNotSupportedException ex) {
            throw new RuntimeException("Cloning failed");
        }
    }
}
```

It is an application of the Prototype pattern, presented later in this chapter.

Memento class

The implementation of the `Memento` class is very simple: it is a container for a dataset:

```java
public class Memento {
    private State state;
    public Memento(State state) {
        this.state = state;
    }

    public State getState() {
        return state;
    }
}
```

4.3.4.2   Undo without full copies

The previous approach is easy to implement but suffers from a major flaw: you have to copy and memorize all the data to use it. In the case of a game with many data, it can quickly be unmanageable. The problem gets even worse when you want to make advanced Artificial Intelligence, where it is necessary to do and undo many times, resulting in a very large amount of computations.

A first simple solution

One solution is not to memorize a complete state, but only the differences with the previous state. If these differences are invertible, memorize them, then execute them in one direction to move forward, then in the other to go back in time. On this basis, a first solution is to enrich the command pattern with methods to undo:

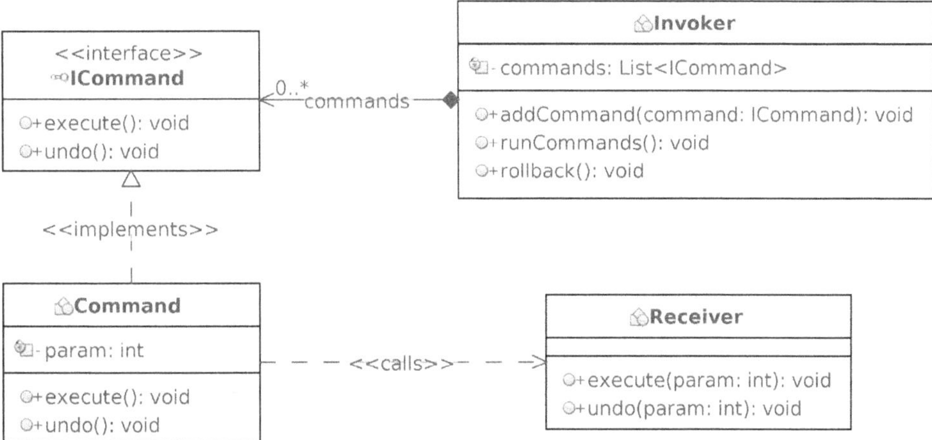

The ICommand interface is enriched with the undo() method; the Receiver class with an undo() method with an argument whose value is supposed to be the inverse of that of the execute() method; and finally the Invoker class has a rollback() method to go back.

This approach suffers, however, a major flaw: the nature of the changes made by the commands must not depend on a context. For example, a command that moves a character to the right can be easily reversed by running the same move to the left. However, we assume that the requested movement is always possible, which is not always the case. Indeed, if we take a look at the implementation of the different commands made for the Pacman example, all commands are subject to conditions. In addition, some commands execute changes that are functions of various factors. For example, Pacman only goes into super mode if he eats a super gum.

It is not possible to delete all the tests and conditions of execution within the commands, nor to move them in the part that generates the commands. In the opposite case, all the advantages obtained in terms of robustness and extensibility would be lost. It is also not possible to copy all or a large part of the data to be able to guess the nature of the changes that was made.

A robust solution

An approach that does not present these defects is based on the addition of a new range of commands, called actions here:

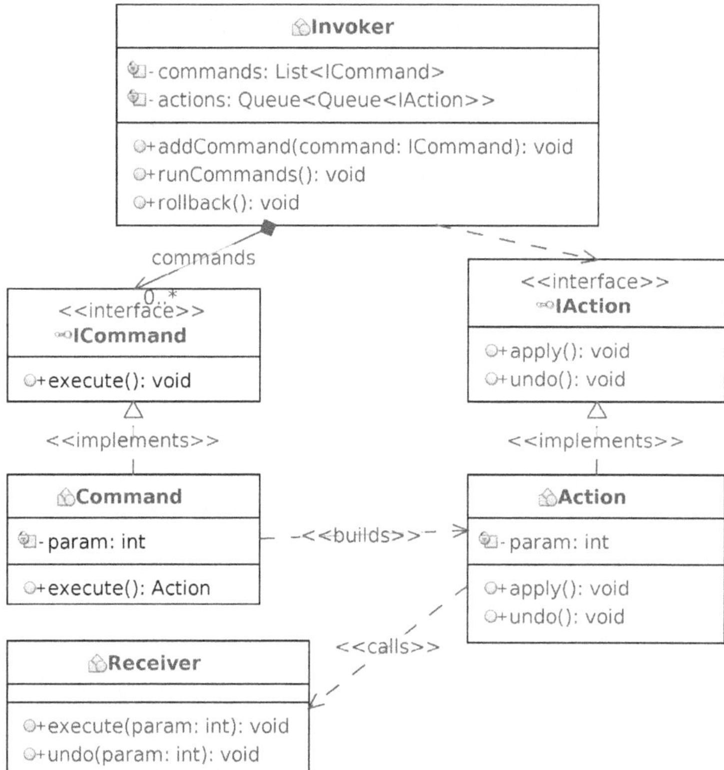

The idea is to manage on one side all the conditions with implementations of the `ICommand` interface, then to carry out the modifications without any conditions with implantations of a new `IAction` interface. The above example is a simple case: the `execute()` method returns an `Action` depending on the context. This action can be executed via the `apply()` method of the `IAction` interface. This uses a `Receiver` class to run the changes.

Contrary to commands, the operations performed by an action do not depend on a context: they are executed whatever happens. They are canceled without conditions. The fact that they do not perform any checks is not a problem when the commands that produce them have already checked everything beforehand. For example, if a move command to a position has produced an action for that move, then the move can take place safely.

The `runCommands()` method of the `Invoker` class executes the current commands and collects the produced actions in its `actions` attribute. There can be several commands per game update, and therefore several actions per game update. The `rollback()` method, on the other hand, retrieves the last batch of stored actions and calls the `undo()` method of those actions to go back.

It is not mandatory to produce an action class for each command class. The same command class can produce different types of actions, and different commands can produce the same actions. A single command can also produce multiple actions, as in the Pacman game example below.

Example with the Pacman game

The principle is implemented for the Pacman example game. The `Rules` class still acts as an invoker, and is modified accordingly:

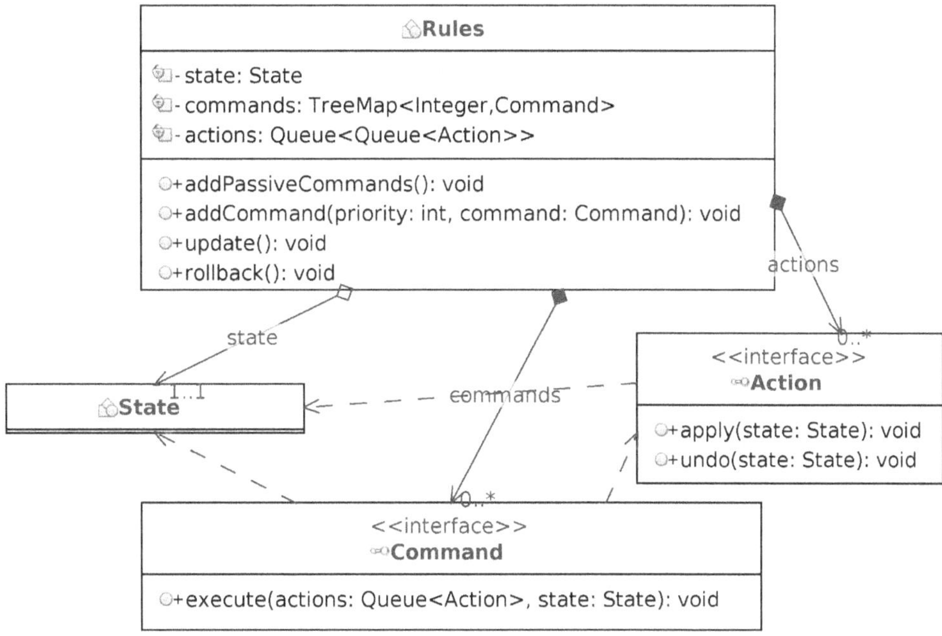

The `execute()` method of the `Command` interface is modified with an additional argument `actions`, which allows adding actions to an action stack. The `Action` interface is added with an `apply()` method to execute the action, and an `undo()` method to cancel the action. The command classes are all moved in the `rules.commands` package. Their `execute()` methods are modified to perform only checks and then create actions when necessary. Some examples of implementations are presented below.

Action classes

Many child classes of `Action` are defined to follow the approach. In each situation, the execution does not depend on the context and only the data necessary for the inversion is stored:

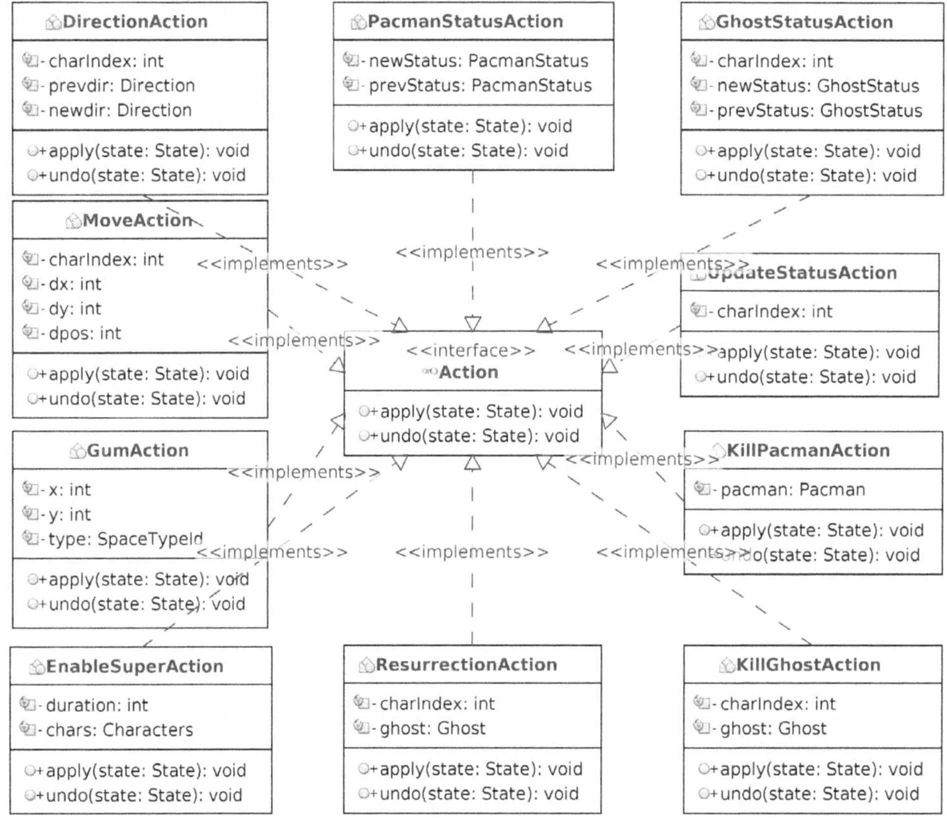

- `DirectionAction`: Changes the direction of a character to `newdir`. The previous direction is stored in the `prevdir` attribute.
- `MoveAction`: Moves a character according to a coordinate vector (dx,dy) and a positional difference `dpos`. To invert, subtract the vectors instead of adding them.
- `GumAction`: Removes a gum at the coordinates (x, y). The previous gum type (normal or super) can be restored thanks to the `type` attribute.
- `EnableSuperAction`: Changes the status of all characters when Pacman becomes super. The duration of the new statuses is defined in the `duration` attribute. The `chars` attribute is a complete copy of all characters, allowing you to restore them if you have to reverse. Attention: it is a complete copy, whose implementation is detailed in the section **Deep copy (Prototype Pattern)**. This action is quite rare, and it is not too expensive to copy all the

characters.
- `PacmanStatusAction` and `GhostStatusAction`: Changes either the Pacman status or the status of a ghost.
- `UpdateStatusAction`: Decrements the status time of a character. To invert, increment it.
- `KillPacmanAction`: Changes Pacman to dead status, and passes the status time to a value depending on the death animation. Death can occur at any time; Pacman is then fully copied.
- `KillGhostAction`: Shifts a ghost to eye status and its status time to zero. A copy of the ghost allows the inversion.
- `ResurrectionAction`: Shifts a ghost to a hunting status and its status time to zero. A copy of the ghost allows the inversion.

GumsCommand

The method of the `GumsCommand` class presents a typical command case that produces actions. It always starts by checking if Pacman exists and if it is alive. If there is a problem, the method ends immediately, and no action is produced:

```java
public void execute(Queue<Action> actions,State state) {
    Characters chars = state.getChars();
    Pacman pacman = chars.getPacman();
    if (pacman == null) {
        Logger.getLogger("rules").log(Level.SEVERE,"No Pacman");
        return;
    }
    if (pacman.getStatus() == PacmanStatus.DEAD)
        return;
```

If Pacman is exactly on a cell, he can eat a gum. The same tests are conducted to determine if this is possible:

```java
    if (pacman.getPosition() == 0) {
        int x = pacman.getX();
        int y = pacman.getY();
        World world = state.getWorld();
        StaticElement se = world.get(x,y,Direction.NONE);
        if (se instanceof Space) {
            Space space = (Space)se;
            SpaceTypeId type = space.getSpaceTypeId();
            if (type == SpaceTypeId.GUM
              || type == SpaceTypeId.SUPERGUM) {
```

At this step, Pacman is on a gum that he can eat. A `GumAction` action is created with the coordinates of the gum to eat. The type of gum is also given so that the action is invertible:

```
Action action = new GumAction(x,y,type);
```

This action is then immediately executed. This is necessary because, after each action, the state changes, and thus the conditions of implementation of the following commands:

```
action.apply(state);
```

Finally, the action is added to the action stack for this command:

```
actions.add(action);
```

An `EnableSuperAction` action can be produced if the gum is a super gum. The principle is the same as in the previous case: we make the action with all the elements to invert it, apply it, and add it to the stack:

```
if (type == SpaceTypeId.SUPERGUM) {
    action = new EnableSuperAction(
      state.getSuperDuration());
    action.apply(state);
    actions.add(action);
  }
        }
      }
    }
}
```

We could have combined `GumAction` and `EnableSuperAction` in a single action. However, this is less interesting for different reasons. First, there is always and again the principle of division: here there are two distinct tasks, and complex enough to justify separation. Second, reversing the `EnableSuperAction` action is quite expensive in memory compared to the `GumAction` action, since it changes the status of all characters. From a memory usage point of view, it is more efficient to store this information only in the rare cases where Pacman goes into super status.

MoveAction

This action is a typical case of modification through a difference. It is based on differences between numerical values. For example, if the coordinates of a character go from (3,10) to (5,4), the difference vector is (5-3,4-10), e.g. (dx = 2, dy = -6) . To implement this displacement, it suffices to add this difference vector to the current coordinates (the principle is the same for the position):

```
public void apply(State state) {
    Characters chars = state.getChars();
    if (charIndex >= chars.size()) {
        Logger.getLogger("rules").log(
            Level.WARNING,"No character "+charIndex);
```

```
        return;
    }
    MobileElement me = chars.get(charIndex);
    if (me == null) {
        Logger.getLogger("rules").log(
            Level.WARNING,"No character "+charIndex);
        return;
    }
    me.setPosition(me.getPosition() + dpos);
    me.setX(me.getX() + dx);
    me.setY(me.getY() + dy);
    state.notifyCharacterChanged(charIndex);
}
```

To reverse this change, just subtract the differences:

```
public void undo(State state) {
    Characters chars = state.getChars();
    if (charIndex >= chars.size()) {
        Logger.getLogger("rules").log(
            Level.WARNING,"No character "+charIndex);
        return;
    }
    MobileElement me = chars.get(charIndex);
    if (me == null) {
        Logger.getLogger("rules").log(
            Level.WARNING,"No character "+charIndex);
        return;
    }
    me.setPosition(me.getPosition() - dpos);
    me.setX(me.getX() - dx);
    me.setY(me.getY() - dy);
    state.notifyCharacterChanged(charIndex);
}
```

The diagrams in this example are available in the "Class Diagrams/chap04/command04"
folder of the sample UML project. The code is present in the "exam-
ples/chap04/command04" folder of the sample Java project. If the "carriage return"
key is pressed, the game is replayed upside down, until it returns to the beginning
of the game.

4.3.5   Test the rules engine

The purpose of this section is to implement tests that validate the rules engine. To
achieve this, two features are required: deep copy and comparison. These make it

possible to copy the state of the game at each time, then to compare it to a state of the game reconstructed by the engine.

4.3.5.1   Deep copy (Prototype Pattern)

References and contents

A copy of an object in Java consists of copying the references, not the referenced content. If we consider the following class:

```java
class Value {
    public int x;
    public Value(int x) {
        this.x = x;
    }
}
```

Then the creation of two instances, followed by the display of their values:

```java
Value v1 = new Value(1);
Value v2 = new Value(2);
System.out.println("v1="+v1.x+",v2="+v2.x);
```

The display obtained is the one expected:

```
v1=1,v2=2
```

If v2 is copied into v1:

```java
v2 = v1;
System.out.println("v1="+v1.x+",v2="+v2.x);
```

The display is natural, v1 and v2 have the same attribute value x:

```
v1=1,v2=1
```

Then, if you modify the x attribute of v1:

```java
v1.x = 3;
System.out.println("v1="+v1.x+",v2="+v2.x);
```

The values of the attributes of the two variables seem to have been modified:

```
v1=3,v2=3
```

This result is quite normal for all languages like Java, C#, Python, etc. whose variables on objects are systematically references. At the beginning of this example, the v1 and v2 variables each refer to a different object, one with the x = 1 attribute and the other with the x = 2 attribute. Then, after the expression v2 = v1, v2 references the same object as v1. It is therefore normal that the values displayed in the end are identical (x = 3).

To get the desired behavior, where v2 contains the same values as v1, but without referencing the same object, you need to do a copy:

```java
Value v1 = new Value(1);
Value v2 = new Value(2);
System.out.println("v1="+v1.x+",v2="+v2.x);
v2 = new Value(v1.x);
System.out.println("v1="+v1.x+",v2="+v2.x);
v1.x = 3;
System.out.println("v1="+v1.x+",v2="+v2.x);
```

The resulting display is the desired one, v1 has been changed to 3, and v2 kept the value 1 copied from the initial v1:

```
v1=1,v2=2
v1=1,v2=1
v1=3,v2=1
```

Prototype Pattern

Copying all the attribute values of one class from one instance to another becomes quickly tedious. In addition, if there are containers, it is also necessary to copy the contained objects, which themselves may have containers, etc. A very effective way to get a deep copy of an object is in the *Prototype Pattern*:

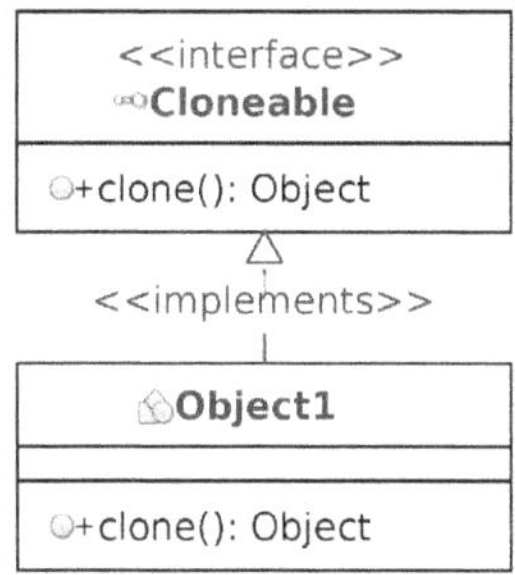

The pattern is based on a unique `clone()` method, whose role is to make a new object, all attributes of which are copies (or clones) of the instance. The Java language has a `Cloneable` interface that already has the `clone()` method. Besides, to duplicate an object without references, it is possible to use the implementation of the `clone()` method of the `Object` class of the language. For example, to implement the pattern for all the child classes of `Element`, call the `clone()` method of the `Object` class via the `super.clone()` expression:

```java
public abstract class Element implements Cloneable {
    @Override
    public Element clone() {
```

```
        try {
            return (Element)super.clone();
        } catch (CloneNotSupportedException ex) {
            throw new RuntimeException();
        }
    }
}
```

The `clone()` method of the `Object` class can throw a `CloneNotSupportedException` exception. In the above implementation, it was chosen to capture it and throw a `RuntimeException`.

This solution works for all the child classes of Element: the `clone()` method of the `Object` class is able, through introspection, to identify and copy all the attributes of the current instance. It is particularly fast.

However, we must be very careful: this copy does not call the `clone()` methods of contained objects. For these cases, manual implementation is required. For example, for the `Characters` class:

```
public Characters clone() {
    Characters other = new Characters();
    for (MobileElement me : chars) {
        other.chars.add((MobileElement)me.clone());
    }
    return other;
}
```

The same goes for the `World` and `State` classes.

4.3.5.2 Deep compare

For the same reasons as with copying, the comparison of two variables compares the two references and not the two referenced objects. So, if we take the `Value` class from the previous section:

```
Value v1 = new Value(1);
Value v2 = new Value(1);
System.out.println(v1 == v2);
```

The resulting display is:

```
false
```

In other words, according to the expression `v1 == v2`, the two variables are different. It is perfectly true: each variable references a different object, and are therefore different, even if the content of the two objects is identical.

To compare the contents of two objects, you need a specific procedure. In Java, as in many other languages with references, the `equals()` method is considered as the one that plays this role. It must return `true` if the instance and the object in the argument have the same content, and `false` otherwise. For example, for the `Value` class:

```java
class Value {
    public int x;
    public Value(int x) {
        this.x = x;
    }
    @Override
    public boolean equals(Object obj) {
        if (this == obj) {
            return true;
        }
        if (obj == null) {
            return false;
        }
        if (getClass() != obj.getClass()) {
            return false;
        }
        final Value other = (Value) obj;
        if (this.x != other.x) {
            return false;
        }
        return true;
    }
}
```

The above implementation compares all possibilities, if the objects exist, if they have exactly the same class, and if they have the same values. The above code was produced by Netbeans, via the context menu of the class:

→ Right-click in an empty space between the two braces of the class

→ Choose **Insert Code...** from the context menu

→ Choose **equals() and hashCode()...** in the second context menu

→ Check all the attributes to duplicate in the `clone()` method.

→ It is also possible to generate the `hashCode()` method to use the class in a hash table (like `java.util.HashMap`).

→ Click **Generate**

With this `equals()` method, if we display the comparison value:

```java
System.out.println(v1.equals(v2));
```

The desired result is obtained - the two variables have equal content:

```
true
```

For containers, we must be careful as we did for copying. Netbeans generally handles these cases very well when generating code with the contextual menu. For example, for the class World, the table is well compared in-depth with the static method Arrays.deepEquals():

```java
public boolean equals(Object obj) {
    if (this == obj) {
        return true;
    }
    if (obj == null) {
        return false;
    }
    if (getClass() != obj.getClass()) {
        return false;
    }
    final World other = (World) obj;
    if (this.width != other.width) {
        return false;
    }
    if (this.height != other.height) {
        return false;
    }
    if (!Arrays.deepEquals(this.elements,other.elements)) {
        return false;
    }
    return true;
}
```

4.3.5.3　Implement tests

It is possible to create a unit test to validate the rules engine since everything can be automated. The idea is to unroll a mini-game in a specific world, check that the state is the one expected, and memorize copies of the state at each time. Then, the mini-game is reproduced backward with the rollback mechanisms, and the restored states are compared to the memorized states. If any difference is found, the whole is considered invalid.

Entry point of the test

A RulesTest class is added to the 'examples/chap04/pacman' folder of the test
packages of the Java project. It starts by initializing a state in the state attribute of the class with the createState() method which takes the code of
theInitCommandcommand:

```java
@Test
public void test() {
    createState();
```

Then, if the enableDisplay attribute is true, we initialize a rendering engine. This
allows to see the progress of the tests to understand the problems:

```java
    if (enableDisplay) {
        gui = new AWTGUIFacade();
        renderer = new Renderer(gui);
        state.registerObserver(renderer);
        state.notityStateChanged();
    }
```

If the display is off, the update rate of the report is extremely high to make the test
as fast as possible:

```java
    else {
        state.setEpochRate(10000);
    }
```

Finally, we initialize the rule engine and launch the run() method:

```java
    rules = new Rules(state);
    run();
}
```

Run() and update() methods

The run() method of the test class is similar to the run() method of the
PlayGameMode class. The main difference is the optional display: the game can
run with no display at all. It calls an update() method of the RulesTest class that
updates the state of the game. It starts with the usual management of the epoch
rate:

```java
public void update() {
    long now = System.nanoTime();
    if ((now-lastUpdate)>=state.getEpochDuration())
    {
        lastUpdate = now;
```

A `rollback` attribute is used to determine the current direction of updates. If it is `false`, we add a copy (or clone) of the current state to a state stack:

```
if ( !rollback) {
    states.add(state.clone());
```

Then, the `generateCommands()` method adds commands to the engine to simulate a game:

```
generateCommands();
```

The `addPassiveCommands()` method of the rule engine adds the usual passive commands:

```
rules.addPassiveCommands();
```

Finally, the rules engine updates the state of the game:

```
rules.update();
}
```

In the case where the `rollback` attribute is `true`, which means that we have to go back in time, we ask the rule engine to cancel the last commands:

```
else {
    rules.rollback();
```

Then, we check that the state of the game is the same as the one that was memorized on the top of the `states` stack:

```
assertEquals(state,states.poll());
        }
    }
}
```

Commands creation

The `generateCommands()` method called at each state update adds predetermined commands for specific epochs of the game. It contains a large `switch ... case` that adds these commands, and also performs checks. For example, for the very first epoch 0, we first check that the number of gums is equal to 15:

```
switch(state.getEpoch()) {
  case 0:
    assertEquals(15, state.getGumCount());
```

Then the different parameters of Pacman, referenced by the `pacman` variable, are checked:

```
assertEquals(PacmanStatus.NORMAL,pacman.getStatus());
assertEquals(0,pacman.getStatusTime());
```

```
assertEquals(Direction.NONE,pacman.getDirection());
assertEquals(0,pacman.getPosition());
assertEquals(0,pacman.getX());
assertEquals(4,pacman.getY());
```

Finally, we add three commands: one to direct Pacman to the right, the first ghost to the left, and the second ghost to the right:

```
rules.addCommand(0,new DirectionCommand(0, Direction.EAST));
rules.addCommand(1,new DirectionCommand(1, Direction.WEST));
rules.addCommand(2,new DirectionCommand(2, Direction.EAST));
break;
```

The same principle is repeated to check and organize a small scenario where most of the rules are tested: displacement, management of the gums, status of the characters, etc. The scenario can be viewed by running the `RulesTest` class, ensuring that the `enableDisplay` attribute is set to `true`.

4.3.6   Exercises

4.3.6.1   Exercise 3.6.1: Several players on the same keyboard

→ Offer the ability to control a ghost in the Pacman example game with the keyboard, using the Z, Q, S, and D keys.

→ Change the code in the "examples/chap04/command04" folder of the sample Java project.

The solution is short: the purpose of the exercise is to understand how the command pattern was used in the Pacman example game and to find where to add the correct code.

4.3.6.2   Exercise 3.6.2: Checkers game with the command pattern

→ Use the command pattern for the checkers game.

→ You can start with classes in the `examples.chap01.checkers2` package.

This exercise is the simplest possible case of implementation of the command pattern. The expected behavior is the same as that of the program in the `examples.chap01.checkers2` package.

4.3.7   Video game development: rules of the game

→ List the rules of your game.

The ideal form is the one that looks like the list of commands you need for the command pattern. This form is not mandatory, especially at startup, when the rules can be quite uncertain. In any case, do not neglect this step and take the time to think. A bad choice at this stage forces you to re-design and re-code many elements. Do not forget the important parameters, such as the notion of time and the need for commands or passive actions.

→ Implement the command pattern

The use of the command pattern is almost mandatory to obtain a robust and efficient solution. There are different ways to achieve it, with or without features like a rollback. For example, the need to be able to roll back is not always necessary, especially if you don't plan to use advanced artificial intelligence methods. In any case, it is vital to find a conception that separates the commands from their origins.

→ Design and implement commands

Start from your list of rules to design the corresponding set of commands. You can proceed iteratively. Keep in mind that running commands only change the state of the game: it must be possible to remove all the code from the user interface without disturbing the code of the rules engine.

In the Pacman example game, it has few rules, and therefore few commands. For more complex games, there may be a large number of them, in which case they must be "packaged" into packages. Some commands may also require heavy processing, in which case the corresponding ecosystem must be designed.

In any case, the usual rules of design must be followed, and avoid at all costs `execute()` methods with hundreds of lines!

→ Test the rules engine

The first way to test the motor is to observe the corresponding display. Once these primary tests are validated, it is necessary to implement unit tests that follow predetermined scenarios to verify that the rules are followed. Do not neglect this step, a rules engine always evolves during development, and it is very common that the addition of new commands "break" the previous ones. Unit tests make it easy to detect unintended changes. Note that it is not necessary to implement random scenarios; artificial intelligence does it much better.

4.4   Additional features

The complete model that brings together game state, user interface and rule engine makes it easy to implement various features. It includes artificial intelligence or game networking, presented in the following chapters. In this section, other examples are proposed.

4.4.1   Game settings (Builder Pattern)

The menu previously created in the user interface doesn't have any game settings, such as choosing the character played or the level of difficulty. A simple approach is to make a game from the beginning of the menu, via an instance of the `PlayGameMode` class, and modify its settings according to the choices in the menu. This approach causes several problems. These are related to the inevitable need to separate issues. With a simple approach, we mix the collection of parameters and the creation of a new game. In the case of the Pacman game, the creation of a game depends only on one class. There are other cases where several types of games are possible, and therefore as many classes. It would then be necessary to create and destroy the instances of these classes according to the course of the user in the menu.

Builder Pattern

To solve these problems, we use the *Builder Pattern*, which places the collection of parameters on one side, and the creation of objects on the other. This pattern, in its most common form, is as follows:

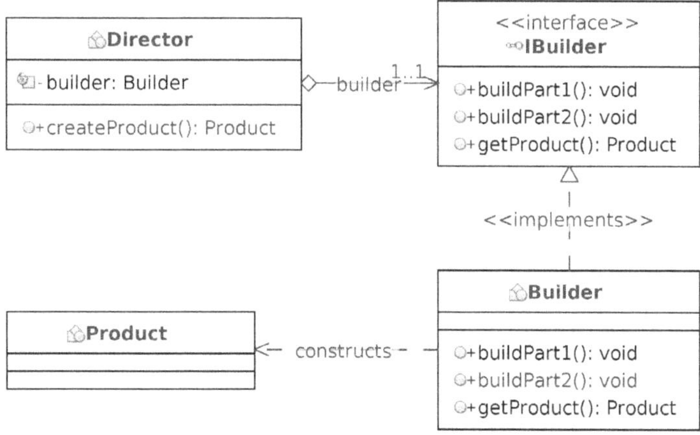

The `Director` class calls the various methods of the `IBuilder` interface to get an instance of the `Product` class. The different methods may or may not have a specific call order, except for the `getProduct()` method that returns the final object. These methods can be build steps, such as `addFoundations()`, `addWalls()`, and `addRoof()` for a house. They can also be simple mutators (*setters*) that define parameters used during the final creation. Finally, there may be several implementations of the `IBuilder` interface, one of which is provided to the `Director` class. In any case, the `Director` class is aware of the call order, and the function of the interface methods. The final user only creates a `Director` instance and requests the creation of the object with the `createProduct()` method.

Use for creating the game

The pattern is implemented to create a new game according to player's choices in the menu. The game settings are very simple, it is also a very simple version of the pattern that is followed. We add a new `GameBuilder` class in the main package:

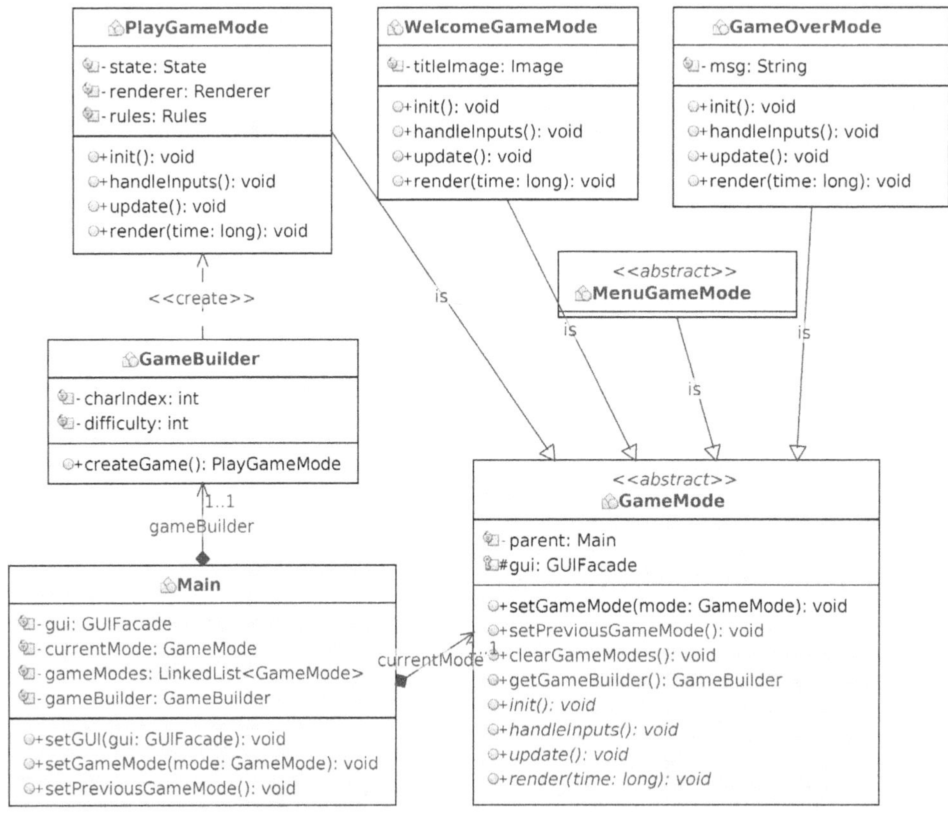

The `GameBuilder` class has two attributes: `charIndex`, which corresponds to the character played, and `difficulty` which corresponds to the level of difficulty. A gameBuilder attribute of this class is added to the Main class, and is made accessible to all modes via the getGameBuilder() method of the GameMode class. The idea is to allow these modes, and especially those that inherit from MenuGameMode, to be able to modify the attributes of gameBuilder, and thus to choose the parameters of the game. For example, in the handleInputs() method of the SelectGhostMenu class, we define the played character (setCharIndex()) according to the selected item in the menu (selectedItem):

```java
public void handleInputs() {
  Keyboard keyboard = gui.getKeyboard();
  switch(keyboard.getLastPressedKey()) {
    case KeyEvent.VK_SPACE:
    case KeyEvent.VK_ENTER:
      keyboard.consumeLastPressedKey();
      getGameBuilder().setCharIndex(selectedItem+1);
      setGameMode(new PlayGhostMenu());
      return;
  }
  super.handleInputs();
}
```

The principle is the same for all other parameters. Once you have reached a final menu step, just before starting a game, call the createGame() method of the GameBuilder class to create the appropriate game mode. For example, for the last step of selecting the difficulty:

```java
public void handleInputs() {
    Keyboard keyboard = gui.getKeyboard();
    switch(keyboard.getLastPressedKey()) {
        case KeyEvent.VK_SPACE:
        case KeyEvent.VK_ENTER:
            keyboard.consumeLastPressedKey();
            GameBuilder builder = getGameBuilder();
            builder.setDifficulty(selectedItem);
            setGameMode(builder.createGame());
            return;
    }
    super.handleInputs();
}
```

The mode created by builder.createGame() is completely unknown from the menu class. It modifies the parameter that concerns it - here the difficulty - then switches to the mode created by GameBuilder. Anything that happened before does not matter, so you do not have to a PlayPacmanMenu and a PlayGhostMenu classes, but a single SelectDifficultyMenu class that can be used both in the menu sequence to play Pacman than in that to play a ghost.

The diagrams in this example are available in the "Class Diagrams/chap04/features01" folder of the sample UML project. The code is present in the "examples/chap04/features01" folder of the sample Java project.

4.4.2   Load a level (Visitor Pattern)

The goal here is to load a level from a file created by "Tiled Map Editor". Before saving the level, XML **Tile layer format** must be selected in the property panel (on the left):

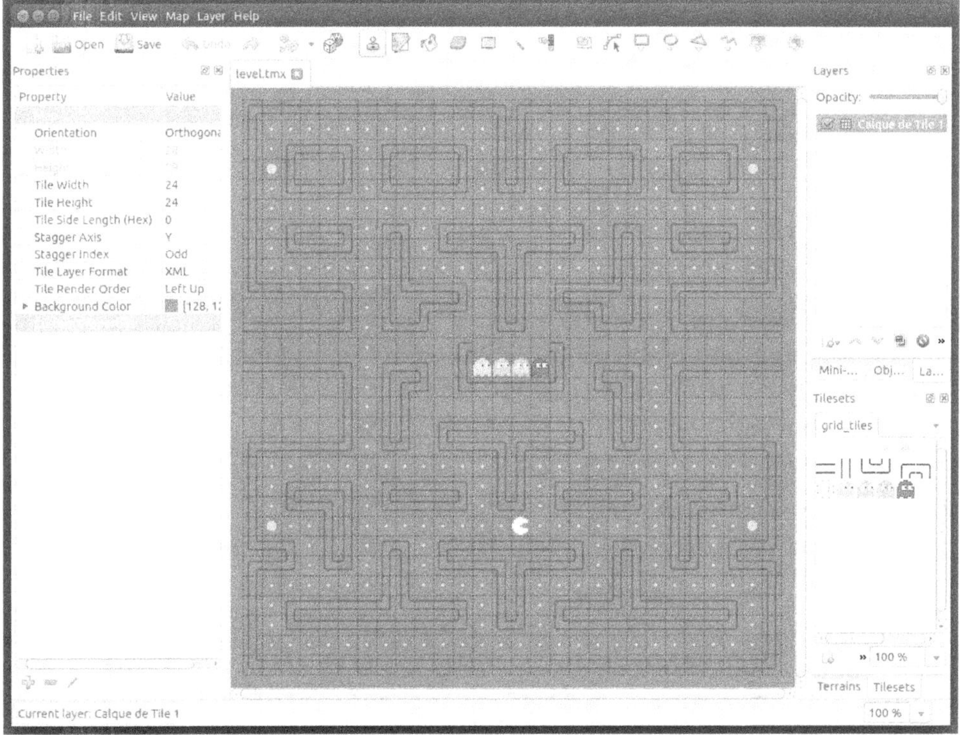

The level is saved in the "level.tmx" file in the "Resources" folder of the Java project (or actual "res" folder). The XML format is chosen because it is easier to decode with existing tools than the CSV format. There are other formats, such as JSON or YAML, and it is also possible to binarize and/or compress the files to reduce their size. In any case, it is advisable to use a format that is based on a structure, such as tags in the formats mentioned, to facilitate the writing and reading of files, but also to increase their robustness.

The XML file is as follows. The first lines define the general parameters:

```
<?xml version="1.0" encoding="UTF-8"?>
<map version="1.0" orientation="orthogonal"
 renderorder="left-up" width="28" height="29"
 tilewidth="24" tileheight="24" nextobjectid="1">
 <tileset firstgid="1" name="grid_tiles"
  tilewidth="24" tileheight="24" tilecount="100">
  <image source="grid_tiles.png" width="256" height="256"/>
 </tileset>
```

The `<layer>` tag contains the level data, starting with its size with the attributes `width` and `height`:

```
 <layer name="Layer 1" width="28" height="29">
```

The cell values are in the `<tile>` tags of the `<data>` tag. The `gid` attribute contains the code of the cell. These are the same codes used until now - the difference here is that they have not been copied and pasted into the java code, but are directly in the XML file:

```
  <data>
   <tile gid="15"/>
   <tile gid="11"/>
   <tile gid="11"/>
   <tile gid="11"/>
   <tile gid="11"/>
   ...etc...
  </data>
 </layer>
</map>
```

Visitor Pattern

To read an XML file, the standard Java library is used. Other libraries exist to decode XML and other structured formats. In almost all cases, they propose the *Visitor Pattern* to browse the data. This pattern makes it easy to browse structured data, just read information, or modify the structure by adding or removing new nodes. Another advantage is that the classes used to represent the data do not need to be modified to add the desired functionality.

This pattern can be presented as follows:

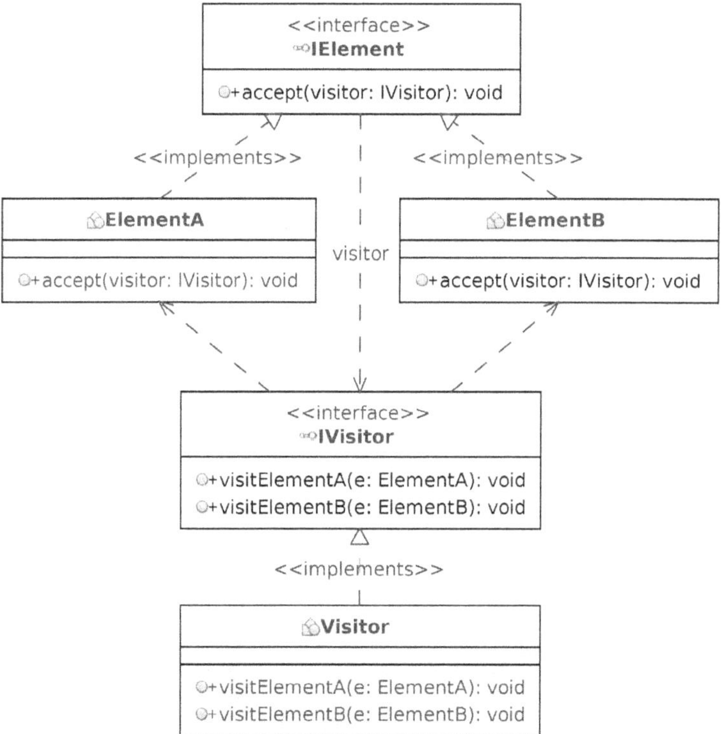

The `IElement` interface represents the elements of the structure. In this example, there are two possible types of objects: `ElementA` and `ElementB`. The interface requires a method like `accept()` which takes as argument a visitor who implements the `IVisitor` interface. There may be several ways to visit the structure, and so many other methods similar to `accept()`. Parameters can also be used to change the course.

The `IVisitor` interface is implemented by the user who wants to browse the structured data. In general, the methods of the interface correspond to the different types of elements that compose it: in this example, they are the classes `ElementA` and `ElementB`. It is quite possible to imagine other cases that may interest a

user, such as being at the beginning or the end of an element. In any case, the
`accept()` method calls the methods of the `IVisitor` interface according to the
cases encountered during its course. Within these methods, the user is free to view
and modify the data.

Reading the level file

A new `LoadLevelCommand` command is added to read a level from a Tiled Map Editor
file. It has a `fileName` attribute with the name of the file to load. Its `execute()`
method uses the XML decoder of the Java standard library:

```java
public void execute(Queue<Action> actions,State state) {
    try {
        SAXParserFactory spf = SAXParserFactory.newInstance();
        SAXParser saxParser = spf.newSAXParser();
        XMLReader xmlReader = saxParser.getXMLReader();
        xmlReader.setContentHandler(new LoadLevelHandler(state)
        );
        URL fileURL = this.getClass()
            .getClassLoader().getResource(fileName);
        xmlReader.parse(fileURL.toString());
    }
    catch(Exception ex) {
        ex.printStackTrace();
        JOptionPane.showMessageDialog(null,
            "Error when loading "+fileName,
            "Error", JOptionPane.ERROR_MESSAGE);
    }
    state.notityStateChanged();
}
```

The decoder is based on a visitor class, in this case, the `LoadLevelhandler` class.

⇒ Note: The XMLReader interface has no `accept()` method as in the typical
visitor pattern realization shown above. Indeed, it is the `setContentHandler()`
method which takes the visitor class as an argument. Then, the `parse()` method
triggers the data traversal process. The principle remains the same, as for the
other patterns, there is no unique form.

The `LoadLevelhandler` class extends the `DefaultHandler` class of the standard
library, which proposes a default implementation of all visit methods:

```java
public class LoadLevelHandler
    extends DefaultHandler {
```

Different attributes are defined to represent the data: `width` and `height` of the
world, the value of the cells of the world (`level`) and coordinates (x, y) of the cell

in decoding course:

```java
State state;
private int width;
private int height;
private int[][] level;
private int x;
private int y;
```

The `startElement()` method is called when the XML traversal algorithm falls on an opening tag:

```java
public void startElement (String uri,
    String localName, String qName,
    Attributes attributes) throws SAXException {
```

We are interested in the `<layer>` tag:

```java
if (qName.equals("layer")) {
```

The width and height of the level are in the `width` and `height`attributes:

```java
width = Integer.parseInt(
    attributes.getValue("width"));
height = Integer.parseInt(
    attributes.getValue("height"));
```

Once the size of the level is known, we initialize the `level` array and the coordinates (x, y) of the next cell:

```java
level = new int[height][width];
x = 0;
y = 0;
}
```

We are interested in the `<tile>` tag:

```java
else if (qName.equals("tile")) {
```

The code of the cell (wall, space, etc.) is in the `gid` attribute:

```java
int id = Integer.parseInt(attributes.getValue("gid")
);
```

The code is copied into the `level` array:

```java
level[y][x] = id;
```

We go to the next cell. If we have reached the end of a line, we move on to the next. If we exit the level, the file is invalid, and an exception is thrown:

```java
x ++;
if (x >= width) {
```

```
                x = 0;
                y ++;
                if (y > height) {
                    throw new SAXException("Error in file");
                }
            }
        }
    }
```

The `endElement()` method is called when the algorithm encounters a closing tag:

```
    public void endElement (String uri,
        String localName, String qName) throws SAXException
    {
```

For the `</layer>` tag, the state is initialized with a new `init()` method of the
State class:

```
        if (qName.equals("layer")) {
            state.init(level, width, height);
        }
    }
}
```

The new `init()` method of the `State` class is similar to the `execute()` method of
the `InitCommand` class, which initializes the game state from an array of cell codes.

The diagrams in this example are available in the "Class Diagrams/chap04/features02"
folder of the sample UML project.   The code is present in the "exam-
ples/chap04/features02" folder of the sample Java project.

4.4.3 Load/Save Game Status (Proxy Pattern)

Serializable interface

A first solution to save and load a game state in a file is to use the serialization
mechanism included in the Java language. To do this, declare all classes of the
game state as implementing the `Serializable` interface. Then you have to add
the `transient` keyword to attributes that can not be saved, such as the list of
observers in the `State` class. With these modifications alone, it becomes possible
to load the entire state of the game, for example, by adding a `save()` method to
the `State` class:

```
public void save(String fileName) {
    try (ObjectOutputStream out = new ObjectOutputStream(
            new FileOutputStream("save.ser"))) {
        out.writeObject(this);
```

```
    }
    catch(IOException ex) {
        ex.printStackTrace();
        JOptionPane.showMessageDialog(null,"Error when saving",
            "Error", JOptionPane.ERROR_MESSAGE);
    }
}
```

Similarly for loading:

```
public static State load(String fileName) {
    State state = null;
    try (ObjectInputStream in = new ObjectInputStream(
            new FileInputStream("save.ser"))) {
        state = (State) in.readObject();
    } catch (Exception ex) {
        ex.printStackTrace();
        JOptionPane.showMessageDialog(null,"Error when loading",
            "Error", JOptionPane.ERROR_MESSAGE);
    }
    return state;
}
```

This approach, however, causes portability problems. Indeed, the slightest modification for one of the classes produces backup files that are no longer compatible with the previous ones. It is not a problem for short file use, as an exchange between two machines on a network. However, in the long term, this is problematic. For example, adding a new patch to the game is likely to make previous backups incompatible.

There are several solutions to overcome this problem. First, by adding a `serialVersionUID` attribute to each class, we allow the loading of classes that are not perfectly identical (the value of `serialVersionUID` does not have any particular meaning, it must just be different for each class):

```
private static final long serialVersionUID =
    27723746661623881071L;
```

In the opposite case, the slightest difference between two classes prohibits the loading, even if from a data point of view, it represents the same data.

Externalizable interface

The `Externalizable` interface can be implemented in place of `Serializable`. It imposes the existence of a constructor without arguments, a `writeExternal()` method for saving and a `readExternal()` method for loading. In addition to allowing us to choose how to load and, this approach does not force the automatic serialization of all contained elements. It is possible to define how these are saved, without passing by the headers created by Java. Finally, how data is encoded, such as integers or strings, can be defined by implementing the `ObjectOutput` and `ObjectInput` interfaces. In the end, it is possible to produce customized backup files, except for headers produced by a Java-specific mechanism.

Proxy Pattern

The usual problem of separation of functionality arises, especially when save and load procedures begin to have some complexity. This complexity may come from the very nature of the data, but also from versioning. Indeed, if we want to read data produced by previous versions, we need to switch to an old version of the loading code, and then to translate it in the new format. Many branches (if, switch case, ...) within the same method is, as always, impossible to maintain in the long term. Other problems are also caused by saving and loading via simple methods, such as security aspects. One way to overcome these problems is to use the *Proxy Pattern*.

The principle of the proxy is very simple: we replace the implementation of features with a new implementation that intercepts and possibly change the nature of these features:

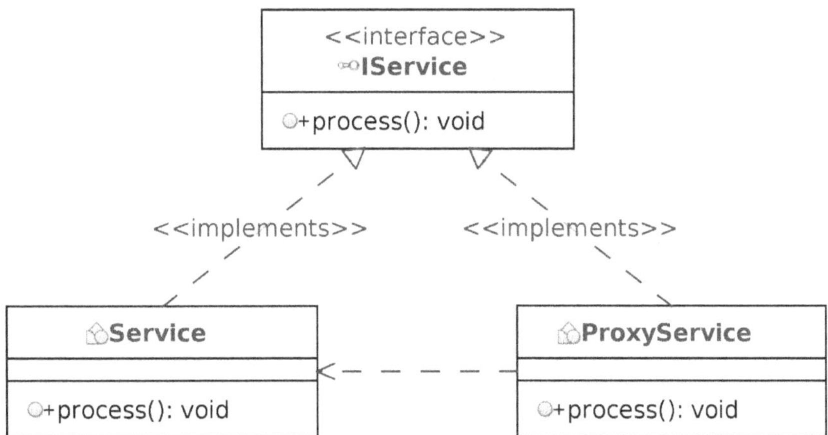

The `IService` interface represents the features: here a simple `process()` method. The `Service` class is an example of implementation. The `ProxyService` class is the proxy of the `Service` class: it also implements the `IService` interface and transfers all calls from the interface to a `Service` implementation. The pattern does not define these transfers: it can be a simple listening, an access control, creation or deletion of the original service, etc. The possibilities are numerous, and in any case, the idea is to replace the original service by its proxy. The end-user must not be bothered by the proxy and must take advantage of the additional features. The way the proxy interacts with the original service is free: it can be by composition, copy, creation, and so on.

Save and Load Proxy

In the case of saving and loading, the targeted features are the two corresponding methods, for example, `writeExternal()` and `readExternal()` from the `Externalizable` interface. By default, the Java language proposes the Proxy pattern via the `writeReplace()` method of the `Serializable` interface. It must return an object able to save and load itself, using the `Serializable` or `Externalizable` interface. For the `State` class of the Pacman example game, it can be used in the following way, assuming the existence of a `StateProxy` proxy class:

```java
public class State implements Serializable {
    private static final long serialVersionUID =
        7832472837472347690L;
    private Object writeReplace() {
        return new StateProxy(this);
    }
    ...
}
```

⇒ Note: It is also possible to implement your backup and load system, and thus to create the proxy classes within this system. In this example, the Java system for saving and loading is used for the sake of simplicity. It is this system that creates a new file, places headers, calls the methods of the `Serializable` interface, etc. It does not remove the benefits of the pattern.

The `StateProxy` class contains a `state` attribute to the state to save or load, a constructor without arguments imposed by the `Externalizable` mechanics, and a constructor that initializes the `state` attribute:

```java
private class StateProxy implements Externalizable
{
    private State state;
    public StateProxy() { }
    public StateProxy(State state) {
        this.state = state;
    }
```

Using a reference to the state to be backed up is the simplest and most convenient, but should be used with caution. For example, the state should not be changed during the backup process. Another approach is to make a deep copy in the constructor.

The `writeExternal` method saves the contents of the state in the `out` argument. This one usually represents a file, but any other output stream can be used:

```java
public void writeExternal(ObjectOutput out)
    throws IOException {
```

We start by writing two integer values: the value 1, then the value 0:

```java
out.writeInt(1);
out.writeInt(0);
```

The idea is to give the version of the created backup. Here is version 1.0. There are many other ways to do it, and in all cases, you have to find a way to identify the format of the data that follow.

The different attributes of the state are saved in a specific order. For objects, like `world` and `chars`, this is only possible if they implement the `Serializable` interface:

```java
out.writeInt(state.epoch);
out.writeInt(state.epochRate);
out.writeInt(state.gumCount);
out.writeInt(state.superDuration);
out.writeObject(state.world);
out.writeObject(state.chars);
}
```

The `readExternal()` method loads the information from the `in` input stream:

```java
public void readExternal(ObjectInput in)
    throws IOException, ClassNotFoundException {
```

It begins by decoding the version of the file, following the format chosen in the `writeExternal()` method:

```java
int versionMaj = in.readInt();
int versionMin = in.readInt();
```

It follows a discussion, depending on the versions. In this example, there is only one possible version:

```java
if (versionMaj != 1 && versionMin != 0)
    throw new UnsupportedEncodingException(
        "Unsupported file version");
```

In the case where there are several possible versions of the file, two possibilities may arise. If the changes are simple, then some branches are enough to manage the case properly. On the other hand, if the changes are important, it becomes interesting to have several proxies, each dedicated to a version of the backup format, then to call the most adapted.

The rest of the method produces a new state, and then loads the attributes following the order used during the backup:

```java
        state = new State();
        state.epoch = in.readInt();
        state.epochRate = in.readInt();
        state.gumCount = in.readInt();
        state.superDuration = in.readInt();
        state.world = (World)in.readObject();
        state.chars = (Characters)in.readObject();
    }
```

The `readResolve()` method is used by the Java save and load system, like the `writeReplace()` method. Its role is to return an object loaded by the `readExternal()` method:

```java
    private Object readResolve() {
        return state;
    }
}
```

Saving up and loading a container

The `World` and `Characters` classes have containers, which reference many objects. For these cases, it is possible to let Java save each of these objects, by implementing the `Serializable` interface to the `Element` class - also with proxy classes. It is also possible to manage these backups ourselves, mainly to reduce the file size.

For example, for the `World` class, we use the same approach as the `State` class with the creation of a proxy class `WorldProxy`, then we implement the `writeExternal()` method for the backup:

```java
public void writeExternal(ObjectOutput out)
    throws IOException {
```

We start by saving the size of the world:

```java
    out.writeInt(world.getWidth());
    out.writeInt(world.getHeight());
```

Then, for each element with coordinates (x,y) of the world:

```java
    for (int y=0;y<world.getHeight();y++) {
        for (int x=0;x<world.getWidth();x++) {
            StaticElement se = world.get(x,y,Direction.NONE);
```

If it's a wall, we write the letter w, then the code of the wall:

```java
        if (se instanceof Wall) {
            Wall wall = (Wall)se;
            out.writeChar('w');
            out.writeInt(wall.getWallTypeId().getCode());
        }
```

If it's a space, we write the letter s, then the code of the space:

```java
        else if (se instanceof Space) {
            Space space = (Space)se;
            out.writeChar('s');
            out.writeInt(space.getSpaceTypeId().getCode());
        }
```

In other cases, there is a problem:

```java
        else {
            throw new IOException(
              "Unable to serialize an element");
        }
      }
    }
}
```

Loading in the readExternal() method starts with loading the world size:

```java
public void readExternal(ObjectInput in)
    throws IOException, ClassNotFoundException {
    int width = in.readInt();
    int height = in.readInt();
    world = new World(width,height);
```

For each coordinate (x,y) of the world, we load a letter in the variable type:

```java
    for (int y=0;y<world.getHeight();y++) {
        for (int x=0;x<world.getWidth();x++) {
            char type = in.readChar();
```

If the letter w is found, then it is a wall: we build an instance according to the
loaded code:

```java
        if (type == 'w') {
            WallTypeId id =
              WallTypeId.fromCode(in.readInt());
            world.set(x, y, new Wall(id));
        }
```

Similarly for the letter s and the case of spaces:

```java
        else if (type == 's') {
            SpaceTypeId id =
```

```java
      SpaceTypeId.fromCode(in.readInt());
    world.set(x, y, new Space(id));
  }
```

Finally, if the loaded letter is not known, there is a problem:

```java
    else {
      throw new IOException(
        "Unable to deserialize an element");
    }
  }
  }
}
```

The same principle is reproduced for the `Characters` class. With this approach, the `Element` classes do not need to implement `Serializable`, or even know how to be saved or loaded. The state of the game can be saved and loaded using the `save()` and `load()` methods presented at the beginning of this section.

The diagrams in this example are available in the "Class Diagrams/chap04/features03" folder of the sample UML project. The code is present in the "examples/chap04/features03" folder of the sample Java project. The state of the game can be saved by pressing the F6 key, and loaded by pressing the F7 key. When loading, the characters are not teleported to the saved coordinates but moved very quickly to these coordinates. It is the result of the interpolation system of the display, which smooths the movements between two states of the game. To avoid this, we can add a pause of the display during one epoch, and then reset sprites.

4.5   Exercise Solutions

4.5.1   Exercise 2.4.1: Build a galaxy

A solution is proposed in the "examples/chap04/stellaris" folder of the source packages, as well as unit tests in the same folder in the test packages.

The non-dependence on planetary types is based on the use of the Abstract Factory pattern to create these:

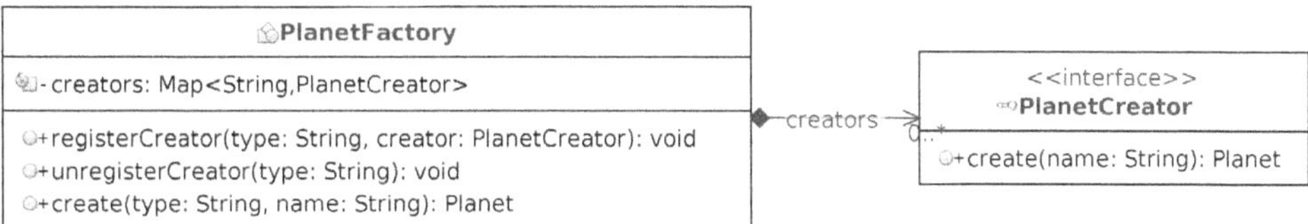

The planet factory follows the usual pattern, knowing that the name of the planet must be provided during its construction. The `create()` method of the factory has two arguments: the type and name of the planet.

```java
public class PlanetFactory {
    private Map<String, PlanetCreator> creators = new HashMap();
    public void registerCreator(String type,
        PlanetCreator creator) {
        creators.put(type, creator);
    }
    public void unregisterCreator(String type) {
        creators.remove(type);
    }
    public Planet create(String type,String name) {
        return creators.get(type).create(name);
    }
}
```

The `GalaxyLoader` class is set to load a galaxy from a `String` list. It does not depend on the `Planet` child classes. It contains a factory default, that can be modified at runtime:

```java
public class GalaxyLoader {
    private final String[] data;

    private int i;

    private PlanetFactory factory = new PlanetFactory();

    public GalaxyLoader(String[] data) {
```

```java
        this.data = data;
        factory.registerCreator("Habitable",
        new PlanetCreator() {
            @Override
            public Planet create(String name) {
                return new Habitable(name);
            }
        });
        factory.registerCreator("Gaseous",new PlanetCreator() {
            @Override
            public Planet create(String name) {
                return new Gaseous(name);
            }
        });
    }

    public Galaxy load() {
        Galaxy galaxy = new Galaxy();
        i = 0;
        while(i < data.length) {
            if (data[i].equals("End"))
                break;
            if (!data[i].equals("System"))
                throw new RuntimeException("Invalid format");
            i ++;
            if (i >= data.length)
                throw new RuntimeException("Invalid format");
            String systemName = data[i++];
            System system = galaxy.createSystem(systemName,0,0);
            loadSystem(system);
        }
        return galaxy;
    }

    private void loadSystem(System system) {
        while(i < data.length) {
            if (data[i].equals("End"))
                break;
            String planetType = data[i++];
            if (i >= data.length)
                throw new RuntimeException("Invalid format");
            String planetName = data[i++];
            Planet planet = factory.create(planetType,planetName
            );
            system.addPlanet(planet);
```

```
        }
        i ++;
    }
}
```

Finally, the loader can be validated via unit tests:

```java
public class GalaxyLoaderTest {
  public static String[] data = {
    "System", "Alpha","Habitable", "Alpha1","Gaseous", "Alpha2",
        "End","System", "Beta","Gaseous", "Beta1","Gaseous", "Beta2",
        "Gaseous", "Beta3","End","System", "Gamma",
        "Habitable", "Gamma1","End","End"
  };
  @Test
  public void test() {
    Galaxy g = new GalaxyLoader(data).load();

    assertEquals("Alpha",g.getSystem(0).getName());
    assertEquals("Beta",g.getSystem(1).getName());
    assertEquals("Gamma",g.getSystem(2).getName());

    System a = g.getSystem(0);
    assertTrue(a.getPlanet(0) instanceof Habitable);
    assertTrue(a.getPlanet(1) instanceof Gaseous);
    System b = g.getSystem(1);
    assertTrue(b.getPlanet(0) instanceof Gaseous);
    assertTrue(b.getPlanet(1) instanceof Gaseous);
    assertTrue(b.getPlanet(2) instanceof Gaseous);
    System g = g.getSystem(2);
    assertTrue(g.getPlanet(0) instanceof Habitable);
  }

}
```

4.5.2   Exercise 2.4.2: Move an army

A solution is proposed in the "examples/chap04/army" folder of the source packages, as well as unit tests in the same folder in the test packages.

The solution is based on the Composite pattern:

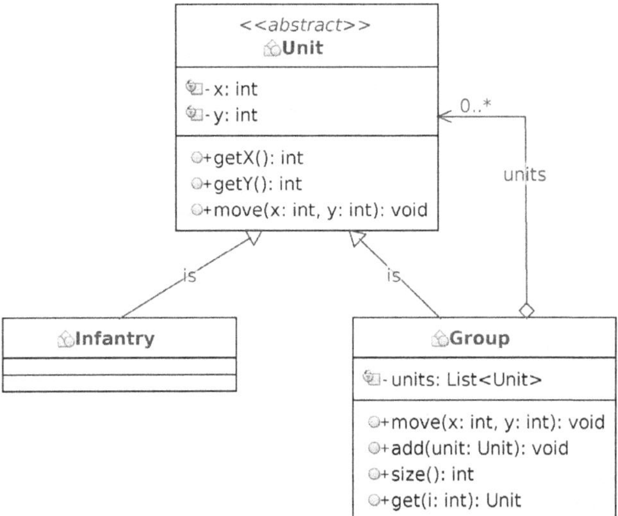

Thanks to this pattern, a group of units can be formed with the Group class. More-over, this class can be manipulated as if it were a simple unit:

```java
public class Group extends Unit {
    private List<Unit> units = new ArrayList();
    public void move(int x, int y) {
        for (Unit unit : units) {
            unit.move(x, y);
        }
    }
    public void add(Unit unit) {
        units.add(unit);
    }
    public int size() {
        return units.size();
    }
    public Unit get(int i) {
        return units.get(i);
    }
}
```

It can be validated with the following unit tests. The groupAsUnit variable demonstrates the property you are looking for:

```java
public class GroupTest {
    @Test
    public void testSomeMethod() {
        Unit unit1 = new Infantry();
        Unit unit2 = new Infantry();
        Unit unit3 = new Infantry();
        Unit unit4 = new Infantry();

        unit1.move(1, 4);
        unit2.move(2, 3);
        unit3.move(3, 2);
        unit4.move(4, 1);

        assertEquals(1,unit1.getX());
        assertEquals(2,unit2.getX());
        assertEquals(3,unit3.getX());
        assertEquals(4,unit4.getX());
        assertEquals(4,unit1.getY());
        assertEquals(3,unit2.getY());
        assertEquals(2,unit3.getY());
        assertEquals(1,unit4.getY());

        Group group = new Group();
        group.add(unit1);
        group.add(unit2);
        group.add(unit3);
        group.add(unit4);

        Unit groupAsUnit = (Unit)group;
        groupAsUnit.move(1, -1);
        assertEquals(2,unit1.getX());
        assertEquals(3,unit2.getX());
        assertEquals(4,unit3.getX());
        assertEquals(5,unit4.getX());
        assertEquals(3,unit1.getY());
        assertEquals(2,unit2.getY());
        assertEquals(1,unit3.getY());
        assertEquals(0,unit4.getY());
    }
}
```

4.5.3 Exercise 3.6.1: Several players on the same keyboard

Just add the following lines in the `handleInputs()` method of the `PlayGameMode` class:

```java
if (keyboard.isKeyPressed(KeyEvent.VK_D)) {
    rules.addCommand(1,new DirectionCommand(1,Direction.EAST));
}
if (keyboard.isKeyPressed(KeyEvent.VK_Q)) {
    rules.addCommand(1,new DirectionCommand(1,Direction.WEST));
}
if (keyboard.isKeyPressed(KeyEvent.VK_S)) {
    rules.addCommand(1,new DirectionCommand(1,Direction.SOUTH));
}
if (keyboard.isKeyPressed(KeyEvent.VK_Z)) {
    rules.addCommand(1,new DirectionCommand(1,Direction.NORTH));
}
```

4.5.4 Exercise 3.6.2: Checkers game with the command pattern

Since there is only one possible action (moving a pawn), a single `MoveCommand` command class is defined. A `Rules` class is also added to handle this command:

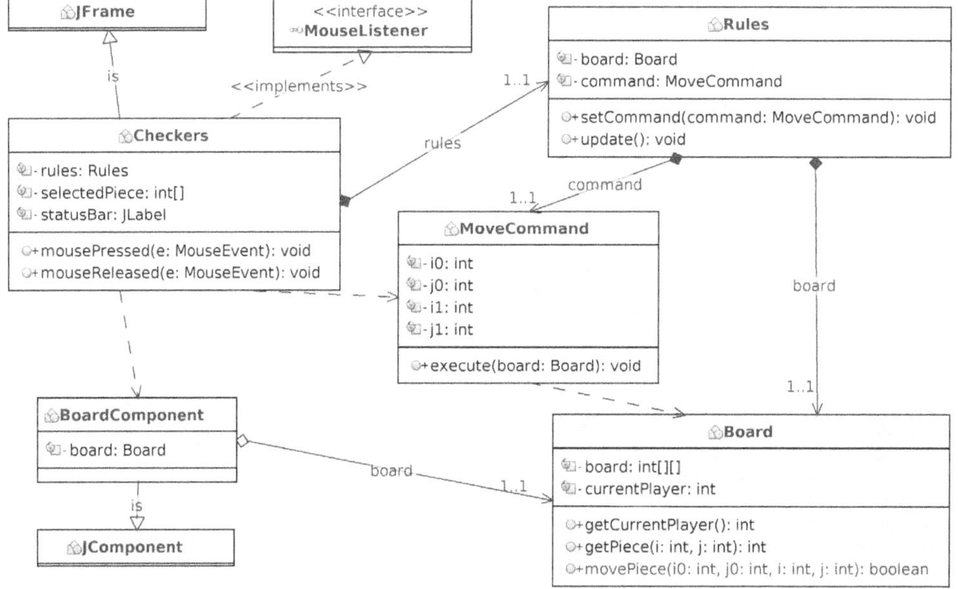

The `MoveCommand` class contains the coordinates of the pawn to move (i0, j0), and the destination coordinates (i1, j1). Its execute() method invokes the movePiece() method of the Board class:

```java
public void execute(Board board) {
    board.movePiece(i0, j0, i1, j1);
}
```

The Rules class memorizes a MoveCommand command, then executes it with its update() method:

```java
public void update() {
    if (command != null) {
        command.execute(board);
        command = null;
    }
}
```

Finally, the mouseReleased() method of the Checkers class is modified to use the pattern mechanisms:

```java
public void mouseReleased(MouseEvent e) {
    if (selectedPiece == null) {
        return;
    }
    int i = e.getX() / 80;
    int j = e.getY() / 80;
    rules.setCommand(new MoveCommand(selectedPiece[0],
            selectedPiece[1], i, j));
    rules.update();
    redraw();
    selectedPiece = null;
}
```

⇒ Note: Calling the redraw() method in the above method is not always necessary. For example, if the requested move is not possible, there is nothing to redraw. The solution to this problem is to use the Observer pattern: the Board class is observed by the Checkers class, which redraws the window if it receives a notification.

With these changes, the Checkers class no longer has complete control over the nature of game changes: it can only ask for it. The changes are now the subject of the Rules and MoveCommand classes.

The entire solution code is available in the "examples/chap04/checkers" folder of the sample Java project.

CHAPTER 5

Artificial Intelligence

5.1 Preparation

Before starting the design and implementation of artificial intelligence, some preparations are required. Firstly, we need to design a read-only game state to avoid unintentional errors. Secondly, we need to define an interface for artificial intelligence (AI), to separate AI internal mechanics from its use.

5.1.1 Immutable game state

So far, the game state has always been editable by any component, including those who have no reason to change it. For example, the rendering engine should not change the state of the game. Similarly, artificial intelligence must not change the state of the game, except in the case where it is allowed to cheat.

There are two main approaches to ensure that an object can not be changed: trusting members of your team or making changes impossible. In the first case, even the most rigorous developers can sometimes make mistakes, especially when a method modifies the data in a counter-intuitive or undocumented manner. This kind of scenario is common after several years of development, where the project is made up of thousands of classes.

The safest approach is to make changes impossible. In this section, we propose two approaches, one when the classes to be protected are not modifiable (ex: external library), and the other when the classes can be modified.

5.1.1.1 Approach with the Proxy Pattern

When the classes to protect are not modifiable, it is possible to use the Proxy pattern. As a reminder, this one consists in defining a new class which copies the contents of the classes to be processed, while providing the same interface. Then, we replace the objects with their proxy: the users of the targeted class do not see the difference, except for the added features. In this case, all methods that do not modify the attributes are unchanged, and those that modify them throw an exception.

Classes without containers

Here is a first example with the `Wall` class of the Pacman game state. We define an `ImmutableWall` class that inherits from the `Wall` class:

```java
public class ImmutableWall extends Wall {
    public ImmutableWall(Wall wall) {
        super(wall.getWallTypeId());
    }
    public void setWallTypeId(WallTypeId wallTypeId) {
        throw new IllegalAccessError();
    }
}
```

There is only one copy constructor, which duplicates the unique attribute of the class and its parent classes. Then, only the setter `setWallTypeId()` of the attribute is redefined to return an exception stating that the use of this method is forbidden.

Classes with containers

We repeat this principle for all classes without a container, such as `Space`, `Pacman` and `Ghost`. For classes with a container, we have to be careful, especially if some getters return a container, like the `getChars()` method of the `Characters` class:

```java
public List<MobileElement> getChars() {
    return chars;
}
```

Although this does not modify the `chars` attribute, it does not prohibit modifying its content. To prevent this, for example, you can throw an exception for this method, and then add accessors for items in the `chars` list. You can also return another proxy from the list. The standard library already provides such a proxy in the `Collections` class with the `unmodifiableList()` static method:

```java
public List<MobileElement> getChars() {
    return Collections.unmodifiableList(chars);
}
```

It is also possible to build this non-modifiable list directly in the constructors of the class, to avoid repeating their creation if we often use the accessor.

Warning: the container elements must not also have containers, in which case the protection is not complete.

For accessors in a container class, such as the `get()` method of the `Characters` class, we must also make sure that the returned objects are unmodifiable:

```java
public MobileElement get(int index) {
    MobileElement me = chars.get(index);
    if (me instanceof Pacman) {
        return new ImmutablePacman((Pacman)me);
    }
    if (me instanceof Ghost) {
        return new ImmutableGhost((Ghost)me);
    }
    throw new RuntimeException("Invalid type");
}
```

Use

To use the proxy, create non-editable versions when necessary. For example, when the state notifies changes, the supplied state is a non-editable version:

```java
public void notityStateChanged() {
    ImmutableState roState = new ImmutableState(this);
    for (StateObserver observer : observers) {
        observer.stateChanged(roState);
    }
}
```

Thus, the rendering engine can not change the state unintentionally.

The diagrams of this example are available in the "Class Diagrams/chap05/immutable01" folder of the sample UML project. The code is present in the "examples/chap05/immutable01" folder of the Java sample project.

5.1.1.2   Approach with the Decorator Pattern

The proxy pattern is relevant when the classes to be protected can not be changed (like external libraries). However, it has some drawbacks. The first is that we must not forget to redefine the mutators in the proxy class. When we add new features, it is usual to forget these redefinitions or to postpone them. One way to ensure that protections are still in place is to define an interface and two implementations: one with all access and modification features, and the other with only access features. The other problem is the overhead generated by the proxy pattern. The proposed solution makes it possible to overcome these two problems.

The decorator pattern is very interesting to define a read-only class. As a reminder, it consists in defining a class with an attribute of the type of the class to decorate (or several if necessary), then to implement the same interface by calling the methods of the attribute. These calls can be without modifications, or with modifications. It is also possible to add new methods. For example, for element classes, the class hierarchy is reproduced with interfaces:

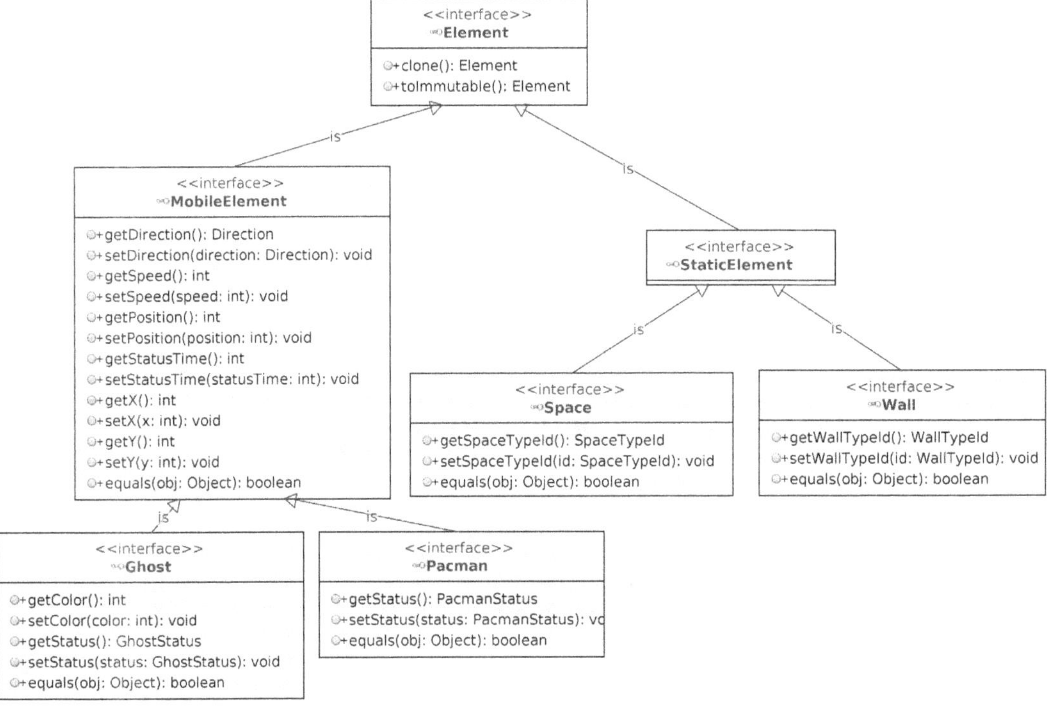

We can notice the `toImmutable()` method of the `Element` class, which did not exist in the initial interface. This method returns a non-editable version of the object and is very useful in several cases presented below.

Editable classes

Editable classes implement these interfaces and are named `MutableXXX`, for example `MutablePacman` for the `Pacman` class. The implementation is identical to the initial version, except for the `toImmutable()` methods. For example, for non-abstract classes like `MutableWall`, a decorated version is returned:

```java
public Element toImmutable() {
    return new ImmutableWall(this);
}
```

Non editable classes without containers

Non-modifiable classes also implement these interfaces and are named `ImmutableXXX`. Classes without a parent, such as the `ImmutableElement` class, have a unique attribute that points to a mutable object:

```java
public class ImmutableElement implements Element
{
    protected final MutableElement element;
```

A single constructor is used to initialize the attribute:

```java
    public ImmutableElement(MutableElement element){
        this.element = element;
    }
```

For the `clone()` method, we can safely return an editable copy since the copies are deep (see the previous Chapter):

```java
    public Element clone() {
        return element.clone();
    }
```

The `toImmutable()` method returns a non-modifiable version of the object, which is itself:

```java
    public Element toImmutable() {
        return this;
    }
}
```

For non-abstract classes, such as `ImmutableWall`, we use the attribute to implement getters, for example:

```java
public WallTypeId getWallTypeId() {
    return ((MutableWall)element).getWallTypeId();
}
```

And for the setters, we throw an exception:

```java
public void setWallTypeId(WallTypeId wallTypeId) {
    throw new IllegalAccessError();
}
```

In addition, we declare non-modifiable classes as final. It means that all their methods are final, and can not be redefined:

```java
public final class ImmutableWall ... {
    ...
}
```

This information allows the compiler to optimize calls to the decorated methods, in many cases removing the intermediate call.

Non-editable classes with containers

For classes with containers, we must care as in the previous case, and ensure that the elements contained are also non-modifiable. For example, for the get() method of the Characters class:

```java
public MobileElement get(int index) {
    MobileElement me = chars.get(index);
    return (ImmutableMobileElement)me.toImmutable();
}
```

The use of non-modifiable classes with the decorator pattern is the same as with the proxy pattern.

The diagrams in this sample are available in the "Class Diagrams/chap05/immutable02" folder of the sample UML project. The code is present in the "examples/chap05/immutable02" folder of the Java sample project.

5.1.2   Artificial Intelligence Interface

Before starting the design of artificial intelligence, an environment is created to ease their management.

5.1.2.1   List the possible commands (Strategy Pattern)

To be able to propose artificial intelligence with an architecture based on the command pattern, it is enough to propose commands for the artificial players. For example, for the Pacman game, it is enough to propose an orientation command evaluated as the most effective to win.

Before being able to make a choice, we need to know the list of possible commands for a given game state. This task is not artificial intelligence, and it depends on the rules of the game. These rules can vary according to different options, and it is more effective for an AI to delegate this task to a third party. We can use the strategy pattern to get this result.

Strategy Pattern

The *Strategy Pattern* allows you to change the behavior of a process while the program is running. It can be presented as follows:

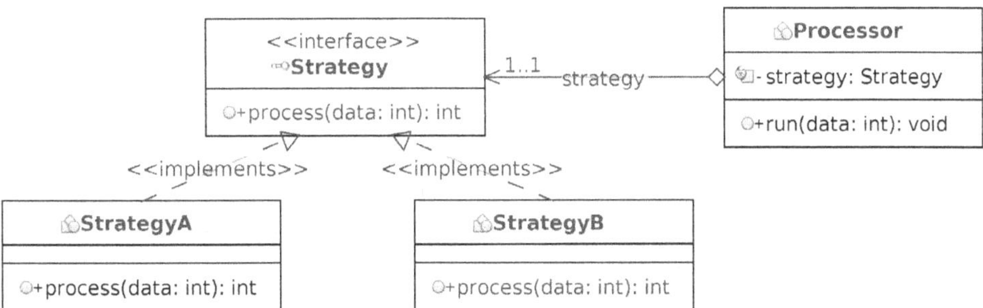

The `Strategy` interface defines the sub-processes that can be modified during program execution. In this illustration, there is only one `process()` method, but we can add other methods with the arguments of our choice. There are two implementations of the interface in this example, `StrategyA` and `StrategyB`. Then, a `Processor` class handles all the processing logic. It uses an implementation of the `Strategy` interface blindly: it knows only the methods of this interface. It can use the implementation that it references with its attribute in a free way.

The typical example of using the Strategy pattern is that of sorting data. Indeed, the algorithm is usually fixed - such as *quick sort* or *binary heap*, but the way you compare data may vary. In the standard library, the `Collections.sort()` static method has two arguments: the list to be sorted and one implementation of the `java.util.Comparator` interface. This interface is the equivalent of the `Strategy` interface in the illustration above.

Use the list of possible commands

The Strategy pattern can be used to separate the logic of artificial intelligence from the process of determining possible commands. We define a CommandsLister interface that acts as a strategy and a DefaultCommandsLister implementation that provides the commands with the default rules. Then, the implantations of an AI interface manages the logic of the AI by making use of a CommandsLister implementation:

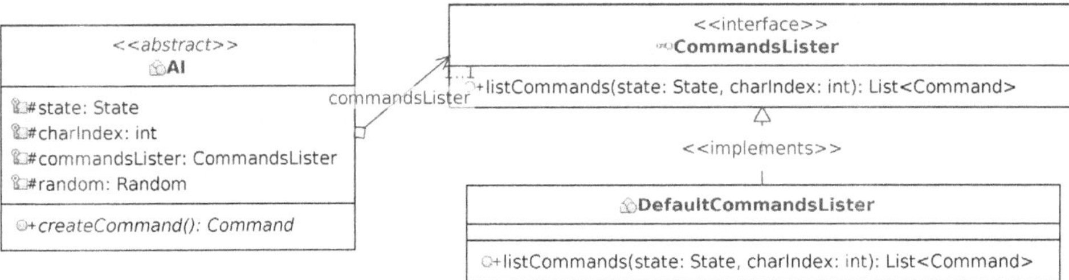

Implementations of the createCommand() method return the best command for the charIndex index character based on the data in state.

⇒ Note: Words and their meaning: the "strategy" in the sense of the pattern in this example is not the strategy of artificial intelligence, but the nature of the commands that can be considered, regardless of any intelligence algorithm.

⇒ Note: In the proposed example, the CommandsLister interface and its implementations are present in the artificial intelligence part of the project. A more complex but more consistent design is naturally to place its elements in the rules engine part, and to enrich the engine so that it is a factory of CommandsLister.

5.1.2.2   Random behavior

Implementation of a random AI

A first artificial intelligence is created to test implementations. It consists of making random choices among the possible commands. For the Pacman example game, a RandomAI class implements the AI interface:

```java
public class RandomAI extends AI
{
    public RandomAI(State state, int charIndex,
        CommandsLister lister, Random random) {
        super(state, charIndex, lister, random);
    }
```

The `createCommand()` method asks for the possible commands and then chooses one at random:

```java
public Command createCommand() {
    List<Command> list = commandsLister
        .listCommands(state, charIndex);
    if (list.isEmpty())
        return null;
    int index = random.nextInt(list.size());
    return list.get(index);
}
}
```

Using the AI

Random AI is used for all characters. An `ais` list of `IA` is added to the `PlayGameMode` class, and is initialized in the `init()` method:

```java
Random random = new Random();
CommandsLister commandsLister = *
    new DefaultCommandsLister();
Characters chars = state.getChars();
ais = new AI[chars.size()];
ImmutableState imState = new ImmutableState(state);
for(int index=0;index<chars.size();index++) {
    ais[index] = new RandomAI(imState,index,
            commandsLister,random);
}
```

We give a non-modifiable state `ImmutableState` to the AIs to prohibit changes.

Then, AIs are invoked for all non-played characters when updating the game in the `update()` method of the `PlayGameMode` class:

```java
Characters chars = state.getChars();
for(int index=0;index<chars.size();index++) {
    if (index == currentChar)
        continue;
    Command command = ais[index].createCommand();
    if (command != null) {
        rules.addCommand(index, command);
    }
}
```

To play non-player characters (whose index is different from `currentChar`), ask the associated AI to make a command and then add it to the game engine if it exists.

⇒ Note: Additional use of the Strategy pattern is made here: the `AI` interface defines the methods of the strategy, and the `PlayGameMode` class contains the general logic of the processing.

The execution of these random AIs when Pacman is played seems quite coherent: ghosts roam the maze in a usual way. However, when a ghost is played by pressing a key between F2 and F5, Pacman has a behavior that makes no sense, it comes and goes aimlessly. It is related to the fact that Pacman can turn around, unlike ghosts.

The diagrams in this sample are available in the "Class Diagrams/chap05/ai01" folder of the sample UML project. The code is present in the "examples/chap05/ai01" folder of the Java sample project.

5.1.2.3 Evaluation

Qualitative evaluation of an AI is possible in trivial cases - especially when AI is particularly inefficient. In other cases, qualitative evaluation is more difficult and can be very long to run. One solution is to simulate games only played by artificial intelligence, and compare their performances.

For the Pacman game, an `AIEval` class is created in the 'pacman/ai' folder of the test packages. It runs many games using AI for all characters. We implement different AI combinations, but for this stage of preparation, we only use a random AI. Statistics are computed, knowing that we are primarily interested in Pacman's AI:

- Difficulty: it defines the speed of ghosts. The greater the difficulty, the faster the ghosts.
- Victories: The number of times that Pacman managed to eat all the gums without being killed by a ghost.
- Victory time: the average number of game epochs to achieve victory. The lower it is, the better the AI.
- Defeat time: The average number of game times when Pacman is killed. The higher it is, the better the AI.
- Gums: The average number of gums when Pacman is killed. The lower the number, the closer AI gets to victory.

Unsurprisingly, random AI never manages to get a victory. Concerning defeats, they are only later with a reduced difficulty:

Pacman	Ghost	Diff.	Victories	Time	Time	Gums
Random	Random	Easy	0	0	739	213
Random	Random	Normal	0	0	570	217
Random	Random	Hard	0	0	399	222

5.1.3 Exercises

5.1.3.1 Exercise 1.3.1: Immutable galaxy

→ Implement a non-modifiable version of the galaxy from the previous exercise, whose sources are in the folder "examples/chap02/stellaris". You can use the Proxy or the Decorator pattern, or try both.

5.1.3.2 Exercise 1.3.2: Connect 4 with a simple AI

→ Propose and implement a design for two AIs for the connect 4 game: one random, and one that always chooses the first possible column from the left.

→ Challenge these two AIs in competition.

You can use your own "connect 4" implementation, or use the one available in "examples/chap05/connect4noai". If you use this example, here is a description of classes and methods that can be useful:

- Board class:
    - It contains a grid of 7 columns with 6 cells. It also contains the current player: 1 for the red player and -1 for the yellow player.
    - `void reset(int player)` method: starts a new game and selects `player` as the first player to play.
    - `boolean isWinner(int player)` method: returns `true` if the player `player` (1 or -1) has aligned 4 pawns.
    - `Boolean isOver()` method: returns `true` if the game is over (a player won, or the grid is full).
    - `boolean canPlay(int column)` method: returns `true` if it is possible to add a pawn in the `column` column.
- Command class:
    - Implements a minimalist version of the command pattern
    - `Command(int column)` constructor: constructs a command whose action is to add a pawn to the `column` column.
    - `void execute(Board board)` method: implements the embedded action. If the action is not possible or is already executed, nothing happens.
    - `void rollback(Board board)` method: cancels the embedded action. If the action was not executed, nothing happens.

5.1.4 Video Game Development: AI Preparation

Before starting to design an artificial intelligence, it is strongly advised to build a framework. It allows you to focus on issues specific to AI and not other implementation details.

This preparation has already begun with the command pattern: it allows us to abstract the running the game. For example, it makes it possible to draw up the list of the possible shots, then to handle them formally, as it was done above to propose a random AI. Besides, if the command pattern has a rollback mechanism, it is possible to simulate sequences of moves to see what happens, and then restore the initial state.

Other preparations are also needed, especially if the game rules are not simple. For simple games like the checkers or Mario, the process is in one step: one shot per player and turn/epoch. Other games are based on several stages. For example, most war games have a management stage, where units are recruited, and a battle stage, where the units are moved. It is strongly recommended to add the necessary elements so that all the AIs can identify the current step, as well as the possible commands according to these steps. The resulting framework must be independent of the AI.

5.2 Artificial Intelligence without planning

The first category of artificial intelligence is presented in this section. It concerns AIs that make a decision based on the current state of the game, without projecting into the future.

5.2.1 Simple heuristics

The simplest AI to implement are those based on heuristics, e.g. functions designed to solve a very specific problem. Their effectiveness depends on the level of cleverness that can be demonstrated by their creator. They generally offer no guarantee of success for all situations, but they promise to be better than random.

For the Pacman example game, a simple heuristic is to choose, among the possible Pacman commands, those that have no ghost insight. For example, if there is a ghost in the cells close to Pacman's right, we avoid this direction. It can be implemented as follows in the `createCommand()` method of a new `ExplorationAI` class that implements the `AI` interface. This one starts by asking the list of the possible commands for the current state of the game:

```java
public Command createCommand() {
    List<Command> list = commandsLister
        .listCommands(state, charIndex);
    if (list.isEmpty())
        return null;
```

The different commands are analyzed one by one:

```java
    Characters chars = state.getChars();
    MobileElement me = chars.get(charIndex);
    Command oppositeCommand = null;
    List<Command> commands = new ArrayList();
    for (Command command : list) {
        if (!(command instanceof DirectionCommand))
            continue;
        DirectionCommand dirCommand = (DirectionCommand)command;
```

If a character is found in the near area in the direction of the command, then we continue:

```java
        Direction direction = dirCommand.getDirection();
        if (findCharacter(dirCommand.getDirection()))
            continue;
```

The `findCharacter()` method is implemented to determine if an area contains a ghost. It is a simple parsing of cells in the area.

If the command is in the opposite direction of Pacman, we also pass. It means that U-turns are not wanted: the goal of this heuristic is also to let Pacman explore the world while avoiding ghosts:

```java
if (direction.isOppositeOf(me.getDirection())) {
    oppositeCommand = command;
    continue;
}
```

If all conditions are met, you can add the candidate command in a list:

```java
    commands.add(command);
}
```

If the selection has not eliminated everything, one of the command candidates is chosen at random:

```java
if (!commands.isEmpty()) {
    int index = random.nextInt(commands.size());
    return commands.get(index);
}
```

If the selection has eliminated all the possibilities, we allow a half-turn, if it is possible:

```java
if (oppositeCommand != null) {
    return oppositeCommand;
}
```

In the latter case, the heuristic is unable to make a decision:

```java
    return null;
}
```

The diagrams in this example are available in the "Class Diagrams/chap05/ai02" folder of the sample UML project. The code is present in the "examples/chap05/ai02" folder of the Java sample project.

This first very simple AI is evaluated using the protocol presented previously. Its results are very unstable, and it is necessary to launch a very large number of simulations to have stable statistics. Unlike the random approach, this AI can find victory, but in a low proportion. It also takes a lot of time to eat all the gums:

Pacman	Ghost	Diff.	Victories	Time	Time	Gums
Simple	Random	Easy	61%	6379	3384	55
Simple	Random	Normal	46%	6137	3098	65
Simple	Random	Hard	19%	5498	2668	73

5.2.2   Distance maps

There is no single recipe for creating heuristics for all games. However, some tools are useful in many cases, such as distance maps. These maps make it possible to carry out different tasks, like choosing the direction that leads as quickly as possible to a goal or a target. They are useful in all games where characters move in a world, but also to facilitate choices in a set of possibilities, such as dialogue trees.

Here is an example of a distance map for the Pacman game. The presented map has Pacman as the only target:

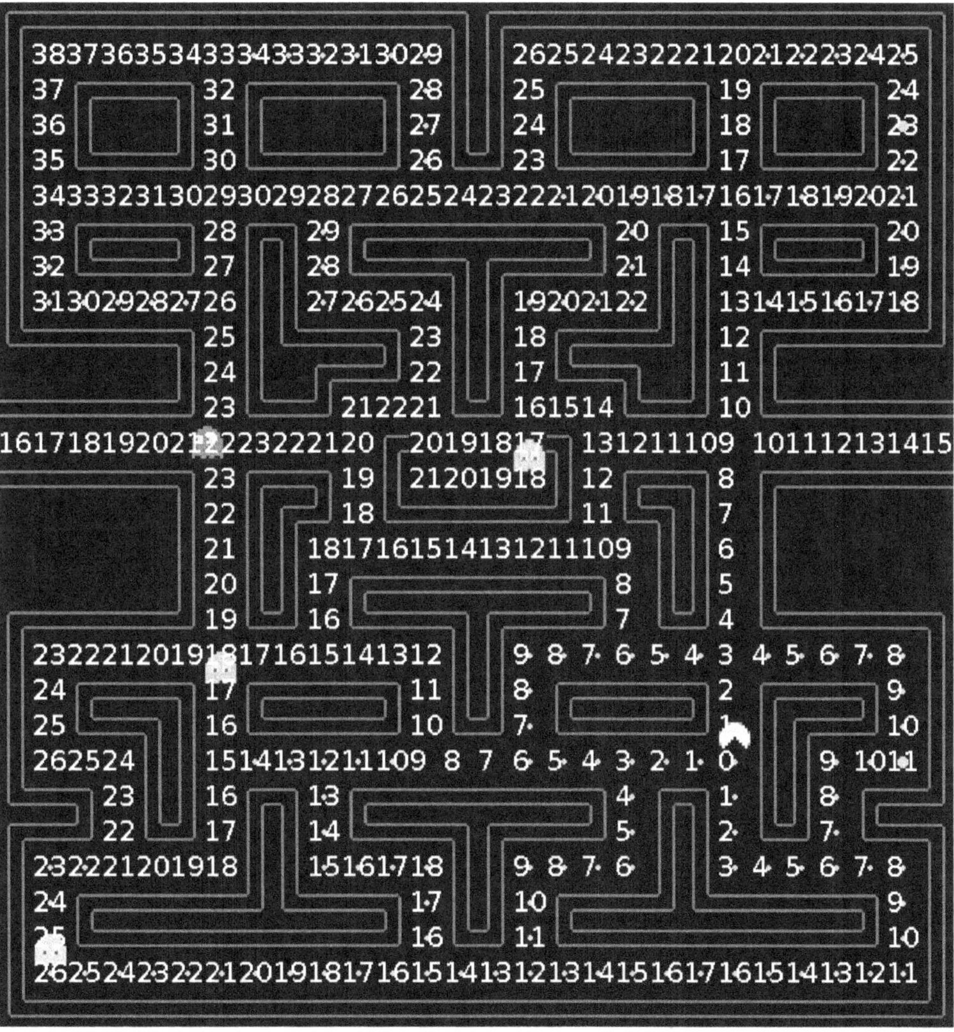

Each value on cells is the number of cells that must be traveled to reach Pacman as quickly as possible. At the Pacman position, the value is 0. The adjacent squares have value 1, and the next ones value 2, etc. To get closer to Pacman as quickly as possible, choose the adjacent cell that has a lower value than the current one. For example, for the red ghost, which is on a cell with the value 22, choose the cell to its left with the value 21. Then, we repeat the same principle until reaching the cell with the value 0.

The following sections present the tools and algorithms for computing these maps.

5.2.2.1 Reminders on graphs

The methods for computing distance maps do not only apply to regular worlds. They can be computed on any world represented by a graph. Before presenting the algorithms that make it possible to compute distance maps, this section presents some reminders on graphs.

Directed and undirected graph

There are two main families of graphs: directed graphs and undirected graphs:

- A directed graph is formed by a pair (V, A), where V is a set of vertices, and A is a set of arcs. An arc connects two vertices with one or more directions;
- An undirected graph is formed by a pair (V, E), where V is a set of vertices and E is a set of edges. An edge connects two vertices but without a direction.

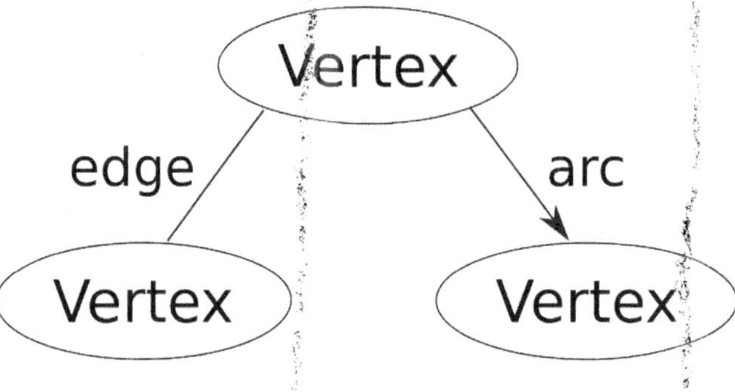

Valued graph and adjacency matrix

Each vertex of a graph has or represents information. For games, it's usually a position in the world, like a cell in the Pacman game.

Arcs and edges may have a value, usually numeric. Then, one says that the graph is valued. In games, these values usually represent the distance between two vertices, or the time required to travel from one vertex to another. In the Pacman example game, the graph is valued, and the value of each edge is always 1: it always takes the same time to go from one cell to another.

Here is an example of valued graph:

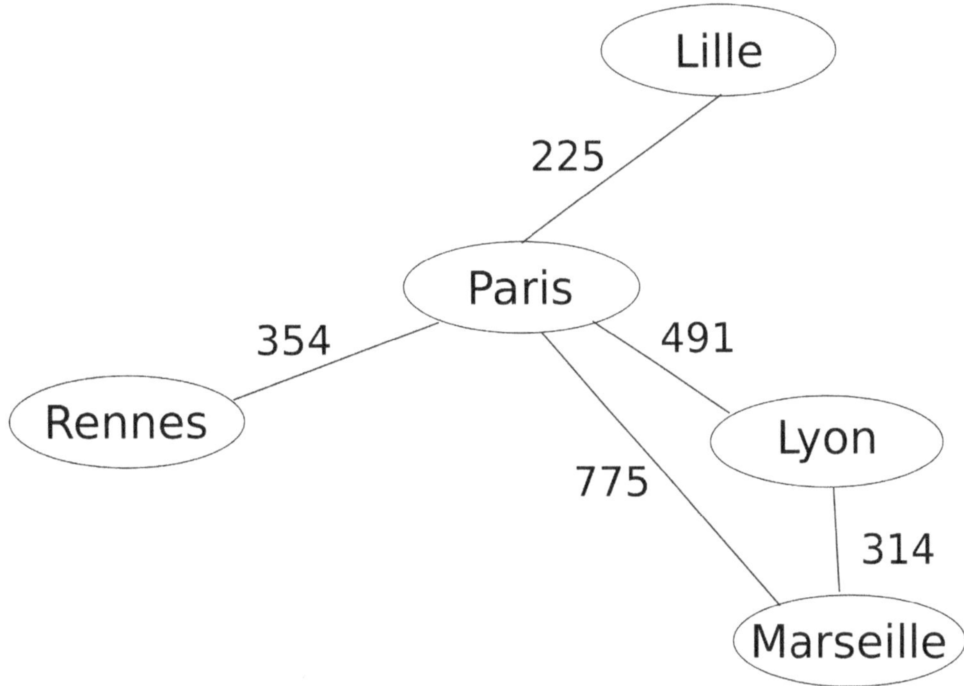

⇒ Note: The position of vertices of the graph in the illustration above is not part of the graph. For example, the vertex "Marseille" can be drawn on the top left, without modifying the graph. This illustration is only one representation, among others.

An adjacency matrix can contain all values of an undirected graph. For example, if we assign a position in a list of edges/cities above, such as {Paris, Lille, Rennes, Lyon, Marseille}, then we can define the following adjacency matrix:

0	225	354	491	775
225	0	0	0	0
354	0	0	0	0
491	0	0	0	314
775	0	0	314	0

⇒ Note: Unvalued graphs can also be represented by an adjacency matrix, in which case values are equal to 0 or 1. Adjacency matrices can also be considered for directed graphs, assuming that there is at most one arc between two vertices.

Chain and cycle/path and circuit

In a graph, we are often interested in sequences of connected vertices. Whatever the graph kind (directed or not), these sequences used to be called walks.

When it's an undirected graph, walks are called chains. For example, in the graph above with cities, the sequence {Lille, Paris, Marseille} forms a chain. The same vertex can appear several times in the chain. If the first and last vertex of the chain is the same, then we speak of a cycle. For example, the chain {Paris, Lyon, Marseille, Paris} is a cycle.

For the directed graphs, the same notions exist, but with different vocabulary: the chains are called paths, and the cycles are called circuits.

Connected graphs

An undirected graph is said to be connected if there is always a chain connecting any pair of vertices. The graph above with cities is connected. For video games, the graphs that represent the world are usually connected: this means that a character can go from any place in the world to any other. However, if a way is blocked, the graph loses its property of connectivity: it is then formed of two so-called connected components.

For directed graphs, the same notions exist, knowing that we must find paths, and therefore sequences of directed arcs that connect any pair of vertices. These are strongly connected graphs and strongly connected components.

Trees and hierarchies

Trees are special cases of undirected, connected graphs without cycles. Hierarchies are the equivalent for directed, connected, and circuit-less graphs. In practice, there is often an abuse of language, and the hierarchies are called trees.

The vertices of trees and hierarchies are often called nodes. Hierarchies (and by abuse trees) always have a node called root, pointed by any arc. If a node points to other nodes, then the pointed nodes are child nodes, and the node that points children is their parent. Finally, if a node does not point to any other node, it is called a leaf.

5.2.2.2 Computation of distance maps

To compute distance maps, there are two main algorithms: Ford's, which is simple but slow, and Dijkstra's, which is a bit more complicated but very fast.

In all cases, we aim at computing a value for each vertex: all these values are the distance map. These principles are illustrated with the following valued graph:

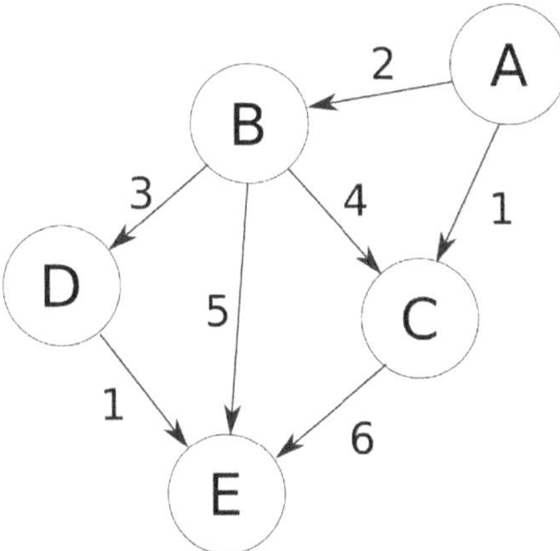

Each vertex of the graph represents a place in space, time, the domain of possibilities, etc. Arcs represent distance, cost, weight, etc. between each vertex.

Initialization

To initialize these algorithms, we first set one or more vertex as targets (or *sinks*) with value 0, and set all others with infinity value. In this example, we chose the vertex A at the top right as the target:

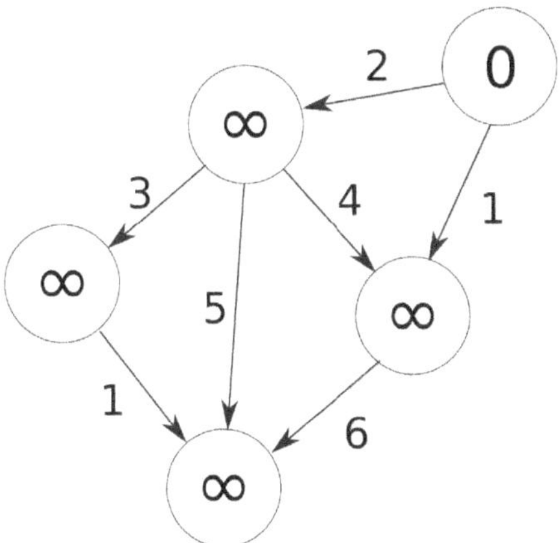

Both algorithms are based on a so-called relaxation operation. This one is applied on a vertex and modifies the vertices that its arcs point. For each pointed vertex, if the sum of vertex value with arc value is lower than the value of the pointed vertex, then the pointed vertex takes the value of the sum. Relaxing the vertex A gives the following result:

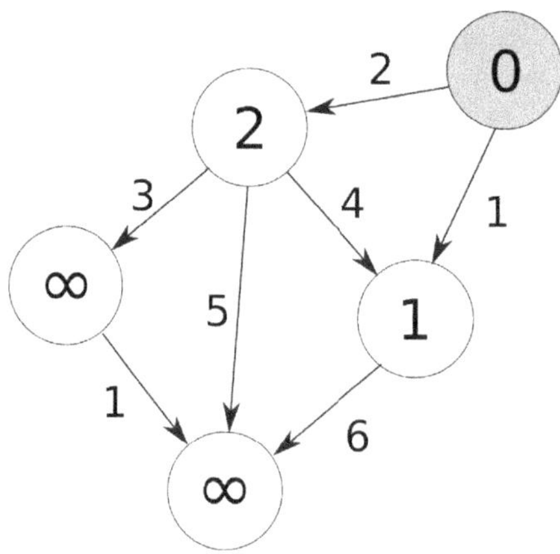

For the vertex B pointed with the arc of value 2, the sum $0 + 2 = 2$ is less than infinity, the vertex B then takes the value $0 + 2 = 2$. For the vertex C pointed with the arc of value 1, the sum $0 + 1 = 1$ is less than infinity, the vertex C then takes the value $0 + 1 = 1$.

Ford algorithm

Ford algorithm allows computing all vertices values thanks to the execution of relaxation on all vertices until convergence. Convergence is established when relaxation on all vertices leads to no change. Repetition is necessary because even if relaxation is applied from a target vertex to a starting vertex, there is no guarantee that it is the shortest path. Indeed, there may be a shorter path, which is found by the Ford algorithm during additional relaxations on the same vertices.

Ford algorithm is very slow: its complexity is quadratic with the number of vertices. For example, if there are a thousand vertices, which corresponds to a relatively small game world, it takes on average 1 million relaxations, which requires several milliseconds with an average processor core.

Dijkstra algorithm

Dijkstra algorithm allows computing the values of all vertices with linear complexity. For the same example, with a thousand vertices, it only takes a few microseconds. To achieve this, Dijkstra has shown that by applying relaxation in a certain order, we are guaranteed to converge with a small number of relaxations. More precisely, if one always first processes vertices whose value is the lowest, then the algorithm converges very quickly.

Be careful, there is a trap: for the algorithm to be effective, we must be able to find the vertex whose value is the lowest quickly. With a naive approach, this vertex is searched exhaustively in the list of vertices, which leads to an algorithm of complexity similar to that of Ford. The common solution is to use a data structure that can quickly store and return an element that minimizes a criterion, such as priority queues. Specifically, whenever the value of a vertex is changed, it is added to the queue. Then, at each iteration, the queue returns the vertex whose value is the lowest.

We initialize the Dijkstra algorithm by placing the vertex A in the queue. Then, it is removed from the queue and processed, and the vertices B and C are added to the queue. The vertex C having the smallest value, this one is chosen. The vertex E then takes the value $1 + 6 = 7$ and is placed in the queue:

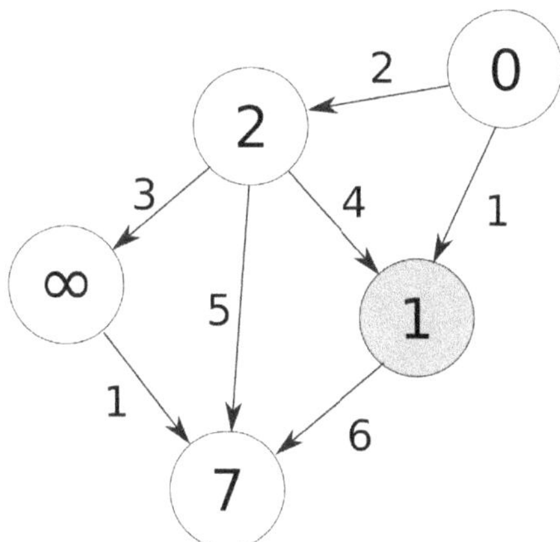

During the next iteration, vertices C and E are left unchanged, since the sum of B value with each arc value is not lower than pointed vertices. The vertex D takes the value 5 and is placed in the queue, since $2 + 3 = 5$ is less than infinity:

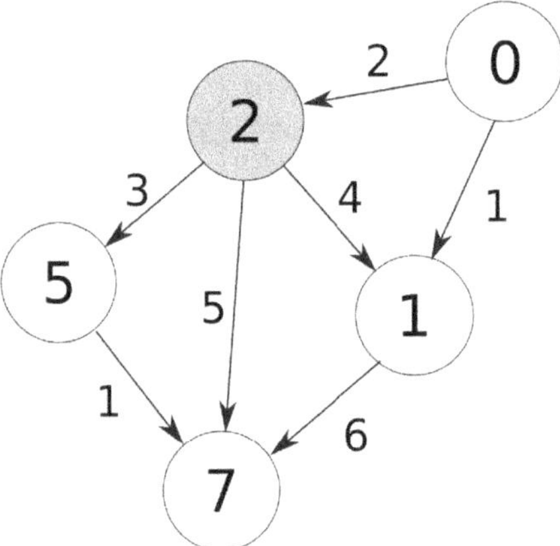

Then, the value of vertex E is changed, since the value of D (5) added to arc D to E (1) is lower than the one of E (7). The new value of E is therefore $5 + 1 = 6$:

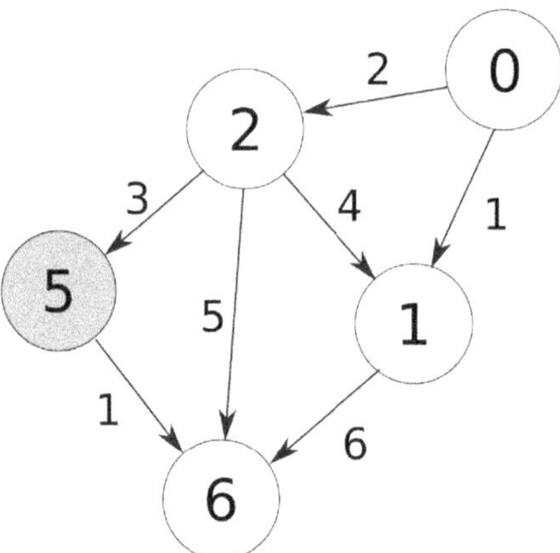

Finally, E is placed in the queue and processed. Its processing does lead to any modification since it does not point to any vertex. The queue is empty, and the algorithm ends.

5.2.2.3   Implementation

The implementation of the algorithm depends on the nature of the world, for example, whether it is on a regular grid or not, in two or three dimensions, etc. A version for regular worlds like Pacman's is available in this section. The principle remains the same with other types of worlds. In all cases, the algorithm is based on a priority queue, which contains the vertices to be processed. As a reminder, priority queues have two operations: *add* which places a vertex in the queue, and *remove/poll* which returns the vertex which minimizes a criterion. To represent a vertex with the associated comparison criterion, we define a `Point` class that implements `Comparable`:

```java
public class Point implements Comparable<Point> {
```

For two-dimensional cases like the Pacman world, two x and y attributes are defined:

```java
    public final int x;
    public final int y;
```

In all cases, you need a value/weight/distance/*etc.* attribute, here called `weight`:

```java
    public final int weight;
```

The `compareTo()` method of the `Comparable` interface returns the difference between the weight of the instance and the weight of another point. It is equivalent to say that a `Point` A with a weight lower than `Point` B is 'smaller' than B:

```java
    public int compareTo(Point point) {
        return this.weight - point.weight;
    }
```

A convenience method `transform()` is added to create adjacent points:

```java
    public Point transform(Direction d,int weight) {
      switch(d) {
        case NONE: return this;
        case EAST: return new Point(x+1,y,weight);
        case WEST: return new Point(x-1,y,weight);
        case NORTH: return new Point(x,y-1,weight);
        case SOUTH: return new Point(x,y+1,weight);
      }
      throw new IllegalArgumentException("Invalid d");
    }
}
```

A `Dijkstra` class is created to produce distance maps:

```java
public class Dijkstra {
```

First of all, access to world data is required, explicitly or implicitly represented by a graph structure. In games like Pacman, there is no explicit graph, vertices and edges are formally considered: space corresponds to a vertex, and adjacent spaces correspond to edges:

```java
private World world;
```

It is necessary to have a container for storing the weights calculated by the algorithm. The first approach is to put this information in the state. From a conceptual point of view, this usually does not make sense. Indeed, this information is not the direct result of the rules of the game and is only used by specific actors, such as AI. This kind of data created from "true" data is usually called *metadata*. So it's best to dedicate a class to do this, called `DistanceMap` in this example:

```java
private DistanceMap map;
```

The `DistanceMap` class is an array of two-dimensional integers decorated with various convenience methods, such as access, modification, etc.

Finally, a priority queue contains the weighted vertices to process:

```java
private PriorityQueue<Point> queue = new PriorityQueue();
```

When constructing an instance of the class, the distance map is initialized with the largest integer value `Integer.MAX_VALUE`, which is like assuming that all vertices are infinite:

```java
public Dijkstra(World world,DistanceMap map) {
    this.world = world;
    this.map = map;
    map.init(Integer.MAX_VALUE);
}
```

The `addSink()` method adds a target. The algorithm can compute the shortest paths to a target set. For each target, add in the queue the corresponding vertex with a zero weight:

```java
public void addSink(int x, int y) {
    queue.add(new Point(x,y,0));
    map.setWeight(x,y,0);
}
```

The `run()` method is the core of the algorithm. It is based on a loop that repeats itself as long as the queue is not empty, in other words, that there is at least one vertex to relax:

```java
public void run() {
    while(!queue.isEmpty()) {
```

Each iteration begins by getting the vertex whose weight is the smallest. It is where the strength of the algorithm lies: by processing the vertices in this order, we are guaranteed to converge very quickly:

```java
        Point point = queue.poll();
```

Some nodes may have been added several times in the priority queue, with weights getting smaller and smaller. When the weight is not as interesting as when it was added, there is no point in processing it:

```
if (map.getWeight(point.x, point.y,
    Direction.NONE) < point.weight) {
    continue;
}
```

The rest is the relaxation operation. For all directions:

```
for (Direction direction: Direction.allButNone){
```

If the adjacent cell in the current direction is a space:

```
if ((world.get(point.x, point.y, direction)
    instanceof Space)
```

And if the weight of the adjacent cell is strictly greater than the weight of the processed cell plus the cost of displacement (here always 1):

```
&& (map.getWeight(point.x, point.y, direction) >
    point.weight+1)) {
```

Then we add to the queue the vertex corresponding to the adjacent cell, with the weight of the shortest path, e.g. the weight of the cell plus the cost of displacement (here always 1):

```
Point point2 = point.transform(direction,point.weight+1);
queue.add(point2);
map.setWeight(point2.x, point2.y, point2.weight);
}
}
}
}
```

5.2.3 Management of distance maps computations

5.2.3.1 Follow a character

Distance maps allow various behaviors, the first of which is to follow a character. To illustrate it, we define a `TrackAI` class which implements AI to do this:

```
public class TrackAI extends AI {
```

Concerning attributes, we define the character to follow (`trackIndex`), as well as its current coordinates (`trackX` and `trackY`):

```
private int trackIndex;
private int trackX;
private int trackY;
```

A distance map is also held: it is only updated if the tracked character moved:

```java
private DistanceMap map;
```

The `createCommand()` method starts by asking for the list of possible commands given the current state of the game:

```java
public Command createCommand() {
    List<Command> list = commandsLister
        .listCommands(state, charIndex);
    if (list.isEmpty())
        return null;
```

The `updateMap()` method is called to update the distance map:

```java
    updateMap();
```

The weight at the current coordinates of the character led by this AI is read from the distance map:

```java
    Command bestCommand = null;
    Characters chars = state.getChars();
    MobileElement me = chars.get(charIndex);
    int minWeight = map.getWeight(
        me.getX(), me.getY(), Direction.NONE);
```

Be careful: there are two characters in this process: the character led by this AI (`charIndex` attribute) and the tracked character (`trackIndex`). Besides, the weight read in the distance map is equal to the number of cells that the controlled character must travel to reach as quickly as possible the tracked character.

For each direction command:

```java
    for (Command command : list) {
        if (!(command instanceof DirectionCommand))
            continue;
        DirectionCommand dirCommand = (DirectionCommand)command;
        Direction direction = dirCommand.getDirection();
```

The weight of a cell adjacent to the position of the controlled character is read:

```java
        int weight = map.getWeight(me.getX(), me.getY(), direction);
```

If this weight is smaller than the smallest weight ever found, it means that a better path was found:

```java
        if (weight < minWeight) {
            minWeight = weight;
            bestCommand = command;
        }
    }
```

Special case where no solution was found:

```
    if (bestCommand == null) {
        int index = random.nextInt(list.size());
        bestCommand = list.get(index);
    }
```

The best order is returned:

```
    return bestCommand;
}
```

The `updateMap()` method launches the computation of the distance map:

```
private void updateMap() {
```

If the tracked character did not move, there is no need to recompute the map:

```
    Characters chars = state.getChars();
    MobileElement me = chars.get(trackIndex);
    if (trackX == me.getX() && trackY == me.getY()) {
        return;
    }
    trackX = me.getX();
    trackY = me.getY();
```

The end of the method uses the `Dijkstra` class to run the computation:

```
    World world = state.getWorld();
    if (map == null) {
        map = new DistanceMap(world.getWidth(),world.getHeight());
    }
    Dijkstra dijkstra = new Dijkstra(world,map);
    dijkstra.addSink(me.getX(), me.getY());
    dijkstra.run();
}
```

The diagrams in this example are available in the "Class Diagrams/chap05/ai03" folder of the sample UML project. The code is present in the "examples/chap05/ai03" folder of the Java sample project. All ghosts follow Pacman, which seems to be difficult for Pacman, and but easy because it is enough to go to a super gum to make this strategy obsolete. The F8 key displays the distance map.

5.2.3.2 Service provider

Before creating different AI based on distance maps, more design is required. Indeed, the same maps can be used by several AIs, as in the previous example where each ghost computes the same distance map. In addition, there are aspects of regular updating of each map, depending on its targets.

Design

To enable effective management of these different aspects, a distance map provider is designed:

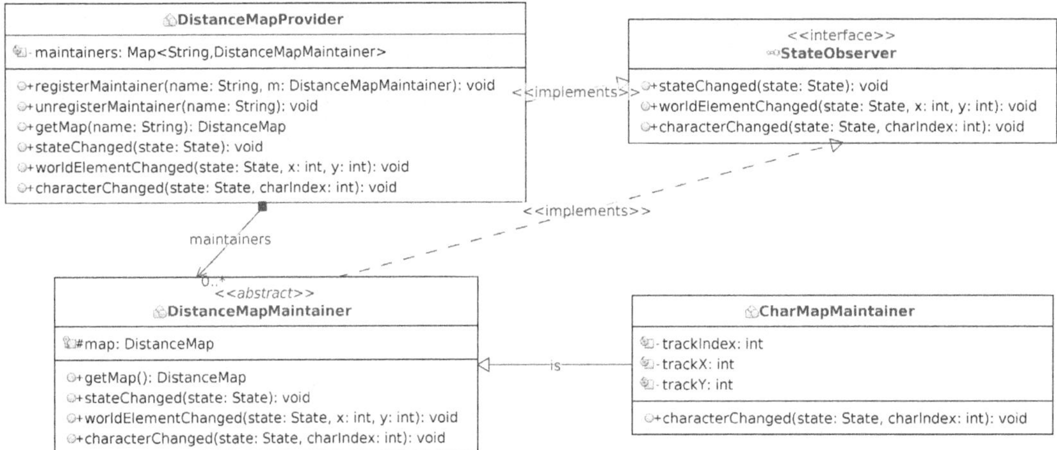

The `DistanceMapProvider` class allows you to add, remove, and request instances of `DistanceMapMaintainer`. These are intended to contain a distance map, but also to update them when notifications are received via the `StateObserver` interface methods. Finally, the `CharMapMaintainer` class is an example of the `DistanceMapMaintainer` class, which is a distance map to follow a character.

This design does not correspond to a particular pattern, and at the same time, uses several ideas from standard patterns. The `DistanceMapProvider` class looks like an Abstract Factory pattern, while the `DistanceMapMaintainer` class does not return new instances each time a card is requested. The latter looks like a flyweight since it manufactures an object if it does not exist, or returns the existing. However, it is not a Flyweight since the returned object is not static. Finally, the two abstract classes are clients of the Observer pattern.

This design is a good illustration of the fact that, although very common, patterns do not respond to every conceivable case. There comes a time when the designer has to invent his solutions. Standard patterns are an excellent source of inspiration, as well as the more general principles grouped so far under the banner of "divide and conquer".

⇒ Note: The proposed map provider follows a kind of "unofficial pattern" that is quite common in different areas, such as operating systems. However, he is not popular enough to have won the official pattern design title - just like the "Game Loop Pattern".

Use of the provider

The best way to understand the provider is to present its use. To begin, a `DistanceMapProvider dmProvider` attribute is added to the `PlayGameMode` class. Then, the `init()` method of this class is enriched to initialize this provider:

```
dmProvider = new DistanceMapProvider();
```

In this case, a single map maintainer is registered with the name "Pacman" with a `CharMapMaintaner` implementation which computes the distance map to Pacman:

```
dmProvider.registerMaintainer("Pacman",new CharMapMaintainer(0)
);
```

The provider is also declared as an observer of the state of the game, which allows him to notify the map maintainers it contains:

```
state.registerObserver(dmProvider);
```

⇒ Note: It is also possible for a map user to save the maps he or she needs. Be careful: you have to agree on the names of these maps and the associated targets.

With this provider, any component can request a map. For example, if you want to have the map that targets Pacman:

```
DistanceMap map = dmProvider.getMap("Pacman");
```

The `TrackAI` class developed in the previous section is modified by replacing its map attribute with a provider and then calling the provider to obtain the map of interest. With this change, the ghosts share the same map, which leads to a reduction in computation and memory used.

DistanceMapProvider implementation

The `DistanceMapProvider` class has an associative array, which to a name, maps a maintainer:

```
public class DistanceMapProvider implements StateObserver {
    private Map<String, DistanceMapMaintainer>
        maintainers = new HashMap();
```

The `registerMaintainer()`, `unregisterMaintainer()` and `getMap()` methods are similar to those typically found in an Abstract Factory:

```
    public void registerMaintainer(String name,
        DistanceMapMaintainer m) {
        maintainers.put(name, m);
    }
    public void unregisterMaintainer(String name) {
        maintainers.remove(name);
```

```java
    }
    public DistanceMap getMap(String name) {
        DistanceMapMaintainer maintainer = maintainers.get(name);
        return maintainer.getMap();
    }
```

The three methods of the `StateObserver` interface pass notifications to the map maintainers:

```java
    public void stateChanged(State state) {
        for (DistanceMapMaintainer m :
            maintainers.values()) {
            m.stateChanged(state);
        }
    }
    public void worldElementChanged(State state,int x, int y) {
        for (DistanceMapMaintainer m :
            maintainers.values()) {
            m.worldElementChanged(state,x,y);
        }
    }
    public void characterChanged(State state,int charIndex) {
        for (DistanceMapMaintainer m :
            maintainers.values()) {
            m.characterChanged(state,charIndex);
        }
    }
}
```

CharMapMaintainer implementation

The class `CharMapMaintainer` takes some of the code of the `TrackAI` class, like the attributes of the tracked character and the `updateMap()` method:

```java
public class CharMapMaintainer
    extends DistanceMapMaintainer {
    private int trackIndex;
    private int trackX;
    private int trackY;

    public CharMapMaintainer(int trackIndex) {
        this.trackIndex = trackIndex;
    }
    public void characterChanged(State state,int charIndex) {
        if (charIndex != trackIndex)
```

```
        return;
    Characters chars = state.getChars();
    MobileElement me = chars.get(trackIndex);
    if (trackX == me.getX() && trackY == me.getY()) {
        return;
    }
    trackX = me.getX();
    trackY = me.getY();
    World world = state.getWorld();
    Dijkstra dijkstra = new Dijkstra(world,map);
    dijkstra.addSink(trackX, trackY);
    dijkstra.run();
  }
}
```

It is another example of problem division into subproblems: the `ChapMapMaintainer` class focuses on map update aspects and the `TrackAI` class on its use. In addition, other AIs may also use the same type of map.

The diagrams in this example are available in the "Class Diagrams/chap05/ai04" folder of the sample UML project. The code is present in the "examples/chap05/ai04" folder of the Java sample project. The F8 key displays the distance map.

5.2.4 Behavior AI

5.2.4.1 Principle

A family of usual artificial intelligence methods is behavior AIs. These define many possible behaviors or strategies. Then, following certain rules, one of the behaviors is selected from the others.

The simplest methods are based on a graphical representation of the different behaviors. Each vertex corresponds to a behavior, and each arc corresponds to the condition necessary to pass from one behavior to another.

Other methods rely on a tree representation of different behaviors. The idea is to go through the behavior tree until you find a solution. A global solution is found when the root of the tree has found a solution among its children, who have solved theirs, and so on. Each node of the tree can have a different strategy to find a solution, including the root. For example, make sure that at least one of the child nodes has found a solution, or make sure that all the child nodes have found a solution. This approach is very common in the field of video games and is very interesting because it allows dividing behaviors in a sequence of elementary behaviors.

The last family of behavioral methods is based on a notion of utility. The idea here is to compute a score for each possible behavior, then choose the behavior that has the highest score.

5.2.4.2   Example with Pacman

Behavior classes

For the Pacman example game, different behaviors are implemented as independent AIs. The TrackAI class used with the Pacman distance map can be considered a behavior where the character follows Pacman. It is also possible to use the same principle to go to the nearest gum. To do this, the class GumsMapMaintainer is defined to manage and compute the distance map with targets all the gums of the level. Then, the TrackAI class is used with this map to define this behavior. The TrackAI class does not need to be modified for this new behavior. It can direct a character to any set of targets, as long as the corresponding distance map is provided. The same principle applies to moving to a graveyard cell with the GraveyardMapMaintainer class, and to the nearest ghost with the GhostsMapMaintainer class.

Distance maps can also be used to escape danger. The choice of movement direction is then almost the same, except that it is the adjacent vertex of greater value that is chosen and not that of smaller value. The FleeAI class is defined with the following createCommand() method, which chooses the adjacent cell with the highest value:

```java
public Command createCommand() {
    List<Command> list = commandsLister
        .listCommands(state, charIndex);
    if (list.isEmpty())
        return null;
    DistanceMap map = dmProvider.getMap(mapName);
    Command bestCommand = null;
    Characters chars = state.getChars();
    MobileElement me = chars.get(charIndex);
    int maxWeight = map.getWeight(
        me.getX(), me.getY(), Direction.NONE);
    for (Command command : list) {
        if (!(command instanceof DirectionCommand))
            continue;
        DirectionCommand dirCommand = (DirectionCommand)command;
        Direction direction = dirCommand.getDirection();
        int weight = map.getWeight(
            me.getX(), me.getY(), direction);
        if (weight > maxWeight) {
            maxWeight = weight;
            bestCommand = command;
        }
    }
}
```

```
    if (bestCommand == null) {
        int index = random.nextInt(list.size());
        bestCommand = list.get(index);
    }
    return bestCommand;
}
```

Combination of behaviors

We use the tree method in its simplest version to combine the behaviors. Indeed, there is only one level to the tree, and the root chooses the first valid behavior. For example, for Pacman, a dedicated `PacmanAI` class is defined:

```
public class PacmanAI extends AI {
```

It contains three AIs, each corresponding to a behavior: to go to the nearest gum (`eatAI`), to hunt a terrified ghost (`trackAI`) and to flee a normal ghost (`fleeAI`):

```
private AI eatAI;
private AI trackAI;
private AI fleeAI;
```

AIs are instances of `TrackAI` and `FleeAI` with the distance maps corresponding to the expected behavior. We assume that these maps are available from the map provider:

```
public PacmanAI(State state,
    CommandsLister commandsLister, Random random,
    DistanceMapProvider dmProvider) {
    super(state, 0, commandsLister, random);
    this.dmProvider = dmProvider;
    eatAI = new TrackAI("Gums",state,charIndex,
        commandsLister,random,dmProvider);
    trackAI = new TrackAI("FleeingGhosts",state,
        charIndex,commandsLister,random,dmProvider);
    fleeAI = new FleeAI("TrackingGhosts",state,
        charIndex,commandsLister,random,dmProvider);
}
```

The `createCommand()` method relies on criteria to choose a particular behavior. The first criterion checks the distance between Pacman and normal ghosts. This distance is computed using the ghost distance map with a "track" status:

```
public Command createCommand() {
    Characters chars = state.getChars();
    Pacman pacman = chars.getPacman();
    DistanceMap map = dmProvider.getMap("TrackingGhosts");
```

```
if (map.getWeight(pacman.getX(),
    pacman.getY(), Direction.NONE) < 5) {
```

If a tracking ghost is too close, Pacman moves away from it:

```
    return fleeAI.createCommand();
}
```

If Pacman is in "super" status and there is still some time, Pacman tries to eat the closest terrified ghost:

```
if (pacman.getStatus() == PacmanStatus.SUPER
 && pacman.getStatusTime() > 5) {
    return trackAI.createCommand();
}
```

Finally, if no previous condition is met, Pacman goes to the nearest gum:

```
    return eatAI.createCommand();
}
```

The ghosts have a similar AI:

- If a ghost is terrified, it flees Pacman;
- If a ghost is dead, it goes to the graveyard to be resurrected;
- Otherwise it randomly walks in the level.

Results

The diagrams in this example are available in the "Class Diagrams/chap05/ai05" folder of the sample UML project. The code is present in the "examples/chap05/ai05" folder of the Java sample project. The F8 key is used to display the distance maps.

An AI by behavior that uses distance maps offers good performance, even with a high level of difficulty. Besides, the average time to eat all the gums is considerably reduced compared to the simple method. Note that ghosts also have higher intelligence, while remaining reasonable to give Pacman a chance.

Pacman	Ghost	Diff.	Victories	Time	Time	Gums
Behavior	Behavior	Easy	77%	2030	1053	99
Behavior	Behavior	Normal	70%	1978	1080	93
Behavior	Behavior	Hard	65%	1950	1021	98

5.2.5 Exercises

5.2.5.1 Exercise 2.5.1: Shortest Path in the Galaxy

→ Propose an implementation of the Dijkstra algorithm to compute a distance map in a galaxy defined by the classes in the "examples/chap02/stellaris" folder. Unlike the Pacman example, the galaxy is not represented by a regular grid, but by a graph.

You can use the example graph in section 2.2.2 to check your implementation:

```
Galaxy galaxy = new Galaxy();
galaxy.createSystem("A", 10, 0);
galaxy.createSystem("B", 7, 2);
galaxy.createSystem("C", 8, 4);
galaxy.createSystem("D", 0, 3);
galaxy.createSystem("E", 6, 6);
galaxy.connectSystems("A", "B", 2);
galaxy.connectSystems("A", "C", 1);
galaxy.connectSystems("B", "D", 3);
galaxy.connectSystems("B", "C", 4);
galaxy.connectSystems("B", "E", 5);
galaxy.connectSystems("C", "E", 6);
galaxy.connectSystems("D", "E", 1);
```

5.2.5.2 Exercise 2.5.2: Connect 4 with a heuristic IA

→ Propose an AI that relies on a heuristic. For instance, the AI can select the column that leads to a connect 4. Otherwise, it can select a column that prevents the opponent from getting a connect 4. Finally, if no simple case arises, it plays at random.

To propose a solution, start with the code you did for exercise 1.3.2.

5.2.6 Video game development: AI without planning

To add artificial intelligence to your game, the methods and approaches in this section meet most expectations. It is especially true for characters and elements that are not usually played by a human, such as roaming monsters, boss strategies, semi-automated moves, and so on.

It's hard to come up with unique recipes for all games, other than common tools like distance maps. We arrive at a stage of the book where you must be creative while keeping in mind the essential rules of separation of problems into subproblems.

So be careful not to end up after months or years of work with an unmanageable mix of features.

Finally, do not neglect aspects of validation and evaluation, preferably with as much automation as possible, to consider the greatest number of possibilities.

5.3   Artificial Intelligence with planning

This section is very difficult and can be ignored by beginners.

The previous approaches make decisions based on the current state of the game. They do not take into account the consequences of the choices made. The range of methods presented in this section proposes to explore the different possibilities by modifying the state of the game as if commands were actually executed.

5.3.1   Browse future states

5.3.1.1   State graphs

Imagining or simulating the consequences of an action can be formalized in the form of state graphs. The idea is to represent each particular state of the game by the vertex of a graph, and each possible change by an arc.

For example, a vertex of this graph for the sliding puzzle game in 3x3 can be presented as follows:

$$\begin{array}{|c|c|c|}\hline 1 & & 3 \\\hline 4 & 2 & 6 \\\hline 7 & 5 & 8 \\\hline\end{array}$$

This vertex contains all game data, e.g. 9 values from 0 to 8.

If digit 2 is moved, a new state is created, to which a new vertex can be associated. The arc representing the transition between these two vertices then corresponds to the displacement of the number 2 from the central cell to the top middle one:

$$\begin{array}{|c|c|c|}\hline 1 & & 3 \\\hline 4 & 2 & 6 \\\hline 7 & 5 & 8 \\\hline\end{array} \rightarrow \begin{array}{|c|c|c|}\hline 1 & 2 & 3 \\\hline 4 & & 6 \\\hline 7 & 5 & 8 \\\hline\end{array}$$

For a given game state, several moves can be possible. For instance, from the second vertex with no digit in the middle, digits 4 and 5 can be moved:

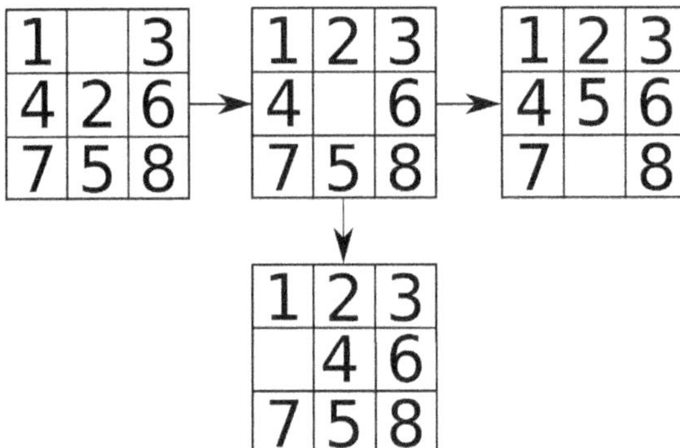

This principle can be repeated again and again, as long as there is a possible movement between vertices.

From a computer point of view, vertices are instances of classes that contain game data, such as the `State` class of the Pacman example game. Arcs are the set of commands that, when applied to the rules engine, transform one state of the game into another. In the Pacman example game, implementations of `Command` interface are the values of these arcs.

The graphs and its vertices are purely formal. It is rare to be able to store as many states of the game as vertices of the state graph, even if their number is finite. Most often, only one state exists and represents the current position in the state graph.

5.3.1.2 Search trees

Search trees are very efficient formal tools to traverse state graph. The role of this one is to represent all the paths that it is possible to produce, starting from a vertex of the state graph.

For the previous example, the search tree is:

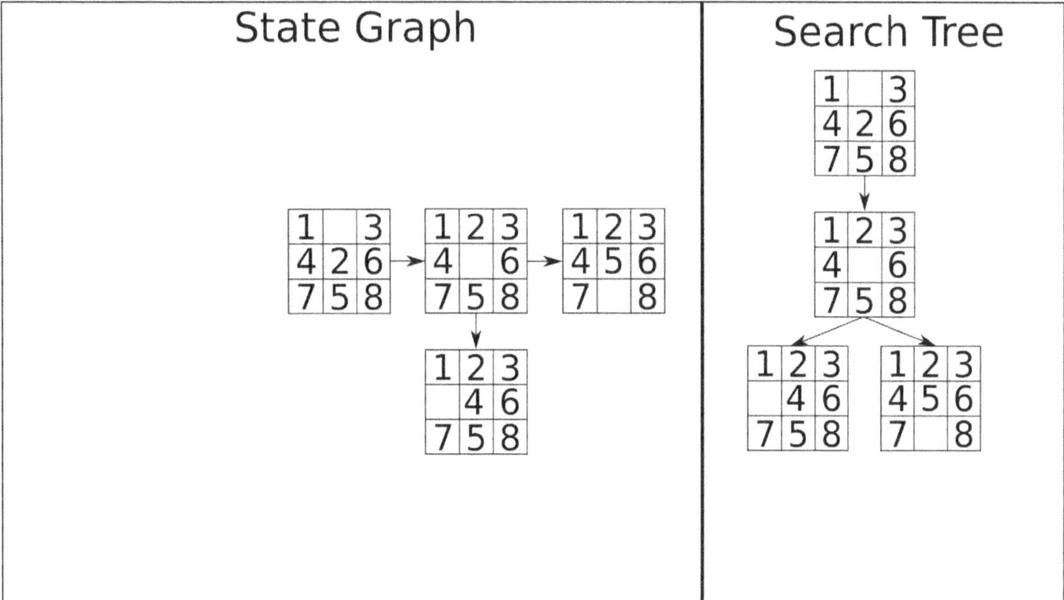

The root of the search tree is the vertex used as the starting point, with the number 2 in the center. The only child of the root of the search tree is the second vertex considered, with no digit in the middle. The children of this one are the two possibilities proposed before when 4 or 5 is moved.

The exploration of the state graph can continue for example, by developing the circled node below:

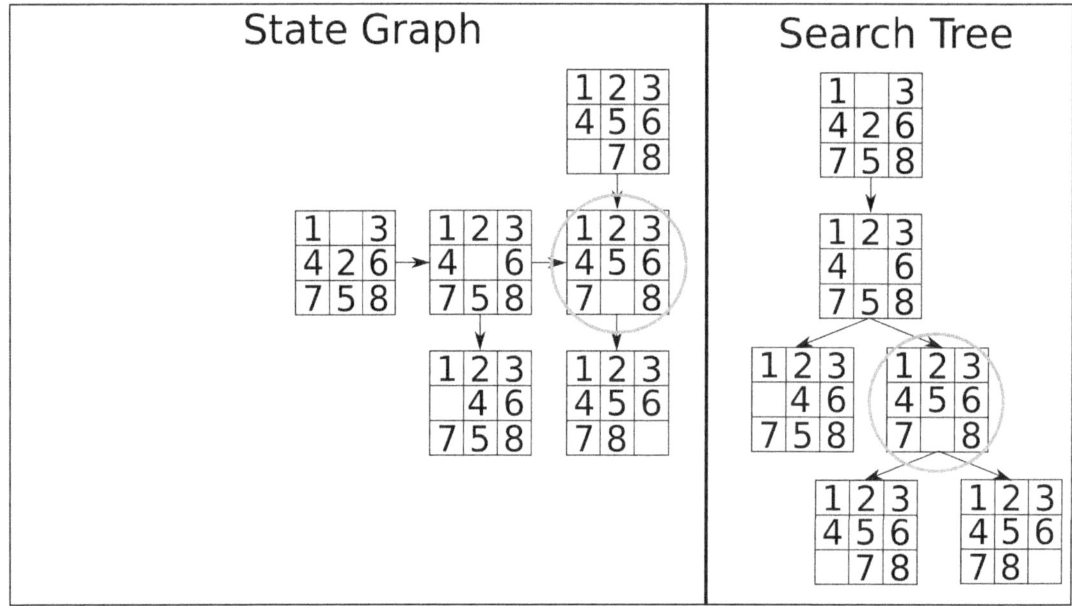

Two movements are presented: one moves digit 8, and the other digit 7. In the case of digit 8, we found a solution of the game: the corresponding node in the search tree is then a leaf.

To win the game, traverse the search tree, until you find a leaf. Besides, the path from the root of the search tree to a leaf gives the set of commands required to transform the game to a solution state.

Search trees can find solutions but also find the best solutions. For example, to reach the solution from the initial state, there are several possibilities:

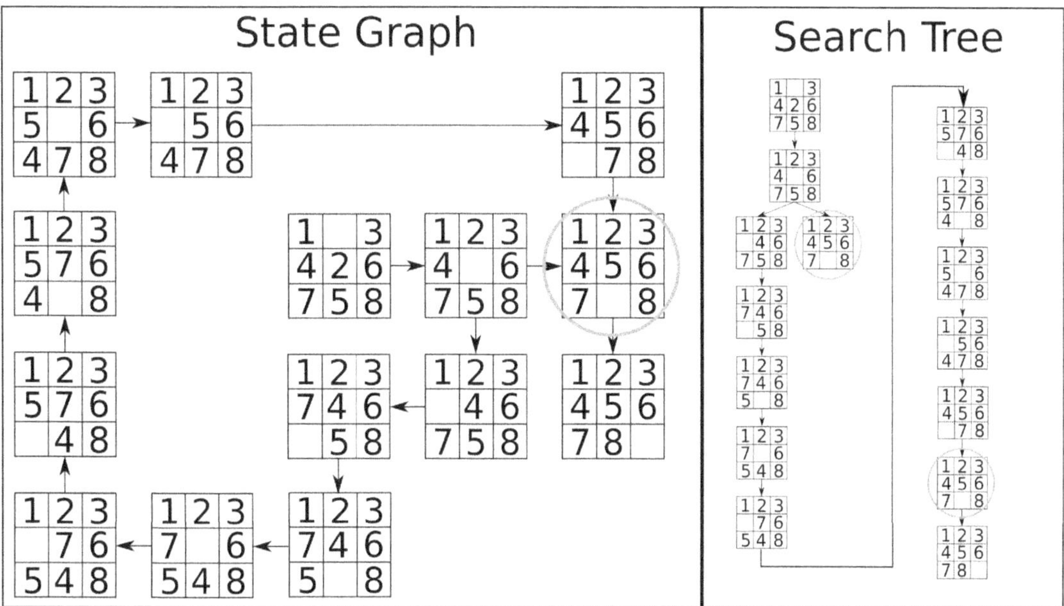

For the state graph, each vertex contains unique data: there can not be two vertices with identical states. There is no way to represent different routes. On the other hand, with the search tree, this is possible. In the example above, the surrounded vertex can be found with the first path found, but also thanks to many moves that "turn around" digits 4,5,7. In the graph, there is only one circled vertex, while in the search tree, the circled vertex is present twice. The difference between these two nodes with identical content lies in their position in the tree. The first is at a shallow depth and can be reached with few moves. The second is much deeper and requires many actions. In addition, to browse the possible paths, the search tree allows you to find the most interesting ones.

5.3.1.3 Traversal algorithms

Depth-first

The search for an interesting state in the graph is equivalent to traverse the search tree. The simplest algorithm for traversing a tree is the one based on recursion. It consists of calling the search method on each child of the current node. For example, using the following class to represent a node:

```java
public class Node {

    private Node parent;
    private int depth;
    private int value;
    private List<Node> children = new ArrayList();

    ... Constructors, getters and setters ...

    public void show() {
        for (int k=0;k<depth;k++) {
            System.out.print("   ");
        }
        System.out.println(value);
    }
}
```

The following method print the tree values following a depth-first traversal using recursion:

```java
public static void depthFirst_rec(Node node) {
    if (node == null) {
        return;
    }
    node.show();
    List<Node> children = node.getChildren();
    for (Node child : children) {
        depthFirst_rec(child);
    }
}
```

The approach is said recursive because it calls itself. The path is depth-first because the algorithm descends as much as possible in the tree before processing all the children of the root.

For example, for the following tree:

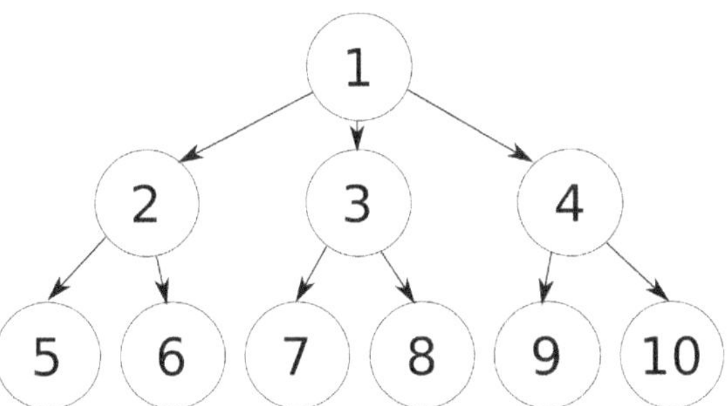

The following display is obtained:

```
1
   2
      5
      6
   3
      7
      8
   4
      9
      10
```

The algorithm goes directly to leaf 5, then processes leaf 6, before going back to 3, and so on.

Breadth-first

Another type of tree traversal is the breadth-first one. It consists of first processing the child nodes before going into the depths of the tree. To implement it, it is not possible to use a trick like recursion. You have to rely on a queue to memorize the nodes to be processed. We start by creating a queue:

```java
public static void breadthFirst(Node node) {
    Queue<Node> queue = new ArrayDeque();
```

Then the root is added to the queue:

```java
    queue.add(node);
```

As long as there is a node to process:

```java
    while(!queue.isEmpty()) {
```

Take the node at the beginning of the queue:

```java
        node = queue.poll();
```

Display this node:

```
node.show();
```

Children of the current node are added to the queue:

```
List<Node> children = node.getChildren();
for (Node child : children) {
    queue.add(child);
}
    }
}
```

On the previous tree, we obtain the following result:

```
1
  2
  3
  4
    5
    6
    7
    8
    9
    10
```

The root is processed, then all the nodes of depth 1, and finally, all the nodes of depth 2.

The algorithm used follows a usual scheme that relies on a data structure, such as that of Dijkstra. Using a stack instead of the queue, you can get a depth-first approach. This implementation is interesting because it no longer depends on the size of the system stack:

```
public static void depthFirst(Node node) {
    Queue<Node> queue =
        Collections.asLifoQueue(new ArrayDeque());
    queue.add(node);
    while(!queue.isEmpty()) {
        node = queue.poll();
        node.show();
        List<Node> children = node.getChildren();
        for (Node child : children) {
            queue.add(child);
        }
    }
}
```

5.3.2 Minimax

In video games, there are always opponents, whether other players or non-player characters. It is necessary to represent the two points of view: the player wishes to win the victory, while his enemies want his defeat. The Minimax algorithm allows you to manage these aspects.

5.3.2.1 Exhaustive version

The minimax algorithm is an algorithm for searching and evaluating the search tree in the state graph. Each node always represents a state of the game, but with different points of view. In the two-player version, we assume that the roles are alternated: one time the first player plays, then the second one, and so on. We also assume that there is a notion of gain or score: the player wants to maximize this value to win, and his opponent wants to minimize it. The definition of the score is totally specific to the game.

The ultimate goal of the minimax algorithm is to find the best move (or best command) to use for the current game state (e.g., not the future ones). It determines the best score that can be expected for each move. The algorithm starts by going down as deep as possible in the search tree to meet a node whose all threads are leaves. For instance, the leftmost node of depth 2 in the following tree has leaves with values 2 and 5:

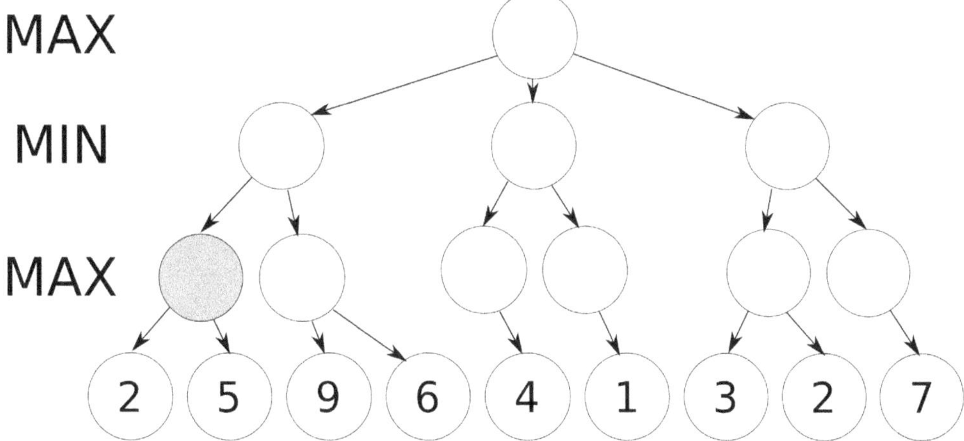

Since this depth is associated with the current player, the largest value is used for this node:

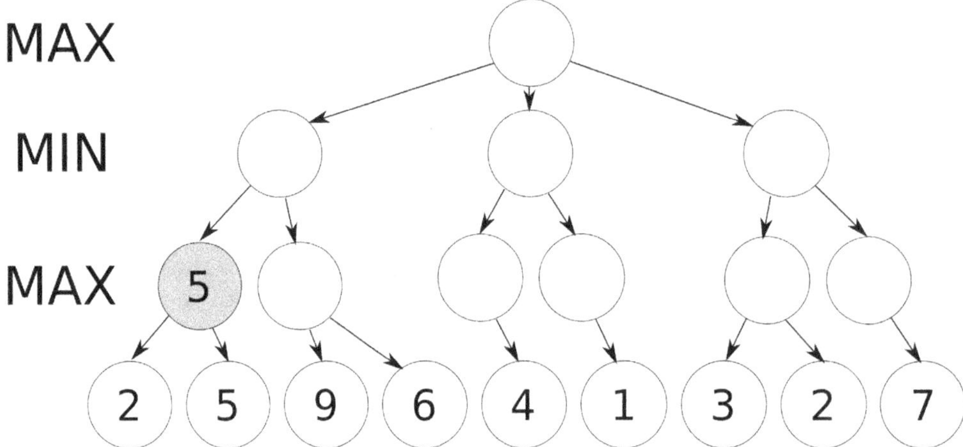

The same rule is applied for the following node:

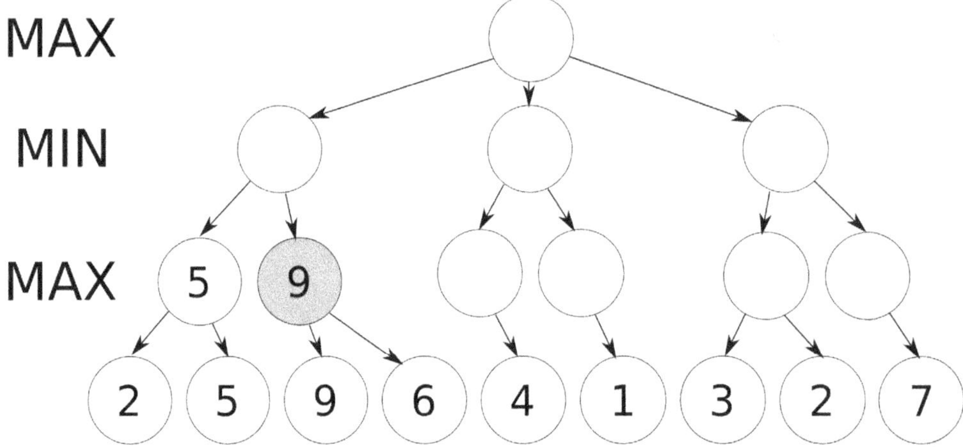

The next node is a depth where the opponent plays: the node then takes the minimum value of its children:

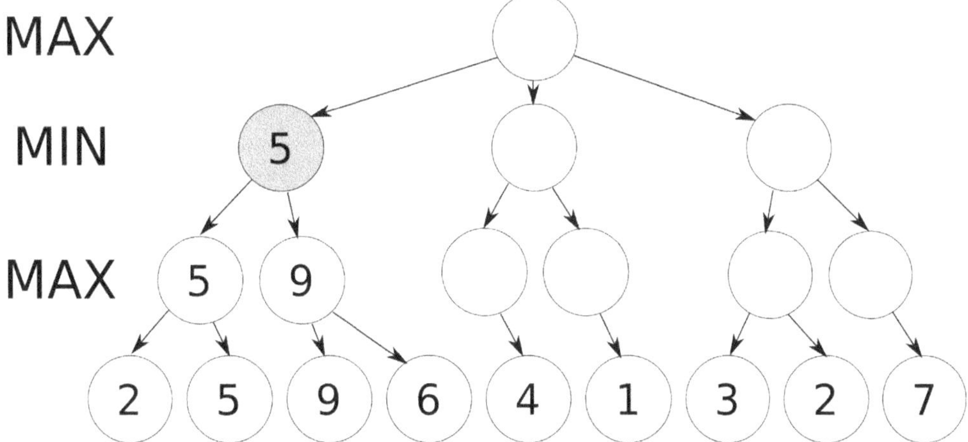

The same processing is repeated for all nodes, up to the root. Once root children all have a value, we can select the best move for the current game state. In this example, it is the command that leads to the state represented by the child node to the left of the root:

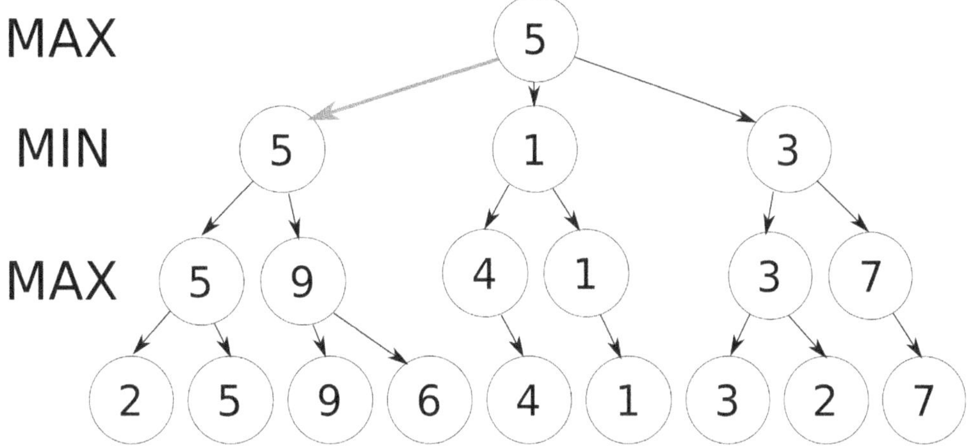

⇒ Note: Nodes and leaves values are computed in two different ways. The Minimax algorithm does not compute the values of leaves, they have to be computed by an algorithm specific to the game. Non-leaf node values, on the other hand, are fully computed by the algorithm.

5.3.2.2 Implementation

The algorithm is based on a depth-first traversal, of which two processing can be distinguished. The first one explores the tree, descending the deepest to reach the leaves. The second one computes node values going up in the tree. A usual implementation relies on a recursion-based algorithm. To better meet the principles of design, a richer approach is proposed in this section.

Abstract tree

First of all, the notion of tree is formalized to be able to create an implementation able to process many cases. An abstract class **Node** is defined:

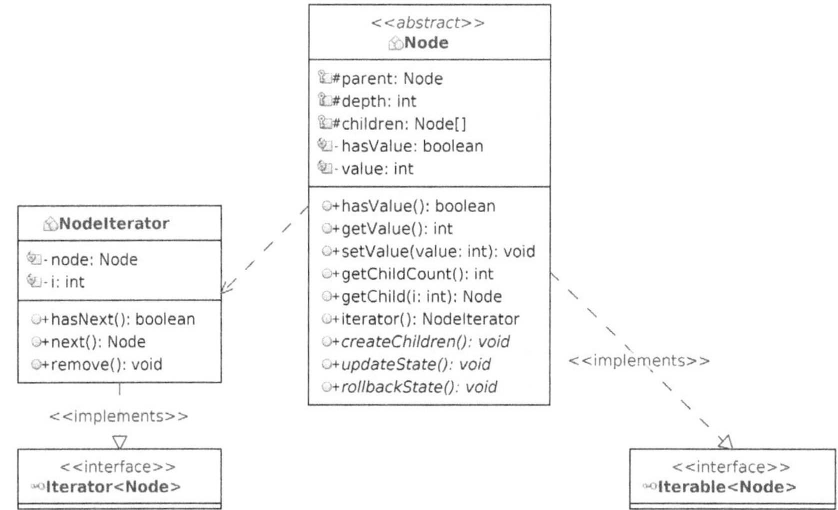

This class contains the usual information like the parent node, the depth of the node, the list of its children, a boolean that indicates if the node has a value (`hasValue`), and the value (`value`). The different getters and setters are also defined, as well as the iterator pattern to be able to browse the children with the `NodeIterator` class and associated interfaces. Finally, an abstract `createChildren()` method is implemented by the `Node` child classes to fill the list of children. Children are created on-demand, for instance, when the `getChildCount()` method is called:

```java
public int getChildCount() {
    if (children == null) {
        createChildren();
    }
    return children.length;
}
```

All of these attributes and methods are a very common approach in the field of computer science to formalize the manipulation of trees, even if it does not have an "official" name. For example, the path algorithms presented in the **Traversal Algorithms** section work with this abstract class, and thus with all trees implemented as a `Node` child class. For tree whose implementation already exists and that can not be modified, it is possible to use this scheme thanks to the decoration of the nodes of the existing implementation (Decorator pattern). This approach does not require the explicit existence of all the nodes of the tree: they can be created during the traversal when the `createChildren()` method is called.

Two other more specific abstract methods are also present: `updateState()` and `rollbackState()`. Their role is to go down and up the tree. Indeed, in our case of video games, it is not possible to produce a new state of the complete game for each node of the search tree. The method used is to use a single game state modified by the application of commands or a rollback. The application of commands corresponds to go down in the search tree, and the rollback corresponds to go up in the search tree. From a traversal algorithm perspective, which knows nothing about the details of the game and its state, descending is done by calling `updateState()`, and going up is done by calling `rollbackState()`.

Minimax

The traversal algorithms generally follow a similar scheme: a list contains the nodes to be processed, and the main loop processes each node of the list, until emptying it. Each algorithm processes the nodes differently. For usual traversals, the same processing is always applied. For the Minimax algorithm, different processing is applied, depending on the nature of the nodes (min or max).

This can be formalized in the following way:

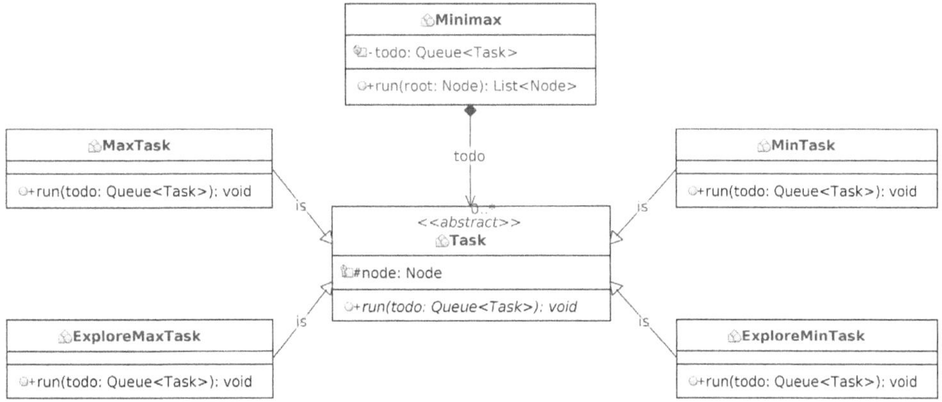

The `Minimax` class contains the `todo` list of nodes to process and the `run()` method with the main processing loop. It relies on implementations of the `Task` abstract class to process the nodes. In this case, there are four kinds of processing: go down from a max node (`ExploreMaxTask` class), compute max values and go up (`MaxTask` class), go down from a min node (`ExploreMinTask` class), compute min values and go up (`MinTask` class).

Knowing that the goal of Minimax is to compute and recover root child nodes with the best score, the `run()` method works like this:

```java
public List<Node> run(Node root) {
```

It begins by creating a new node list - more precisely a node stack since a depth-first approach is required:

```java
todo = Collections.asLifoQueue(new ArrayDeque());
```

Knowing that the root of the tree is a max node, the stack is initialized with processes that descend to each child of the root:

```java
for (Node child : root) {
    todo.add(new ExploreMinTask(child));
}
```

The main loop repeats as long as the stack is not empty. This one takes a task in the stack, and executes it:

```java
while (!todo.isEmpty()) {
    Task task = todo.poll();
    task.run(todo);
}
```

The end of the method computes the highest score among the root children:

```java
int max = Integer.MIN_VALUE;
for(Node child : root) {
    if (!child.hasValue())
        throw new RuntimeException("No value");
    int value = child.getValue();
    if (value > max) {
        max = value;
    }
}
```

Then it forms the list of nodes with this maximum value (there can be several movements with the same score):

```java
ArrayList<Node> bestNodes = new ArrayList();
for(Node child : root) {
    if (child.getValue() == max) {
        bestNodes.add(child);
    }
}
```

```
root.setValue(max);
return bestNodes;
}
```

ExploreMin/ExploreMax processing

The `ExploreMaxTask` class handles descent from a max node, which is the player's turn:

```
public class ExploreMaxTask extends Task {
    public ExploreMaxTask(Node node) {
        super(node);
    }
```

The `run()` method starts by calling the `updateState()` method of the node, which goes down in the search tree:

```
    public void run(Queue<Task> todo) {
        node.updateState();
```

If the node has a value, then the node is a leaf: it is no longer necessary to continue, and the `rollbackState()` method is called to go up in the tree:

```
        if (node.hasValue()) {
            node.rollbackState();
            return;
        }
```

⇒ Note: The processing of a leaf during the descent of the tree is a small optimization that avoids having to instantiate a `MaxTask` task for this particular case.

If the node has no value, it is a node with children. Max processing (`MaxTask` class) is added to the stack:

```
        todo.add(new MaxTask(node));
```

Then, an exploration (`ExploreMinTask` class) is added for each child:

```
        for (Node child : node) {
            todo.add(new ExploreMinTask(child));
        }
```

Knowing that `todo` is a stack, the exploration tasks are executed before the task that computes the max. In doing so, all nodes have a value when computing the max.

```
    }
}
```

The `ExploreMinTask` class is identical to this one, except the min and max are inverted.

Min/Max processing

The `MaxTask` class computes the max between all the child nodes:

```java
public class MaxTask extends Task {
    public MaxTask(Node node) {
        super(node);
    }
```

The `run()` method scans the children to determine the largest value:

```java
    public void run(Queue<Task> todo) {
        int max = Integer.MIN_VALUE;
        for(Node child : node) {
            if (!child.hasValue())
              throw new RuntimeException("No value");
            int value = child.getValue();
            if (value > max) {
                max = value;
            }
        }
```

The current node takes this maximum value:

```java
        node.setValue(max);
```

The `rollbackState()` method is called to go up in the tree:

```java
        node.rollbackState();
    }
}
```

The code is present in the "examples/chap05/ai06/ai/tree/minimax" folder of the Java sample project.

5.3.2.3 Alpha Beta optimization

The basic Minimax algorithm requires an exhaustive traversal of the search tree, whose size grows exponentially with its depth. An optimization called "Alpha Beta" can significantly reduce the number of nodes explored, while computing the same result (no approximation).

Alpha Beta

This optimization makes it possible to ignore some branches of the tree without modifying the final result. It is based on the analysis of values of nodes in an area:

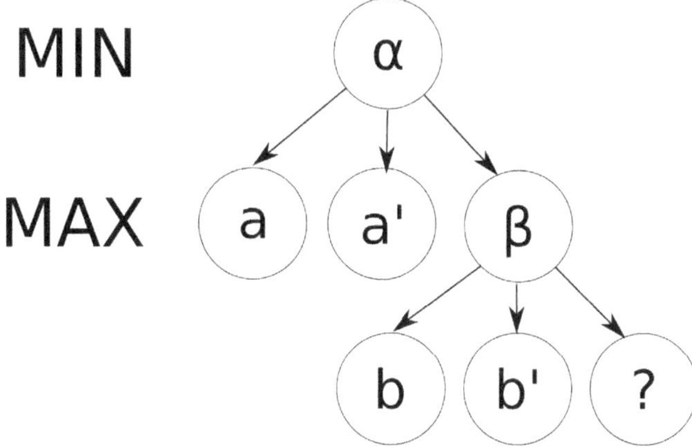

- The *alpha* node, at the very top of the hierarchy in this example, is currently being processed. His first two children *a* and *a'* have already been processed, and the current value of *alpha* is the minimum between *a* and *a'*. It may be lower after the processing of his last child *beta*. The only assumption that can be made is that *alpha* can not take a greater value.
- The *beta* node is also being processed. Its first two children *b* and *b'* have already been processed, and the current value of *beta* is the maximum between *b* and *b'*. It may be larger after the processing of its last child. The only assumption that can be ensured at the moment is that *beta* can not take a smaller value.
- The last child of *beta* with a question mark is the one whose processing is being discussed. There are two cases:
    - If *beta* is greater than *alpha*, then node processing is useless, since *alpha* can not increase, and *beta* can not decrease. So, whatever happens, *beta* is always larger than *alpha*.
    - If *beta* is smaller than or equal to *alpha*, nothing can be concluded, the processing must take place.

The optimization is the same when min and max nodes are inverted: in this case, the question mark node is not processed if *alpha* is greater than *beta*.

Applied to the previous example tree, it leads to the following optimizations, represented as red lines:

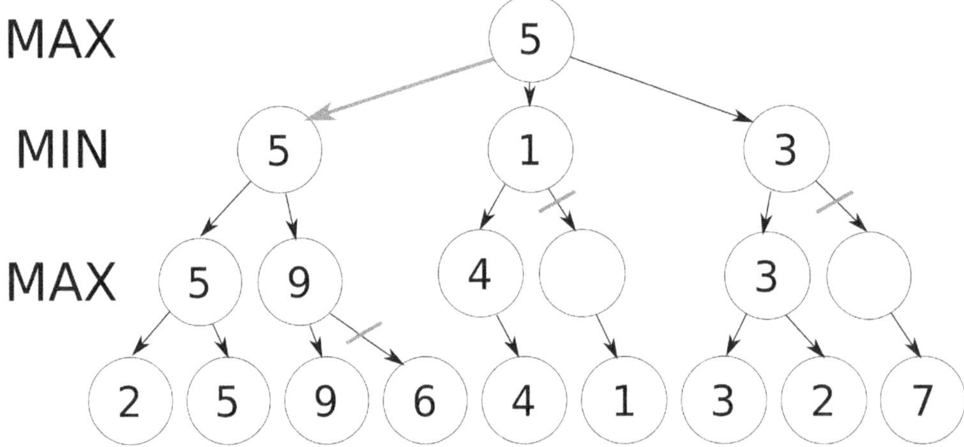

Implementation

The Alpha Beta optimization forces us to compute node values in an unexpected order. To do this, two moveMaxValueUp() and moveMinValueUp() convenience methods are added to the Task class. Their role is to move up the current value of the node to its parent, according to the nature of the node (min or max). For example, the moveMaxValueUp() method move up the value to a max node:

```
protected void moveMaxValueUp() {
    Node parent = node.getParent();
    if (parent != null) {
        if (!parent.hasValue()
          || parent.getValue() < node.getValue()) {
            parent.setValue(node.getValue());
        }
    }
}
```

The moveMinValueUp() method is similar.

The MinTask and MaxTask tasks are simplified since it is no longer necessary to compute the min or max of children values. For example, for MaxTask, go up in the tree with the rollbackState() method of the node, then move up the current value to the parent node with the moveMinValueUp() method:

```java
public class MaxTask extends Task {
    public void run(Queue<Task> todo) {
        node.rollbackState();
        moveMinValueUp();
    }
}
```

For exploration tasks like `ExploreMaxTask`, the main novelty is the cancellation of processing if the Alpha Beta condition is true:

```java
public void run(Queue<Task> todo) {
    if (node.getDepth() > 2) {
        Node beta = node.getParent();
        Node alpha = beta.getParent();
        if (beta.hasValue() && alpha.hasValue()
         && beta.getValue() < alpha.getValue()) {
            return;
        }
    }
```

The rest is similar to the case without Alpha Beta, except for the need to move up the value to the parent node:

```java
    node.updateState();
    if (node.hasValue()) {
        node.rollbackState();
        moveMinValueUp();
        return;
    }
    todo.add(new MaxTask(node));
    for (Node child : node) {
        todo.add(new ExploreMinTask(child));
    }
}
```

The code is present in the "examples/chap05/ai06/ai/tree/alphabeta" folder of the Java sample project.

5.3.2.4   Validation with the Tic Tac Toe game

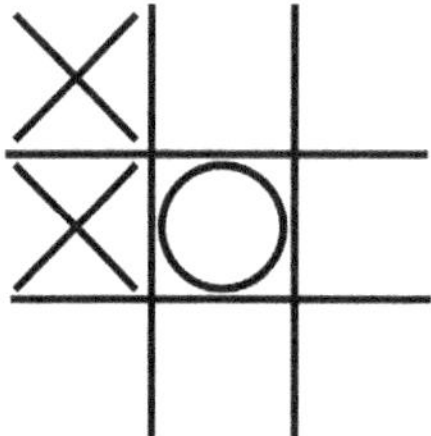

The implementation of Minimax with Alpha/Beta optimization does not depend on a particular game. We use the Tic Tac Toe game to validate it. The motivation is always the same: to divide the problems into sub-problems. Validating the implementation of the Minimax with the Pacman game is a complex problem, whereas with the Tic Tac Toe game, it is much simpler. With this game, it is possible to visualize a very large number of states of the game. In addition, there are known strategies to ensure victory, defeat, and draws.

Game state

A Tic Tac Toe game state is required, made of the current epoch, and a 3x3 array of integers:

```java
public class TicTacToe {
    public int epoch;
    public int[][] cells= {{0,0,0},{0,0,0},{0,0,0}};
```

The array has three possible values: 1 for player symbols 1, -1 for player symbols -1, and 0 for no symbols.

Two methods of convenience are proposed, the first to detect victory:

```java
    public boolean hasWon(int player) {
        // returns true if player aligned 3 symbols
    }
```

And the second to show the state of the game:

```java
    public void show() {
        // console display ...
    }
}
```

Because the game is very simple, the command pattern is not used, and there is no equivalent to the `Rules` class in the Pacman example game.

Node of the search tree

The abstract class Node is extended to define a TicTacToeNode class that represents a node in the search tree:

```java
public class TicTacToeNode extends Node
{
```

Each node has a reference to the state of the game:

```java
private final TicTacToe state;
```

Warning: this is not a copy of this state; there is only one state of the game throughout the execution of the algorithm.

An epoch attribute is defined to identify the time of the game. It is related to the depth in the tree, and is used to do checks:

```java
private final int epoch;
```

The player attribute informs about the player played by the AI: it is the one we want to see winning. This value is the same for all nodes of the tree:

```java
private final int player;
```

The three attributes currentPlayer, x and y indicate the move represented by the node: which player (1 or -1) and which coordinate in the grid:

```java
private final int currentPlayer;
private final int x;
private final int y;
```

The createChildren() method fills the children array of the Node parent class with the child nodes. They correspond to all the possible moves from the current state, e.g. all the currently empty cells. For this to work, the state of the game must be the expected one. Comparing the epoch of the game to the expected one allows to (partially) check this property:

```java
public void createChildren() {
    if (state.epoch != epoch)
      throw new RuntimeException("Internal error");
    ArrayList<Node> list = new ArrayList();
    for (int j=0;j<3;j++) {
      for (int i=0;i<3;i++) {
        if (state.cells[i][j] == 0) {
            list.add(new TicTacToeNode(
                this,state,player,i,j,-currentPlayer));
        }
      }
    }
}
```

```java
    children = list.toArray(new Node[0]);
}
```

The `updateState()` method must apply the move represented by the node:

```java
public void updateState() {
```

We start by checking that the state epoch is the expected one:

```java
    if (state.epoch != epoch)
        throw new RuntimeException("Internal error");
```

Then we make sure that the move has not been played yet:

```java
    if (state.cells[x][y] != 0)
        throw new RuntimeException("Internal error");
```

The move is applied, and epoch is incremented:

```java
    state.cells[x][y] = currentPlayer;
    state.epoch ++;
```

The following lines determine whether the node is a leaf, and assign a value if any. For example, if the move just played leads to a victory:

```java
    if (state.hasWon(currentPlayer)) {
```

If the current player is the one defended by the AI, a positive value is assigned:

```java
        if (player == currentPlayer) {
            setValue(10-state.epoch);
        }
```

This value is greater if the depth is low, which means that we prefer to win as quickly as possible.

Otherwise, a negative value is assigned:

```java
        else {
            setValue(-state.epoch);
        }
    }
```

If the state is at the time 9, the grid is filled, and it is a draw:

```java
    else if (state.epoch == 9) {
        setValue(0);
    }
}
```

The `rollbackState()` method cancels the move, and thus restores the previous state, which is equivalent to go up in the search tree:

```java
public void rollbackState() {
    if (state.cells[x][y] != currentPlayer)
      throw new RuntimeException("Internal error");
    if (state.epoch != epoch+1)
      throw new RuntimeException("Internal error");
    state.cells[x][y] = 0;
    state.epoch --;
```

The child nodes are destroyed to avoid overloading the memory:

```java
    children = null;
}
```

Validation tests

The Tic Tac Toe game code is present in the "pacman/ai/tictactoe" folder of the Java sample project test packages. A class of unit tests `MinimaxTest` is also present in the folder 'pacman/ai'. It tests the implantations of Minimax, with or without Alpha/Beta optimization.

5.3.2.5   Minimax with Pacman

The use of Minimax for Pacman is more complex than with a game like the Tic Tac Toe. The main difficulty comes from the size of the search tree, which grows exponentially with the number of possible movements of the characters. Furthermore, we must make a decision very quickly - 12 times per second depending on the setting - we have to find solutions to prune the search tree. A usual solution to achieve this is to have a heuristic to determine interesting nodes to develop. Like any heuristic, there is little chance that it is perfect, in which case the Minimax algorithm could not work properly. However, this is usually enough. To be convinced of this, it must be remembered that the primary goal is only to select a single command for Pacman for the current game epoch, and a similar process is restarted for the next epoch. Thus, even if there is some randomness in the heuristic, any bad choice in the depths of the search tree will not have disastrous consequences. Besides, ghosts are moving, and bad predictions made several times before will no longer be when the present time has come. Finally, the main idea of search tree exploration is to have an approximative view of the consequences of each move. If a choice always leads to death, even a bad heuristic detects it.

Settings

Before defining `Node` child classes, the many parameters are grouped within a `Parameters` class. It eases the creation of nodes, but also reduces the memory footprint:

```java
public final class Parameters {
```

The first parameters make it possible to know and modify the state of the game: `rules` engine, game `state`, `list` command generator, and `random` generator:

```java
public final Rules rules;
public final State state;
public final CommandsLister lister;
public final Random random = new Random();
```

The following two attributes make it possible to use third-party AIs for ghosts. The goal is to use these AIs to predict ghost behavior:

```java
public final DistanceMapProvider dmProvider;
public final AI[] ais;
```

The following parameters control the depth and the number of maximum updates, in order to stop the algorithm if it is too long:

```java
public int minDepth = 20;
public int maxDepth = 40;
public int updateCount;
public int maxUpdateCount = 10000;
}
```

Pacman node

For readability, two child classes of `Node` are defined. One is dedicated to the max nodes when Pacman plays, and the other to the min nodes, when the ghosts play. The `PacmanNode` class contains the parameter set, as well as the move command for Pacman:

```java
public class PacmanNode extends Node
{
    private final Parameters parameters;
    private final Command command;
```

The `createChildren()` method produces ghost nodes. We consider two approaches. The first one considers all possible commands for ghosts. This approach is quickly problematic because the number of possibilities becomes very large. In addition, many obvious combinations will not lead to a gain for ghosts. The second one considers that ghosts are pretty smart and well-coordinated. It is not the case in the game, which would become impossible for Pacman. However, in the current situation, the goal is to avoid the worst situations for Pacman. Added to the fact that this leads to a small number of combinations, this second approach is very interesting.

To get some ghost intelligence, a target-tracking AI is chosen (as in the **Follow a character** section). Thus, it is assumed that all ghosts rush to Pacman, the worst situation that can be imagined:

```java
public void createChildren() {
    State state = parameters.state;
    Characters chars = state.getChars();
    Command[] commands = new Command[chars.size()];
    for (int index=1;index<chars.size();index++) {
        Command command = parameters.ais[index].createCommand();
        commands[index] = command;
    }
    Node node = new GhostsNode(this,parameters,commands);
    children = new Node[] { node };
}
```

The `updateState()` method adds the command for Pacman. There is no update of the state of the game since all the characters play during the same epoch. Also, there is no value assigned to the node: a Pacman node is never a leaf:

```java
public void updateState() {
    if (command != null) {
        parameters.rules.addCommand(0, command);
    }
}
```

The `rollbackState()` method has nothing to cancel since no state change has taken place:

```java
public void rollbackState() {
}
```


Ghost nodes

Ghost nodes also have access to the set of parameters, as well as the list of commands for all ghosts:

```java
public class GhostsNode extends Node
{
    private final Parameters parameters;
    private final Command[] commands;
```

The `createChildren()` method produces the nodes for Pacman. Except for the very first level of the tree, a very simple heuristic is followed: all possible directions are considered, except the U-turn. If the U-turn was added to the list, the search tree would grow considerably. The U-turn at the root of the tree is still considered, to allow Pacman to flee a ghost that goes in his direction. The only drawback of this

choice is the fact that Pacman does not consider trajectories where he approaches
a point, turns around, then leaves:

```java
public void createChildren() {
    List<Command> list = parameters.lister.listCommands(
            parameters.rules.getState(), 0);
    if (!list.isEmpty()) {
      if (depth != 0) {
        State state = parameters.rules.getState();
        Pacman pacman =state.getChars().getPacman();
        Iterator iterator = list.iterator();
        while (iterator.hasNext()) {
          DirectionCommand command =
            (DirectionCommand)iterator.next();
          if (command.getDirection().isOppositeOf(
            pacman.getDirection()))) {
            iterator.remove();
          }
        }
      }
    }
}
```

The end of the method translates the list created in a native array:

```java
    if (list.isEmpty()) {
        children = new Node[1];
        children[0] = new PacmanNode(this,parameters,null);
    }
    else {
        children = new Node[list.size()];
        for (int i=0;i<list.size();i++) {
            children[i] = new PacmanNode(this,parameters,list.get(i));
        }
    }
}
```

The `updateState()` method starts by adding ghost commands:

```java
public void updateState() {
    for (int i=1;i<commands.length;i++) {
      if (commands[i] != null) {
        parameters.rules.addCommand(i, commands[i]);
      }
    }
}
```

Knowing that the parent Pacman node has already added a Pacman command, the
game state can be updated:

```
parameters.rules.addPassiveCommands();
parameters.rules.update();
parameters.updateCount ++;
```

The following discussions determine whether the current node can be considered as a leaf:

```
State state = parameters.state;
Pacman pacman = state.getChars().getPacman();
```

If there are no more gums, Pacman wins, and a high value/score is given to the node:

```
if (state.getGumCount() == 0) {
    setValue(10000);
}
```

If Pacman is dead, a low value is given to the node. It is relative to the depth of the node. That is to say that among the possible deaths, we prefer those that arrive as late as possible:

```
else if (pacman.getStatus()==PacmanStatus.DEAD){
    setValue(-10000 + depth);
}
```

The last situation is a calculation to determine if a certain depth is reached or if the algorithm takes too much time. When this happens, the value is a high value relative to the number of gums. That is to say that we prefer a future where more gums were eaten:

```
else if (depth >= parameters.maxDepth
  || (depth >= parameters.minDepth
    && parameters.updateCount >= parameters.maxUpdateCount)) {
        setValue(10000 - state.getGumCount());
    }
}
```

The `rollbackState()` method is very simple, thanks to the preliminary work with the command pattern. In addition, child nodes are removed to reduce memory usage:

```
public void rollbackState() {
    parameters.rules.rollback();
    children = null;
}
```

Results

The diagrams in this example are available in the "Class Diagrams/chap05/ai06" folder of the sample UML project. The code is present in the "examples/chap05/ai06" folder of the Java sample project.

The Minimax with the proposed pruning allows obtaining very high victory rates, especially when the ghosts are slower than Pacman (easy and medium levels). This result is very satisfactory given the simplicity of the heuristics used. Better results can be obtained with greater depth of exploration but at the cost of large computations. It is also and certainly possible to do even better, using more efficient pruning heuristics.

Pacman	Ghost	Diff.	Victories	Time	Time	Gums
Minimax	Behavior	Easy	90%	1396	834	93
Minimax	Behavior	Normal	74%	1400	941	79
Minimax	Behavior	Hard	76%	1414	1027	55

5.3.3 Other usual approaches in Artificial Intelligence

Monte Carlo approaches

A natural extension for the exploration of a search tree are those called "Monte Carlo" (*Monte Carlo Tree Search*). These begin with the complete exploration of a small number of levels in the search tree. Then, for each node at the last level, complete - or very long - games are played. The first way to play these games is to make random choices. A second, more efficient approach is to use heuristics with a very low computation cost to select the moves. Finally, a third approach is to use another AI, provided that its complexity is low. In all cases, a score is computed based on the success of these games. This score is used to give a value to the node at the deepest level of the tree. The same principle is repeated for all nodes of the same depth, and then the classical Minimax algorithm is applied.

The main advantage of this approach is that the function that plays the games from the deep nodes of the tree does not need to be very smart. It makes it possible to offer AIs for games whose complexity is such that no effective heuristics could be proposed, like the game of Go. With the Monte Carlo approach, good AIs can be proposed, while being very simple to understand and implement.

Machine learning approaches

Another usual set of AI algorithms is machine learning. The first idea is to conceive heuristics no longer but to let the computer learn these heuristics by playing against humans or against itself. Most approaches rely on methods derived from statistical learning. The most recent approaches in this area are so-called *deep learning* methods, the most popular of which are *Convolutional Neural Networks*. Most of these methods work on vector representations: you have to translate the state of the game as a set of values. Similarly for decisions: these methods learn numerical parameters, which must then be linked to the game data. A simple first approach to "vectorize" the game data is to compute parameters such as the size of the armies, the amount of gold, etc., then to consider macro parameters, such as the level of aggressiveness or the level of priority of construction. Even with rather crude values, current learning methods are so powerful that they are able to find correlations where they do not seem to exist - provided that a very large number of games are simulated (millions).

Combining approaches

The best solutions are usually a combination of existing techniques, depending on the game played. For example, for the Go game, which was a challenge for decades, a solution combining Minimax with Monte Carlo and deep learning has achieved excellent results. In this solution, deep learning is used as a heuristic to play games from the deepest nodes of the search tree. For the Mario game, a method that won the 2009 international competition uses a search tree combined with an AI by behavior. The nodes of the tree are no longer precise commands, but a choice at a given time between different possible behaviors.

5.3.4 Exercises

5.3.4.1 Exercise 3.4.1: Traversal with the Node interface

→ Propose a traversal interface and two implementations to browse the trees described by the `pacman.ai.tree.Node` class, using the Visitor pattern. The first traversal implementation is a depth first/recursive approach. The second traversal implementation is a depth first/iterative approach. To test, you can use the implantation for the Tic Tac Toe game in the `pacman.ai.tictactoe` package (in test packages). Here is an example of an initial state of the game:

```
TicTacToe state = new TicTacToe();
state.epoch = 6;
state.cells = new int[][] {{1,-1,0},{-1,1,0},{1,-1,0}};
Node node = new TicTacToeNode(state,-1);
```

Even if you test with the Tic Tac Toe game, your solutions must work with any other implementation of `pacman.ai.tree.Node`.

5.3.4.2 Exercise 3.4.2: Connect 4 with an AI with planning

→ Design and implement an AI by planning for the Connect 4 game. Start with the solution of exercice 1.3.2.

For Minimax implementation, you can implement it yourself, or use the implementation in the Pacman example game, available in "pacman/ai/tree". This implementation does not depend on any game. To use it, you have to implement a child class of `pacman.ai.tree.Node`, and then use the `pacman.ai.tree.alphabeta.AlphaBeta` class, as it was done for the Tic Tac Toe game and Pacman.

⇒ Note: If you do not use the implementation of Connect 4 proposed in the folder "examples/chap05/connect4noai", you need to implement a solution that allows finding alignments of 4 pawns in the grid quickly. In the opposite case, your AI will be very slow, and you will be limited to small depths of the search tree.

5.3.5 Video game development: AI with planning

To efficiently use search trees, you must first manage their size, exploration time, and available time. For example, for a game like Pacman, the tree quickly grows but not necessarily in an interesting way, and the processing window is very short (a few milliseconds). For the tactical part of a game like Heroes of Might and Magic, the tree is not very large, and the computation time can be very long(several seconds). For the strategic part, where you have to develop your cities and move your heroes, the tree is very large, and the processing time can be very long (one minute).

Different levels can be considered. In the Pacman example, the lowest level is considered, e.g. player controls. Nothing prohibits interest in higher levels, such as the overall behavior of a player, or macro parameters. For example, if we take the strategic part of Heroes of Might and Magic, it is useless to consider all possible and imaginable movements of the heroes on the map. It is more interesting to work with macro-commands, like "approaching an enemy hero", knowing that these macro-commands include a series of commands over several epochs of the game.

Once the overall strategy is devised and put on paper, good design is also very important for this part. The more the IA is divided into independent, modular, and interchangeable features, the easier it is to try out possibilities and find the best ones. In this scope, the usual patterns are always welcome, and their combinations even more. At this point in the development of your video game, you should normally start to feel comfortable with the usual patterns. So it's time to start being creative and to come up with new designs, tailored to your needs. It is what we did to serve distance maps in the **Service Provider** section, and for the implementation of Minimax in this section. Finally, the validation steps are also very important, especially if it is possible to evaluate or put in competition the AI.

5.4 Exercises solutions

5.4.1 Exercise 1.3.1: Immutable galaxy

The version with the decorator pattern is presented here. The complete solution is in the "examples/chap05/stellaris01" folder of the Java sample project. Only the salient points are presented here.

For each class, an interface is defined with the same methods, then an editable class with the name `MutableXXX`, and a non-modifiable class with `ImmutableXXX`. Besides, an additional `toImmutable()` method is defined to allow you to create a non-editable version from any object.

For example, the `Building` interface is defined as follows:

```java
public interface Building {
    public BuildingType getType();
    public int getLevel();
    public void setType(BuildingType type);
    public void setLevel(int level);
    public ImmutableBuilding toImmutable();
}
```

The editable version uses the original code:

```java
public class MutableBuilding implements Building {
    private BuildingType type;
    private int level;
    public MutableBuilding(BuildingType type,int level) {
        this.type = type;
        this.level = level;
    }
    public BuildingType getType() {
        return type;
    }
    public int getLevel() {
        return level;
    }
    public void setType(BuildingType type) {
        this.type = type;
    }
}
```

```java
    public void setLevel(int level) {
        this.level = level;
    }
    public ImmutableBuilding toImmutable() {
        return new ImmutableBuilding(this);
    }
}
```

The last `toImmutable()` method returns a non-editable version that has decorated it.

The non-modifiable version is defined as follows:

```java
public final class ImmutableBuilding implements Building {
    private final MutableBuilding building;
    public ImmutableBuilding(MutableBuilding b) {
        this.building = b;
    }

    public BuildingType getType() {
        return building.getType();
    }
    public int getLevel() {
        return building.getLevel();
    }
    public void setType(BuildingType type) {
        throw new IllegalAccessError();
    }
    public void setLevel(int level) {
        throw new IllegalAccessError();
    }
    public ImmutableBuilding toImmutable() {
        return this;
    }
}
```

The last `toImmutable()` method returns `this` since it is already unmodifiable.

When an object is returned from a non-editable class, always make sure that it is a non-editable version. For example, for the `getPlanet()` method of the `ImmutableSystem` class, the planet found is converted to a non-editable version via the call to the `toImmutable()` method:

```java
public Planet getPlanet(int index) {
    return system.getPlanet(index).toImmutable();
}
```

When a container is returned, you must also ensure that the content is not editable.

For example, for the `getBuildings()` method of the `ImmutablePlanet` class:

```java
public ArrayList<Building> getBuildings() {
    ArrayList<Building> list = new ArrayList();
    MutableHabitable h = (MutableHabitable)planet;
    for (Building building : h.getBuildings()) {
        list.add(building.toImmutable());
    }
    return list;
}
```

This method returns an editable list of immutable buildings. However, since it was created during the call, modifying it does not change the list of buildings on the planet, which is the end goal.

5.4.2 Exercise 1.3.2: Connect 4 with a simple AI

The solution is in the "examples/chap05/connect4" folder. The AIs are located in the ai subfolder, and follow the same design scheme as the one presented with the Pacman game:

AI class: Abstract class to represent an AI. It proposes a `listCommands()` convenience method which allows obtaining the list of possible commands given the current state of the game:

```java
public List<Command> listCommands() {
    List<Command> commands = new ArrayList();
    if (board.getWinner() == 0) {
        for (int j=0;j<7;j++) {
            if (board.canPlay(j)) {
                commands.add(new Command(j));
            }
        }
    }
    return commands;
}
```

RandomAI class, child of AI: implements a random AI. The `createCommand()` method selects a command at random:

```java
public Command createCommand() {
    List<Command> list = listCommands();
    if (list.isEmpty())
        return null;
    int index = random.nextInt(list.size());
    return list.get(index);
}
```

FirstAI class, child of AI: implements an AI that always selects the first playable column:

```java
public Command createCommand() {
    List<Command> list = listCommands();
    if (list.isEmpty())
        return null;
    return list.get(0);
}
```

AIs are competing in the Connect4Test class in the 'examples/chap05/connect4' folder of the test packages. It offers a battle() method that lets you play two AIs against each other. This method is independent of the exact nature of the chosen AIs, and relies solely on the AI class:

```java
public void battle() {
    wins1 = 0;
    wins2 = 0;
    evens = 0;
    int startingPlayer = 1;
    for (int repeat=0;repeat<100;repeat++) {
        board.reset(startingPlayer);
        System.out.println("Game "+(repeat+1)+"/100...");
        while(true) {
            if (board.isWinner(1)) {
                wins1 ++;
                break;
            }
            if (board.isWinner(-1)) {
                wins2 ++;
                break;
            }
            if (board.isOver()) {
                evens ++;
                break;
            }
            Command command = null;
            if (board.getCurrentPlayer() == 1) {
                command = ai1.createCommand();
            }
            else {
                command = ai2.createCommand();
            }
            if (command == null) {
                evens ++;
                break;
```

```
        }
        command.execute(board);
    }
    startingPlayer = -startingPlayer;
  }
}
```

Faced with the random AI, the simple AI wins very often (4 games won out of 5 on average). This result is consistent since the simple AI tries to form a vertical alignment on the first column of the grid. Random AI cancels this alignment only by chance, which happens rarely.

5.4.3   Exercise 2.5.1: Shortest path in the galaxy

We must first assign values to the vertices of the graph that represents the galaxy. The simplest way is to add an attribute to the System class that represents a system in the galaxy. This approach is not very elegant from a conceptual point of view since the System class is loaded with additional functionality. In addition, it does not allow us to have several distance maps at the same time. Another solution is to decorate the system class to add this new attribute. This approach is the most versatile because it can adapt the map when the galaxy changes but is more complex to implement. An alternative proposed here is to use an associative array to associate systems and values. For example, we can associate the index of a system with its weight:

```
HashMap<Integer,Integer> weights = new HashMap();
```

To initialize the Dijkstra algorithm, we must first give the infinite value to all the vertices:

```
for (int i=0;i<galaxy.getSystemCount();i++) {
    weights.put(i, Integer.MAX_VALUE);
}
```

The algorithm is based on a priority queue that contains the vertices to be processed, along with their weight. A ValuedSystem class is defined for this:

```
public static class ValuedSystem
    implements Comparable<ValuedSystem> {
    public int index;
    public int value;
    public ValuedSystem(int index, int value) {
        this.index = index;
        this.value = value;
    }
    public int compareTo(ValuedSystem other) {
        return this.value - other.value;
```

```
    }
}
```

It must implement `Comparable`, so that the priority queue can order the vertices according to their value (here the `value` attribute).

Before starting the computations, you must also add each target system with the weight 0:

```
int index = galaxy.findSystem(systemName);
queue.add(new ValuedSystem(index,0));
weights.put(index,0);
```

The implementation of the algorithm is then very close to the case with a grid, except for the neighbors who are obtained with methods of the `Galaxy` class, like `findLeftConnections()`, which returns all the connections for a given system:

```
while(!queue.isEmpty()) {
    ValuedSystem vs = queue.poll();
    if (vs.value >
        weights.get(vs.index))
        continue;
    for (Connection connection :
        galaxy.findLeftConnections(vs.index)) {
        int newWeight = vs.value + connection.getParsecs();
        int curWeight = weights.get(connection.getSystem2());
        if (curWeight > newWeight) {
            queue.add(new ValuedSystem(
                connection.getSystem2(),newWeight));
            weights.put(connection.getSystem2(),newWeight);
        }
    }
}
```

The complete solution is available in the folder "examples/chap05/stellaris02".

5.4.4   Exercise 2.5.2: Connect 4 with a heuristic AI

The solution is in the "examples/chap05/connect4" folder. The requested AI is located in the `HeuristicAI` class of the sub-folder 'ai'. It follows the proposed strategy (to make an alignment, to prevent an alignment or to play at random) relying on the commands and their ability to cancel a move:

```
public Command createCommand() {
```

This initial step returns the list of possible commands, each corresponding to a column:

```
List<Command> list = listCommands();
if (list.isEmpty())
    return null;
```

The following operations try to find a move that leads to a connect 4:

```
Command found = null;
int player = board.getCurrentPlayer();
for (Command command: list) {
```

Each possible command is executed:

```
command.execute(board);
```

If the state of the game finds a winner, and the winner is the current player, then a winning move has been found:

```
if (board.isWinner(player)) {
    found = command;
}
```

In any case, the command is reversed to restore the state of the game:

```
command.rollback(board);
```

If a winning order was found, it is returned:

```
if (found != null) {
    return found;
}
}
```

The following lines follow the same principle to prevent a move that offers an alignment for the opponent. This time, two moves are imagined: a command move for the player, then a command2 move for the opponent. In any case, it must be ensured that the orders are canceled:

```
for (Command command: list) {
    command.execute(board);
    List<Command> list2 = listCommands();
    for (Command command2: list2) {
        command2.execute(board);
        if (board.isWinner(-player)) {
            found = command2;
        }
        command2.rollback(board);
    }
    command.rollback(board);
    if (found != null) {
        return found;
```

```
        }
    }
```

Default case: a command is chosen at random:

```
    int index = random.nextInt(list.size());
    return list.get(index);
}
```

⇒ Note: This solution is not dedicated to the Connect 4 game. It works with any game that has a move to end the game with a winner.

5.4.5   Exercise 3.4.1: Traversal with the Node interface

The solution presented here is based on the following classes and interfaces:

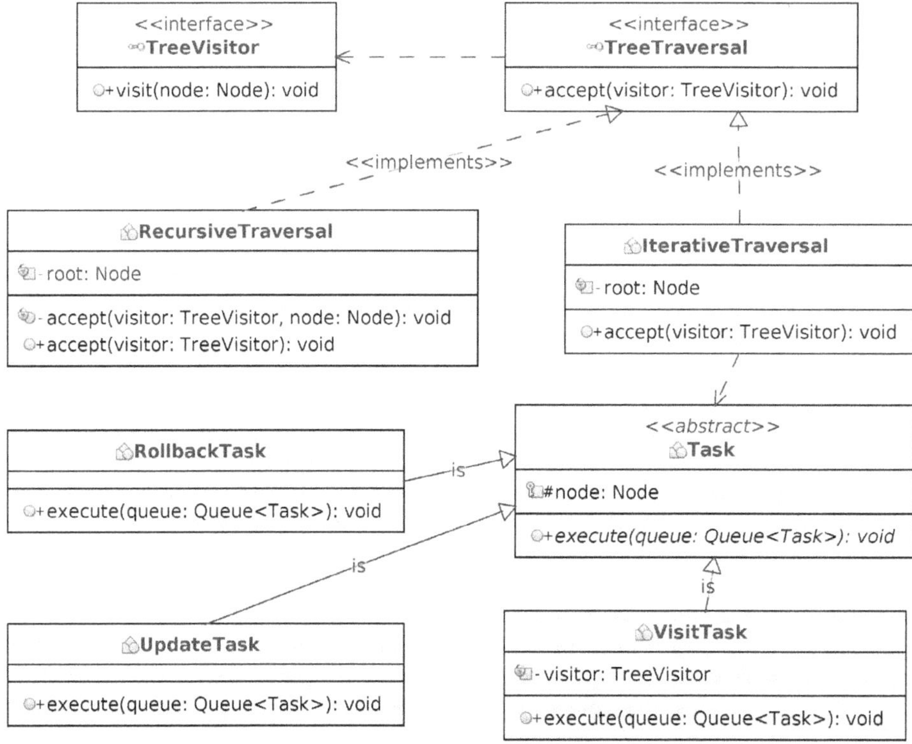

TreeVisitor

The TreeVisitor interface must be implemented by the user to perform the desired tasks for each node. For example, if you want to display the state of the Tic Tac

Toe game at each node visit:

```java
class MyVisitor implements TreeVisitor {
    public void visit(Node node) {
        TicTacToeNode tttNode = (TicTacToeNode)node;
        TicTacToe state = tttNode.getState();
        state.show() ;
    }
}
```

TreeTraversal

The TreeTraversal interface allows you to implement various strategies for traversing the tree. Once the user chooses an implementation, he has to call the accept() method with the visitor of his choice, like the MyVisitor class above, so that all nodes are visited.

RecursiveTraversal

The RecursiveTraversal class is a depth-first traversal with a recursive algorithm. The accept() method with a single argument process the root:

```java
public void accept(TreeVisitor visitor) {
    visitor.visit(root);
    for (Node child : root) {
        accept(visitor,child);
    }
}
```

This method calls the accept() method with two arguments for each child node in the root.

The accept() method with two arguments processes all the other nodes of the tree, calling itself recursively:

```java
private void accept(TreeVisitor visitor,Node node) {
    if (node == null) {
        return;
    }
    node.updateState();
    visitor.visit(node);
    for (Node child : node) {
        accept(visitor,child);
    }
}
```

```
        node.rollbackState();
}
```

IterativeTraversal

The `IterativeTraversal` class performs a depth-first traversal with an iterative algorithm. In this case, use its stack instead of the system stack. An abstract `Task` class is defined to represent the tasks to be performed later. The `accept()` method of the `IterativeTraversal` class adds a first initial task to queue, and then executes tasks until queue is empty:

```java
public void accept(TreeVisitor visitor) {
    Queue<Task> queue =
        Collections.asLifoQueue(new ArrayDeque());
    queue.add(new VisitTask(root,visitor));
    while(!queue.isEmpty()) {
        Task task = queue.poll();
        task.execute(queue);
    }
}
```

The three implementations of the `Task` class represent the three tasks encountered in the process: going down the tree with `UpdateTask`, visiting the node with `VisitTask`, and going up in the tree with `RollbackTask`.

For the `UpdateTask` and `RollbackTask` classes, the operation is very simple: either call the `updateState()` method of the node to go down in the search tree or call the `rollbackState()` method of the node to go up.

For the `VisitTask` class, the first operation is to call the visitor. Then, in a specific order, new tasks are added for each child of the current node:

```java
public void execute(Queue<Task> queue) {
    visitor.visit(node);
    for (int i=node.getChildCount()-1;i>=0;i--) {
        Node child = node.getChild(i);
        queue.add(new RollbackTask(child));
        queue.add(new VisitTask(child, visitor));
        queue.add(new UpdateTask(child));
    }
}
```

Tasks are added in an order that takes into account that a stack is used: it is always the last added task that is executed first. Thus, when you add the `RollbackTask`, `VisitTask`, and `UpdateTask` tasks, the last one is executed first, then the visit, and finally `RollbackTask`. Similarly, the children are traversed from the last to the first to obtain a similar traversal order to that by recursion. It is not mandatory since the children of the same node can be traversed in any order; the traversal remains depth-first.

The solution is proposed in the "examples/chap05/treevisitor" folder of the Java project example. Validation tests are offered in the same folder in the test packages.

5.4.6   Exercise 3.4.2: Connect 4 with an AI with planning

The solution is in the "examples/chap05/connect4" folder. The requested IA is implemented in the `MinimaxAI` and `BoardNode` classes in the `ai` subfolder. This implementation is based on that of Minimax used for Pacman and Tic Tac Toe.

The `BoardNode` class is a child class of the `pacman.ai.tree.Node` class. The `createChildren()` method lists the possible child nodes from the current node. Each of its nodes corresponds to a possible move/command:

```java
public void createChildren() {
  ArrayList<Node> list = new ArrayList();
  for (int j=0;j<7;j++) {
    if (board.canPlay(j)) {
      list.add(new BoardNode(this,new Command(j)));
    }
  }
  children = list.toArray(new Node[0]);
}
```

The `updateState()` method executes the command contained in the node, and handles the different cases of leaves:

```java
public void updateState() {
    if (command == null) {
        return;
    }
    command.execute(board);
```

If the player has won, the score awarded is even greater than the depth is low, which is to prefer to win as soon as possible:

```java
    if (board.isWinner(player)) {
        setValue(42 - depth);
    }
```

If the opponent has won, the score awarded is even larger than the depth is large, which is to assume that the opponent prefers to win as soon as possible:

```java
    else if (board.isWinner(-player)) {
        setValue(depth - 42);
    }
```

If the depth is greater than 7, the exploration is stopped. This depth allows a computation of Minimax lasting about 100 milliseconds on an average machine. The score of 0 represents a lack of evaluation. A heuristic proposed at this level would improve the AI, both in terms of its quality and speed of execution, the score 0 does not allow Alpha-Beta to work fully:

```java
else if (depth >= 7) {
    setValue(0);
}
```

If the game is over, and there is no winner, it is a draw:

```java
else if (board.isOver()) {
    setValue(0);
}
}
```

The `MinimaxAI` class, via its `createCommand()` method, applies the Minimax algorithm with Alpha/Beta optimization to find a set of interesting moves. Then, one of these moves is randomly chosen:

```java
public Command createCommand() {
    if (board.getWinner() != 0) {
        return null;
    }
    AlphaBeta alphabeta = new AlphaBeta();
    BoardNode root =
      new BoardNode(board,board.getCurrentPlayer());
    List<Node> bestNodes = alphabeta.run(root);
    if (bestNodes.isEmpty()) {
        return null;
    }
    BoardNode bestNode = (BoardNode)bestNodes.get(
        random.nextInt(bestNodes.size()));
    return bestNode.getCommand();
}
```

CHAPTER 6

Concurrent execution and networking

6.1 Concurrent execution

Before we start designing solutions for network gaming, we must first be able to run the rules engine in a separate thread. Furthermore, the rules engine should run without any UI component. Ultimately, the goal is to run an engine in a different process on a remote machine.

This section also introduces several common approaches and associated patterns for managing concurrent execution of processing, for example, the parallelization of tree search for planned AIs.

6.1.1 Separate rules engine and user interface

6.1.1.1 Interaction between components

If we want to parallelize processing, we can emphasis the following components:

- The rules engine that changes state using commands;
- The rendering engine that draws the state and produces commands;
- A component which orchestrates the interactions, embodied by the `PlayGameMode` class in the Pacman example game.

These components need common information, such as game state data. Some components modify these shared data, which makes reading this data impossible during the changes. Other components produce messages, such as the rules engine that notifies status changes or the user interface that produces commands. Finally, the whole is subject to real-time constraints, such as the rendering that must be performed at 60 frames per second.

For each type of interaction, a solution must be found to allow access or modification of the data, without errors or blocking. Another usual problem in concurrent execution is *data race*. It occurs when multiple components want to view or edit the same information at the same time. It does not necessarily lead to blocking, but slow down the program. In these situations, components are constantly waiting. The latency generated by these conflicts also comes with scheduling problems: the order in which data is read and written is generally not predictable, which can lead to erratic behavior.

All the work in this section is to identify the problems associated with parallel processing and then find ways to minimize or remove them.

6.1.1.2 Rules engine thread

The first separation step in this chapter is to place the rules engine in a dedicated thread. Hence, it is necessary to determine where is the game state, or more precisely, who "owns" and controls access to the game data. There is no concurrent processing in the rules engine, and it is the only one that changes the game state. As a result, we consider that the rules engine is the sole owner of the game state, and to access it, you have to ask for it. In the opposite case, where there are concurrent accesses to data, as it is the case in conventional databases, it would be necessary to separate and synchronize the parts that modify the database of those that store them.

We define a `RulesThread` class in the `sync` package to manage access to the rules engine and its state. An alternative would have been to enrich the `Rules` class. However, from a conceptual point of view, it gives too much responsibility to this class. Just as methods must be separated into sub-methods when they become too large, it is strongly advised to divide classes that have too many features.

Rules engine thread

The `RulesThread` class handles the execution of the game state updates in the background. The `run()` method of the `Thread` class is implemented, and contains a loop that continuously calls an `update()` method, as long as the `running` attribute is true:

```java
public void run()
{
    while(running) {
        update();
    }
}
```

The `running` attribute is used to control the stopping of updates and the life of the thread. A `stopRunning()` method is defined to trigger the end of the thread:

```java
public void stopRunning() {
    running = false;
}
```

The `running` attribute is declared `volatile` to ensure that it is modifiable by all threads. It also ensures that there is no risk that there are multiple copies with different values in the caches of the processor cores. It is not necessary to declare the `stopRunning()` method as `synchronized` since the only access to the `running` attribute is in the `run()` method. Concerning these accesses, there are two possible scenarios. In the first scenario, another thread modifies the attribute by calling the `stopRunning()` method during the while loop of the `run()` method: no problem. In the second scenario, the modification is during the while test of the `run()` method: there is then a data run, and therefore a slight block (a few nanoseconds). Since the goal is to stop the game, it only happens once and presents no problem for the user. However, it remains relevant to have thought about this before making a decision, knowing that the synchronization of the `stopRunning()` method would have unnecessarily blocked its callers.

⇒ Note: This usual approach does not allow you to terminate the thread during an update. For a game like Pacman, which updates are very fast, it's not a problem. For other games, it is necessary to place tests to know if the stop is requested regularly. A good approach is to use the mechanism of thread interruption integrated into the Java language. To interrupt a thread, the `interrupt()` method of the Thread class is called. Within the update, the `isInterrupted()` method of the Thread class can be periodically checked to see if the game has to stop.

Update the game state

The `update()` method of the `RulesThread` class updates the game state at the defined frequency. This one starts by watching if the time spent since the beginning of the last update is sufficient:

```java
private long lastUpdate = 0;
public void update()
{
    long now = System.nanoTime();
```

```java
State state = rules.getState();
if ((now-lastUpdate)<state.getEpochDuration()) {
    return;
}
lastUpdate = now;
```

It follows the update of the state. This one is synchronized, to prohibit any access during the update:

```java
synchronized(this) {
    rules.update();
}
```

The end of the method pauses the unused time so as not to make the processor work unnecessarily:

```java
long elapsed = System.nanoTime() - lastUpdate;
long milliSleep = (state.getEpochDuration()-elapsed)/1000000;
if (milliSleep > 0) {
    try {
        Thread.sleep(milliSleep);
    } catch (InterruptedException ex) {
    }
}
}
```

Simple reading of the rules engine

If another thread needs to read data in the rules engine, a simple getter is too dangerous. Even synchronized, it would offer no guarantee on non-concurrent access to data. A simple but inefficient solution is to create a synchronized method with a lambda function:

```java
public synchronized void processRules(
    Consumer<Rules> consumer) {
    consumer.accept(rules);
}
```

To use this method, we provide a lambda function with a `Rules` type argument. For example, to save the game state in the `PlayGameMode` class:

```java
public void saveState(String fileName) {
    rulesThread.processRules((rules) -> {
        State state = rules.getState();
        state.save(fileName);
        savedState = state.clone();
```

```
    });
}
```

The `processRules()` method of the `RulesThread` class executes all lambda code with the assurance that the rules engine is locked all the way through. So, if the update is in progress, the other thread is waiting. If the other thread is running this method, the update must wait before starting. This simple solution is relevant in cases where these locks are not troublesome, such as saving or loading the game state.

6.1.1.3 Transfer commands (Double Buffer)

The user interface produces commands when the user interacts. For example, in the `handleInputs()` method of the `PlayGameMode` class, the keyboard is consulted to see if the arrows are pressed. If it is the case, a corresponding command is produced.

A basic approach to transfer these commands to the rules engine thread is to create a synchronized method in the `RulesThread` class to add commands, or directly use the `processRules()` method presented above. This approach causes many locks. Indeed, the keyboard is consulted 60 times per second, and each time, if a command is added with this approach during an update, the main thread is then blocked. The display is then frozen, and the entire game seems to pause the time of the update. In the case where the update took the maximum allowed time, the duration of the pause is as long. For the Pacman example game, where the update can take up to 80 milliseconds, it's still playable, but the display is unstable. For games with much larger updates, it completely wipes out the user experience.

A usual solution in the field of parallel execution is to use a *double buffer*. It's not an "official" design pattern, but it's still very popular. The first example in this book is the case of the double buffer presented for display in **Chapter 3**. When the graphics card transfers the data from one buffer to the screen, the other can be modified without any blocking. This principle was also used for the rendering engine, with display data placed in layers (e.g., `Layer` child classes). The processor freely modifies this data and then copied it into the graphics card. The difference with the previous case is that there is a copy of one buffer to another and not a swap of the two buffers. Unlike the copy, swapping is extremely fast and therefore leads to the shortest possible blocking time.

For the transfer of commands, the solution is to create a command array `commands` in the `PlayGameMode` class. Then, in the `handleInputs()` method of the `PlayGameMode` class, when an arrow is pressed, a new command is added to that array:

```
synchronized(commands) {
    if (keyboard.isKeyPressed(KeyEvent.VK_RIGHT)) {
        commands.put(currentChar,new DirectionCommand(
```

```
                    currentChar,Direction.EAST));
    }
    if (keyboard.isKeyPressed(KeyEvent.VK_LEFT)) {
        commands.put(currentChar,new DirectionCommand(
            currentChar,Direction.WEST));
    }
    if (keyboard.isKeyPressed(KeyEvent.VK_DOWN)) {
        commands.put(currentChar,new DirectionCommand(
            currentChar,Direction.SOUTH));
    }
    if (keyboard.isKeyPressed(KeyEvent.VK_UP)) {
        commands.put(currentChar,new DirectionCommand(
            currentChar,Direction.NORTH));
    }
}
```

We synchronize the whole on the `commands` array: thus, the array can be safely modified without causing an error if another thread tries to access it.

Subsequently, the rules engine thread adds these commands to the game engine at the best time just before the update. Then, it empties the commands array, which no longer has any interest in referencing the added commands. The blocking time then corresponds to the maximum time between the creation of commands (like in the `synchronized` block above) and that of the transfer of the commands, e.g. at most a few hundred nanoseconds. In terms of data structures, there are two arrays: the one in the rules engine and the one in the `PlayGameMode` class. So there is a copy of the references from one array to another, but not commands: it is a hybrid case of double-buffer, between copy and permutation.

6.1.1.4 Efficient reading of the rules engine (Observer Pattern)

For many components, it is necessary to have access to the rules engine and the game state. As noted above, it is not feasible to leave free access to this data. It is also not efficient to very frequently request an access window, as we did with the `processRules()` method of the `RulesThread` class. In general, it seems complicated to allow components which require access to the data to request it at any time. The simplest way is to let the data owner choose these moments.

To get it, we use the Observer Pattern again. The owner of the rules engine, `RulesThread`, is made observable:

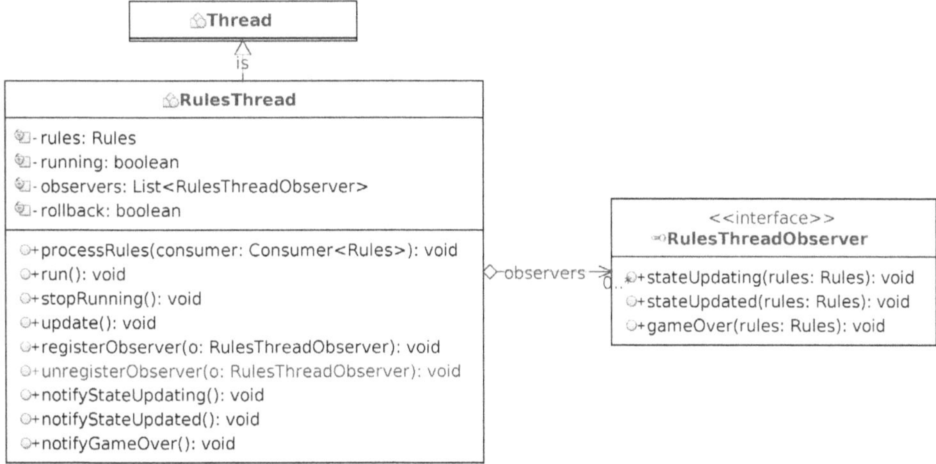

We consider three notification categories:

- `stateUpdating()` when the update is about to be started;
- `stateUpdated()` when the update has just finished;
- `gameOver()` when the game and the thread are finished.

The `notifyXXX()` methods call the corresponding methods with the rules engine as an argument.

Operations before the update

The `PlayGameMode` class, as the main orchestrator, is the best candidate to observe the rules engine. For the `stateUpdating()` method, called before a new state update, the main aim is to add commands. The first commands to be added are the ones caused by the player (e.g., the ones stored in the `commands` array):

```java
public void stateUpdating(Rules rules) {
    synchronized(commands) {
        commands.entrySet().forEach((command) -> {
            rules.addCommand(command.getKey(),
                command.getValue());
        });
        commands.clear();
    }
}
```

The operation is synchronized with the `commands` array, to ensure that it is not changed during the operation.

Then, we add the commands of the AIs, which also makes it possible to run them in the thread of the rules engine (the `stateUpdating()` method of the observers are called by the `notifyStateUpdating()` method, itself called by the rules engine when it is about to update the state):

```java
for(int index=0;index<5;index++) {
    if (index == currentChar)
        continue;
    Command command= ais[index].createCommand();
    if (command != null) {
        rules.addCommand(index, command);
    }
}
}
```

Operations after the update

The `stateUpdated()` method, called just after an update, determines whether the game is over. If this is the case, the `stopRunning()` method of the `RulesThread` class is called to terminate the rules engine thread:

```java
public void stateUpdated(Rules rules)
{
    State state = rules.getState();
    if (state.getGumCount() == 0) {
        rulesThread.stopRunning();
    }
    Characters chars = state.getChars();
    Pacman pacman = chars.getPacman();
    if (pacman != null && pacman.getStatus() == PacmanStatus.DEAD
      && pacman.getStatusTime() == 0) {
        rulesThread.stopRunning();
    }
}
```

End-of-game operations, such as changing the game mode, can not take place until a rules engine thread is running. It is the reason why the above method merely asks to stop it.

Operation after the end of the rules engine thread:

The `gameOver()` method, called just before the end of the engine thread, performs the game mode change operations. The different cases of victories and defeats are the same as before:

```java
public void gameOver(Rules rules) {
   State state = rules.getState();
    if (state.getGumCount() == 0) {
      if (currentChar == 0) {
        setGameMode(new GameOverMode("Victory !"));
      }
      else {
        setGameMode(new GameOverMode("You failed"));
      }
    }
    Characters chars = state.getChars();
    Pacman pacman = chars.getPacman();
    if (pacman != null && pacman.getStatus() == PacmanStatus.DEAD
     && pacman.getStatusTime() == 0) {
      if (currentChar == 0) {
        setGameMode(new GameOverMode("You lost !"));
      }
      else {
        setGameMode(new GameOverMode("Congrats !"));
      }
    }
}
```

6.1.1.5 Cache notifications

For the rendering engine, we can also follow the previous approach: when the update is complete, it consults the state to modify its graphic data. However, it does not consult the state but is notified of the changes it has undergone. It makes it possible to reduce the computations, avoiding a complete state reading for each update of the display.

Leaving the state notifying the rules engine is risky, even with synchronizations to avoid conflicts. With this type of approach, every change of the rules engine that results in notification causes a lock with the rendering engine. Besides, these notifications can be numerous, which gives rise to a strong loss of resources, since a large number of locks requires many processor cycles.

One solution in this section is to intercept rules engine notifications, store them, and then start them at the right time. In doing so, there are no locks during the state update. The only blocking is the delayed execution of all notifications, which is the bare minimum that can be considered. The operation is an asynchronous execution; in other words, a non-immediate call of a method in the near future. Several design patterns incorporate this type of mechanics, but no "official" that corresponds to the present case. The underlying mechanics remain usual and widely used in the field of concurrent execution.

A cache for notifications

A `CachedStateObserver` class is defined, and implements the `StateObserver` interface. However, this class is not a standard state observer: it does not process notifications, but stores the necessary information to be able to run them later:

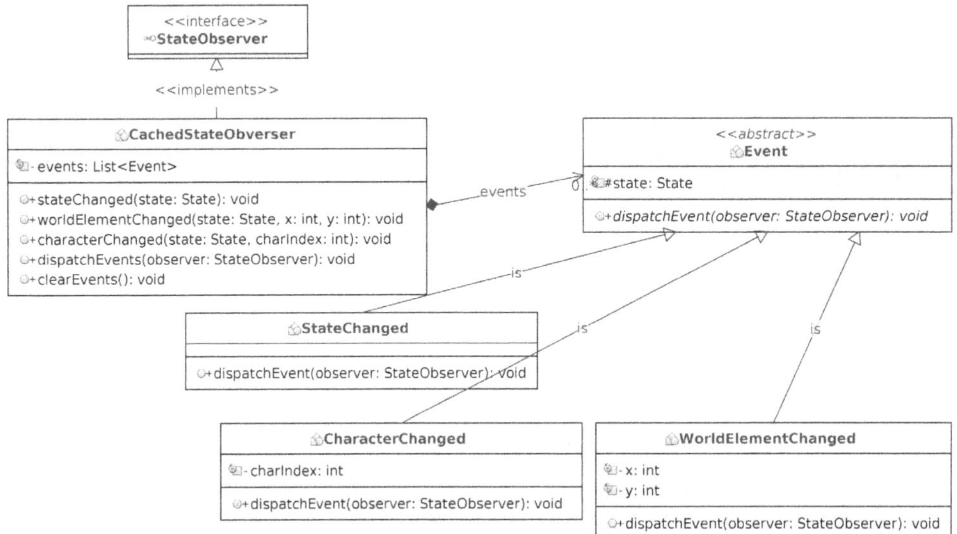

The `events` attribute contains the list of received notifications. We represent each notification type by a child class of `Event`. For example, a `characterChanged()` notification is represented by an instance of the `CharactedChanged` class with the `charIndex` attribute value received during the notification. This instance is built and added to the array during a notification:

```java
public void characterChanged(State state, int c) {
    events.add(new CharacterChanged(state,c));
}
```

The principle is the same for other types of notification.

The `dispathEvents()` method of the `CachedStateObserver` class is used to send all stored notifications to a state observer:

```java
public void dispathEvents(StateObserver observer) {
    for (Event event : events) {
        event.dispathEvent(observer);
    }
}
```

It uses implementations of the `dispatchEvent()` method of the `Event` class, for example for `CharacterChanged`:

```java
public void dispatchEvent(StateObserver observer) {
    observer.characterChanged(state,charIndex);
}
```

Finally, the `clearEvents()` method of the `CachedStateObserver` class is used to delete all stored notifications.

Use for the rendering engine

When initializing in the `PlayGameMode` class, the renderer no longer observes the game state. Instead, a `CachedStateObverser` is made, and observes the game state:

```java
public void init() {
    ...
    cachedStateObserver = new CachedStateObverser();
    state.registerObserver(cachedStateObserver);
    ...
}
```

Then in the `stateUpdating()` method, called just after a state update, the stored notifications are sent to the rendering engine and then deleted:

```java
public void stateUpdating(Rules rules) {
    synchronized(renderer) {
      cachedStateObserver.dispatchEvents(renderer);
      cachedStateObserver.clearEvents();
    }
    ...
}
```

Both operations are synchronized with the rendering engine to avoid sending notifications while drawing.

Finally, the drawing takes place as before, except for the synchronization on the rendering engine, to avoid the drawing during the reception of notifications:

```java
public void render(long time) {
    synchronized (renderer) {
        renderer.render(beginEpoch,time,beginEpoch+epochDuration
        );
    }
}
```

The diagrams in this sample are available in the "Class Diagrams/chap06/threads01" folder of the sample UML project. The code is present in the "examples/chap06/threads01" folder of the Java sample project.

6.1.2   Parallelize processing

This section introduces advanced notions that beginners can ignore.

The previous section presents a higher-level concurrent execution context when components exchange large amounts of data. In addition, there is no precise control of exchange time. For example, it is not possible to predict when a user presses a key. The issues are more about synchronization aspects, where everyone must be able to perform their tasks without blocking or being blocked by others.

In this section, we are interested in another context of concurrent execution, where the main objective is the execution of heavy processing, whose course is known and controlled. This processing usually comes down to performing a function, which on input data returns output data. For instance, compute the sum of two arrays, or execute an AI to find the best move according to the current game state.

The following sections present the most popular approaches in this area, as well as the corresponding design patterns. The field of concurrent execution being less practiced than the domains of the preceding chapters, there is not always a consensus on the exact name and definition of these patterns. Despite this lack of consensus in terms of vocabulary, the underlying principles remain the same and remain fundamental to address the problems of parallel execution.

6.1.2.1   Asynchronous calls (Observer and Future Patterns)

Most approaches are generally based on the delayed execution of many sub-processing. The calls being executed on different cores of processors, the parallelism is obtained naturally. The user only has to wait until all the calls are finished to merge all the results of the sub-processing, and thus deduce the final result. This principle can be repeated if the computation is decomposed into several parallelizable steps. It is also possible that a sub-process generates other sub-processes, in which case it is paused until its subprocesses are completed.

Observer pattern

To implement these asynchronous calls, there are many ways to launch them, to schedule them, and to be informed of their execution status. The oldest and most common approach is to start a thread for each task and then be notified of their status via a notification, usually called *callback*.

For example, an observer interface can be defined to inform the execution state of a task, in the first place its end:

```java
private interface TaskObserver {
    public void taskCompleted(Task process);
}
```

Each task references an observer (or more if the context requires it):

```java
private class Task implements Runnable
{
    private final TaskObserver observer;
    ...
```

When performing the computations, the methods of the interface are called, for example, at the end:

```java
public void run() {
    ... Computations ...
    observer.taskCompleted(this);
}
}
```

A main class can then start the tasks, and react to notifications/callbacks. For example, the run() method of the following class starts two tasks, each in a different thread, and waits for the threads to finish:

```java
private class Process implements TaskObserver
{
    public void run() throws InterruptedException
    {
        System.out.println("Run thread 1");
        Thread thread1 = new Thread(new Task(this,1));
        thread1.start();
        System.out.println("Run thread 2");
        Thread thread2 = new Thread(new Task(this,2));
        thread2.start();
        thread1.join();
        System.out.println("End of thread 1");
        thread2.join();
        System.out.println("End of thread 2");
    }
```

This class is an observer of the two tasks; it receives the notifications, like the end of execution:

```java
    public void taskCompleted(Task task) {
        System.out.println(
            "Computation "+task.getX()+" completed");
    }
}
```

In the case where the second task is faster than the first one, the following display is produced:

```
Run thread 1
Run thread 2
Computation 2 completed
Computation 1 completed
End of thread 1
End of thread 2
```

This approach is implemented in the Java standard library with the `CompletableFuture` class of the `java.util.concurrent` package.

Future Pattern

The *Future Pattern* manages the end of sub-processing in a simpler way than with the Observer pattern. It is based on a thread manager that, when submitting a task, returns a "future" object. The future object has methods that allow you to wait for the execution to finish. The standard Java library has different versions of this pattern through implementations of the `ExecutorService` interface in the `java.util.concurrent` package. Here is the equivalent of the previous example with this approach. We start by creating an `ExecutorService` which contains two threads:

```java
ExecutorService executor = Executors.newFixedThreadPool(2);
```

Both tasks are submitted to the executor, which returns an object of type `Future`:

```java
System.out.println("Launch computation 1");
Future future1 = executor.submit(new Task(1));
System.out.println("Launch computation 2");
Future future2 = executor.submit(new Task(2));
```

At this step, both tasks are already running, each in a dedicated thread.

By calling the `get()` method of the `Future` class, we then ask to wait for the end of the corresponding process:

```java
future1.get();
System.out.println("End of computation 1");
future2.get();
System.out.println("End of computation 2");
```

Once the processing is complete, we close the executor to free the resources consumed by the threads:

```java
executor.shutdown();
```

In this example, future objects do not return an object because the considered processes do not. However, it is possible to directly obtain the result of a process via the future object by defining tasks that implement `java.util.Callable` instead of `java.util.Runnable`. There are also other interesting features, detailed in the standard documentation.

Note that, on the contrary to the Observer pattern, we do not exactly know when processing is completed. With the Future pattern, we can only know when processing is completed and its result ready to be used.

6.1.2.2 Threads Pool Pattern

The previous cases were very simple: one thread is created per task. There are, however, many situations where this approach is insufficient. For example, when the number of tasks is very important, it is not possible to create as many threads: the operating systems have a limit, and even we don't reach it, the resources consumed by the management of threads can quickly use many CPU resources. There are also cases of processing where the number of tasks is unknown in advance or evolves during the execution. The creation and regular destruction of threads would then lead to unnecessary consumption of resources.

Threads Pool Pattern

A usual solution is to use the Thread Pool pattern. It relies on a main class that contains and manages threads. The number of threads and the nature of their management is free and depends on the needs. The class also has a way to handle submitted tasks. In general, it takes the form of a queue, so that the first tasks submitted are the first executed. On the interface side, the minimal case is one method to submit one task, then another to wait for the completion of the tasks. The pattern is usually combined with other patterns, like those presented previously.

In the standard Java library, different versions of this pattern are proposed as implementations of `ExecutorService` interface in the `java.util.concurrent` package. The `Executors` class allows to instantiate these different cases via the following static methods:

- `Executors.newFixedThreadPool()`: returns a fixed pool of threads. In the example above, we create a 2-thread pool. This pool works by using a non-blocking queue of tasks. It means that we can submit a large number of tasks without creating as many threads. The number of threads is fixed, and they process simultaneously as many tasks as possible, while other tasks are waiting. It is a viable solution when tasks can be submitted in advance, and the size of tasks in memory is not important.

- `Executors.newCachedThreadPool()`: Returns a variable thread pool. Threads are created on-demand, depending on the number of submitted tasks. If a thread is finished, however, it can be reused if a task is submitted a few moments later, which avoids a thread deletion/creation in a short time. This approach is interesting if there are not many tasks, and their number is very variable.
- `Executors.newScheduledThreadPool()`: returns a fixed pool of threads. This pool implements the `ScheduledExecutorService` interface, an extension of `ExecutorService`. It allows you to submit tasks with a delay, and the execution can be repeated.
- `Executors.newWorkStealingPool()`: Returns a variable thread pool. It is a `ForkJoinPool` presented in the next section.

It is also possible to create other types of thread pools using the `ThreadPoolExecutor` class or defining new child classes.

Processing with reduction or expansion

The previous solutions are capable of handling a large number of cases, but not those where tasks generate tasks. The usual processing that leads to this type of behavior is reductions and expansions. In both cases, we can see the processing can as the traversal of a tree, either from the leaves for reduction or from the root for expansions.

Sum parallelization is an example of reduction. All values of an array are seen as the leaves of a tree. Then, grouping these values/leaves, usually two by two, a first node level is created. These nodes are also grouped to form a second level. We repeat the process until we obtain a single node, the root of the tree. For instance, for an array with values { 1, 2, 3, 4, 5, 6 }, the following tree is imagined:

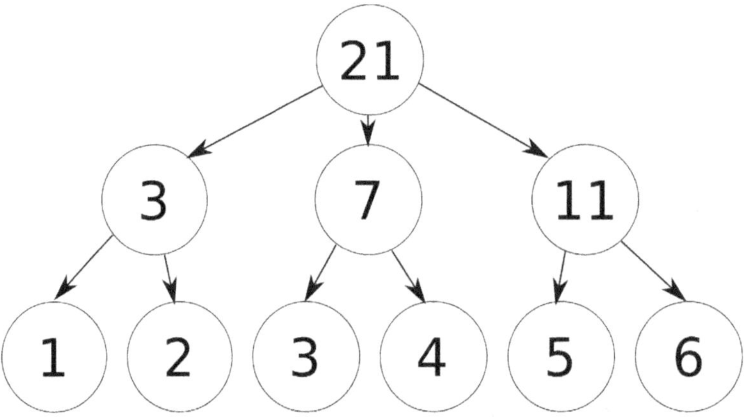

Parallelizing is equivalent to processing each level of the tree from the deepest. With the example above, 3 tasks are used to calculate sums 1 + 2, 3 + 4 and 5 + 6.

Finally, one last task is used to compute the final sum $3 + 7 + 11$.

Sort parallelization is an example of expansion. To do so, we start by dividing array values into two parts, where values in the first part are always lower than the values in the second part. This first step can be seen as the creation of two child nodes at the root of the tree: the root is the complete array, the left child is the part with the lower values, and the right child is the part with the higher values. Then, the same processing is run on each node, until arriving at parts small enough to be ordered sequentially.

Previous thread pools do not well handle reduction and expansion. Indeed, to carry out these processing, each task that corresponds to a node in the tree generates threads for as many tasks, which themselves generate threads... In the end, a large number of tasks generate threads waiting for the generated subtasks to end. With a fixed pool of threads, the process is quickly completely blocked, and with a variable pool, the amount of threads explodes without using the core of the processor: most tasks are waiting!

Thread Pool pattern with thread stealing

The solution is to use pools with thread stealing. The idea is: if you run out of threads, and there is a thread waiting, then you wake it up to modify its execution while keeping a record of the position within your past processing. In doing so, it is no longer necessary to have a large number of threads, while being able to handle a large number of tasks created.

The standard Java library includes a thread-stealing pool implementation in the `ForkJoinPool` class in the `java.util.concurrent` package. To use it, you need to implement `ForkJoinTask`. For most cases, implementations are available in the standard library: `RecursiveAction` for non-return value processing, `RecursiveTask` for return value processing. The `CounterCompleter` class is also available to handle more complex cases.

Here is an example of the parallel computation of the sum of array values. We first define a task as a child class of `RecursiveTask`:

```
class ForkJoinRecursiveSum
    extends RecursiveTask<Long> {
```

Each task has to compute the sum of values between `low` (included) and `high` (excluded) index:

```
private final long[] values;
private final int low, high;
```

The `compute()` method of the `RecursiveTask` class must return the result of the computation:

```java
protected Long compute() {
```

If the number of values is small, it is better to sum sequentially:

```java
    if (high - low <= 10) {
        long sum = 0;
        for (int i=low;i<high;i++) {
            sum += values[i];
        }
        return sum;
    }
```

For the parallel case, we compute the center index between the `low` and `high` index:

```java
    else {
        int center = (high+low)/2;
```

Two new tasks are created, one to sum values left to `center`, and one to sum values right to `center`:

```java
        ForkJoinRecursiveSum left =
            ForkJoinRecursiveSum(values,low,center);
        ForkJoinRecursiveSum right =
            new ForkJoinRecursiveSum(values,center,high);
```

The `fork()` method of the `ForkJoinTask` class starts the job in the background and immediately returns. It is used to schedule the left sum:

```java
        left.fork();
```

For the right sum, it is not necessary to compute in another thread, and the current one is available:

```java
        long rightSum = right.compute();
```

Before summing all values, the left sum must be complete. To do this, the `join()` method of the `ForkJoinTask` class allows you to wait for the result to finish:

```java
        long leftSum = left.join();
        return leftSum + rightSum;
    }
}
```

The class above is tested to compute the sum of the first integers explicitly. An array is defined, with all integers from 1 to 100 million:

```java
long[] values = new long[100000000];
for (int i=0;i<values.length;i++) {
    values[i] = 1+i;
}
```

We create a thread pool:

```
ForkJoinPool pool = new ForkJoinPool();
```

Parallel computation is started via the invoke() method of the ForkJoinPool class with the argument ForkJoinRecursiveSum on the array, with index from 0 to the size of the array:

```
long sum = pool.invoke(
    new ForkJoinRecursiveSum(values,0,values.length));
```

The following checks that the commutation is correct:

```
long n = values.length;
System.out.println("Sum: "+sum+", check: "+(n*(n+1))/2);
```

6.1.2.3 Producer/Consumer Pattern

The *Producer-Consumer Pattern* is another use case in the field of parallel execution. It assumes that there are two types of tasks: producers and consumers. The whole is controlled by a manager who coordinates the tasks. Producers perform quick processing and submit consumer tasks to the manager. Then, either they continue if the queue is not saturated, or they are paused waiting for resources to be released. Consumers are executed if there are enough threads available; otherwise they wait.

The main interest of this pattern is the ability to handle two levels of tasks, one being faster (producers) and the other slower (consumers), without blocking everything. An example is the network servers. These have producers who intercept the network packets and submit the corresponding processing. Consumers process information submitted by producers. Thus, even if the consumer processing queue is full, the producers are still available to react to incoming network packets. In the case of a usual pool, the server may lose packets if the queue is full, or if the time to process the current tasks is too long.

Example of implementation

A simple example of the implementation of the pattern is proposed here. It is based on the following elements:

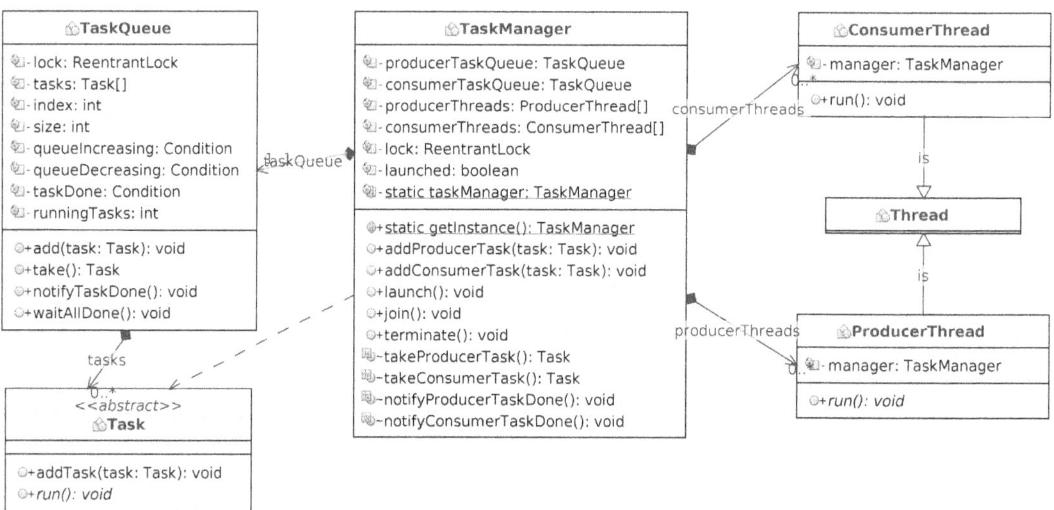

The `TaskManager` class is the main manager that controls the whole. It has the following attributes:

- A `producerTaskQueue` dedicated to production tasks;

- A `consumerTaskQueue` dedicated to consumer tasks;
- A list of `ProducerThread`. These threads are instances of the `ProducterThread` class, which execute the production tasks in the `producerTaskQueue`;
- A list of `ConsumerThread`. These threads are instances of the `ConsumerThread` class, which execute consumer tasks in the `consumerTaskQueue`;
- A recursive mutex `lock`. This type of mutex avoids the parallel execution of some of the code, as with the keyword `synchronized`. It is not blocking if it is the same thread that is trying to acquire it. It is used by both queues to manage concurrent access;
- A `launched` boolean allows you to know if the threads are already started;
- A static `taskManager` attribute references the only possible manager. In this implementation, we want to use a single manager, to limit the number of threads by design. The idea is to prevent users from creating many managers, and hence many threads. Coupled with the `getInstance()` static method, the Singleton pattern is implemented. This one makes the manager during his very first call:

```java
public static TaskManager getInstance() {
    synchronized(TaskManager.class) {
        if (taskManager == null) {
            taskManager = new TaskManager();
        }
    }
    return taskManager;
}
```

The operation is synchronized with the class, in case multiple threads try to call it at the same time.

The `addProducerTask()` method adds a new production job to the `producerTaskQueue` queue. It adds the task if there is room; otherwise it waits for a place to be released:

```java
public void addProducerTask(Task task) {
    producerTaskQueue.add(task);
}
```

The principle is similar for the `addConsumerTask()` method.

The `launch()` method builds and starts all threads. It acquires the `lock` mutex with the `lock()` method to ensure that there are no other executions in parallel. It follows a `try ... finally` block, which ensures that the mutex is released with the `unlock()` method, regardless of the outcome of the processes. It is the manual equivalent of the `synchronized` keyword applied to the method:

```java
public void launch() {
    lock.lock();
    try {
```

```java
            if (launched)
                return;
            launched = true;
            for (int i=0;i<producerThreads.length;i++) {
                ProducerThread producer = new ProducerThread(this);
                producerThreads[i] = producer;
                producer.start();
            }
            for (int i=0;i<consumerThreads.length;i++) {
                ConsumerThread consumer = new ConsumerThread(this);
                consumerThreads[i] = consumer;
                consumer.start();
            }
        }
        finally {
            lock.unlock();
        }
    }
```

The `join()` method waits for all jobs to complete, both producers and consumers:

```java
public void join() throws InterruptedException {
    producerTaskQueue.waitAllDone();
    consumerTaskQueue.waitAllDone();
}
```

The `terminate()` method interrupts all threads. This operation is possible if all mutex acquisitions by threads can be interrupted:

```java
public void terminate() {
    lock.lock();
    try {
        if (!launched)
            return;
        launched = false;
        for (int i=0;i<producerThreads.length;i++) {
            producerThreads[i].interrupt();
        }
        for (int i=0;i<consumerThreads.length;i++) {
            consumerThreads[i].interrupt();
        }
    }
    finally {
        lock.unlock();
    }
}
```

The `takeProducerTask()`, `takeConsumerTask()`, `notifyProducerTaskDone()`, and `notifyConsumerTaskDone()` methods pass the request to the corresponding queue. They all have access at the package level, which means that the pattern users can not use them.

TaskQueue class

The `TaskQueue` class is a blocking queue: if you try to add an item when there is no more room, it pauses the thread. Similarly, if you try to take an item while the queue is empty, the thread is also paused. It is very close to the `ArrayBlockingQueue` class of the standard Java library.

It has a `lock` mutex, initialized with the one created by the task manager. The objective is to have a common mutex for the three components: the task manager, the producer queue, and consumer queue. The `tasks`, `index`, and `size` attributes allow you to implement a fixed size queue using a classic circular array algorithm. The three conditional variables `queueIncreasing`, `queueDecreasing`, and `taskDone` are defined to notify the addition of a task, the removal of a task, and the end of a task. Finally, the `runningTasks` attribute stores the current number of running tasks. When it goes to zero, and the queue is empty, all jobs in the queue are complete.

The `add()` method adds a task to the queue if it is possible, otherwise waits for a place to free:

```java
public void add(Task task)
    throws InterruptedException {
```

It starts with the acquisition of the `lock` mutex shared by all queues. The acquisition is obtained via the `lockInterruptibly()` method which allows another thread to interrupt the current thread:

```java
lock.lockInterruptibly();
try {
```

As long as the queue is full, the thread is waiting for a signal from the `queueDecreasing` conditional variable. The wait continues until another thread calls `queueDecreasing.signal()`:

```java
while (size == tasks.length)
    queueDecreasing.await();
```

The following is the addition in a circular array:

```java
tasks[index] = task;
index ++;
if (index >= tasks.length)
```

```
        index = 0;
    size ++;
```

The condition variable `queueIncreasing` tells the threads that are monitoring it that a task has just been added to the queue:

```
        queueIncreasing.signal();
    } finally {
        lock.unlock();
    }
}
```

The `takeTask()` method allows you to take a task in the queue. It waits as long as the queue is empty, and responds to `queueIncreasing` signals. Then, it removes a task, increases the `runningTasks` counter, and reports with `queueDecreasing` that the queue has just decreased:

```
public Task take() throws InterruptedException {
    lock.lockInterruptibly();
    try {
        while (size == 0)
            queueIncreasing.await();
        index --;
        if (index < 0) {
            index = tasks.length - 1;
        }
        Task task = tasks[index];
        size --;
        runningTasks ++;
        queueDecreasing.signal();
        return task;
    } finally {
        lock.unlock();
    }
}
```

The `notifyTaskDone()` method is used to indicate that a task has just been completed. It decrements the task counter, and sends a signal:

```
public void notifyTaskDone()
        throws InterruptedException {
    lock.lockInterruptibly();
    try {
        runningTasks --;
        taskDone.signal();
    } finally {
        lock.unlock();
    }
```

```java
}
```

The `waitAllDone()` method first waits for the queue to be empty, and then the number of running tasks to drop to zero:

```java
public void waitAllDone()
        throws InterruptedException {
    lock.lockInterruptibly();
    try {
        while (size != 0)
            queueDecreasing.await();
        while (runningTasks != 0)
            taskDone.await();
    } finally {
        lock.unlock();
    }
}
```

ConsumerThread class

This thread loops to infinity, trying to take a consumer task. As soon as there is one available, it executes it, then informs the manager when it is finished:

```java
public void run() {
    try {
        while (true) {
            Task task = manager.takeConsumerTask();
            task.run();
            manager.notifyConsumerTaskDone();
        }
    } catch (InterruptedException ex) {
    }
}
```

The `ProducerThread` class works similarly.

The complete code for this example is present in the "examples/chap06/threads02/mt" folder of the Java sample project.

6.1.2.4 Minimax parallelization

In this section, the goal is to parallelize the Minimax algorithm for artificial intelligence. It has two main principles: the first one that goes down in the search tree to the leaves, and the second that goes up in the tree by calculating either the min or the max of the child nodes. These properties are driven by a strategy of sequentially exploring the search tree. Each time we reach a node at a given depth, we duplicate the game state, and a task is started in parallel to process the entire subtree from the reached node. Besides, to be able to apply the second Minimax principle of raising values in the tree, a second tree is built when the search tree is searched. This tree is very simple and has only values and no game state. It avoids having to go back through the search tree to find the calculated values. We define this additional tree as a `PrecomputedNode` class child of `ai.tree.Node`, whose values and threads are defined by a user, not by itself.

As part of its use for the AI of a video game, it is necessary to limit as much as possible the copies of the game state, the size of which is generally quite large. It is necessary to find a solution so as not to duplicate the game state too many times. One solution is to use the Producer-Consumer pattern with blocking queues, as implemented in the previous section. The traversal of the search tree to a given depth is the only producer. When it finds a node at a given depth, it launches a consumer task that consists of exploring the search subtree. Consumers apply the Minimax algorithm on these subtrees, which allows obtaining the value of the starting node. By using blocking queues, we pause the producer when there are too many running consumer tasks. Knowing that each task start is a copy of the game state, the size of the blocking queue determines the maximum number of state copies.

ParallelMinimax class

The main part of the algorithm is located in the `ParallelMinimax` class. Its `run()` method starts by creating a `MinimaxProducer`:

```java
public List<Node> run(Node root)
{
    TaskManager manager = TaskManager.getInstance();
    MinimaxProducer producer =
        new MinimaxProducer(root, parallelDepth);
```

This producer explores the search tree from `root` to `parallelDepth` depth, and then submits tasks to process the subtrees. The `join()` method of the handler is called to wait for the end of all the processes:

```java
    try {
        manager.addProducerTask(producer);
        manager.join();
    } catch (InterruptedException ex) {
        throw new RuntimeException();
    }
```

Once the computations are complete, the `MinimaxProducer` class has created a mirror tree of the search tree, all of whose leaves have a value:

```java
Node precomputedRoot = producer.getPrecomputedRoot();
```

The sequential algorithm can be applied to the mirror tree, like any tree whose nodes are child classes of `ai.tree.Node`:

```java
AlphaBeta minimax = new AlphaBeta();
minimax.run(precomputedRoot);
```

The values of the children of the root of the mirror tree are copied to those of the root of the search tree. The goal is to lure the users of the algorithm who need these values:

```java
for (int i=0;i<root.getChildCount();i++) {
    Node child = root.getChild(i);
    Node precomputedChild = precomputedRoot.getChild(i);
    child.setValue(precomputedChild.getValue());
}
```

The end is the same computation of the best nodes:

```java
int max = Integer.MIN_VALUE;
for(Node child : root) {
    if (!child.hasValue())
        throw new RuntimeException("No value");
    int value = child.getValue();
    if (value > max) {
        max = value;
    }
}
ArrayList<Node> bestNodes = new ArrayList();
for(Node child : root) {
    if (child.getValue() == max) {
        bestNodes.add(child);
    }
}
root.setValue(max);
return bestNodes;
}
```

The producer

The `MinimaxProducer` class builds a `precomputedRoot` mirror tree from the root search tree to a maximum `parallelDepth` depth:

```java
public class MinimaxProducer extends Task
{
    private final Node root;
```

```java
private final int parallelDepth;
private PrecomputedNode precomputedRoot;
```

The `run()` method is called through the task manager. It launches an exploration of the search tree by recursion via the `explore()` method:

```java
public void run() {
    try {
        precomputedRoot = new PrecomputedNode();
        explore(root,precomputedRoot);
    } catch (InterruptedException ex) {
    }
}
```

The `explore()` method traverses the search tree to a `parallelDepth` depth. The algorithm followed is a simple recursion: it is sufficient since few nodes are explored. It has two arguments: a node in the search tree and its equivalent in the mirror tree:

```java
private void explore(Node node,PrecomputedNode precomputedNode)
    throws InterruptedException {
```

Recursion stops when a node with we found a value. The corresponding mirror node then takes on its value:

```java
if (node.hasValue()) {
    precomputedNode.setValue(node.getValue());
}
```

Recursion also stops when the depth is `parallelDepth`. In this case, a task is started in the background. It is this one which, at the end of its processing, assigns a value to the mirror node. This step uses a new `createRoot()` method in the `Node` interface, which returns the root of the search subtree from the current node. This trick allows the task to process the subtree as an independent tree. It is also at this moment that the game state is duplicated:

```java
else if (node.getDepth() >= parallelDepth) {
    addTask( new MinimaxConsumer(precomputedNode,node.createRoot()
        ));
}
```

In other cases, we apply recursion to all child nodes. We create the same number of child nodes in the mirror node. For each of them, we explore a mirror child node using a recursive call. Finally, the `updateState()` and `rollbackState()` methods of the node in the search tree are used to go down and then go up in it:

```java
else {
    PrecomputedNode[] precomputedChildren =
        new PrecomputedNode[node.getChildCount()];
    for (int i=0;i<node.getChildCount();i++) {
```

```java
        Node child = node.getChild(i);
        child.updateState();
        precomputedChildren[i] = new PrecomputedNode(precomputedNode);
        explore(child,precomputedChildren[i]);
        child.rollbackState();
      }
      precomputedNode.setChildren(precomputedChildren);
    }
}
```

Consumers

The MinimaxConsumer class implements the task executed in parallel. It contains
the root of a search tree that corresponds to a subtree in the main search tree. It
also contains the precomputedNode node in the mirror tree that must receive the
value of the root after Minimax was applied:

```java
public class MinimaxConsumer extends Task {
    private final PrecomputedNode precomputedNode;
    private final Node root;
```

The run() method, called by one of the task manager consumer threads, launches
a sequential Minimax and then transfers the value from its root to the mirror node:

```java
    public void run() {
        AlphaBeta minimax = new AlphaBeta();
        minimax.run(root);
        precomputedNode.setValue(root.getValue());
    }
}
```

Use

The ParallelMinimax class is used like the other classes that implement the
Minimax, except for the choice of the depth of creation of the parallel tasks. For
the Pacman example game, a depth of 24 was chosen, because it leads on average
between 2 and 4 tasks, ie as many copies of the state of the game.

The diagrams in this example are available in the "Class Diagrams/chap06/threads02"
folder of the sample UML project.   The code is present in the "exam-
ples/chap06/threads02" folder of the Java sample project.

6.1.3 Exercices

6.1.3.1 Exercise 1.3.1: Parallelize the exhaustive search for collisions

Collision detection between objects is a common task in the field of video games, in two as in three dimensions. Generally, objects are not directly compared for reasons of computational speed. Instead, *Axis Aligned Bounding Box (AABB)* are compared. These boxes can include a whole object or a part of this object, according to its form. The bounding boxes in 2D are rectangles and those in 3D parallelepipeds. In either case, the principles, problems, and solutions are similar.

The purpose of this exercise is to work on these boxes, and more specifically, to parallelize the search for collisions. In this exercise, the scenes used to be filled with a large number of objects or parts of objects, which are quickly counted in millions. To manipulate the boxes, you can either implement it yourself or use the code present in the "examples/chap06/collisions" folder, which includes the following elements:

- `AABB` class: represents a bounding box in 2D, in the form of a coordinate rectangle (x0,y0) for the upper left corner, and (x1,y1) for the bottom right corner. This class contains several convenience methods; the one that is useful to you is the `collides()` method which returns `true` if the box collides with another one.
- `Collider` interface: defines the `collides()` method, which, to any bounding box, returns the list of bounding boxes that collide.
- `ExhaustiveCollider` class: implements the `Collider` interface with an exhaustive search strategy. It is this strategy that is asked to parallelize in this exercise.
- `TreeCollider` class: implements the `Collider` interface with a binary tree search strategy. This class is useful for the following exercise. It uses the `TreeColliderNode` class.
- `Display` class: allows viewing of bounding boxes, as well as a particular box that is moved with the arrow keys.

The displaced box is green, the collided boxes are red, and the other boxes are white:

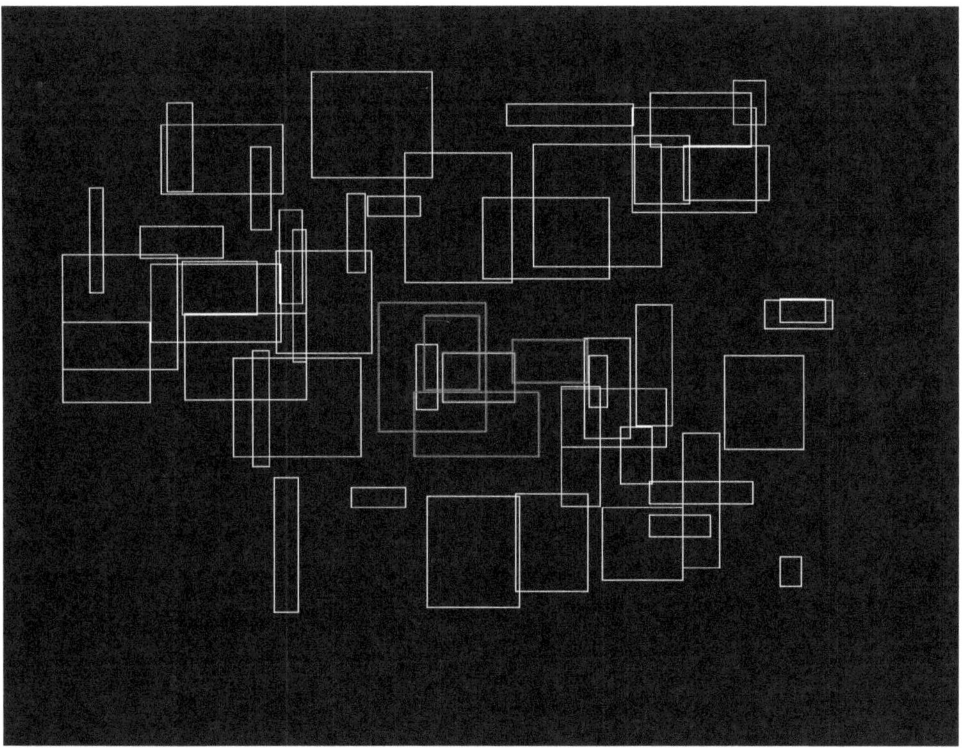

The `Display` class allows checking implementation of `Collider` visually.

→ Implement a parallel version of the exhaustive collision search. Several implementations are possible, with or without the tools of the standard library. Also, implement unit tests to check that the collisions found by your parallel solution are the same as the one found by the sequential one.

6.1.3.2 Exercise 1.3.2: Parallelize the indexed search for collisions

This exercise is similar to Exercise 1.3.1, but with a search strategy for collisions based on a binary tree. Beforehand, a binary tree is built to store enclosing boxes. Each leaf of this tree is a bounding box, and each node is a bounding box that includes all the boxes of its descendants. In other words, for any node d descendant of a node n, the bounding box of n includes that of d. This property makes it possible to find more quickly the boxes which are in collisions with a candidate box. This is recursively implemented in the `collides()` method of the `TreeColliderNode` class in the "examples/chap06/collisions" folder:

```java
public void collides(List<AABB> result, AABB aabb) {
```

If the current node is a leaf, we compare the candidate box aabb with that of the node: if they collide, it is added to the list result of the boxes in collision:

```java
if (isLeaf()) {
    if (this.aabb.collides(aabb)) {
        result.add(this.aabb);
    }
}
else {
```

If the current node is not a leaf, we look if its box is in collision with the candidate box. If this is not the case, there is no chance of finding a colliding box in its descendants: it is no longer necessary to continue:

```java
if (!this.aabb.collides(aabb))
    return;
```

The search for collisions recursively continues for each child node of the current node:

```java
if (leftChild != null) {
    leftChild.collides(result, aabb);
}
if (rightChild != null) {
    rightChild.collides(result, aabb);
}
    }
}
```

→ Implement a parallel version of the search for collisions indexed with a binary tree. Also, implement unit tests that check that the collisions found by your parallel solution return the same as the one returned by a sequential one.

6.1.4 Video game development: concurrent execution

Even if a multiplayer game is not targeted, the parallelization of the processing usually improves the user experience. Besides, most machines have at least two physical cores, which allows for more processing, whether for display or game logic.

The main difficulty lies in the parallel execution with a minimum of locks. We must avoid that each thread blocks the others, with finally one and only one thread running, which does not lead to any parallel execution. Other types of locks can directly affect the user experience, especially the display. Any blocking beyond the millisecond in the game's main loop is quickly uncomfortable for the user. Finally, the last type of blocking is the one that increases the latency of the game. Even with a perfectly smooth display, the user has the feeling that the game does not react, which does not improve his experience either.

To effectively implement concurrent executions, the following components have been presented in this section, and are relevant solutions in many situations:

- **Locks**, either with the `synchronized` keyword or with a mutex (like the `ReentrantLock` class). The first objective is to ensure that concurrent access never takes place at the same time. Attempts to read and write data at the same time quickly lead to unpredictable behavior or errors.
- **Double buffer**. This approach solves many cases. It duplicates the data, one copy can be manipulated by one thread, and the other by another thread, and without any blocking. The blocking only appears when exchanging or copying from one buffer to the other. This approach can be generalized with more buffers, depending on the case. The only flaw in this approach is that it is only conceivable in two situations. The first assumes that the data is not large and can be duplicated quickly. The second assumes that data can be reconstructed from scratch, in which case a copy is not needed, and a simple exchange of references is enough.
- **Notifications**. Blocking problems are usually related to the fact that it is not possible to know when access is taking place. Once these accesses are known or controllable, it becomes easier to know the times when a thread can access the data without requiring blocking. This approach has been illustrated in this section to access to the game state. Knowing that the rules engine is the owner of the state, it is best placed to know or even decide when a third party can handle it. It is implemented with an observer pattern, where the observed rules engine tells observers when the state can be accessed. This approach is only possible if the observers can be interrupted at any time: it has only reversed the initial situation, where the data or their owner can be interrupted at any time.
- **Combine approaches**. It is not always possible to interrupt the data manager and its users. This case is illustrated with the rules engine and the rendering engine: both of them, when they are working on the game state, it is not possible to interrupt them. It is not possible to duplicate the game state, nor to rebuild it with each frame. In this kind of situation, you have to be creative and combine approaches to find a solution. For our engines, the initial trick is to notify the game state changes to the rendering engine. These notifications form a kind of "diff" between the game state at one time and the next. These can not be sent directly to the rendering engine since there can be multiple renditions during a single update of the game state. The solution proposed was to cache these notifications, like a double buffer approach. In doing so, the only blocking is the transfer of notifications between two game state updates. Changes from one state to another being few, blocking is very short.

In the cases considered above, the processing is supposed to run continuously, each in a thread. It exists cases where scheduling is more complex. For these cases, there are also solutions:

- **Asynchronous execution**. Sometimes it is necessary to execute single isolated processing without blocking the general flow. An example is shown in this chapter for performing background network queries. Knowing that a network request may take several tens of milliseconds to obtain a response from a server, synchronous execution unnecessarily blocks the application. It is more interesting to execute the query asynchronously, in which case two types of scenarios are usually encountered. In the first one, the result is required after several tasks. It is possible to carry out other operations in the meantime, but following these, the answer to the request is necessary. For this scenario, the Future pattern is perfect. In a second scenario, it is only necessary to be informed of the end of the request. In this case, the Observer pattern is the best one.
- **Single Thread pool**. The best way to control the order of tasks is to self-manage the threads that execute them. As discussed in the Threads Pool section, there are several types of pools available in the standard Java library that can meet many needs. For example, the `ScheduledExecutorService` class allows you to run a task on a regular basis and can be used to run regular queries to a server for status, without blocking the application. Other types of pools help to facilitate the parallelization of complex processes, such as recursive processes. The `ForkJoinPool` classes in the standard Java library solve this type of problem.
- **Thread pools**. The preceding processes assume that all the tasks are of the same kind and that it is possible to saturate the thread pool without any problem. There are, however, situations where this is not the case. The best example is that of a server that must respond to different requests. An approach with a single pool can quickly lead to server saturation: as soon as the thread pool is full of requests, the server is no longer able to respond, not even with responses indicating that it is full. One solution is to use the Producer/Consumer pattern. In this case, the producing part receives the requests, and plans their processing in the consumer part, if this is possible. Otherwise, it returns a message indicating saturation. These production tasks are very fast; hence a very large number of requests is required to saturate the server. In the consumer part, requests are processed at their own pace. This pattern was illustrated in a simple version in the previous section. There are many other possibilities, for example, with thread pools with different priority levels, or the ability to pause tasks to execute others, and so on.

In conclusion, it is difficult to cover all the problems related to concurrent execution. However, with the elements given here, it is already possible to offer a very satisfying user experience - knowing that the creative mind remains the best asset to succeed in any situation.

6.2   Network communication

In this chapter, the implementation of multiplayer games on a network is proposed. The approach followed is based on HTTP REST type web services, all via a TCP/IP protocol. This approach brings together very popular technical solutions in all areas of networks. It was chosen for its simplicity while ensuring all the usual criteria of robustness and stability. Besides, using widely tested protocols on a large scale offers guarantees, while avoiding having to reinvent the wheel. It meets the needs of most video games, whatever the platform (PC, smartphone, etc.). The only games whose use is possible but suboptimal are games that require very low latency and a very high rate of updating the game data, such as FPS or fighting games. For these, a very basic approach via UDP also presented, is sufficient.

6.2.1   Essentials

This section presents the technical elements required to understand the designs proposed later. These presentations are far from covering the totality of the network notions, and some are very approximate but sufficient for our needs.

6.2.1.1   Network layers

The communication between machines on a network is based on the exchange of batches of data, generally called *packets*. Different types and scales of packets are considered during these exchanges, and in each case, a packet is accompanied by a header. Each header is specific to the corresponding network layer and allows to obtain or set the information that refers to it. These headers usually stack one after the other: for a packet, the first part is the header of the lowest layer, then the second part is the header of the next layer, etc., until to the last, which precedes the data. There are also packet scales: a packet of a high layer can be formed by a set of packets of a lower layer. There is thus a header for the high layer and a header for each packet of the low layer.

In terms of layers, two main levels can be distinguished: the hardware layers and the software layers. The hardware layers are usually managed by electronic chips that can not be programmed. For example, switches are independent electronic devices that manage these low layers. Although it is possible to modify certain aspects of their behavior, they generally work in a completely autonomous way, without the intervention of the software that uses them to communicate. Software layers, on the other hand, are fully programmable and fully driven by the programs that use them.

The hardware layers considered in the approach followed in this chapter are the following (from the lowest to the highest):

- Data link layer: Ethernet. It manages the exchange of data at the lowest level, without any notion of location or connection;
- Network layer: IP. It makes it possible to identify the machines on the networks;
- Transport layer: UDP. It is the simplest transport layer. It does not handle the connection.
- Transport layer: TCP. It mainly makes it possible to manage the connection and the sending of segmented data in several packets.

The software layers considered in this chapter are the following ones:

- Transport layer: HTTP. It is like the software version of TCP. It offers a very wide range of features.
- API layer: REST. It allows defining *stateless* services.
- Format layer: JSON. It makes it possible to produce universally transportable data representations.

6.2.1.2   Ethernet

The header of an Ethernet packet contains the MAC address of the sending machine and that of the destination machine. These addresses identify machines on the same network but do not locate them. Besides, there is no particular security around these addresses: any machine can choose the MAC address of its choice.

The header also contains a checksum, which can detect transmission errors. If on receiving the packet is detected as erroneous, it is ignored, and nothing is done to ask for the sending of the original packet.

An Ethernet packet contains between 46 and 1500 bytes of data. This property is very important when designing messages to exchange. Indeed, the cost of sending an Ethernet packet is the same, regardless of the amount of data it contains. On the other hand, sending multiple Ethernet packets is more expensive than sending one. As long as the data is less than 1500 bytes, it is not worth looking for savings by reducing them. It is also more interesting to group the data within the same package. For example, it is more efficient to send 4 100-byte messages grouped in the same Ethernet packet rather than sending 4 Ethernet packets, each containing one of the messages. When designing API for machine-to-machine communication, this is not to be overlooked and can play a significant role in service quality and user experience. Warning: when calculating the data size of an Ethernet packet, do not forget the size of the headers of the following layers.

6.2.1.3   IP (Internet Protocol)

The role of this layer is primarily to locate the source machine and the destination machine via IP addresses. There are two types of IP addresses: IPv4 and IPv6. The size of the IPv4 header is 20 bytes, and that of the IPv6 is 40 bytes. The principles necessary for this chapter are common to both types: IPv4 is used here to illustrate them. The IPv4 addresses are formed by 4 digits between 0 and 255, for example, 1.0.100.255.

IP addresses have two parts: a network part, which identifies the network, and a host part, which identifies the machine within its network. The network address is defined internationally: if you want to obtain a network address, you must ask the relevant organizations. The network administrator freely sets the host address. Therefore, to make servers for a video game accessible on the Internet, obtain a network address, then choose for each of them a host address. The simplest way to do this is to rent server machines in a data center with associated IP addresses.

Address classes

There are 5 classes of IP addresses. The first three allow you to divide the number of digits for the network address and the host address in different ways:

- Class A: addresses from 1.0.0.0 to 127.255.255.255. The first number is the network address (from 1 to 127), and the next three is the host address.
- Class B: addresses from 128.0.0.0 to 191.255.255.255. The first two numbers are the network address (from 128.0 to 191.255), and the last two are the host address.
- Class C: addresses from 192.0.0.0 to 223.255.255.255. The first three numbers are the network address (from 192.0.0 to 223.255.255), and the last one is the host address.

The other two classes are special cases that are rarely used.

Special addresses

Some addresses are special. For example, the address 127.0.0.1 systematically designates the current machine. For each of the first three classes of addresses, there are network addresses that systematically designate the local network:

- Class A: network address 10, ie the addresses 10.0.0.0 to 10.255.255.255
- Class B: Network Addresses 172.16 to 172.31, which is 172.16.0.0 to 172.31.255.255
- Class C: 192.168.0 to 192.168.255 network addresses, which is 192.168.0.0 to 192.168.255.255

These addresses are considered by all routers as local addresses and are never sent to the Internet. So it's a good way to detect a local network.

Routing and Network Address Translation (NAT)

The machines of a local network, for example, those of the players connected to the Internet box, necessarily have local addresses. The Internet box also has a local IP address and an Internet IP address. The box can be reached from any machine on the Internet. On the other hand, local machines do not have an Internet address, and can not be reached directly from outside. To reach a local machine from the Internet, there are several solutions; for example, ask the box to redirect some of the traffic to a specific machine, making believe then that the targeted machine is the box.

For the reception of the response of a request sent by a local machine, it is not necessary to activate particular functionalities. When a machine sends a request to a server on the Internet, the IP header contains the local IP address of the machine, as well as the IP address of the server. Then, the box replaces the local IP address of the machine: thus, when the server sends back its request, it arrives on the box. Then, via a mechanism not detailed here, the box transforms the destination IP address in the header of the response to the IP address of the local machine. These transformations are the result of *Network Address Translation (NAT)*.

To summarize: when a local machine sends a request to the Internet, the response comes back to it via automatic mechanisms. On the other hand, if a machine on the Internet wishes to send a request to a machine of a local network, it is necessary to set up routing solutions.

To ease understanding, the approach followed in this chapter is without requests from a server on the Internet to the player's machine on a local network. It implies that the server can not send messages to players' machines: they must continually ask the server if something has happened. In the context of video games, where real-time matters, the exchanges are permanent: there is no change from this point of view. The main defect lies in the extra latency caused by sending a request from the player's machine. In this case, the information on the server takes twice as long to arrive: the time between the client and the server, and the time of the return of the response. If the server can go directly to the clients, there is only the time between the server and the client. It is not a problem for most games, except those that require an extremely fast response time, such as FPS or fighting games. For these cases, it is better to send the data directly from the server, by programming the network at the UDP or TCP socket level, and by handling the routing problems.

Domain Name System (DNS)

A common function related to the IP layer is the *Domain Name System (DNS)*. This allows you to assign an IP address to domain names of the type "<name>.<extension>", such as "wikipedia.org" which is assigned to the address

91.198.174.192. Warning: any other element added to a domain name does not modify this assignment by the DNS. For example, the subdomains fr.wikipedia.org and en.wikipedia.org continue to designate the same IP address. It does not prevent being finally redirected to another IP address, which is possible, but not via the DNS.

To know these assignments, the Internet box asks a DNS server to resolve the cases that it does not know, or whose validity has expired. For example, the first time the page en.wikipedia.org is requested, the box asks a DNS server for the IP address. It should be kept in mind that communication is only possible with IP addresses: no packet will find its destination with a domain name. This rule also applies to DNS servers whose IP addresses are known to boxes.

To obtain an assignment between a domain name and its game server, it is necessary to go through an operator who makes the necessary to spread it on all the DNS servers of the world. This operation is inexpensive, between 5 and 7 dollars per year. This assignment can be changed at any time, which allows changing the game server without disrupting the service. It is preferable that the game communicates with servers identified by a domain name, and not directly their IP address. Thus, if a server fails, it is enough to modify the assignment to a backup server, without having to modify the clients. The failure then lasts the time of propagation, which is quite fast at the scale of a country (generally one hour) and slower at the scale of the world (one day).

6.2.1.4 UDP (User Datagram Protocol)

The UDP layer introduces the notion of *port*. The ports are numbers between 0 and 65535 that allow you to assign packets to a particular service or program on the machine. There are many standard ports, for example, port 80 is considered to be the default port that receives HTTP requests. When a browser like Firefox or Chrome asks for a web page, the port used is 80. However, it is possible to specify another one, for example, myserver.game:8080 to indicate that port 8080 should be used instead of 80. The ports can be seen as an extension of the IP address, with an additional number.

The routers can redirect these ports, for example, one can ask a router to transform all packets to port 80 to port 8080. It is also possible to route ports and IP addresses. For example, a box may be requested to redirect all packets whose destination port is 80 to port 8080 of a particular local machine. Thus, it is believed that the box is a classic HTTP server on port 80, while it is a local machine on port 8080 which is the HTTP server. In the case where direct communication between the Internet server and the local machine is required, it is this type of routing that must be put in place.

The UDP header has a size of 8 bytes and contains the source port, the destination port, the data size, and a checksum. Nothing is done to handle the loss of packets:

the erroneous packets are just deleted. This protocol is interesting in cases where the losses are not problematic, or when the correction is not of interest. For example, in Internet telephony (*Voice over IP*), the loss of a few milliseconds of voice does not prevent its understanding. Also, pausing the signal to allow the reception of lost packets is more unpleasant for the user than a slight barely noticeable hash. Naturally, if the losses are large, the voice becomes incomprehensible, and whatever the protocol, with or without loss, the discussion is compromised.

The UDP protocol is interesting for games whose action is extremely fast, and whose entire game state can be transmitted in a packet. It is the case of FPS and fighting games, whose game state can usually be summarized as the position of a dozen players and some characteristics (life, weapon, etc.). All this information comes in a single Ethernet packet and can be lost between two frames: the player only sees a brief pause, much more tolerable than a latency. It remains a special case: even for real-time games, like many MMORPGs, these low latencies are not essential. Only *Street Fighter* experts count the frames of each move. Besides, placing all the data needed to update the immediate environment of MMORPG players in 60 Ethernet packets per second quickly becomes impossible.

6.2.1.5   TCP (Transmission Control Protocol)

The TCP layer is an extended version of the UDP layer. It introduces the concept of connection. This concept of connection is very low level: for example, there is no identification of the person who issues the requests. The connection allows the client as well as the server to keep track of their exchanges, mainly in the form of numbers that they increment. These mechanisms make it possible to keep the order of the packets, but also to cause the retransmission of unacknowledged packets. Other services are also included, such as congestion management.

All these features are automatic for programs, which can reasonably assume that any TCP/IP message sent is always received and results in a response, even if late. Otherwise, we consider that the server is no longer accessible for access denial or failure. If this happens, the behavior of the clients is to patiently wait for the server to respond again, and to ask the users if they wish to abandon the game. In terms of design, it is better to run queries in the background, so as not to block the entire game when a lost packet leads to latency.

6.2.1.6   HTTP (Hypertext Transfer Protocol)

The HTTP protocol offers a very large number of features, of which only a few are presented here. Before you begin, it may be useful to distinguish it from the HTML (*Hypertext Markup Language*) format, which is often linked to it. Indeed, when an Internet page is requested to an HTTP server, it returns a page in HTML format. The HTML format allows us to create page layouts and has nothing to do with the

HTTP protocol. It is quite possible to return via HTTP any data format, and it is possible to make HTML documents without the Internet or HTTP.

HTTP request format

The format of an HTTP request is textual, with properties distributed by lines:

```
<Method> <URI> HTTP/<Version>
[<Header field>:<Value>]
[<Header field>:<Value>]
[...]
[<Data>]
```

The first line always contains the method (GET, POST, ...), an Internet address called URI, and the version of the HTTP protocol. The following lines may optionally contain header fields that provide additional information about the query. Finally, data can accompany the request. If present, it is always preceded by an empty line.

Here is an example of an HTTP request without associated data:

```
GET /index.html HTTP/1.0
Accept : www/source
Accept : text/html
User-Agent : Lynx/2.2 libwww/2.14
From : alice@wonderland.net
```

Here is an example of an HTTP request with associated data:

```
POST /update.html HTTP/1.0
Accept : www/source
Accept : text/html
User-Agent : Lynx/2.2 libwww/2.14
From : alice@wonderland.net
Content-Length : 31

firstname=Paul&lastname=Durant
```

HTTP response format

The format of an HTTP response is slightly different from that of the request:

```
HTTP/<Version> <Status> <Status comment>
[<Header field>:<Value>]
[<Header field>:<Value>]
[...]
```

```
[<Data>]
```

The first line is different: it starts with the version of the protocol, then a status code that informs about the success of the request, and finally, a textual description of this status. The following consists of a sequence of header fields. If the response contains data, they are also placed after a blank line.

Here is an example of an HTTP response with associated data:

```
HTTP/1.0 200 OK
Content-type : text/html
Date : Wed, 02 Feb 97 23:04:12 GMT
Last-modified : Mon, 15 Nov 96 23:33:16 GMT
Content-length : 2345

<HTML><HEAD><TITLE>
...
</BODY></HTML>
```

The different data types in these HTTP packets are presented in the following.

URI (Uniform Resource Identifier)

An HTTP request always contains an Internet address or URI (*Uniform Resource Identifier*). A URI makes it possible to identify an element (or resource) on the Internet. This notion of element or resource is abstract, and it does not necessarily correspond to a file or something stable over time. The strict notion of URI is broad; only a rough definition is proposed here. A URI can usually be split into two parts: URL (*Uniform Resource Locator*) and parameters. The URL part often refers to a rather stable element, such as a file, and the parameter part used to modify the shape or content of the stable element. A question mark "?" separates both. For example, for the following URI:

```
https://en.wikipedia.org/w/index.php?title=Special:CreateAccount
    &returnto=Main+Page
```

The URL part is:

```
https://en.wikipedia.org/w/index.php
```

The parameters part is:

```
title=Special:CreateAccount
returnto=Main+Page
```

The URL starts with the protocol used, in the above secure HTTP (`https://`). Then, a domain or subdomain name precedes a file path. In the example above, the subdomain is `en.wikipedia.org`, and the path is `/w/index.php`. The path does not necessarily refer to a file that exists.

The parameters are usually separated by the symbol "&", and each parameter is defined by a pair (name, value) separated by the symbol "=". In the example above, there are two parameters: `title` with the value `Special:CreateAccount` and `returnto` with the value `Main+Page`. The purpose of parameters is often to change the default behavior of the object targeted by the URL. In this example, the `title` parameter instructs the index.php file to present a page that creates an account, and the `returnto` parameter reprograms the action of the `previous page` button.

HTTP methods

The HTTP protocol adds another layer of routing, thanks to methods. Added to the concept of IP address and port, these allow to route requests to different services. They take the form of a string of characters, freely defined, as for the expected service. These choices are at the ones of clients and servers: when the same person designs both, the freedom of choice is not a problem. If not, you have to adapt or agree. There are some very popular choices, like the following four used in this chapter:

- GET method: type of request without data, and with data in return. The purpose of this method is to return information. The typical example is that of an Internet browser that requests a web page: it is a GET request on the URL of the site, and the Internet page is the data returned.
- POST method: type of query with data, and without data back. The purpose of this method is to modify a piece of information. Forms on web pages are a common example of this type of request. For example, when you press the "submit" button in a form where the name, first name, address, etc. have been filled in, the browser sends a POST request with the name, first name, etc., as data.
- PUT method: type of query with data, and with data in return. The purpose of this method is to request the creation of a new object. For example, when you want to add a new row in a database. The data sent is that of the object to be created, and the data returned is generally the elements resulting from the creation, such as the identifier (or "primary key") of the new line in the database.
- DELETE method: type of query without data or feedback. The purpose of this method is to request the destruction of an object, for example, the destruction of a file on the server.

There are many other standard methods, as well as the ability to create all possible methods, as long as clients and servers have the same interpretation.

HTTP Status code

HTTP requests systematically return a number that characterizes the behavior of the latter. These numbers are divided into different categories:

- Codes between 100 and 199: The request is usually not completed. For example :
    - Code 100: *Continue*. The server waits for the rest of the request.
    - Code 102: *Processing*. The request is in progress.
- Codes between 200 and 299: The query is a success. The code indicates the nature of it, for example:
    - Code 200: *OK*. The response contains data.
    - Code 201: *Created*. The item has been created.
    - Code 204: *No content*. The response has no data.
- Codes between 300 and 399: The query could not be executed for routing issues.
- Codes between 400 and 499: The request is erroneous: the client made a mistake, for example:
    - Code 400: *Bad request*. The request is not correct.
    - Code 403: *Forbidden*. The request is correctly formulated, but the requested operation is impossible.
    - Code 404: *Not found*. The requested element does not exist.
- Codes between 500 and 599: There is an error, but server-side:
    - Code 500: *Internal Server Error*. The server has experienced an internal error (for example, an exception was thrown).
    - Code 501: *Not implemented*. The feature is not implemented.

The above codes are standard codes, but just like the methods, it is quite possible to vary their meaning or to invent others, as long as clients and servers follow the same conventions.

HTTP header fields

Within an HTTP request, it is possible to add header fields, in the form of pairs (name, value). These headers are present in the request, but also in the response. The client can add information in its requests, and the server can add details in its response. Components between the client and the server can also read and modify these headers for interesting features, such as caching, redirection, or data compression/decompression.

Among the most usual headings, we find:

- *Content-Length* header: indicates the size of the associated data. This header is almost mandatory when data accompanies the HTTP packet (request or response). Warning: this size is in bytes, it is not the number of characters of a string. Here is an example :

```
Content-Length: 23
```

- *Content-Type* header: indicates the format of the data, for example to indicate an HTML format with characters in UTF8:

```
Content-Type: text/html; charset=utf-8
```

  The data type format is a MIME type, in the form `<category>/<subclass>; <options>`. For example, `image/png` represents the MIME type for a PNG image. These types are well described on many sites on the Internet.

- *Last-Modified* header: indicates the date of the last modification of the data. For example :

```
Last-Modified: Tue, 15 Nov 1994 12:45:26 GMT
```

- *WWW-Authenticate*: Specifies the authentication method to use. For example, for a basic method:

```
WWW-Authenticate: Basic
```

HTTP Features

From all the possibilities offered by the HTTP protocol, many features are possible. These include load distribution, fault management, query caching, packet traversal optimization within a server cluster, data compression, identification, securing with the HTTPS extension, etc.

From a video game designer's point of view, and even from applications in general on the network, this protocol makes it possible to manage the many problematic cases without having to reinvent anything. Indeed, there are existing and widely proven solutions like Apache servers or node.js that can be used to manage all common problems. To do this, these servers are at the forefront of the scene and directly receive requests from clients. Then, via proxy mechanisms, requests can be redirected to the servers of the video game (or application). Without even looking at features such as load balancing or fault management, this approach helps protect game servers from common attacks on the Internet.

Of course, and if you have the required resources, it can be interesting to develop all network features yourself. It is why, in the design presented later in this chapter, the usual approach of separating the different features is followed. With this kind of approach, there is only one step to swap one implementation with another.

6.2.1.7 REST Web API (Representational State Transfer)

To be able to interact with a server, it is necessary to be able to request the implementation of tasks and the retrieval of information. The previous layers already make it possible to handle a large part of the communication, but with a low level of interaction. A higher level is the one used in programming languages, for example via a function and its arguments. An even higher level and even more comfortable is via object programming, with a class and its methods. In any case, an idea of API appears as the simplest and most effective solution to communicate between clients and servers.

Remote Method Invocation (RMI)

Ideally, the simplest API to communicate is a fully transparent API. For example, if you want to bring players together for a game, a `Game` class with methods like `addPlayer()`, `setPlayer()`, and so on is an API that works well. However, communication can not take place directly between the Java code of the client and that of the Server. The call to a method must be transformed to go through the Internet pipes, and then be reformed on the server side. The same goes for the answer.

The standard Java library provides a solution for making remote method calls via the *Remote Method Invocation (RMI)* system. This system makes it possible to deport the call of the methods of a class from one machine to another. This approach is possible, but also debatable. If it works very well on a private network, as in a server cluster, things are much more complicated on the Internet. Managing a set of clients whose versions differ, as well as the java virtual machines being used, complicates this approach. Finally, the lack of access to a certain level of implementation prohibits many possible optimizations. Other similar solutions follow this approach, and the same remarks can also be made.

In this book, a low-level approach is proposed to overcome all these problems - which remain questionable depending on the situation. Besides, this does not constrain the solutions to the Java language and remains in the general context of object-oriented languages. Finally, this is also an opportunity to understand and manipulate the network layers, and therefore produce designs better adapted to these hardware constraints.

The REST approach

The REST approach can be used to perform the equivalent of calling functions or methods, but with an approach closer to hardware constraints than solutions like RMI. This approach relies entirely on the HTTP protocol, which it uses the resource and method principle. Path in the URI identifies each resource, and the HTTP method used in the request indicates the nature of the operation. For example, a `GET /player` is like saying 'I want to receive player information'. The GET method indicates the desire to receive the information, and `/player` indicates the "player" resource. A `PUT /player` indicates that you want to add a player.

The path of the URL is the same, but the method changes the "get" operation to "add". It is also possible to request particular information, for example, thanks to a GET /player/3, which requests the information of the player number 3. This works because the expression /player/3 unambiguously indicates the concerned player. Similarly, if you want to change this player, a POST /player/3 allows it. The resource identification principle can be expanded in many other ways. For example, a GET /player?name=Paul can identify all players whose name is 'Paul'. Combinations are also possible, for example /player/3/phone/2/number can refer to the second phone number of the third player. Everything is possible, as long as the resource is well identified.

The REST approach also considers each URI as the identifier of an accessible and/or modifiable *stateless* resource. It means that if a client requests the /player resource, the response does not depend on the previous requests, nor is waiting for a future request. For a relatively simple element like the list of players, this does not seem to be a strong constraint. Things are different when the resource can not be accessed or modified via a single query. This resource can be particularly important, and therefore not received in one answer.

The resource can be formed in several stages, called a transaction. For example, when registering on a website, there are usually several pages to complete before you can create an account. With a variable state approach, it is possible to resolve these cases by placing the server in a certain state and then evolving according to the progress in the task. For example, to receive a large file, the server goes into a "file transmission" state, then "10% file transmission", and so on, until you return to a state "ready for any new request". The problem is resolved, but the server blocks other requests in the meantime. Also, the management of states is not trivial and quickly gives rise to various problems, such as the management of a client canceling before the end of the transaction.

With a REST approach, the server is always in the same state, e.g. "no state". Fault management is also simplified since there is no processing being lost - if a file has started to be transferred to 20% from a server, the following steps can be immediately handled by another server.

How REST works

There are various architectures for REST deployment; here are the most common with a quick description. A single "scheduler" server receives all client requests. It redirects these requests to "service" servers. This task is very simple and quick to execute, and a single "scheduler" server can handle a very large number of requests. The "service" servers interpret the requests and then eventually retrieve or modify the data on the "database" servers. The "service" servers receive high-level REST HTTP requests that are analogous to method calls. The operations of these queries can be complex, and these servers check that the queries are valid, such as the respect of the rules of a game. The "database" servers receive low-level queries that correspond to "atomic" operations. These operations are extremely simple, such as changing the value of the attribute of a class. Low-level queries are very fast and subject to no validity checks, in the sense of business logic. When the load is low, it is possible to group everything on the same machine, in which case the servers are threads: we have a "scheduler" thread, "services" threads, and a "database" thread.

With this architecture, when the /player resource is requested by a client, the "scheduler" server assigns it to a "service" server. The latter asks the "database" server, which contains the players to return the list, most certainly in a low-level format. Then, the assigned "service" server encodes the data in a transportable format over the Internet and sends its response to the client. For the communication between "service" and "database" servers, an approach like RMI does not cause any problems since everything circulates locally.

In the case of transactions, which groups transactions into multiple queries, such as creating a multi-step account on a website, the common solution for remaining stateless is to create and manipulate a resource "creating a new account". The client starts by requesting the creation of this resource, for example, via a PUT /accountcreation. This request returns, for example, the identifier 12. Then, the client requests a first batch of data, for example, first and last name, and sends the request to POST /accountcreation/12/names. This request modifies the first and last name for the request to create a login account 12. Then the client does the same for the address, with a POST /accountcreation/12/address request. Finally, the last step allows creating the account with a request of the type PUT /account, with data accountcreation=12. The server creates a new account using the data stored in the accountcreation resource 12. The client could also have changed his mind and no longer want to create an account. In which case, it can cancel with a DELETE /accountcreation/12 request. In all case, no request requires a particular state of the server. The notion of state is, in a way, transformed into a notion of resource, here /accountcreation.

The mechanics of REST is most often used with an HTTP protocol, as it is done in this chapter. However, nothing forbids using these same principles of resources and "stateless" with a personal protocol, created for a specific game.

6.2.1.8 Data formats

To pass data over the network, you have to use a data format that does not depend on the machines that produce and consume them. The problem is similar to the one discussed for saving the state of the game, but with an even stronger constraint. Therefore, we must not depend on information related to the execution of a program, such as a memory address or reference values. It is also not possible to depend on the version of the program or the version or type of virtual machine being used.

One solution is to follow the serialization principle presented at the end of Chapter 4 for saving and loading the game state. To do this, we must get rid of dependencies on the tools of the standard Java library. This approach, at a lower level, is the most optimal but also the most expensive in development, especially to manage different versions of data format. Such a level of optimization is not necessarily interesting for the multiplayer game. Indeed, in general, very small amounts of information are transmitted for the synchronization (the commands), and the latencies of the networks are such that a gain of a few nanoseconds of coding/decoding time is not interesting.

Another approach is to use a standard format. Of these, the most popular are XML, JSON, and YAML. All rely on fairly similar principles and differ mainly in the way they encode the data. The XML format is very verbose and looks like HTML. It is the oldest format and has many features. The YAML format is, on the contrary, very compact and less easy to read. Finally, the JSON format is a kind of compromise that is chosen for this chapter.

JavaScript Object Notation Format (JSON)

The JSON format is a subset of the JavaScript language. It allows representing data in the form of a hierarchy. Here is an example that represents a list of two players:

```
{
  "players":[
    {
      "id": 1,
      "name": "Sophie",
      "ready": true
    },{
      "id": 2,
      "name": "Paul",
      "ready": false
    }
  ]
}
```

The representation starts with an opening brace {: this means that the root of the data is an object. An object in JSON is a set of attributes, each having a value or null. In this example, the root object has a unique players attribute. This attribute is an array since it starts with an opening bracket [. Each element of this array is an object since we find braces. The first object has three attributes:

```
{
  "id": 1,
  "name": "Sophie",
```

```
  "ready": true
}
```

The first `id` attribute is a number and is set to 1. The second `name` attribute is a string and is set to 'Sophie'. Finally, the last `ready` attribute is a boolean and is set to `true`.

In a more general way, the possible values of a JSON are: object, number, character string, array, boolean, and null. Objects are defined in braces {} and arrays in square brackets []. The other types are immediate values.

Validation scheme

In JSON, as in other formats, it is possible to define the shape of the expected data with a validation scheme. These diagrams make it possible to automate the verification of the layout of the received data. Thus, any errors are detected upstream, before the operations using these data take place.

The validation schema is also in JSON format. For the previous example, a validation scheme can be:

```
{
  "type": "object",
  "properties": {
    "players": {
      "type": "array",
      "items": {
        "type": "object",
        "properties": {
          "id": {
            "type": "integer",
            "minimum": 1
          },
          "name": {
            "type": "string",
            "pattern": "([A-Za-z]+)"
          },
          "ready": {
            "type": "boolean"
          }
        }
      }
    }
  }
}
```

The `type` attribute of the schema root indicates that the expected root object must be an object. Then, the `properties` attribute indicates the nature of this object. It must contain a `players` array:

```
"players": {
  "type": "array",
  "items": {
    ...
  }
}
```

Then, each element of the array is defined by the `items` attribute. They must be objects, with an `id` integer attribute with a minimum value of 1, a `name` string with only letters, and finally a `ready` boolean.

6.2.2 Implement Web Services

In this section, simple Web services are implemented with the elements of the standard Java library.

6.2.2.1 Create an HTTP server

Creating an HTTP server is very easy using the `HttpServer` class in the `com.sun.net.httpserver` package. To do this, you have to build a new instance on a given port (here 8080):

```java
public static void main(String args[])
    throws IOException {
  HttpServer httpServer = HttpServer.create(
      new InetSocketAddress(8080), 0);
```

Then, a handler is used to react to requests on a given path. In this example, we use a handler via the `Handler` class defined below. This manager receives all requests from the root path "/":

```java
  httpServer.createContext("/", new Handler());
  httpServer.start();
}
```

Query Manager

The `Handle` class receives the parameters of the HTTP request via an `exchange` argument of type `HttpExchange`:

```
class Handler implements HttpHandler {
public void handle(HttpExchange exchange)
    throws IOException {
```

In this example, the server systematically responds with the message "Successful execution" and the status code HTTP 200 (OK). This message is first placed in an array of bytes named `reponseData`:

```
String response = "Successful execution";
byte[] responseData = response.getBytes();
```

It is easier to go through an array of bytes because the memory footprint of a string is not necessarily equal to the number of letters that compose it: it depends on the format of the characters. With an array of bytes, there is no more ambiguity: the size in bytes of the string is equal to that of the array returned by the `getBytes()` method of the `String` class.

The `sendResponseHeaders()` method of the `HttpExchange` class is used to define the HTTP status code of the response, as well as the length of the transmitted data:

```
exchange.sendResponseHeaders(200, responseData.length);
```

It is also possible to indicate that there is no data to send, in which case it is necessary to give a data length equal to -1.

The end of the method sends the data, via an output stream returned by the `getResponseBody()` method. This stream is a standard `java.io.OutputStream` and is used like any other stream of this type:

```
OutputStream os = exchange.getResponseBody();
os.write(responseData);
os.close();
}
```


Server test

The code is present in the "examples/chap06/restserver/E01Server.java" folder of the Java sample project. To test it, just run it, then use an internet browser like Firefox or Chrome, by entering the following address: `http://localhost:8080/` or `http://127.0.0.1:8080/`. The message appears in the browser.

6.2.2.2 HTTP Headers and Data Format

To indicate the format of the data sent, use the `Content-Type` HTTP header. This one expects a *MIME* type which used to be two words separated by a slash "/". For example, for simple text, the MIME type is `text/plain` and for a png image `image/png`. It is also possible to add options after a semicolon. In the following example, the server returns JSON data, and the chosen character set is the UTF8, the most common format: `application/json; charset=utf-8`.

The implementation in the `handle()` method can then take the following form. It starts by adding the `Content-Type` header with the JSON MIME type using UTF8:

```
Headers headers = exchange.getResponseHeaders();
headers.set("Content-Type","application/json; charset=utf-8");
```

For the sake of consistency, the data to be transmitted must use the declared character format (by default, the character set in Java is UTF16, less used than UTF8). Data in JSON format is converted to an array of UTF8 bytes using the `getBytes()` method of the `String` class:

```
String response = "{ \"message\": \"Successful execution\" }";
byte[] responseData = response.getBytes(Charset.forName("UTF8"));
```

The `getBytes()` method can take a `Charset` type argument that defines a set of characters. There are sets already present in the standard library, accessible via the static `forName()` method of the `Charset` class.

The end of the method remains the same and transmits the data to the client:

```
exchange.sendResponseHeaders(200, responseData.length);
OutputStream os = exchange.getResponseBody();
os.write(responseData);
os.close();
```

The code is present in the "examples/chap06/restserver/E02Server.java" folder of the Java sample project. Once the server is viewed in a browser, there are no problems if you send a message with special UTF8 characters. Note that some browsers can interpret the JSON format, and offer non-textual rendering, in the form of lists or trees, so you may not see the raw JSON text.

6.2.2.3 Produce JSON (Factory and Builder Patterns)

If we want to produce data in JSON format, it is better to use a library instead of directly writing the text that represents it. It is much more robust, and often faster in execution. The standard Java library provides a standard API available for the `javax.json` package. The implementation is free, and in this book, JSONP implementation, available at `https://javaee.github.io/jsonp/` was chosen. It is important to remember that the choice of implementation does not influence the programs that use it: they only see the standard API. If an implementation causes problems, it is possible to use another one without modifying the programs which exploit it.

Factories

The standard JSON API is very interesting and intelligently uses several design patterns. First, it frequently uses the Factory pattern to instantiate its elements. For example, to create an instance of `JsonWriter` that converts from formal JSON to plain text, we use a `JsonWriterFactory`, literally a `JsonWriter` factory. To do this, a `createWriterFactory()` static method is available in the `Json` class:

```
JsonWriterFactory jsonWriterFactory =
    Json.createWriterFactory(<options>);
```

`<options>` allows you to customize the shape of the text produced, such as adding an indentation or not.

Once the factory is available, it is possible to obtain a `JsonWriter` very easily:

```
JsonWriter jsonWriter =
    jsonWriterFactory.createWriter(<destination>);
```

Other types of factories can be created with other static methods of the `Json` class.

Builders

To build JSON content, the standard API relies on builders, like the `StringBuilder` class in the standard library. These builders allow you to define the elements of a JSON and then produce the final JSON. Each type of builder is dedicated to a JSON value type: `JsonObjectBuilder` for objects, and `JsonArrayBuilder` arrays. Each type of builder is created via a factory method of the Json class, for example:

```
JsonBuilderFactory jsonBuilderFactory =
    Json.createBuilderFactory(null);
JsonObjectBuilder responseObjectBuilder =
    jsonBuilderFactory.createObjectBuilder();
```

To summarize: a builder factory is instantiated, usually one for the whole program (or one per thread in case of parallel execution). Then, for each JSON object creation, the factory is used to get a builder.

The builder is used in a rather intuitive way, for example, to add the `message` attribute with the value "Successful execution":

```
responseObjectBuilder.add("message", "Successful execution");
```

The JSON object can then be obtained using the `build()` method:

```
JsonObject responseObject = response.build();
```

Once converted to plain text, the above object takes the following form:

```
{
  "message": "Successful execution"
}
```

Server with Json builders

An equivalent of the previous server code can be written using the standard
JSON API. The following code for the handle() method uses jsonBuilderFactory
and jsonWriterFactory attributes that reference a builder factory and a JSON
converter factory:

```
Headers headers = exchange.getResponseHeaders();
headers.set("Content-Type","application/json; charset=utf-8");

JsonObjectBuilder responseObjectBuilder =
    jsonBuilderFactory.createObjectBuilder();
responseObjectBuilder.add("message", "Successful execution");

StringWriter responseWriter = new StringWriter();
JsonWriter jsonWriter =
    jsonWriterFactory.createWriter(responseWriter);
jsonWriter.write(responseObjectBuilder.build());
byte[] responseData = responseWriter.toString().getBytes(utf8);

exchange.sendResponseHeaders(200,responseData.length);
OutputStream os = exchange.getResponseBody();
os.write(responseData);
os.close();
```

The code is present in the "examples/chap06/restserver/E03Server.java" folder of
the Java sample project. The observed behavior is the same as the previous one.

6.2.2.4   HTTP method and client

HTTP method

In the previous examples, the HTTP method is not read, and we react as if
the method was always GET. The method of a query is available through the
getRequestMethod() method of the HttpExchange class. The preceding code is
modified to respond normally when the method is GET, and return an error message
with the BAD_METHOD HTTP status code when this is not the case:

```
int httpStatusCode;
JsonObjectBuilder response =
```

```java
    jsonBuilderFactory.createObjectBuilder();
String method = exchange.getRequestMethod();
if (method.equals("GET")) {
    httpStatusCode = HttpURLConnection.HTTP_OK;
    response.add("message", "Successful execution");
}
else {
    httpStatusCode = HttpURLConnection.HTTP_BAD_METHOD;
    response.add("error","Invalid or unsupported HTTP Method");
}
```

This step is also an opportunity to start implementing a process that systematically produces HTTP status code and JSON data. Ultimately, the goal is to focus on JSON data and to handle encoding issues in a single place.

The code is present in the "examples/chap06/restserver/E04Server.java" folder of the Java sample project. To get the error message, you need to use a program or browser that can produce non-GET HTTP requests. In this chapter, an HTTP client is programmed in Java to do this.

HTTP client

The standard Java library has tools for building HTTP requests in the `java.net` package. These tools are not perfect but meet most needs. The creation of a query starts with the creation of a URL, for example, here `http://localhost:8080`:

```java
URL url = new URL("http","localhost",8080,"");
```

Then, the `openConnection()` method of the URL class makes it possible to build a request to the address it contains. In general, these URLs can be seen as query factories:

```java
HttpURLConnection connection =
    (HttpURLConnection)url.openConnection();
```

The object returned by the method is converted to `HttpURLConnection` because the URL protocol is HTTP. For other protocols, another type of connection is returned.

Then, the method and type of expected content are specified:

```java
connection.setRequestMethod("GET");
connection.setRequestProperty("Content-Type", "application/json"
);
```

Any cache system is disabled:

```java
connection.setUseCaches(false);
```

In the opposite case, the server may not be consulted during a consecutive request, depending on the value of the default parameters.

The purpose of the following lines is to retrieve the transmitted data, via the incoming stream returned by the `getInputStream()` method of the `HttpURLConnection` class:

```java
InputStream is = connection.getInputStream();
BufferedReader rd = new BufferedReader(new InputStreamReader(is)
);
String line;
while ((line = rd.readLine()) != null) {
    System.out.println(line);
}
rd.close();
```

The code is present in the "examples/chap06/restserver/E04Client.java" folder of the Java sample project. If the server is running, this program displays the JSON data. If the method is modified, this program displays an exception with code 405, which is BAD_REQUEST.

6.2.2.5   GET service

The objective of this section is the implementation and validation of a /user REST service limited to the GET method. This must be able to return one or more sets of information about the users of a database.

Decoding the URL path

The URL paths considered are:

- Path /user: concerns all users
- Path /user/<id>: refers to the user of identifier <id>

Besides, any identifier less than or equal to 0 is considered to represent all users. For example /user/0 and /user/-1 are equivalent to /user.

We use regular expressions to decode this information. More specifically, a pattern is prepared to detect paths with an identifier:

```java
Pattern servicePattern = Pattern.compile("(/[^/]+)/(\\d+)");
```

The pattern is formed by two sub-patterns separated by a slash: (/[^/]+) and (\\d+). Valid paths must begin with the first sub-pattern, followed by a slash, and end with the second sub-pattern. The first subpattern looks for a slash followed by any character that is not a slash. The second sub-pattern looks for numbers.

The pattern can be exploited as follows. First, the path of the URL is placed in the `serviceName` variable, and a `serviceId` variable is set to 0:

```
URI uri = exchange.getRequestURI();
String serviceName = uri.getPath();
int serviceId = 0;
```

The goal is that at the end of the decoding processes, `serviceName` contains the name of the service (like `/user`) and `serviceId` the corresponding identifier, knowing that the value 0 represents the absence of ID.

The pattern is then searched in the current path:

```
Matcher matcher = servicePattern.matcher(serviceName);
```

If the pattern is found, the values corresponding to the two sub-patterns define our two variables:

```
if (matcher.matches()) {
    serviceName = matcher.group(1);
    serviceId = Integer.parseInt(matcher.group(2));
}
```

In the opposite case, it is assumed that there is no identifier. Only small processing is applied to remove a possible slash at the end of the path:

```
else {
    if (serviceName.endsWith("/")) {
        serviceName = serviceName.substring(
            0, serviceName.length() - 1);
    }
}
```

Routing according to the service requested and the method

Once the path is decoded, it becomes possible to route according to the requested service. For example, if the service is `/user`:

```
if (serviceName.equals("/user")) {
```

Depending on the HTTP method, different operations are possible. In this example, only the GET method is considered, and handled by a `getUser()` method presented below:

```
String method = exchange.getRequestMethod();
switch(method) {
    case "GET":
        httpStatusCode = getUser(response,serviceId);
        break;
```

For other methods, a `HttpException` is thrown. It is an exception type defined specifically for this server. Its role is to contain an HTTP status code and a message:

```java
        default:
            throw new HttpException(HttpURLConnection.HTTP_BAD_METHOD,
                "Method "+method
                +" is invalid or unsupported");
    }
}
```

Similarly, if the service is not recognized, the same type of exception is thrown:

```java
else {
    throw new HttpException(HttpURLConnection.HTTP_BAD_REQUEST,
        "Service "+serviceName
        +" is invalid or unsupported");
}
```

These exceptions allow to interrupt the request processing at any time and to define the code and the message corresponding to the error. Then, the `handle()` method intercepts these exceptions to build a valid HTTP response.

GET /user/ service

For this example, a micro user database is defined. It is based on a `User` class with the name and age of a user, as well as an associative array `TreeMap<Integer,User> users = new TreeMap()`. The array matches a user ID with a user.

A `getUser()` method is implemented to respond to the `/user/<id>` service. The idea is to be as independent as possible from the form of the request. The method receives via its arguments a JSON builder `response` to fill, as well as a user ID `serviceId`:

```java
public int getUser(JsonObjectBuilder response,
    int serviceId) throws HttpException {
```

If the identifier is strictly greater than 0, then there is an identifier:

```java
    if (serviceId > 0) {
```

If the identifier is invalid, an exception is thrown:

```java
        if (!users.containsKey(serviceId)) {
            throw new HttpException(
                HttpURLConnection.HTTP_NOT_FOUND,
                "User "+serviceId+" not found");
        }
```

If the identifier is valid, the JSON is built with the name and age of the corresponding user:

```java
        User user = users.get(serviceId);
        response.add("name", user.name);
        response.add("age", user.age);
    }
```

If `serviceId` is negative or null, all users are requested:

```java
    else {
```

The lambda syntax is used: it is equivalent to a usual for ... each:

```java
        users.entrySet().forEach((user) -> {
```

For each user, a JSON builder is created and filled with the user's information:

```java
        JsonObjectBuilder jsonUser =
         jsonBuilderFactory.createObjectBuilder();
        jsonUser.add("name",user.getValue().name);
        jsonUser.add("age", user.getValue().age);
```

The JSON object is added to the general response object:

```java
        response.add(String.valueOf(user.getKey()),
            jsonUser.build());
        });
    }
    return HttpURLConnection.HTTP_OK;
}
```

The code is present in the "examples/chap06/restserver/E05Server.java" folder of the Java sample project. Via an internet browser, the server responds to requests of the type `http://localhost:8080/user` or `http://localhost:8080/user/1`.

Client

On the client side, the code for the GET /user request type is gathered in a `getUser()` method. This one contains code similar to the previous one, except the decoding of the data in JSON format, which allows returning a JSON object directly:

```java
public static JsonObject getUser(int id)
{
    JsonReader jsonReader = null;
    JsonObject jsonObject = null;
    try {
        URL url = new URL("http","localhost",8080,"/user/"+id);
```

```java
        HttpURLConnection connection = null;
        connection = (HttpURLConnection)url.openConnection();
        connection.setRequestMethod("GET");
        connection.setRequestProperty(
            "Content-Type", "application/json");
        connection.setUseCaches(false);
        int httpStatusCode = connection.getResponseCode();
        if (httpStatusCode == HttpURLConnection.HTTP_OK) {
            InputStream is = connection.getInputStream();
            BufferedReader rd = new BufferedReader(
                new InputStreamReader(is,utf8));
            jsonReader = Json.createReader(rd);
            jsonObject = jsonReader.readObject();
        }
    }
    catch(Exception ex) {
    }
    finally {
        if (jsonReader != null)
            jsonReader.close();
    }
    return jsonObject;
}
```

The decoding of JSON is similar to its encoding, replacing the output stream with an input stream, and `JsonWriter` by `JsonReader`.

⇒ Note: The `getUser()` methods on the server side and the client side have almost identical arguments. When the client calls its `getUser()` method, it is reasonable to think of calling the server's `getUser()` method directly. The whole process between the two is almost a technical formality, keeping in mind that the two methods can not access any common object at the program level. The only means of communication lie in the arguments of the methods.

This method makes it possible to use the various cases of the service: to obtain a user, to obtain all the users, and finally to ask for an invalid user:

```java
System.out.println("Request user 1 data");
JsonObject user1 = getUser(1);
System.out.println(" * Name: "+user1.getString("name")
    +", age: "+user1.getInt("age"));

System.out.println("Request all users data");
JsonObject users = getUser(0);
users.entrySet().forEach((pair) -> {
    JsonObject user = pair.getValue().asJsonObject();
    System.out.println(" * Name: "+user.getString("name")
```

```
            +", age: "+user.getInt("age")));
});

System.out.println("Request an invalid user");
JsonObject nullUser = getUser(3);
if (nullUser == null)
    System.out.println(" * No user returned");
```

The code is present in the "examples/chap06/restserver/E05Client.java" folder of the Java sample project.

6.2.2.6 POST service

The goal here is to implement and test a POST /user/<id> service that allows you to modify a user's information.

Server

A postUser() method is implemented in the server to allow service management. The idea is the same as before: to be independent of the coding and decoding processes. The method receives via its arguments the data to be modified in JSON format, as well as the identifier of the user to modify:

```
public int postUser(JsonObject request,
    int serviceId) throws HttpException {
```

In this implementation, only the case with a valid identifier is managed:

```
    if (!users.containsKey(serviceId)) {
        throw new HttpException(
            HttpURLConnection.HTTP_NOT_FOUND,
            "User "+serviceId+" not found");
    }
```

An extension of this method may consider a negative or null identifier to modify all users at once.

The found user is modified according to the parameters in the JSON object:

```
    User user = users.get(serviceId);
    if (request.containsKey("name")) {
        user.name = request.getString("name");
    }
    if (request.containsKey("age")) {
        user.age = request.getInt("age");
    }
```

```
        return HttpURLConnection.HTTP_NO_CONTENT;
}
```

The code is present in the "examples/chap06/restserver/E06Server.java" folder of the Java sample project.

Client

A `postUser()` method is implemented on the client side to allow the creation of a query modifying a user. This one takes the JSON data to modify as input, as well as the identifier of the user. Unlike the GET service, data is sent and not received: *readers* have become *writers*. Regarding this point, it is important to specify that there is outgoing data with the `setDoOutput()` method of the `HttpURLConnection` class:

```java
public static boolean postUser(JsonObject jsonObject,int id) {
    JsonWriter jsonWriter = null;
    try {
        URL url = new URL("http","localhost",8080,"/user/"+id);
        HttpURLConnection connection = null;
        connection = (HttpURLConnection)url.openConnection();
        connection.setRequestMethod("POST");
        connection.setRequestProperty(
            "Content-Type", "application/json");
        connection.setUseCaches(false);
        connection.setDoOutput(true);
        BufferedOutputStream bw = new BufferedOutputStream(
                connection.getOutputStream());
        jsonWriter = Json.createWriter(bw);
        jsonWriter.write(jsonObject);
        jsonWriter.close();
        int httpStatusCode = connection.getResponseCode();
        if (httpStatusCode ==
            HttpURLConnection.HTTP_NO_CONTENT) {
            return true;
        }
    }
    catch(Exception ex) {
    }
    finally {
        if (jsonWriter != null)
            jsonWriter.close();
    }
    return false;
}
```

The services and their use can be tested as follows:

```java
System.out.println("Modify user 1");
JsonObjectBuilder builder1 = Json.createObjectBuilder();
builder1.add("name", "Peter");
builder1.add("age", 34);
if (postUser(builder1.build(),1)) {
    System.out.println("Success");
}

System.out.println("Request user 1 data");
user1 = getUser(1);
System.out.println(" * Name: "+user1.getString("name")
    +", age: "+user1.getInt("age"));

System.out.println("Modify an invalid user");
JsonObjectBuilder builder2 = Json.createObjectBuilder();
builder2.add("name", "Peter");
builder2.add("age", 34);
if (!postUser(builder2.build(),Integer.MAX_VALUE)) {
    System.out.println("Modification failed");
}
```

The code is present in the "examples/chap06/restserver/E06Client.java" folder of
the Java sample project.

6.2.3 Exercises

6.2.3.1 Exercise 2.3.1: Creating a chat with sockets

The goal of this exercise is to create a chat between two machines, one as a server
and the other as a client. Each machine can type a message in the console, which
is then sent and displayed on the console of the other. The server and client roles
differ in the order of establishing connections: the server must be launched first
and wait for the client. Then, the client is started and connects to the server.
Subsequently, both actors have symmetrical roles.

It is necessary to go down to the socket level. The standard Java library provides
tools for this in the `java.net` package. At start, the server makes an instance of
`ServerSocket` on a particular port, and then waits for the client to connect:

```java
// Server side
ServerSocket serverSocket = new ServerSocket(port);
Socket socket = serverSocket.accept();
```

Once the client is connected, the `accept()` method returns a `Socket` that allows you to send and receive data.

The client can then open a socket on the server address and port (for example, the current machine):

```java
// Client side
Socket socket = new Socket("localhost",port);
```

Once these two sockets are connected, each component acts in the same way: the messages typed on the keyboard are sent, and the received messages displayed.

To enter a message on the keyboard, the `Scanner` class of `System.in` does the trick:

```java
Scanner userInput = new Scanner(System.in);
String message = userInput.nextLine();
```

Then, we get the output stream of the socket, then write the data there. For example, if we want to write text data line by line:

```java
PrintWriter outputWriter =
    new PrintWriter(socket.getOutputStream());
outputWriter.println("Message sent");
outputWriter.flush();
```

To receive data from a socket, we get the input stream from the socket and read the data there. For example, if you want to read textual data line by line:

```java
BufferedReader inputReader = new BufferedReader(
    new InputStreamReader(socket.getInputStream()));
String message = inputReader.readLine();
```

Finally, to terminate the connection, you must close the sockets with the `close()` method.

For the whole to run, the data send and receive operations must be in separate threads.

→ Implement a chat between two machines. Choose a word to enter to end the conversation.

6.2.3.2 Exercise 2.3.2: Implementing a nano HTTP server

This exercise aims to implement a minimalist HTTP server via TCP sockets. This exercise allows seeing the element required to implement a low-level solution, with all the optimizations dedicated to the developed game. This exercise is based on the notions seen in the previous exercise, which it is strongly recommended to do before this one.

The implementation of a server at the TCP socket level is based on a main loop that repeats waiting for connections from a `ServerSocket` of `java.net`:

```java
while(true) {
    Socket socket = serverSocket.accept() ;
    // Handling of the new connection
}
```

Processing a new connection through the socket returned by the `accept()` method follows the following procedure:

- The HTTP header is read and decoded from the input stream of the socket
- According to the HTTP method, and if data is present, these are read and decoded from the input stream of the socket
- The processing requested by the request are then implemented; For this exercise, the following one as requested:
    - For a GET method: send a message, preferably with special characters to check encoding problems;
    - For a POST method: read and decode the data that accompanies the query, and check their contents.
- According to the HTTP method, response data is also formed.
- Once the processing is completed, you must form the HTTP response header, with the status code (200 = OK, 400 = BAD_REQUEST, etc.). If there is data to return, do not forget the "Content-Length" header.
- Finally, the header and any data are sent via the output stream of the socket.

→ Implement a minimalist HTTP server that responds to GET and POST methods using a single thread. Also add unit tests to ensure proper implementation.

→ Implement a multi-threaded version of your server. There are several solutions to do this: here is one. Use a Producer/Consumer blocking queue: For example, you can use `pacman.mt.TaskManager`. When a new socket is returned by the `accept()` method of the `ServerSocket` class, run a producer thread that parses the HTTP header. If all is correct, run a consumer thread (or better: move the current thread into the consumption pool) that processes the request.

With this kind of approach, the server can respond to significant peaks of queries, and it is difficult to overload it. With the production pool, HTTP requests are immediately processed. Fast filtering can be done at this level, either because a request is invalid, or because the consumption queue is saturated. The server is thus able to propose a response, including a negative one, when there is a very large number of requests.

6.3   Network Gaming

6.3.1   Principles

This section looks at the distribution of a video game on several machines, one of which acts as a server and the others as graphical clients. There are two main approaches to synchronize all these components: one is to propagate the entire game regularly, and the other to propagate only the information that has changed.

The first approach is the simplest to implement. To do this, you must be able to convert the game state in a transportable format on the network, like the JSON format previously seen. Unfortunately, this approach is only possible when the memory footprint of the game data is very small. Indeed, it is difficult to imagine spreading several megabytes dozens of times per second on current networks. This also prohibits all optimizations that rely on the notification of minor changes in the game state, as it was done in the Pacman example game with the rules engine that notifies the rendering engine. For games that require this approach, such as extremely fast games like FPS and fighting games, the game state is very small, and a simple broadcast of it is fully appropriate.

The second approach is more complex to implement unless the design has already been prepared. Indeed, if the update of the game state is based on a command pattern, there is already a mechanism that allows knowing what was changed. To be more precise, this mechanism makes it possible to know not what was modified, but what modifies the game state, namely the commands. These are small and scarce because human beings produce them: even the greatest players of Starcraft never exceed 1000 commands per minute, which is far beyond normal human capacities but remains low at a computing scale. Therefore, it is enough for a server to receive the commands of the players, possibly to validate them, then to propagate these commands to all interested components (players and spectators). For the whole to work, each component must have its state and its rules engine, and the implementation of these commands must always be the same, regardless of the machine.

To summarize, each player does not apply his commands in his rules engine. Each player sends his orders directly to the game server. Then, he regularly checks the server to see if any orders are available for the next game epoch. If so, he uses them in his own rules engine. Among the orders received, some are his own commands, and some are commands from other players, human or AI. For its part, the server receives and stores commands. It has its own rules engine, which contains a game state at a given epoch. During a game state update, the last received commands are applied, possibly validated, associated with the current game epoch, and then stored by the server. In parallel, if a player requests the commands, whether past or recent, the server returns them. It allows players to know the latest orders received and passed by the server's rule engine, but also to retrieve the entire history of the game. Thus, if a player joins a game or is disconnected, he can reconstruct the state of the game by applying all the commands from the beginning of the game.

In this section, this last approach is illustrated through the Pacman example game. This process is easily generalizable to most other games and does not depend on the Pacman game, except in the name and values of the commands. The first approach is illustrated in Exercise 3.5.1.

6.3.2　Serialize commands

This section is interested in the serialization of commands in JSON, to allow us to transfer them on the network. Regardless of any network considerations, this feature also allows you to save and replay games.

6.3.2.1　Serialization (Proxy Pattern)

Serialization of a class

To abstract the serialization process, a `toJson()` method is added to the `Command` interface, similar to the `writeExternal()` method of the `Externalizable` interface. Thus, it is possible to ask any class that implements `Command` to produce a serialized version. For example, for the `DirectionCommand` class:

```java
public void toJson(JsonObjectBuilder builder) {
    builder
        .add("type", "Direction")
        .add("charIndex",charIndex)
        .add("direction",direction.toString());
}
```

This method adds a `type` attribute that will allow decoding to know that it is a directional command. Then, the values of the `charIndex` and `direction` attributes are added as attributes of the same name in the JSON.

The other command classes are similar and do not involve any particular operations.

Serialization of all commands of a game

The `PlayGameMode` class is enriched with a new `replay` attribute that references an array of JSON objects, with one object per game epoch. An array is chosen in place of a JSON array builder so that we can easily add and remove elements when using the rollback feature. In the following, the JSON object and array builder factories are considered available.

The very first `replay` element is initialized by the serialization of the initial command contained in the `initCommand` attribute. A `jsonCommand` JSON object builder is used by the `toJson()` method of the initial command to obtain a serialized version:

```
JsonObjectBuilder jsonCommand =
    jsonBuilderFactory.createObjectBuilder();
initCommand.toJson(jsonCommand);
```

For each game epoch, there are possible commands, each associated with a priority level. The set of commands of an epoch can thus be represented by a JSON object whose attributes are the priority levels with the corresponding commands.

For the first element of `replay`, there is only one command, whose priority is arbitrarily set to 0:

```
JsonObjectBuilder jsonEpochCommands =
    jsonBuilderFactory.createObjectBuilder();
jsonEpochCommands.add("0", jsonCommand);
```

The text version of `jsonEpochCommands` gives something like:

```
{
    "0":{
        "type":"LoadLevel",
        "fileName":"level.tmx",
        "pacmanSpeed":2,
        "ghostSpeed":4
    }
}
```

Finally, the `replay` array can be initialized with the first set of commands contained in `jsonEpochCommands`:

```
replay = new ArrayList();
replay.add(jsonEpochCommands.build());
```

Serialization of the following commands

The commands that follow the first one are serialized in the `stateUpdating()` method, called just before the game state update. That's when the player's commands are transferred from the `commands` buffer, and then the AI commands are produced. At each call to the rules engine `addCommand` method, the added command is also serialized and added to a JSON object for all commands of the current game epoch. Finally, these commands are added to the `replay` array.

Another approach is to place the recording of the commands in the rules engine and enrich the `addCommand()` method to serialize and store commands. It can be discussed since we add a role to the rules engine, which already has many. An additional, more elegant, but more expensive, approach to development is to create a class that decorates the rules engine by adding the command recording functionality (Decorator Pattern). One motivation for moving to one of these approaches can be triggered by the size of the `PlayGameMode` class, which, if it has too many features, must be split.

Save a replay

Finally, to save the replay, we use the plain text translation processes presented previously:

```java
Map<String,Boolean> options = new HashMap();
options.put(JsonGenerator.PRETTY_PRINTING, true);
JsonWriterFactory writerFactory =
    Json.createWriterFactory(options);
JsonWriter jsonWriter = writerFactory.createWriter(
        new FileWriter("replay.json"));
JsonArrayBuilder replayBuilder =
    jsonBuilderFactory.createArrayBuilder();
for (JsonObject json : replay) {
    replayBuilder.add(json);
}
jsonWriter.write(replayBuilder.build());
jsonWriter.close();
```

6.3.2.2　Deserialization

To build Java commands from JSON, a first approach might be to add a `fromJson()` method to the `Command` interface, like the `readExternal()` of `Externalizable` interface. In this case, all the classes to deserialize must have a constructor without arguments. Then, we need an independent method, able to produce an instance of the right class, before calling its `fromJson()` method.

Deserialization of a command

Another approach followed here is to implement a constructor from a JSON object for each command class. Efficiency motivates this choice: the direct construction of an object with the right parameters is always faster than a default construction followed by a modification of the parameters. For example, for the `DirectionCommand` class, the following constructor is added:

```java
public DirectionCommand(JsonObject json) {
    this.charIndex = json.getInt("charIndex");
    this.direction = Direction.valueOf(
        json.getString("direction"));
}
```

It also requires an independent method to call the right constructor of the right class. The simplest is a discussion based on the `type` attribute of JSON objects, which is implemented in the static method `fromJson()` of theCommandinterface:

```java
public static Command fromJson(JsonObject json) {
    String type = json.getString("type");
    switch(type) {
    case "Collisions":
        return new CollisionsCommand(json);
    case "Direction":
        return new DirectionCommand(json);
    case "Gums":
        return new GumsCommand(json);
    case "Init":
        return new InitCommand(json);
    case "LoadLevel":
        return new LoadLevelCommand(json);
    case "Move":
        return new MoveCommand(json);
    case "Resurrection":
        return new ResurrectionCommand(json);
    case "UpdateStatus":
        return new UpdateStatusCommand(json);
    }
    throw new ClassCastException(
        "Type "+type+" invalid or unsupported");
}
```

Another more automatic approach is to use dynamic instantiation tools within the Java language. These tools make it possible to build objects from the name of a class. However, this approach is slow enough in execution.

A final approach is based on an abstract factory that, at a given command type, maps an instance of the concerned class from a JSON object. This approach does not exclude an explicit association between type of command and class but has the benefit of splitting the selection process from the instantiation process. Besides, it is the fastest of all, especially if a hash map is used to find the constructor from the type.

Replay a game

A new game mode is implemented with the `ReplayGameMode` class to replay a game. This one is very close to the `PlayGameMode` class, but with the process of entering commands (player, AI) replaced by the decoding of the commands of a replay.

During initialization, the commands are read from a file and placed in a `replay` JSON array:

```java
JsonReader jsonReader = Json.createReader(
    new FileReader("replay.json"));
replay = jsonReader.readArray();
jsonReader.close();
```

Then, in the `stateUpdating()` method called just before an update of the game state, the commands corresponding to the current epoch are added to the rules engine:

```java
JsonObject initCommands = replay.getJsonObject(state.getEpoch());
initCommands.entrySet().forEach((pairs) -> {
    int priority = Integer.parseInt(pairs.getKey());
    Command command = Command.fromJson(
        pairs.getValue().asJsonObject());
    rules.addCommand(priority, command);
});
```

In doing so, the rules engine and the rendering engine are completely deceived and run as if players or AIs were playing. On the screen, the game is replayed the same way it was played.

The diagrams in this example are available in the "Class Diagrams/chap06/network01" folder of the sample UML project. The code is present in the "examples/chap06/network01" folder of the Java sample project. To test the replay, play a game, leave it, then choose "Replay the last game" in the main menu.

6.3.3   Gather the players

Before starting a multiplayer game, it is necessary to bring together the players, each choosing his role. To implement it a *CRUD (Create, Read, Update, Delete)* web service is set up on the players' resource. This approach is valid for all kinds of games.

6.3.3.1 Definition of the service

The CRUD service via an HTTP REST approach relies on the following four sub-services. We are interested in players identified by their name and at a specific position in the list:

- *Create* service: PUT /player: adds a player, if there is a place left and the name is not already used. Returns the CREATED status code if everything went well, otherwise FORBIDDEN.
- *Read* service: GET /player/<position>: returns player information at <position>, or all player information if <position> is zero or less than or equal to 0. If the operation is successful, return the OK code. If the player is not found, return the NOT_FOUND code.
- *Update* service: POST /player/<position>: changes player information at <position>. If the player's name is already in use, it is swapped with the player at <position>. Returns the NO_CONTENT code if everything went well. Returns NOT_FOUND otherwise.
- *Delete* service: DELETE /player/<position>: Deletes the player at <position>. Returns NO_CONTENT if there are no problems, otherwise NOT_FOUND.

A possible extension is to add services of the type /player/<name>, which allows us to read, modify and delete a player by name. Since the positions are always numbers, and if a number can not be a player name, it is then possible to always distinguish the two cases.

6.3.3.2 Implementation of services

Abstraction of services

An abstract Service class is defined in the server package with the four corresponding operations:

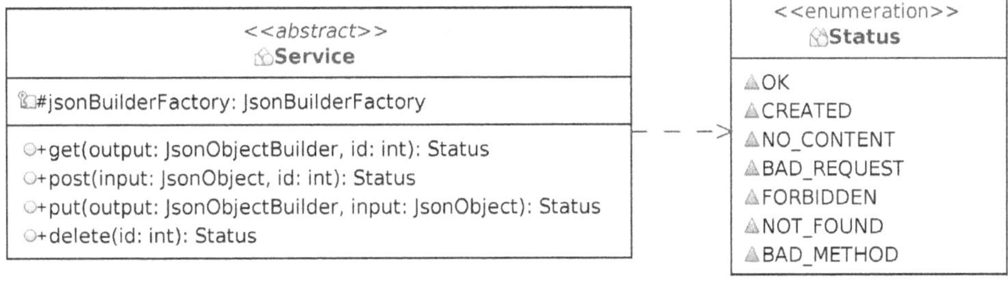

The first motivation behind this design is to separate the problems of encoding and decoding HTTP/JSON from the processing of the players. Thus, the functionalities no longer depend on server aspects, which can be completely re-implemented if necessary, without having to modify the services. The second motivation is based on the need to implement other similar services in the following.

The `Status` enumeration contains the codes returned by the methods. It is defined not to be dependent on an HTTP library, but also to freely define new codes. A `ServiceException` class is also defined to throw exceptions with code, like the `HttpException` class from previous examples.

The methods in the `Service` class are based on the previous examples that illustrated the implementation of REST services:

- `get()` method: builds a JSON response using the `output` constructor. The returned data depends on the value of `id`. Usually returns OK or NOT_FOUND.
- `post()` method: uses the data in `input` to modify the element identified by `id`. Usually returns NO_CONTENT or NOT_FOUND.
- `put()` method: uses data in `input` to add an element. Constructs a JSON response with `output` to identify the added element. Usually returns CREATED or FORBIDDEN.
- `delete()` method: removes the element identified by `id`. Usually returns NO_CONTENT or NOT_FOUND.

The `jsonBuilderFactory` attribute allows implementations to have a JSON object factory.

A very simple service

A service that is always recommended to provide is the one that gets the version of the application. It allows clients to know if they are in sync with their version, and act accordingly. This service only requires a GET. It is implemented via the `VersionService` child class of `Service`, with the redefinition of the `get()` method. This method is very simple, and builds a JSON object with the major version and the minor version whatever the situation:

```java
public Status get(JsonObjectBuilder output,int id) {
    output.add("major", 1);
    output.add("minor", 0);
    return Status.OK;
}
```

CRUD services for the management of players

A PlayerService class, child of Service, is defined to manage the list of players. It contains a list of Player class instances that contains a player's information:

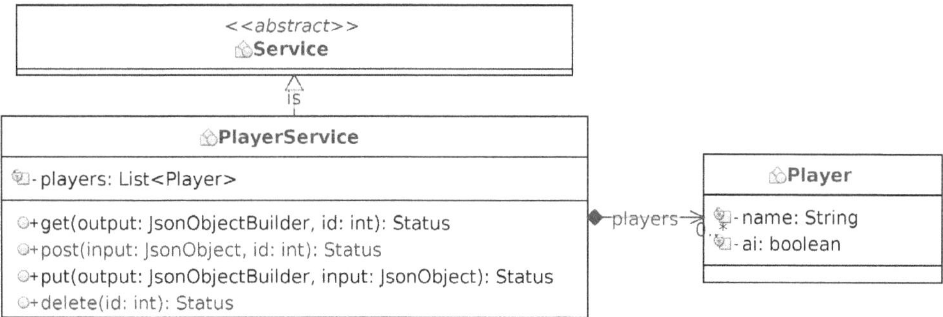

The implementation of PlayerService methods does not have interesting features. They apply the definitions presented above, by consulting and modifying the players player list.

6.3.3.3 Service manager

A service manager is defined as a ServiceManager class. Its role is to route requests to the concerned services. The idea of independence regarding the HTTP library is preserved: the manager takes a type of method (GET, PUT, etc.), a query path (ex: /player/), and JSON input and output data:

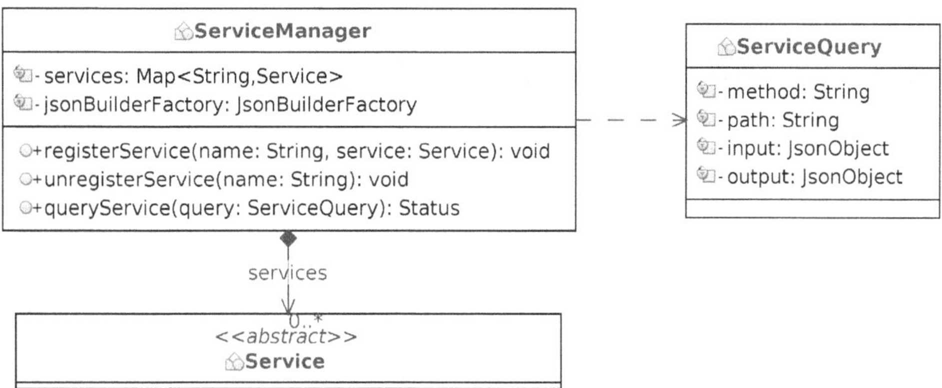

This definition is close to an abstract factory, with the difference that there is no creation of objects, but the implementation of an operation. The class stores Service implementations in the services associative array based on the service base name (such as /player). The registerService() and unregisterService()

methods add and remove services from the array. The `ServiceQuery` class carries all the information in a query - this form is more comfortable than a long list of arguments.

The `queryService()` method is the core of the manager, and selects the requested service:

```java
public Status queryService(ServiceQuery query)
    throws ServiceException {
```

The start-up is similar to what was done in the previous example: paths of type `/name/service/<id>` are expected, and decoded if detected:

```java
String serviceName = query.getPath();
int serviceId = 0;
Matcher matcher = servicePattern.matcher(serviceName);
if (matcher.matches()) {
    serviceName = matcher.group(1);
    serviceId = Integer.parseInt(matcher.group(2));
}
else {
    if (serviceName.endsWith("/")) {
        serviceName = serviceName.substring(0, serviceName.length()-1
        );
    }
}
```

At this stage, the `serviceName` variable contains the name of a service, and the `serviceId` variable a numeric identifier.

The following lines check that the requested service exists:

```java
if (!services.containsKey(serviceName)) {
    throw new ServiceException(Status.BAD_REQUEST,
        "No service "+serviceName);
}
```

The implementation of the service is retrieved, and the sub-service is selected according to the method of the query. Depending on the case, the input and output data in the query are taken into account:

```java
Service service = services.get(serviceName);
switch(query.getMethod()) {
case "GET": {
  JsonObjectBuilder out =
    jsonBuilderFactory.createObjectBuilder();
  Status status = service.get(out, serviceId);
  query.setOutput(out.build());
  return status;
```

```
}
case "POST":
  return service.post(query.getInput(),serviceId);
case "PUT": {
  JsonObjectBuilder out =
    jsonBuilderFactory.createObjectBuilder();
  Status status = service.put(out,query.getInput());
  query.setOutput(out.build());
  return status;
}
case "DELETE":
  return service.delete(serviceId);
}
throw new ServiceException(Status.BAD_METHOD,
  "Method "+query.getMethod()+" invalid");
}
```

This manager is generic enough, and able to handle all cases of simple requests of type /name/service/<id>. It can be easily extended to handle services with more complex paths, such as /name/service/<id1>/fields/<id2>.

6.3.3.4 Service server

To be able to provide the services, only the HTTP server is missing. The proposed implementation in the form of a Server executable class generalizes the elements presented in the previous example.

Concerning attributes, the Server class has a serviceManager reference to the service manager shown above, the utf8 character set, and JSON constructor factories. The service manager is initialized in the constructor with the two previous services for the version and the players:

```
public Server() {
    serviceManager = new ServiceManager(jsonBuilderFactory);
    serviceManager.registerService("/version",
        new VersionService(jsonBuilderFactory));
    serviceManager.registerService("/player",
        new PlayerService(jsonBuilderFactory));
}
```

The Server class implements the HttpHandler interface of the com.sun.net.httpserver package to respond to HTTP requests through the handle() method:

```
public void handle(HttpExchange exchange) {
```

The method starts with defining the headers and then makes an instance of ServiceQuery to hold the query elements:

```java
Headers headers = exchange.getResponseHeaders();
headers.set("Content-Type","application/json; charset=utf-8");
int httpStatusCode;
URI uri = exchange.getRequestURI();
String method = exchange.getRequestMethod();
ServiceQuery query = new ServiceQuery(method,uri.getPath());
```

The following lines add input data to `ServiceQuery` in case the method is POST or
PUT. This data is directly decoded into JSON, so the services don't have to deal
with this task:

```java
try {
  if (method.equals("POST") || method.equals("PUT")) {
    JsonReader jsonReader = null;
    JsonObject input = null;
    try {
      InputStream is = exchange.getRequestBody();
      BufferedReader rd = new BufferedReader(
        new InputStreamReader(is,utf8));
      jsonReader = Json.createReader(rd);
        put = jsonReader.readObject();
    }
    finally {
      if (jsonReader != null)
        jsonReader.close();
    }
    query.setInput(input);
  }
```

The service manager is called to execute the query contained in the `ServiceQuery`.
The `queryService()` method returns the resulting HTTP status code:

```java
  httpStatusCode = serviceManager
    .queryService(query).getCode();
}
```

The following block deals with error cases. First, there are errors directly caused
by services through the `ServiceException`. These exceptions allow us to give a
precise HTTP status code:

```java
catch(ServiceException ex) {
  httpStatusCode = ex.getStatus().getCode();
  JsonObjectBuilder builder =
    jsonBuilderFactory.createObjectBuilder();
  builder.add("error",ex.getMessage());
  query.setOutput(builder.build());
}
```

The general exception case is also handled - in the opposite case, an unexpected exception would crash the entire server. For these cases, we give by default a BAD_REQUEST code. A SERVER_INTERNAL_ERROR code would also have been possible, knowing that the true nature of the error is not known:

```
catch(Exception ex) {
  httpStatusCode = HttpURLConnection.HTTP_BAD_REQUEST;
  JsonObjectBuilder builder =
    jsonBuilderFactory.createObjectBuilder();
  if (ex.getMessage() != null) {
    builder.add("error",ex.getMessage());
  }
  else {
    builder.add("error",ex.toString());
  }
  query.setOutput(builder.build());
}
```

If the service generates output data, it is then encoded in plain text and passed to the client:

```
JsonObject output = query.getOutput();
if (output != null) {
  StringWriter responseWriter = new StringWriter();
  JsonWriter jsonWriter =
    jsonWriterFactory.createWriter(responseWriter);
  jsonWriter.write(output);
  byte[] responseData = responseWriter.toString().getBytes(utf8);
  OutputStream os = null;
  try {
    exchange.sendResponseHeaders(
      httpStatusCode, responseData.length);
    os = exchange.getResponseBody();
    os.write(responseData);
  }
  catch (IOException ex) {
    System.err.println("Error when sending the response");
  }
  finally {
    try {
      if (os != null) {
        os.close();
      }
    } catch (IOException ex) {
      System.err.println("Error when sending the response");
    }
```

```
    }
}
else {
  try {
    exchange.sendResponseHeaders(httpStatusCode, -1);
  } catch (IOException ex) {
    System.err.println("Error when sending the response");
  }
}
}
```

⇒ Note: Only the `Server` class depends on the HTTP library of the standard library, whose performance is not the best. To use another library or to implement network exchanges yourself, you only have to modify this class.

6.3.3.5 Client queries

Generic call to services

To simplify the execution of HTTP requests, a `ServiceQueries` class is defined to execute the four types of requests that the service manager and the services it contains can handle. It contains an attribute for the server address and a port number: all requests from an instance of `ServiceQueries` go to the same server. Then four methods are proposed: `get()`, `post()`, `put()` and `delete()`. They are similar to what was started in the **Implement Web Services** section. For example, for the `put()` method, which handles incoming and outgoing data:

```
public JsonObject put(String serviceName,JsonObject input) {
    JsonReader jsonReader = null;
    JsonWriter jsonWriter = null;
    try {
        URL url = new URL("http",host,port,serviceName);
        HttpURLConnection connection = null;
        connection = (HttpURLConnection)url.openConnection();
        connection.setRequestMethod("PUT");
        connection.setRequestProperty(
            "Content-Type", "application/json");
        connection.setUseCaches(false);
        connection.setDoOutput(true);
        BufferedOutputStream bw = new BufferedOutputStream(
                connection.getOutputStream());
        jsonWriter = Json.createWriter(bw);
        jsonWriter.write(input);
        jsonWriter.close();
        jsonWriter = null;
```

```
            int httpStatusCode = connection.getResponseCode();
            if (httpStatusCode == HttpURLConnection.HTTP_CREATED) {
                InputStream is = connection.getInputStream();
                BufferedReader rd = new BufferedReader(
                    new InputStreamReader(is, utf8));
                jsonReader = Json.createReader(rd);
                return jsonReader.readObject();
            }
        } catch (Exception ex) {
        } finally {
            if (jsonWriter != null) {
                jsonWriter.close();
            }
            if (jsonReader != null) {
                jsonReader.close();
            }
        }
        return null;
}
```

The ServiceQueries class allows very simple execution of queries, for example to make a GET /player/3 on the server 192.168.1.2:8000:

```
ServiceQueries serviceQueries =
    new ServiceQueries("192.168.1.2",8000);
JsonObject output = serviceQueries.get("/player",3);
```

The output variable is null if the request has failed, or it contains a JSON object with the information of player 3. Pay attention to the effects of latency: on a network, it takes at least a few milliseconds for the request to be completed. This point can be blocking in some cases.

Validation

The server is validated with the ServerTest test class in the "pacman" folder of the test packages. It launches a server on port 8080, and then runs and checks multiple queries using ServiceQueries.

6.3.3.6 Graphical menus and network queries

Queries are used to form a team via menus in the game.

Multiplayer menu

A first menu implemented via the `MultiplayerMenu` class allows you to choose a name (randomly initialized), the IP address of the server and the port of the server:

Once the **Connect** item is selected, an instance of `ServiceQueries` is built with the server coordinates:

```
ServiceQueries serviceQueries =
    new ServiceQueries(serverIp,serverPort);
```

Then, a `/player` PUT request with the entered name is started:

```
JsonObject player = Json.createObjectBuilder()
    .add("name", playerName).build();
JsonObject id = serviceQueries.put("/player", player);
```

A few tens or hundreds of milliseconds later - which is not a problem here - the answer is obtained. If it is non-zero, the player could be added, in which case we move to the menu managed by the `LobbyMenu` class:

```
if (id != null) {
    int playerId = id.getInt("id");
    setGameMode(new LobbyMenu(
        serverIp,serverPort,playerName,playerId));
}
```

If not, an error message is displayed:

```
else {
    JOptionPane.showMessageDialog(null,
        "The server is full or does not respond",
```

```
            "Error", JOptionPane.ERROR_MESSAGE);
}
```

List of players menu

The goal of the following menu in the `LobbyMenu` class is to display the list of players, to change characters, and finally to launch or join the game:

The main difficulty in handling this situation is the latency of the network exchanges and the possible problems of server failure.

The list of players can change at any time since other players can join the game. With communications that allow the server to go directly to clients, you must respond to their notifications to update the list. With communications only from clients to the server, as it is the case in this example, you must periodically ask the server if the list has changed. We use the `ScheduledExecutorService` class of the standard library. It allows us to regularly call the `run()` method of a class that implements `Runnable`. An instance of this class is placed in the `updater` attribute with the `newSingleThreadScheduledExecutor()` static method of the `Executors` class:

```
updater = Executors.newSingleThreadScheduledExecutor();
```

A pool with a single thread is chosen to prevent queries from accumulating when the server stops responding. If this happens, the single thread is stuck waiting, and no other operation can be started.

The pool is used to run the `updatePlayers()` method every second:

```
updater.scheduleWithFixedDelay(new Runnable() {
    public void run() {
```

```
        updatePlayers();
    }
}, 0, 1, TimeUnit.SECONDS);
```

The `updatePlayers()` method performs a GET /player, and then uses the returned JSON data to update the menu items that represent a character:

```
public void updatePlayers() {
    JsonObject players = serviceQueries.get("/player");
    if (players != null) {
        updateMenuItem(0,"Pacman",players.getJsonObject("1"));
        updateMenuItem(1,"Blinky",players.getJsonObject("2"));
        updateMenuItem(2,"Pinky",players.getJsonObject("3"));
        updateMenuItem(3,"Inky",players.getJsonObject("4"));
        updateMenuItem(4,"Clyde",players.getJsonObject("5"));
    }
}
```

The query in this method is run in the `updater` thread and does not block, even if the server stops responding. The `updateMenuItem()` method contains operations that update a menu item.

Character change

If the user selects a menu item that corresponds to a character, then a PUT /player query with the player name is executed:

```
JsonObject player = Json.createObjectBuilder()
    .add("name", playerName).build();
boolean success = serviceQueries.post(
    "/player",player,selectedItem+1);
if (success) {
    playerId = selectedItem+1;
    updatePlayers();
}
```

Latency is not a problem here. If the server crashes, the `post()` method of `ServiceQueries` returns `false` after a while, which can cause a slight freeze.

If the user presses the escape key, his participation is canceled via a DELETE /player request:

```
serviceQueries.delete("/player", playerId);
updater.shutdownNow();
setPreviousGameMode();
```

We must not forget to terminate the updater pool, at the risk of consuming more and more resources each time you use this menu.

The diagrams in this example are available in the "Class Diagrams/chap06/network02" folder of the sample UML project. The code is present in the "examples/chap06/network02" folder of the Java sample project. To try the server, you must run the Server class, then run the Main class for each player.

6.3.4 Multiplayer game

6.3.4.1 Server implementation

Two additional services are created to run the multiplayer game,: /game to know and change the status of the game (started or not), and /command to add and view commands. In addition, a Game class is defined as a 'database', which contains all the information shared by the services.

Game class

The Game class handles all aspects of the game: players, AI, and rules engine:

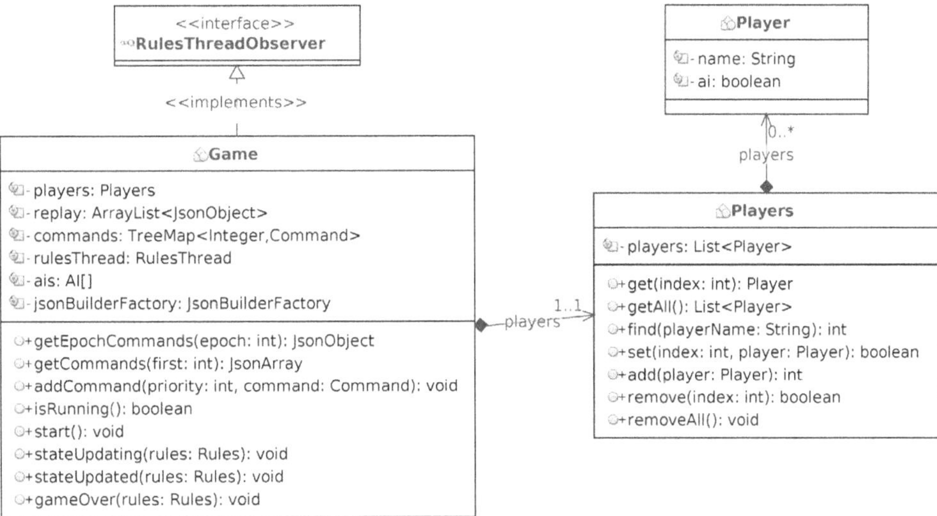

The trickiest part of the implementation concerns concurrent access: several threads may access or modify the information. One has to avoid unnecessary errors and locks.

List of players

The Game class first contains the list of players with the players attribute. The list of players is placed in a separate class to spread features, but also to manage synchronization aspects. All methods of the Players class are synchronized to prevent concurrent access, and they only return copies of players and never return references. It ensures that an instance of Player is never viewed or edited by more than one component at a time. For example, the get() method of the Player class returns a clone from the requested player:

```
public synchronized Player get(int index) {
    if (index >= players.size() || players.get(index) == null) {
        return null;
    }
    return players.get(index).clone();
}
```

It is possible since the memory footprint of an instance of Player is very small. Otherwise, we should return a Player Proxy.

List of commands

For commands management, the Game class keeps a complete history of all commands with the replay attribute, using the same principles as those used above to record the game. A set of commands for a given epoch can be viewed via the getEpochCommands() method:

```
public JsonObject getEpochCommands(int epoch) {
    synchronized(replay) {
        return replay.get(epoch);
    }
}
```

Access is synchronized on replay to manage concurrent access. The JsonObject instances are not modifiable, so there is no risk of returning them. The getCommands() method returns all commands from a given time and is used by the commands service.

For adding a command, it is not possible to directly use the replay array, since JSON objects are not editable. Moreover, these additions could bring unnecessary locks. The proposed solution is similar to the one when synchronizing between the user interface thread and the rules engine thread: a command buffer is filled and then emptied when the game state is updated. The addCommand() method adds the new commands to the commands buffer:

```
public void addCommand(int priority,Command command) {
    synchronized(commands) {
```

```
        commands.put(priority,command);
    }
}
```

Starting the game

The game can be started with the start() method. It performs the usual initializations: game status, AI, rules engine thread, and so on. The specificity, in this case, is based on the initialization of the replay history with an initial command, and the zeroing of the command buffer:

```
Command initCommand = new LoadLevelCommand("level.tmx",2,2);
JsonObjectBuilder jsonEpochCommands =
    jsonBuilderFactory.createObjectBuilder();
JsonObjectBuilder jsonCommand =
    jsonBuilderFactory.createObjectBuilder();
initCommand.toJson(jsonCommand);
jsonEpochCommands.add("0", jsonCommand);
synchronized(replay) {
    replay.clear();
    replay.add(jsonEpochCommands.build());
}
synchronized(commands) {
    commands.clear();
}
```

The isRunning() method then lets you know if the game is in progress.

Update the game state

The Game class is an observer of the rules engine thread and reacts to different notifications. Before a state update, the stateUpdating() method starts by creating a JSON object constructor jsonEpochCommands to gather all the commands of the coming epoch:

```
public void stateUpdating(Rules rules) {
JsonObjectBuilder jsonEpochCommands =
    jsonBuilderFactory.createObjectBuilder();
```

Then, the commands buffer is added to the rules engine:

```
synchronized(commands) {
commands.entrySet().forEach((command) -> {
    rules.addCommand(command.getKey(),command.getValue());
});
```

They are also converted to JSON, and added to `jsonEpochCommands`:

```
commands.entrySet().forEach((command) -> {
  JsonObjectBuilder jsonCommand =
    jsonBuilderFactory.createObjectBuilder();
  command.getValue().toJson(jsonCommand);
  String priority =String.valueOf(command.getKey());
  jsonEpochCommands.add(priority,jsonCommand);
});
```

Finally, the buffer is emptied:

```
commands.clear();
}
```

The players are then reviewed: commands are added for those played by an AI. A copy of the list of players is first obtained:

```
List<Player> playersList = players.getAll();
```

This copy avoids errors if a player is modified or removed at the same time while avoiding a long block.

For each player:

```
for(int index=0;index<playersList.size();index++) {
```

If the player does not exist or is explicitly an AI:

```
    if (playersList.get(index) == null
      || playersList.get(index).isAi()) {
```

AI builds a command:

```
      Command command = ais[index].createCommand();
      if (command != null) {
```

The command is added to the rules engine:

```
        rules.addCommand(index, command);
```

Then converted to JSON and added to `jsonEpochCommands`:

```
        JsonObjectBuilder jsonCommand =
          jsonBuilderFactory.createObjectBuilder();
        command.toJson(jsonCommand);
        String priority = String.valueOf(index);
        jsonEpochCommands.add(priority,jsonCommand);
      }
    }
}
```

Finally, history is enlarged with the content of `jsonEpochCommands`:

```
synchronized(replay) {
    replay.add(jsonEpochCommands.build());
}
}
```

Following these operations, the commands of the future epoch are available, and with minimal locks.

Game over

For the end of the game, the stateUpdated() method detects it and orders the rules engine to stop:

```
public void stateUpdated(Rules rules) {
    State state = rules.getState();
    if (state.getGumCount() == 0) {
        rulesThread.stopRunning();
    }
    Characters chars = state.getChars();
    Pacman pacman = chars.getPacman();
    if (pacman != null && pacman.getStatus() == PacmanStatus.DEAD
      && pacman.getStatusTime() == 0) {
        rulesThread.stopRunning();
    }
}
```

Once the game is over, the thread is destroyed and the players deleted:

```
public void gameOver(Rules rules) {
    rulesThread = null;
    players.removeAll();
}
```

The Game class is then in an initial state, ready to restart a game with the start() method.

Services

The /player services are located in the PlayerService class. The implementation is similar, except for the use of the Players instance in the Game class.

The /game services are implemented in the GameService class: the get() method determines the state of the game via the isRunning() method of the Game class, and the put() method starts a game with the start() method.

The `/command` services are located in the `CommandService` class. The `get()` method returns all commands from a given epoch. This original behavior matches the needs of the client, who require all the commands from their current state to catch up with the server state. A `get()` method that returns only a command set for a single epoch is less efficient: several queries are then required to obtain several sets of commands. Knowing that it is much more interesting to obtain several small batches of data via a single request than via several requests, the proposed approach is more interesting. For example, if the latency of a query is approximately 100 milliseconds, retrieving 3 sets of commands then costs 300 milliseconds with 3 queries and 100 milliseconds with 1 grouped query. It works because the command sets have a low memory footprint.

⇒ Note: There is no verification mechanism: any player can pretend to be another, or disrupt the whole game. These mechanisms are not presented for the sake of clarity.

The services are stateless, in the spirit of REST, and the service manager and server do not need to be changed, except for small details. Indeed, the implementation in `sun.net.httpserver` uses a default delay to send HTTP responses. This is relevant for classic servers, but problematic for a real-time game. To disable it, you must modify the property at the very beginning of the program, in the `main()` function:

```
System.setProperty("sun.net.httpserver.nodelay","true");
```

6.3.4.2   Client implementation

For the implementation of the client-side multiplayer game, a `RemoteGameMode` class is defined. It is also close to the `PlayGameMode` class. The main difference lies in the path traveled by the commands. In the local case, the commands are sent directly to the local rules engine. In the multiplayer version, the commands are sent to the server. Then the client regularly looks if the server has new commands. If so, it executes them with its local rules engine, which triggers the resulting display.

Sending local commands

In the `handleInputs()` method, when an arrow is pressed, a direction command is sent to the server. However, this sending is not immediate: it is executed in a thread in the background. Otherwise, each press of an arrow causes a freeze due to the response time of the server. Besides, it is better to avoid sending a request if the previous one is not yet finished: this quickly leads to high resource consumption.

The Future pattern is used to handle these points. A `commandFuture` attribute of type `java.util.concurrent.Future` is used to track the execution of the query.

If there is no future or if the query is finished, it is then possible to look at the
keyboard and possibly execute a query:

```java
if (commandFuture == null || commandFuture.isDone()) {
  commandFuture = null;
  commandDirection = Direction.NONE;
  if (keyboard.isKeyPressed(KeyEvent.VK_RIGHT)) {
    commandDirection = Direction.EAST;
  }
  else if (keyboard.isKeyPressed(KeyEvent.VK_LEFT)){
    commandDirection = Direction.WEST;
  }
  else if (keyboard.isKeyPressed(KeyEvent.VK_DOWN)){
    commandDirection = Direction.SOUTH;
  }
  if (keyboard.isKeyPressed(KeyEvent.VK_UP)) {
    commandDirection = Direction.NORTH;
  }
```

If a direction is requested, the `sendCommand()` method is executed in the background using the default thread pool present in the virtual machine:

```java
  if (commandDirection != Direction.NONE) {
    commandFuture = ForkJoinPool.commonPool()
      .submit(new Runnable() {
        public void run() {
          sendCommand(commandDirection);
        }
      });
  }
}
```

The `sendCommand()` method builds the data required to send a PUT /command
request and then executes it:

```java
public void sendCommand(Direction direction) {
    JsonObjectBuilder builder =
        jsonBuilderFactory.createObjectBuilder();
    builder.add("priority", playerId-1);
    JsonObjectBuilder commandBuilder =
        jsonBuilderFactory.createObjectBuilder();
    Command command = new DirectionCommand(playerId-1,direction);
    command.toJson(commandBuilder);
    builder.add("command", commandBuilder.build());
    serviceQueries.put("/command", builder.build());
}
```

Recovery of server commands

When the mode is initialized, in the `init()` method, all available commands collected from the server are immediately executed. There is no observer or display, and the execution is as fast as possible. This initialization allows a new player to join the game, but also a player whose client has crashed or whose network connection has been interrupted to return to the game.

As the game progresses normally, a `scheduledCommands` command buffer is used. As long as it has commands that have not yet been executed, it is used to update the game. Then, when all the buffer commands have been used, a GET `/command/<next epoch>` query is executed. This one returns all the commands until the next epoch and then place them in the buffer. This strategy makes it possible to absorb the possible latencies of the network, regular or not. For example, if the network has a latency of 200 milliseconds, a duration much greater than an epoch (80 milliseconds), the game is generally 3 epochs late. With this strategy, the 3 epochs are retrieved in one query, e.g. 200 milliseconds. They are then executed as quickly as possible to catch up. With a strategy that retrieves orders epoch by epoch, it takes 3 queries and 600 milliseconds to recover them. Knowing that epochs are updated much faster, the client can never catch up with the server.

This policy is implemented in the `stateUpdating()` method called before an update of the game state. It starts with transmitting state change notifications to allow the rendering engine to display the current state:

```java
public void stateUpdating(Rules rules) {
    State state = rules.getState();
    synchronized(renderer) {
      epochDuration = state.getEpochDuration();
      beginEpoch = System.nanoTime();
      cachedStateObserver.dispatchEvents(renderer);
      cachedStateObserver.clearEvents();
    }
```

The following lines ask the server for the next batch of commands, as long as the buffer is empty or if all the commands it contains was used. The `currentScheduledCommand` attribute is the index of the next command in the buffer:

```java
    while(scheduledCommands == null || currentScheduledCommand >=
            scheduledCommands.size()) {
```

The GET `/command` request is executed:

```java
        JsonObject response = serviceQueries.get(
            "/command", state.getEpoch()+1);
```

If the command has failed, the game is over, or the server has crashed, and there are no more commands to recover:

```java
if (response == null) {
    return;
}
```

If the request is successful, commands from the next epoch are retrieved:

```java
scheduledCommands = response.getJsonArray("commands");
currentScheduledCommand = 0;
```

If the next epoch has not yet occurred, the commands buffer is empty. In this case, the loop resumes, and a new request is sent.

```java
}
```

The end of the method adds the commands for the next epoch to the rules engine:

```java
JsonObject commands = scheduledCommands.getJsonObject(
        currentScheduledCommand);
commands.entrySet().forEach((pairs) -> {
    int priority = Integer.parseInt(pairs.getKey());
    Command command = Command.fromJson(
        pairs.getValue().asJsonObject());
    rules.addCommand(priority, command);
}
currentScheduledCommand ++;
}
```

Apart from sending commands to the server and then receiving them, there are no other changes to make. The diagrams in this example are available in the "Class Diagrams/chap06/network03" folder of the sample UML project. The code is present in the "examples/chap06/network03" folder of the Java sample project.

6.3.4.3 Improvements

Two-way messages

The latency can be halved if the server sends itself the new commands. A simple but less efficient approach to do this is to make each client a server. Another more expensive but much more cost-effective approach is to develop the network aspects at the socket level and exploit their ability to bidirectionally. Exercise 3.5.1 presents an example of two-way communication using UDP.

Predictions

Latency can also be reduced if the local player's commands are immediately implemented without waiting for the server to return. For this to work, it is also necessary to predict the commands of the other players. If the prediction is wrong, a rollback when receiving the real commands restore the common state. These rollbacks are not annoying if they are rare: they lead to small character "jumps". Otherwise, the user experience may be particularly lowered. To compute predictions, the most common approach is to use an AI to choose a command for other players, until their real commands arrive.

Checksums

The command exchange approach works if all machines have a rules engine that makes the same changes based on the commands. The slightest difference can quickly lead to totally different states and a total loss of synchronization between the machines. It is usually the result of bugs, which are in many cases very difficult to detect.

One solution to prevent these problems is to compute a checksum for each state of each machine. If a machine has a checksum different from the others, it's because a bug has changed the behavior of the rules engine. It may be due to chance, which can be corrected by going back to the last valid state, then running all the commands again, hoping that luck does the rest. If not, we can only warn the players and report the case to the development team to identify the cause.

Concerning algorithms, the Cyclic Redundancy Check (CRC) is quite suitable: it is reliable and very fast. There are no security aspects, algorithms like MD5 or SHA are not needed. Also, it is encouraged to use algorithms that can combine multiple checksums. Indeed, recalculating the checksum over the entire state at each update can be particularly expensive in computations. In this area, the Merkle tree approaches allow the CRC calculation to be distributed according to a tree structure.

6.3.5 Exercises

6.3.5.1 Exercise 3.5.1: Multiplayer with UDP

→ Implement a game with 4 players, each with a color and a position in a window. A possible display can be the following:

A different machine leads each player on the network. At each direction command of a player, a UDP message is sent to a server. The server, meanwhile, constantly sends the position of all players to all machines.

To initialize the game, imagine a simple procedure that allows a player to ask if there is a place left. If so, the server responds positively by assigning a playable color.

UDP with the standard Java library

To communicate over the network with the UDP protocol, you first have to open a UDP socket, represented by the `DatagramSocket` class of the `java.net` package. To do this, several possibilities:

- Open a socket on any port with the constructor without arguments: this is what is usually done by the clients.
- Open a socket on a specific port with the constructor with an argument, for example `new DatagramSocket(8000)`. It is done by the server, whose port should be known to clients.

Once a socket is open, it is possible to send data with the `send()` method. Beforehand, you need to form a data packet, using the `DatagramPacket` class. It requires an array of bytes, its size, the address, and the destination port. Here is a simple example where only one byte is sent:

```
InetAddress address = InetAddress.getByName("localhost");
int port = 8000;
byte[] outputData = new byte[1];
outputData[0] = 23;
DatagramPacket outputPacket = new DatagramPacket (outputData,
    outputData.length, address, port);
socket.send(outputPacket);
```

Similarly, it is possible to receive data with the `receive()` method. The call to this method blocks until a packet is received. After the call, it is possible to know the address and port of the machine that sent the package:

```
byte[] inputData = new byte[1024];
DatagramPacket inputPacket =
    new DatagramPacket(inputData,inputData.length);
socket.receive(inputPacket);
InetAddress address = inputPacket.getAddress();
int port = inputPacket.getPort();
```

6.3.5.2   Exercise 3.5.2: Local stateless multiplayer

The goal of this exercise is to make a network game without duplicating a complete game state on each machine. In this case, each player on each machine only sees and manipulates a subset of the game state. It is only possible if the game allows it, where each screen does not require a large amount of information. It is often the case with economy games, where screens are composed of information about a particular structure, such as a country or a city.

For this exercise, the case of a universe is considered. Several screens are possible:

- The view of the universe, which presents the list of galaxies: only the names of galaxies are required;
- The view of a galaxy, which presents its systems: only the names, positions and connections of the systems are required;
- The view of a system, which presents its planets: only the names of the planets are required;
- The view of a planet, which presents its constructions: only the list of buildings is required.

→ Implement HTTP REST services to manage universe and galaxy views. Other views use the same principles: you can also implement them if it helps you better understand.

No display is expected, only a server with services and unit tests. It is possible to start with the classes in the "pacman/server" folder of the Pacman sample game. It is also possible to use the code in the folder "examples/chap02/stellaris" for the representation of galaxies.

The expected solution must be as versatile as possible. For example, the service management system must be dynamically programmable during execution, as is the case for services in the example with Pacman.

The following paragraphs describe possible services.

CRUD services on galaxies

- GET /galaxy: returns the list of galaxies with names and number of systems, for example:

```
{
    "1": {
        "name": "Milky Way",
        "systems": 2,
        "path": "/galaxy/1"
    }
    "3": {
        "name": "Andromeda",
        "systems": 0,
        "path": "/galaxy/3"
    }
}
```

  The items in the list above also contain a "path" attribute. This attribute has a path that allows you to manipulate the element. For example, "/galaxy/1" is the path to manipulate the first galaxy. It is a common practice in HTTP REST and allows the user to know valid paths without having to compute them.

- GET /galaxy/<id>: returns information about the galaxy <id>, for example:

```
{
    "name": "Milky Way",
    "systems": {
        "1": {
            "name": "Solar",
            "x": 10,
            "y": 50,
            "planets": 2,
            "path": "/galaxy/1/system/1"
        }
        "3": {
            "name": "Alpha Centauri B",
```

```
            "x": 200,
            "y": 30,
            "planets": 2,
            "path": "/galaxy/1/system/3"
        }
    }
}
```

There is more information than in the previous case, and enough for a screen that presents a galaxy. We find a path for each element of a list, for example "/galaxy/1/system/3" allows us to manipulate the identifier system "3" of the galaxy identifier "1".

- PUT /galaxy: adds a galaxy.

  The only data expected in the input is the name of the galaxy. Other data, such as systems, is added via other services.

- POST /galaxy/<id>: changes the name of a galaxy.

- DELETE /galaxy/<id>: deletes a galaxy.

CRUD services on the systems of a galaxy

- GET /galaxy/<id>/system: returns information about the systems of galaxy <id>. It is close to /galaxy/<id> but restricted to system information:

```
{
    "1": {
        "name": "Solar",
        "x": 10,
        "y": 50,
        "planets": 0,
        "path": "/galaxy/1/system/1"
    },
    "3": {
        "name": "Alpha Centauri B",
        "x": 200,
        "y": 30,
        "planets": 0,
        "path": "/galaxy/1/system/3"
    }
}
```

- GET/galaxy/<id1>/system/<id2>: returns information about the <id2> system of galaxy <id1>.

There is a little more information than in the previous case, for example with the list of planets:

```
{
    "name": "Solar",
    "x": 10,
    "y": 50,
    "path": "/ galaxy/1/system/1",
    "planets": {
        "1": {
            "name": "Earth",
            "type": "Habitable",
            "path": "/ galaxy/1/system/1/planet/1"
        }
        "2": {
            "name": "Jupiter",
            "type": "Gaseous",
            "path": "/ galaxy/1/system/1/planet/2"
        }
    }
}
```

- `PUT/galaxy/<id>/system`: add a system.

- `POST/galaxy/<id1>/system/<id2>`: change the information of a system (name and position)

- `DELETE/galaxy/<id1>/system/<id2>`: delete a system

6.3.6 Video game development: Network gaming

Fast action games and UDP/IP

Network gaming depends on the nature of the game. For very fast real-time games, such as FPS or fighting games, UDP/IP is recommended. In these cases, the server constantly sends packets to clients with a complete copy of the game state. For this to be possible, it is required that the state of the game is small, ideally small enough to enter an Ethernet packet (1500 bytes minus the headers). These cases are still quite rare, even for a real-time game like Pacman, it is not necessarily relevant.

Real-time, turn-based games and TCP/IP

For most games, but also for other networking aspects of games such as team creation, it is best to use TCP/IP. This one can manage the order and the loss of packets. Then, the most common synchronization solution is to rely on the command pattern. Thanks to this one, it is not necessary to send all the game state. Besides, humans create these commands: the size and number of commands can not be important, which allows the handling of tens of thousands of players per server. An alternative is to send some "diff" between states, like the `Action` classes in the Pacman sample game, or the notifications sent to the rendering engine. These solutions are debated, depending on the case.

Slow games and partial state

Some games do not necessarily need to have all the data of the game state to be played. It is the case of economy games that looks more like an Excel game than a usual game, like Galactic Civilization. In these cases, each player doesn't need to have a full copy of the game state. It suffices for each screen to have the required data. For example, when viewing a planet from a solar system, only the data for that planet is needed. When viewing a galaxy, only the positions and names of the systems are needed. To implement these cases, ask the server for the data needed for the current screen. For commands, things remain unchanged: when the user sends a command, which is the result of several clicks through various menus and options, the server receives it and changes the game state. Then, the clients receive the necessary data for the current screen.

Protocol and web API

It is necessary to define how network exchanges are operated. In other words, it is necessary to define a protocol, and an API adapted to this context. In this chapter, an HTTP REST approach is chosen for its many qualities. It is possible to rely more or less on existing protocols since only a specific batch of operations is required. In the case of the Pacman sample game, they are implemented in the `Service` class on the server side and in the `ServiceQueries` class on the client side. Both are used independently of the exploited protocols, almost as if the methods of `ServiceQueries` had their equivalent in `Service`.

It can be risky if you plan to create your personal protocol. The many subtle choices within existing protocols handle many network problems: it is hard to predict them all when you are not a network expert. Besides, we must also think about the security aspects. It is a shame to lose players when the game starts to be successful: the number usually attracts bad intentions, which can lead to network attacks. Using an existing protocol, such as HTTP, you can run an existing server (like

Apache) to immediately and easily benefit from a good base of security features. With a home protocol, it is necessary to implement everything, which requires large means.

Format of transmitted data

As far as network communication aspects are concerned, one last choice concerns the format of the data. In the above example, the JSON format was chosen. This format widely used in the field of networks, and meets many specifications. Another popular format is XML. It is more robust but has a larger memory footprint. The YAML format is more and more used. This one looks like a compact version of the JSON. It is less robust but offers a smaller memory footprint.

All these formats can be blamed for their memory footprint and coding/decoding time that is higher than a binary format. These points are to be put in perspective with the rest of the chain. If the processing time of a command by the rules engine is significantly higher than the decoding time of commands in XML or YAML, there is no point in spending energy to pass to a binary format. Similarly, if reducing the memory footprint of serialized commands can solve network bandwidth problems, it may be interesting to switch to a binary format.

One-way and bidirectional communication

In the examples used in this chapter to illustrate the different principles, the communications are unidirectional. Only the client can send requests to the server. The server can not notify the client of a change, and the client must constantly check the server to see if something has happened. This approach is simple and easy to implement, especially if you use the HTTP protocol which is implemented in many free servers. The drawback of this approach lies in the induced latency: to the time of transfer of data from the server to the client, we must add that of sending a request from the client to the server. For all not real-time games, this is not a problem. For slow real-time games, everything is fine as long as network latency is low (up to 50 milliseconds, possibly 80 milliseconds). In other cases, this can be problematic for the user experience.

The solution is to use bidirectional communications where the server can also send messages on its own. In this area, there are no or few free and well maintained libraries. It is necessary to implement a solution yourself by working at the socket level. This level of programming is the lowest that can be achieved in a general application: below, it is system programming, related to the hardware and the operating system used. Using a bidirectional approach, there are also synchronization issues, since each client can be interrupted by server messages. The port access must also be managed, which is now quite simple thanks to the functionalities found in most operating systems.

Once the various choices are made, it is time to move on to class design and implementation. If the concurrent execution work of the first section of this chapter is well done, the synchronization aspects should not be a problem.

6.4　Exercise solutions

6.4.1　Exercise 1.3.1: Parallelize the exhaustive search for collisions

A solution is proposed in the folder "examples/chap06/collisions01mt", and unit tests in the class "ExhaustiveColliderMTTest" in the "examples/chap06/collisions" folder of the test packages. The `ExhaustiveColliderMT` class implements the `Collider` interface defined in the "examples/chap06/collisions" folder. It contains a list of `boxes` to use for the search of collisions.

To parallelize the search, the list of bounding boxes is divided into several chunks, each chunk being processed by a thread:

```java
public List<AABB> collides(AABB aabb) {
```

The `chunkSize` variable sets the size of a chunk in the list. It is divided by 16 to obtain a number a little larger than the number of threads on the most powerful machines:

```java
int chunkSize = boxes.size()/16;
```

This division value does not mean that 16 threads are used: it depends on the thread pool used.

The `chunkIndex` variable contains the index of the first box for the next chunk:

```java
int chunkIndex = 0;
```

A list of futures is defined to track the result of the parallel tasks that are submitted:

```java
ArrayList<Future<List<AABB>>> futures = new ArrayList();
```

As long as all chunks in the list are not scheduled for processing:

```java
while (chunkIndex < boxes.size()) {
```

Computation of the indices of the next chunk:

```java
    int fromIndex = chunkIndex;
    int toIndex = chunkIndex + chunkSize;
    if (toIndex >= boxes.size()) {
        toIndex = boxes.size();
    }
```

Extract the next chunk from the list of boxes:

```
List<AABB> subList = boxes.subList(fromIndex, toIndex);
```

Chunk processing is submitted to the default thread pool in the JVM. The future returned is stored in the `futures` list:

```
futures.add(ForkJoinPool.commonPool()
    .submit(new ColliderThread(subList, aabb)));
```

The `ColliderThread` class implements `Callable<List<AABB>>` and performs an exhaustive search for collisions in the box chunk.

```
chunkIndex += chunkSize;
}
```

The end of the method retrieves and merges the sublists of boxes colliding with the candidate box:

```
ArrayList<AABB> result = new ArrayList<AABB>();
for (Future<List<AABB>> future : futures) {
    try {
```

The `get()` method of `Future` class is waiting for the process to complete before responding:

```
        List<AABB> subResult = future.get();
        for (AABB box : subResult) {
            result.add(box);
        }
    } catch (Exception ex) {
        throw new RuntimeException();
    }
}
return result;
}
```

The parallel implementation is validated with the `ExhaustiveColliderMTTest` class in the 'examples/chap06/collisions01' folder of the test packages:

```
public void testExhaustiveColliderMT() {
    ArrayList<AABB> boxes = new ArrayList();
    Random random = new Random();
    for (int i=0;i<1000000;i++) {
        int x0 = 50+random.nextInt(600);
        int y0 = 50+random.nextInt(400);
        int x1 = x0+10+random.nextInt(100);
        int y1 = y0+10+random.nextInt(100);
        boxes.add(new AABB(x0,y0,x1,y1));
    }
```

```
int x0 = 50+random.nextInt(600);
int y0 = 50+random.nextInt(400);
int x1 = x0+10+random.nextInt(100);
int y1 = y0+10+random.nextInt(100);
AABB aabb = new AABB(x0,y0,x1,y1);
List<AABB> result1 =
  new ExhaustiveCollider(boxes).collides(aabb);
List<AABB> result2 =
  new ExhaustiveColliderMT(boxes).collides(aabb);
assertEquals(result1, result2);
}
```

6.4.2   Exercise 1.3.2: Parallelize the indexed search for collisions

A solution is proposed in the "examples/chap06/collisions01mt" folder and unit
tests in the `TreeColliderMTTest` class in the "examples/chap06/collisions" folder
of the test packages. The `TreeColliderMT` class implements the `Collider` interface
defined in the "examples/chap06/collisions" folder. It contains a `root` attribute
of type `TreeColliderNode` that references the root of a binary tree to search for
bounding boxes. Its `collides()` method starts by making a synchronized version of
a list of boxes in collisions. The synchronization property allows you to manipulate
the list from different threads safely:

```
public List<AABB> collides(AABB aabb) {
    List<AABB> result =
        Collections.synchronizedList(new ArrayList());
```

The processing implemented through the `TreeColliderTask` class is submitted to
the default thread pool in the JVM:

```
    ForkJoinPool.commonPool().invoke(
        new TreeColliderTask(result,root,aabb,0));
    return result;
}
```

The `TreeColliderTask` class represents an explored node in the binary tree of
bounding boxes. It contains :

- A `node` attribute that references the corresponding node in the binary tree;
- A `depth` attribute that contains its depth in the tree;
- An `aabb` attribute that references the candidate box to collide;
- A `result` attribute to store the boxes colliding with `aabb`.

The `compute()` method of `TreeColliderTask` runs the parallel computation. It uses
methods of the `RecursiveAction` class of the `java.util.concurrent` package:

```java
protected void compute() {
```

If the node is a leaf, we can compare the candidate box with that of the node: if they collide, we must add it to the result list:

```java
if (node.isLeaf()) {
    if (node.getAabb().collides(aabb)) {
        result.add(node.getAabb());
    }
}
```

If the depth is large enough, it is best to stop paralleling. In the opposite case, the tasks are too inexpensive in computation for the parallelization to be interesting:

```java
else if (depth >= 10) {
    node.collides(result, aabb);
}
else {
```

If the node is not a leaf, we look at whether it is colliding with the candidate box. If this is not the case, it is not necessary to continue:

```java
if (!node.getAabb().collides(aabb)) {
    return;
}
```

Two new tasks are created: one to explore the subtree on the left, and the other for subtree on the right:

```java
TreeColliderTask leftTask = new TreeColliderTask(result,
        node.getLeftChild(),aabb,depth+1);
TreeColliderTask rightTask = new TreeColliderTask(result,
        node.getRightChild(),aabb,depth+1);
```

The left task is executed in another thread:

```java
leftTask.fork();
```

The task on the right is executed in the current thread:

```java
rightTask.compute();
```

Finally, we wait for the end of the left task:

```java
leftTask.join();
    }
}
```

The parallel implementation is validated with the `TreeColliderMTTest` class in the 'examples/chap06/collisions02mt' folder of the test packages:

```java
public void testTreeColliderMT() {
    ArrayList<AABB> boxes = new ArrayList();
```

```java
    Random random = new Random();
    for (int i=0;i<10000;i++) {
        int x0 = 50+random.nextInt(600);
        int y0 = 50+random.nextInt(400);
        int x1 = x0+10+random.nextInt(100);
        int y1 = y0+10+random.nextInt(100);
        boxes.add(new AABB(x0,y0,x1,y1));
    }
    int x0 = 50+random.nextInt(600);
    int y0 = 50+random.nextInt(400);
    int x1 = x0+10+random.nextInt(100);
    int y1 = y0+10+random.nextInt(100);
    AABB aabb = new AABB(x0,y0,x1,y1);
    List<AABB> result1 = new TreeCollider(boxes).collides(aabb);
    List<AABB> result2 =
        new TreeColliderMT(boxes).collides(aabb);
    assertEquals(result1.size(),result2.size());
    for (AABB box: result1) {
        assertTrue(result2.contains(box));
    }
}
```

6.4.3   Exercise 2.3.1: Creating a chat with sockets

A solution is proposed in the folder "examples/chap06/chat". To test it, you first need to run the `Server` class and then the `Client` class. Entering a phrase in the console sends a message to the other. Entering the word "bye" terminates the conversation.

Aside from using a server-side `ServerSocket`, both classes do the same thing. For example, the client initializes its socket in the constructor with a given address and port:

```java
socket = new Socket(InetAddress.getByName(ip),port);
```

Then, it creates a `PrintWriter` to send data on the socket:

```java
outputWriter = new PrintWriter(socket.getOutputStream());
```

A `BufferedReader` is created for receiving data:

```java
inputReader = new BufferedReader(
    new InputStreamReader(socket.getInputStream()));
```

Two threads are built and run: `listenThread` to receive messages, and `sendThread` to send messages:

```java
Thread listenThread = new ListenThread();
Thread sendThread = new SendThread();
listenThread.start();
sendThread.start();
listenThread.join();
sendThread.join();
```

The receiving thread is waiting for a line to be received. Then, if this line is not empty and is not equal to "bye", it is displayed:

```java
public class ListenThread extends Thread {
public void run() {
    try {
        while(true) {
            String message = inputReader.readLine();
            if (message == null || message.equals("bye")) {
                System.out.println("End of server connection");
                break;
            }
            System.out.println("Server>"+message);
        }
        socket.close();
    }
    catch(SocketException ex) {
    }
    catch (IOException ex) {
    }
}
}
```

Note that among exception cases, the exception SocketException is captured, while no method declares it. It can still happen when the socket is closed: this is a way to know that the connection is complete.

The sending thread enters a line at the console, which is equivalent to asking the user to enter words followed by the enter key. Then, the seized message is sent by writing in the output stream of the socket:

```java
public class SendThread extends Thread {
public void run() {
    try {
        Scanner userInput = new Scanner(System.in);
        while(true) {
            String message = userInput.nextLine();
            outputWriter.println(message);
            outputWriter.flush();
            if (message.equals("bye"))
```

```
                break;
        }
        socket.close();
    }
    catch(SocketException ex) {
    }
    catch (IOException ex) {
    }
  }
}
```

6.4.4   Exercise 2.3.2: Implementing a nano HTTP server

A solution is proposed in the folder "examples/chap06/nanohttpserver". Unit tests are offered in the same folder in the test packages.

This solution uses the implementation of the Producer/Consumer pattern in the `pacman.mt` package. It is formed by the following elements:

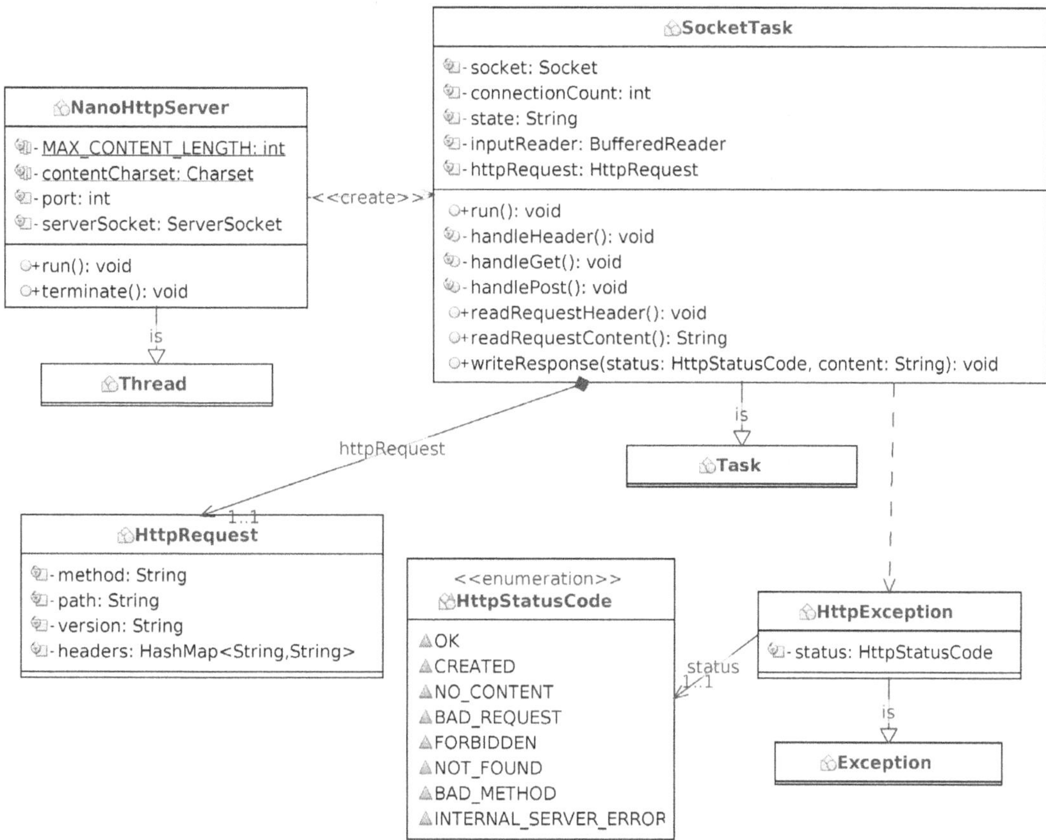

- `NanoHttpServer` class: main thread, waiting for new connections. As soon as a new connection is established, it submits a `SocketTask` to the production queue.
- `SocketTask` class: A task executed by the task manager, initially in the production queue, to decode the HTTP header. Once this header is decoded, it is transferred into the consumption queue to process the request.
- `HttpRequest` class: Contains the information of a HTTP header.
- `HttpStatusCode` enumeration: lists HTTP status codes. Allows to obtain the number (like OK => 200) as well as textual representation.
- `HttpException` class: exception that contains an HTTP status code and message.

NanoHttpServer class

The core of this class is in its `run()` method:

```
public void run() {
```

It starts by creating a `ServerSocket` on the selected port:

```
try {
    serverSocket = new ServerSocket(port);
} catch (IOException ex) {
    System.out.println("Error when creating the socket. "
        +"Does the port "+port+" is free ?");
    return;
}
```

The `connectionCount` variable allows for numbering the connections. This numbering is used to identify the connections:

```
int connectionCount = 0;
```

As long as the thread is not interrupted, a connection is expected:

```
while(!interrupted()) {
```

Two cases of errors are considered: if it is a `SocketException`, the `serverSocket` has been closed, it is necessary to stop the server. For `IOException`, there is an unwanted problem that prevents new connections from being obtained:

```
    Socket socket;
    try {
        socket = serverSocket.accept();
    } catch (SocketException ex) {
        break;
    } catch (IOException ex) {
        System.out.println("Error waiting for a new connection");
        break;
    }
```

A new `SocketTask` task is produced and submitted to the production queue:

```
    Task task = new SocketTask(socket,connectionCount++);
    try {
        TaskManager.getInstance()
            .addProducerTask(task);
    } catch (InterruptedException ex) {
        interrupt();
    }
}
}
```

Note that with a finished-size production queue, if the queue is full, the job is not added, and the thread is asleep until a place is released. It helps protect against overload attacks.

SocketTask class: run() method

The run() method of the SocketTask class is called by the task manager when it joins a processing queue. To be able to move it from the production queue to that of consumption, it uses the State pattern. The state attribute contains the state in which an instance of this class is located: if null, it is an initial state that requires an analysis of the HTTP header. If state is equal to 'GET', then the task must process a method with the same name, and likewise for 'POST':

```
public void run() {
try {
    if (state == null) {
        handleHeader();
    }
    else if (state.equals("GET")) {
        handleGet();
    }
    else if (state.equals("POST")) {
        handlePost();
    }
```

If the state is not correct, a HttpException with INTERNAL_SERVER_ERROR is thrown. When caught, it leads to a HTTP response with this code and the associated message:

```
    else {
        throw new HttpException(HttpStatusCode.INTERNAL_SERVER_ERROR,
            state);
    }
```

Everything went well, the task is over:

```
    return;
```

The following lines handle several error cases. There are many problems to deal with network communications; the minimum is proposed here. The first error case is the interception of an HttpException, which uses the writeResponse() method to produce a response with the status and the message contained in the exception:

```
} catch (HttpException ex) {
    try {
        writeResponse(ex.getStatus(),ex.getMessage());
```

```java
    } catch (IOException ex2) {
    }
```

The following errors are not expected to occur unless there is a bug. A message is displayed to help identify problems:

```java
} catch (SocketException ex) {
    System.out.println("Connection lost with client "
        +connectionCount);
} catch (IOException ex) {
    System.out.println("Error when communicating with client "
        +connectionCount);
} catch (Exception ex) {
    System.out.println("Error with client "
        +connectionCount);
}
```

At this point, something caused an error: a response with a INTERNAL_SERVER_ERROR status and no message:

```java
try {
    writeResponse(HttpStatusCode.INTERNAL_SERVER_ERROR);
} catch (IOException ex) {
}
}
```

SocketTask class: handleHeader() method

```java
private void handleHeader() throws IOException,
    InterruptedException, HttpException
{
```

This method begins by decoding the header with the readRequestHeader() method. The latter fills the httpRequest attribute with the properties of the HTTP header:

```java
readRequestHeader();
```

According to the HTTP method, the current task (this) changes state via the state attribute, then moves to the consumption queue:

```java
TaskManager taskManager = TaskManager.getInstance();
String method = httpRequest.getMethod();
if (method.equals("GET")) {
    state = "GET";
    taskManager.addConsumerTask(this);
}
else if (method.equals("POST")) {
    state = "POST";
```

```
    taskManager.addConsumerTask(this);
}
else {
```

Other types of methods are not supported, and the result is BAD_METHOD:

```
    throw new HttpException(HttpStatusCode.BAD_METHOD,
        "Invalid method "+method);
}
}
```

SocketTask class: handleGet() method

This method performs a process to illustrate and test the HTTP GET method, which does not use data in the query and returns data in the response:

```
private void handleGet() throws IOException {
String message;
```

If the path is "/testget", the message "Test GET passed" is returned. This path is used in unit tests:

```
if (httpRequest.getPath().equals("/testget")) {
    message = "Test GET passed";
}
```

Otherwise, the message is "Successful execution":

```
else {
    message = "Successful execution";
}
```

The writeResponse() method is used to return the message with the OK state:

```
writeResponse(HttpStatusCode.OK, message);
System.out.println("End of connection with client "
    +connectionCount);
}
```

SocketTask class: handlePost() method

This method is an example of POST processing, which uses data in the query and does not return data in the response:

```
private void handlePost() throws IOException,HttpException {
```

The readRequestContent() method decodes the data that accompanies the query:

```java
String content = readRequestContent();
if (content == null) {
    throw new HttpException(
        HttpStatusCode.BAD_REQUEST, "No content");
}
```

If the path is "/testpost", the content must be "x=1,y=2". This path is used in unit tests:

```java
if (httpRequest.getPath().equals("/testpost")) {
    if (!content.equals("x=1,y=2")) {
        throw new HttpException(HttpStatusCode.BAD_REQUEST,
            "Invalid content");
    }
}
```

For other paths, the content is displayed in the server console:

```java
else {
    System.out.println(content);
}
```

A response with status `NO_CONTENT` is returned (without data):

```java
writeResponse(HttpStatusCode.NO_CONTENT);
System.out.println("End of connection with client "
    +connectionCount);
}
```

SocketTask class: readRequestHeader() method

The `readRequestHeader()` method decodes the information from the HTTP header from the input stream of the socket and fills the `httpRequest` attribute accordingly:

```java
private void readRequestHeader()
    throws IOException, HttpException {
```

A `BufferedReader` is open on the input stream of the socket:

```java
inputReader = new BufferedReader(new InputStreamReader(
        socket.getInputStream(),NanoHttpServer.contentCharset));
```

The first line is read:

```java
String line = inputReader.readLine();
if (line == null || line.isEmpty()) {
    throw new HttpException(HttpStatusCode.BAD_REQUEST);
}
```

The format of the first line has 3 parts: The method, the URI, and the version:

```
String[] parts = line.split(" ");
if (parts.length != 3) {
    throw new HttpException(HttpStatusCode.BAD_REQUEST);
}
httpRequest.setMethod(parts[0]);
httpRequest.setPath(parts[1]);
httpRequest.setVersion(parts[2]);
```

The following lines of the input stream are read:

```
while (true) {
    line = inputReader.readLine();
```

A null line means that there is nothing left on the stream, and an empty line that data follows the headers:

```
    if (line == null || line.isEmpty())
        break;
```

The header fields have the format <name>:<value>:

```
    int index = line.indexOf(':');
    if (index < 0) {
        throw new IOException();
    }
    String name = line.substring(0, index).trim();
    String value = line.substring(index+1).trim();
    httpRequest.setHeader(name,value);
}
}
```

SocketTask class: readRequestContent() method

The readRequestContent() method decodes the query data into a String:

```
private String readRequestContent()
    throws HttpException {
```

The procedure followed is based on the existence of a Content-Length header field. The protocol does not impose it in all situations, and the present solution handles the simplest cases:

```
String contentLength = httpRequest.getHeader("Content-Length");
if (contentLength == null) {
    return null;
}
```

If the size of the data is too large, the request is rejected. It is a recommended protection to avoid overloading the server memory:

```
int contentSize = Integer.parseInt(contentLength);
if (contentSize >= NanoHttpServer.MAX_CONTENT_LENGTH) {
    throw new HttpException(HttpStatusCode.BAD_REQUEST,
        "Content too large");
}
```

The data is read from the input stream of the socket and then converted to `String`:

```
try {
    char[] buffer = new char[contentSize];
    inputReader.read(buffer);
    return new String(buffer);
} catch (IOException ex) {
    return null;
}
}
}
```

SocketTask class: writeResponse() method

The `writeResponse()` method sends the header and any data of the response to the output stream of the socket:

```
public void writeResponse(HttpStatusCode status,
String content) throws IOException {
```

The first line is formed here, with the format `<Version> <Status> <Description>`:

```
StringBuilder headerBuilder = new StringBuilder();
headerBuilder.append("HTTP/1.1 ");
headerBuilder.append(String.valueOf(status.getCode()));
headerBuilder.append(" ");
headerBuilder.append(status.toString());
headerBuilder.append("\n");
```

A `Content-Type` header field is added to indicate that the data is plain text in UTF8:

```
headerBuilder.append("Content-Type: text/plain; charset=utf-8\n"
);
```

If there is data, it must be converted into an array of bytes, and add a header field `Content-Length` with the size in bytes (NB: not in character count!):

```
byte[] contentBytes = null;
if (content != null && !content.isEmpty()) {
    contentBytes = content.getBytes(NanoHttpServer.contentCharset);
    headerBuilder.append("Content-Length: ");
    headerBuilder.append(String.valueOf(contentBytes.length));
    headerBuilder.append("\n");
```

```
    headerBuilder.append("\n");
}
```

The header is converted into an array of bytes and sent via the output stream of the socket:

```
String header = headerBuilder.toString();
byte[] headerBytes =
    header.getBytes(NanoHttpServer.contentCharset);
socket.getOutputStream().write(headerBytes);
```

Likewise, for the data, if it is present:

```
if (contentBytes != null) {
    socket.getOutputStream().write(contentBytes);
}
```

Processing is complete, and the connection can be completed:

```
socket.close();
}
```

6.4.5 Exercise 3.5.1: Multiplayer with UDP

A solution is proposed in the folder "examples/chap06/udp".

Message format

To distinguish the nature of the messages, a very simple format is established:

- The first byte of the message is a code that defines the nature of the message;
- If the first byte of the message is 0: it is a message to request a new place in the game. The message in response always contains only one byte: the index of the place if there remains one, or 255;
- If the first byte of the message is 1: the rest of the message contains the coordinates of only one player;
- If the first byte of the message is 2: the rest of the message contains the coordinates of all the players.

These codes are represented by the variables in `MessageCode` enumeration.

Server implementation

The server contains a `Player` class with attributes to hold a player's information:

```
class Player {
    public boolean present = false;
    public InetAddress address;
    public int port;
    public int[] coords = new int[2];
}
```

During initialization, a socket is opened on a particular port. It is then used throughout the program:

```
try {
  socket = new DatagramSocket(8000);
} catch (SocketException ex) {
  System.out.println(
    "Error when opening socket. The port is free ?");
  return;
}
```

Two threads are then launched in the background: the first to receive requests, and the other to continuously send the coordinates of the players.

Server - Listening Thread

The listener thread loops the following lines. It begins by waiting for a packet to be received:

```
byte[] inputData = new byte[1024];
DatagramPacket inputPacket =
    new DatagramPacket(inputData,inputData.length);
socket.receive(inputPacket);
```

Once a packet is received, the address and port of the player who sent it are retrieved. This information is used to find the player in the player list with the findPlayer() method:

```
InetAddress playerAddress = inputPacket.getAddress();
int playerPort = inputPacket.getPort();
int playerIndex = findPlayer(playerAddress, playerPort);
```

To decode the received data, a DataInputStream is created: it reads byte by byte, int by int, etc:

```
ByteArrayInputStream bis = new ByteArrayInputStream(inputData);
DataInputStream dis = new DataInputStream(bis);
```

The first byte of the message is decoded and determines the nature of the message:

```
byte messageCode = dis.readByte();
if (messageCode==MessageCode.NEW_PLAYER.getCode()) {
```

A new player in the game is requested. If the player is not found with his address
and his port, a new player slot is searched with the findFreePlayer() method:

```java
if (playerIndex < 0) {
    playerIndex = findFreePlayer();
}
```

A one-byte response is constructed. If there is no more room, the value 255 is placed
in the response. Otherwise, the index of the new player is put in the response, and
the information of the new player is stored in the list of players:

```java
byte[] outputData = new byte[1];
if (playerIndex < 0) {
    outputData[0] = (byte)255;
}
else {
    players[playerIndex].present = true;
    players[playerIndex].address = playerAddress;
    players[playerIndex].port = playerPort;
    outputData[0] = (byte)playerIndex;
}
```

The response is sent:

```java
DatagramPacket outputPacket = new DatagramPacket(outputData,
        outputData.length,playerAddress,playerPort);
socket.send(outputPacket);
}
```

If the message contains the coordinates of a player, they are updated in the list of
players. There is no expected response for this case:

```java
else if (messageCode == MessageCode.PLAYER_COORD.getCode()) {
    synchronized(this) {
        players[playerIndex].coords[0] = dis.readInt();
        players[playerIndex].coords[1] = dis.readInt();
    }
}
```

Server - Sending thread

The sending thread repeats the following lines, ensuring that they take place
60 times per second (using the same approaches as for the synchronized display). It starts by building data that contains the coordinates of all the players. A
DataOutputStream is used to be able to write byte by byte easily:

```java
byte[] outputData;
synchronized(this) {
```

```java
ByteArrayOutputStream bos = new ByteArrayOutputStream();
DataOutputStream dos = new DataOutputStream(bos);
dos.writeByte(MessageCode.PLAYER_COORDS.getCode());
for (int i=0;i<players.length;i++) {
    dos.writeInt(players[i].coords[0]);
    dos.writeInt(players[i].coords[1]);
}
outputData = bos.toByteArray();
}
```

The same data is sent to each player present in the game:

```java
for (int i=0;i<players.length;i++) {
    if (!players[i].present)
        continue;
    InetAddress playerAddress = players[i].address;
    int playerPort = players[i].port;
    DatagramPacket outputPacket = new DatagramPacket(outputData,
            outputData.length,playerAddress,playerPort);
    socket.send(outputPacket);
}
```

Client implementation

The client makes a `JFrame` with a canvas to display four colored dots as in the
screenshot in the description of the exercise.

It also starts by opening a socket, but without a particular port. This one is used
throughout the program. Then, a message is sent to the server to get a player slot
in the game:

```java
byte[] inputData = new byte[1];
inputData[0] = MessageCode.NEW_PLAYER.getCode();
DatagramPacket inputPacket = new DatagramPacket(
 inputData,inputData.length,serverAddress,serverPort);
socket.send(inputPacket);
```

A response is expected from the server:

```java
byte[] outputData = new byte[1024];
DatagramPacket outputPacket =
  new DatagramPacket(outputData,outputData.length);
socket.receive(outputPacket);
```

There is no guarantee that a response is received, the UDP protocol offering none.
Improvements are needed here to handle this aspect.

The expected response is one byte: if it matches a player's index, all is fine. Otherwise, there are no more slots:

```java
playerIndex = outputData[0];
if (playerIndex < 0 || playerIndex >= 4) {
    System.out.println("Server is full");
    return;
}
```

Client - Listening thread

A listening thread repeats the following lines, which constantly decode the co-ordinates of the players from the server. If the window is visible, the display is refreshed with a call to the render() method:

```java
try {
    byte[] inputData = new byte[1024];
    DatagramPacket inputPacket =
        new DatagramPacket(inputData,inputData.length,
            serverAddress,serverPort);
    socket.receive(inputPacket);
    ByteArrayInputStream bis =
        new ByteArrayInputStream(inputData);
    DataInputStream dis = new DataInputStream(bis);
    byte messageCode = dis.readByte();
    if (messageCode == MessageCode.PLAYER_COORDS.getCode()) {
        for(int i=0;i<players.length;i++) {
            players[i].coords[0] = dis.readInt();
            players[i].coords[1] = dis.readInt();
        }
    }
} catch (IOException ex) {
    ex.printStackTrace();
}
if(isVisible()) {
    render();
}
```

Client - Sending coordinates

Each time an arrow is pressed, the player's coordinates are sent to the server:

```java
ByteArrayOutputStream bos = new ByteArrayOutputStream();
DataOutputStream dos = new DataOutputStream(bos);
```

```
dos.writeByte(MessageCode.PLAYER_COORD.getCode());
dos.writeInt(players[playerIndex].coords[0]+sx);
dos.writeInt(players[playerIndex].coords[1]+sy);
byte[] inputData = bos.toByteArray();
DatagramPacket inputPacket =
    new DatagramPacket(inputData,inputData.length,
        serverAddress,serverPort);
socket.send(inputPacket);
```

The final result allows playing with one server and four clients. Since there are no synchronization techniques implemented, strange behavior can take place. To eliminate these undesirable effects, it is enough to take again the design patterns presented in the book, and combine them with these exchanges in UDP. For aspects of management of the game, like joining or leaving, it is much easier to stay in TCP. To do this, it is quite possible to use multiple ports per machine.

6.4.6   Exercise 3.5.2: Local Stateless Multiplayer

A solution is proposed in the folder "examples/chap06/stellaris". Unit tests are also offered in the same test package folder.

Representation of the galaxy

The classes in the "examples/chap02/stellaris" folder are taken over and enriched. They have a toJson() method, which allows you to populate a JSON object builder with the main data of an element. These methods do not use all element data, only what is needed for the services to implement. For example, for the System class, there is a list of planets but without details about them:

```
public void toJson(JsonObjectBuilder output) {
    output.add("name",name);
    output.add("x",x);
    output.add("y",y);
    output.add("path",getPath());
    JsonObjectBuilder objectBuilder = Json.createObjectBuilder();
    for (int i=0;i<planets.size();i++) {
        Planet planet = planets.get(i);
        if (planet == null) {
            continue;
        }
        JsonObjectBuilder jsonPlanet =
            Json.createObjectBuilder();
        jsonPlanet.add("name",planet.getName());
        jsonPlanet.add("type",planet.getClass().getSimpleName()
```

```
        );
        jsonPlanet.add("path",planet.getPath());
        objectBuilder.add(String.valueOf(i+1),jsonPlanet);
    }
    output.add("planets",objectBuilder);
}
```

Methods are added to modify the information of an element from a JSON representation. For example, the fromJson() method of the System class allows you to
modify the information (out of planets):

```
public void fromJson(JsonObject json) {
    name = json.getString("name");
    x = json.getInt("x");
    y = json.getInt("y");
}
```

getPath() methods are added to get the service path for an object. For example,
for the System class:

```
public String getPath() {
    return galaxy.getPath()+"/system/"+(id+1);
}
```

The implementation is recursive: the getPath() method of System calls that of
Galaxy, which returns /galaxy/ followed by the identifier of the galaxy, which
ultimately gives a path like /galaxy/<galaxy id>/system/<system id>.

Routing services

In addition to the Pacman game-specific services, the classes in the pacman/server folder are reworked and modified to meet the objectives of the exercise. In particular, a dynamic routing system for queries is set up. Instead of systematically interpreting query paths with the form `/<service name>/<id>`, the routing system allows any form of query path. To achieve this, `ServiceRouter` abstract class implementations are queried by the service manager via a `matchService()` method to obtain a corresponding service:

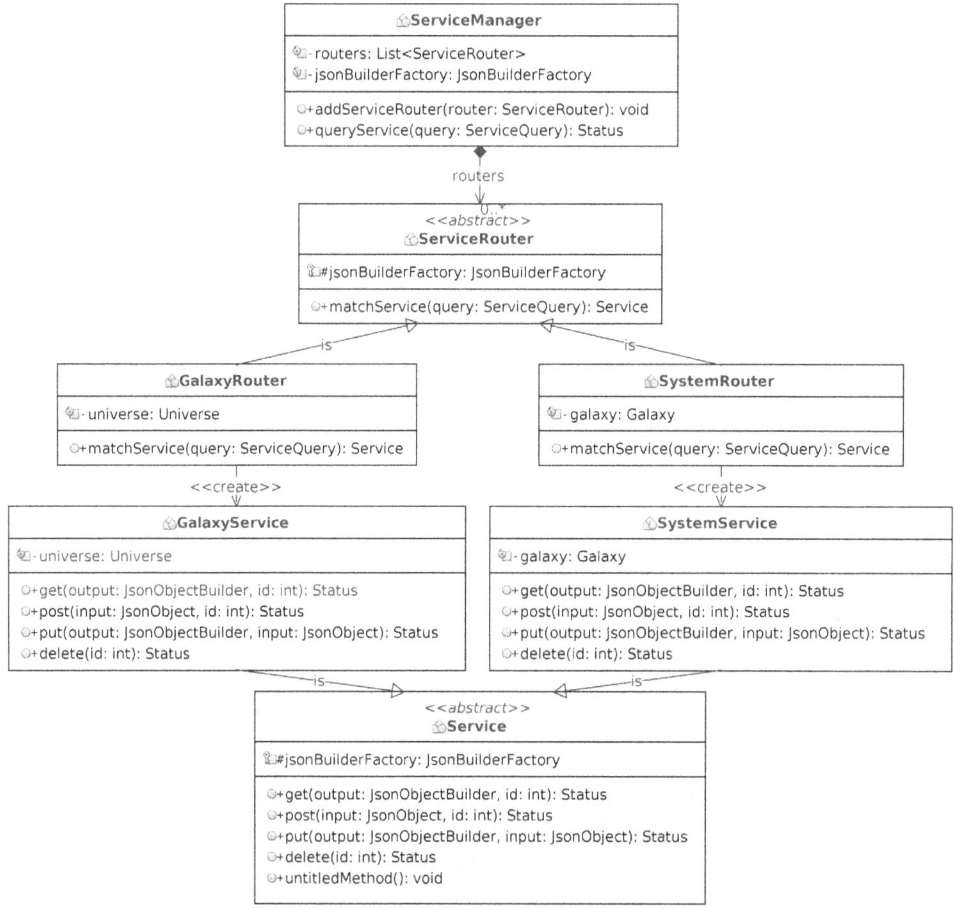

The `queryService()` method of the `ServiceManager` class asks each service router whether it recognizes the path of the request. As soon as a router finds a path that corresponds to it, it returns the corresponding service:

```
Service service = null;
for (ServiceRouter router : routers) {
```

```
    service = router.matchService(query);
    if (service != null) {
        break;
    }
}
```

If no router matches, there is no service available:

```
if (service == null) {
    throw new ServiceException(
        Status.BAD_REQUEST, "Invalid path");
}
```

This mechanism allows all possible forms of routing. In this exercise, simple cases are considered, but nothing precludes more complex possibilities.

Once service is offered by a router, the `queryService()` method of the `ServiceManager` class brings back any path case to a case that may be terminated by a numeric identifier:

```
String path = query.getPath();
int serviceId = 0;
int slashIndex = path.lastIndexOf('/');
if (slashIndex > 0) {
    String ending = path.substring(slashIndex+1);
    try {
        serviceId = Integer.parseInt(ending);
        path = path.substring(0,slashIndex);
    }
    catch(NumberFormatException ex) {
    }
}
```

This manipulation makes it possible to use services that implement the same interface as that proposed with the Pacman example game. For this exercise, two types of paths are considered:

- Path /galaxy/[<id>]: These paths are recognized by GalaxyRouter and the associated services are implemented by GalaxyService.
- Path /galaxy/<id1>/system/[<id2>]: These paths are recognized by SystemRouter and the associated services are implemented by SystemService. The <id1> id is used by SystemRouter to build a SystemService on the galaxy <id1>:

```
final Pattern servicePattern1 =
    Pattern.compile("/galaxy/(\\d+)/system");
final Pattern servicePattern2 =
    Pattern.compile("/galaxy/(\\d+)/system/(\\d+)");
public Service matchService(ServiceQuery query)
```

```java
    throws ServiceException {
    String method = query.getMethod();
    String path = query.getPath();
    Matcher matcher1 = servicePattern1.matcher(path);
    if (matcher1.matches()) {
        if (method.equals("PUT") || method.equals("GET")) {
            int galaxyId = Integer.parseInt(matcher1.group(1));
            Galaxy galaxy = universe.getGalaxy(galaxyId-1);
            if (galaxy == null) {
                throw new ServiceException(
                    Status.BAD_REQUEST, "Galaxy "
                    +galaxyId+" does not exist.");
            }
            return new SystemService(jsonBuilderFactory, galaxy
            );
        }
    }
    else {
        Matcher matcher2 = servicePattern2.matcher(path);
        if (matcher2.matches()) {
            int galaxyId = Integer.parseInt(matcher2.group(1));
            Galaxy galaxy = universe.getGalaxy(galaxyId-1);
            if (galaxy == null) {
                throw new ServiceException(
                    Status.BAD_REQUEST, "Galaxy "
                    +galaxyId+" does not exist.");
            }
            return new SystemService(jsonBuilderFactory, galaxy
            );
        }
    }
    return null;
}
```

The <id2> id, if present, is decoded by the queryService() method of the
ServiceManager class, and then supplied to the SystemService methods that
need it.

It is possible to continue this principle to implement services to more localized
elements. For example, a PlanetRouter class might recognize paths of type
/galaxy/<id1>/system/<id2>/planet/[<id3>], and produce instances of a class
PlanetService for the <id2> system of galaxy <id1>. The identifier <id3> is then
used for services working on a specific planet.